Urban Emancipation

Urban Emancipation
Popular Politics in Reconstruction Mobile, 1860–1890

MICHAEL W. FITZGERALD

Louisiana State University Press

Baton Rouge

Published by Louisiana State University Press
Copyright © 2002 by Louisiana State University Press
All rights reserved
Manufactured in the United States of America

Designer: Barbara Neely Bourgoyne
Typeface: Sabon and Franklin Gothic
Typesetter: Coghill Composition, Inc.

Library of Congress Cataloging-in-Publication Data

Fitzgerald, Michael W., 1956–
    Urban emancipation : popular politics in Reconstruction Mobile, 1860–1890 / Michael W. Fitzgerald.
      p. cm.
    Includes bibliographical references and index.
    ISBN 978-0-8071-2837-4 (pbk. : alk. paper)
    1. African Americans—Alabama—Mobile—Politics and government—19th century. 2. Reconstruction—Alabama—Mobile. 3. Mobile (Ala.)—Race relations. 4. Mobile (Ala.)—Politics and government—19th century. 5. Republican Party (Ala.)—History—19th century. 6. African American leadership—Alabama—Mobile—History—19th century. 7. African American politicians—Alabama—Mobile—History—19th century. I. Title.
    F334.M6F58 2002
    976.12200496073—dc21

2002009885

The paper in this book meets the guidelines for permanence and durability of the Committee on Production Guidelines for Book Longevity of the Council on Library Resources. ∞

To Judy, Alex, and Nate

Contents

Acknowledgments / xi

Abbreviations / xv

Introduction / 1

1 An Influx of "Ignorant Country Darkies": War and Emancipation in Mobile / 9

2 None but Colored Men: The Mobile *Nationalist* and the Dilemmas of Interracial Activism / 49

3 The Most Influential People: Suffrage, Class, and Factionalism / 86

4 The Fruits of Sagacity: Race, Business, and the Radical Ascendancy / 132

5 The Mainspring of It All: The Racial Politics of Federal Employment / 168

6 Let Us Serve the Rich: Black Politics in an Era
   of Diminishing Prospects / 198

   Epilogue: Black Mobile Enters the New South / 246

   Bibliography / 269

   Index / 287

Illustrations

PHOTOGRAPHS

Following page 162

Casual Labor on the Mobile Docks

Creole Fire Station

Albert Griffin

White Racial Attitudes toward Freedmen

1865 Explosion of the U.S. Receiving Magazine

MAPS

Downtown Mobile after the Civil War / 22

Mobile during the Reconstruction Era / 23

Acknowledgments

No author really works alone, and one accumulates an especially large number of obligations in trying to write southern history from Minnesota. But one of the delights of doing a study of this sort is the opportunity to get to know a new community well, and I should thank first the archivists in Mobile who kindly shared their materials, insights, and local knowledge with me. Ned Harkins and his predecessor Jay Higginbotham at the Mobile Municipal Archives have been helpful for the last decade and more. George Ewert and his coworkers at the much improved Museum of Mobile actually interrupted a move to an impressive new building to give me timely access to their holdings. The employees at the University of South Alabama Archives and those of the Mobile Public Library were also quite helpful. I should also thank the staffs of the Mobile School Board offices, the Mobile County Commission, and the Mobile County courthouse. The city has not exactly been deluged with scholars seeking enlightenment, and I would like to thank these government employees for putting up with my somewhat inconvenient presence in their business offices. It must have seemed odd to them, but they were good natured about everything.

I spent a good amount of time in the rest of Alabama over the years, especially in Montgomery at the Alabama Department of Archives and History; thanks to Debbie Pendleton and Rickie Bruner and also the interlibrary loan department. I also appreciate local historian Richard Bailey's general encouragement. Montgomery is an evocative environment for a southern historian, and I have had years of excellent experiences there. I also thank the Hoole Special Collections Library at the University of Alabama, especially former archivist Ellen Garrison for taking great pains on my behalf, and the special collections staff at Auburn as well.

The Midwest was also a fruitful area for researching this project, providing the letters and memoirs of northern soldiers who were in Mobile near the end of the Civil War. The Minnesota Historical Society was a surprisingly rich source for this study, and it has the finest food I have ever encountered in a scholarly facility. Many thanks to the staff there as well as to those of the Indiana, Illinois, Ohio, and Wisconsin historical societies and to the two Iowa state historical societies in Des Moines and Iowa City. I also acknowledge the kind assistance of the employees of the Wilson Library at the University of Minnesota. I have no idea how I could have finished this work had the university not been only fifty miles away and the librarians so helpful. Finally, at my home institution of St. Olaf College, I would like to thank Connie Gunderson, Katarzyna Gonnerman, Sara Leake, and the other employees of the interlibrary loan office. I took ample advantage of their good nature.

The staff of the following institutions also provided assistance: the Manuscript Division at Duke University and the Southern Historical Collection at the University of North Carolina; Barbara Bair and her colleagues at the Library of Congress; and the staff at the National Archives. Leslie Rowland and Susan O'Donovan of the Freedmen and Southern Society Project at the University of Maryland were also most helpful in making the project's collection available to me. Susan in particular was kind enough to trace leads for me on numerous occasions.

Various people subsidized my work by housing me on my research trips. I exploited friends pretty thoroughly to get this written on a liberal-arts college budget, and they probably deserve some acknowledgment. Chip and Carol Hixson housed me for weeks in various cities, as did the economist Don Davis at Columbia. In Tuscaloosa I thank Amilcar Shabazz and his family as well as the family of Guy Hubbs. Also, Steve Salemson, now at the University of Wisconsin Press, was more than generous in opening his home to me in Chapel Hill. Finally, my father, Bill Fitzgerald, and his wife, Rose, put up with me as a research-obsessed houseguest more than once. My sister, Cheryl Berriman, and her husband, Bill, did the same. Many thanks to all of them for their patience.

To continue the exploitation theme, I had research assistance from my former students, several of them now aspiring to greater glory in the profession. Max Grivno, Beth Russey, and Martha Overby all did work in Washington for me. Scott Van Tatenhove also did some laborious microfilm fact checking for me. I also acknowledge the encouragement of my talented undergraduates here in encouraging my work and helping me see it to completion.

Several scholars were kind enough to read the manuscript, most reluctantly my wife and colleague, Judy Kutulas. I thank Chris Waldrep, Lawrence N. Powell, Mitchell Snay, Harriet Doss-Amos, Jenny Wahl, Eric Fure-Slocum, and various anonymous readers of the manuscript or portions of it for their insights. I should also mention Christopher Nordmann for his generous consultation on Mobile's antebellum racial background. My colleagues here in the History Department have heard of my research problems and travails over the years, and I thank them for their insights and patience. My errors are of course my own, but I am sure the work is better for the criticism I have received.

Outside financial support sped the completion of this manuscript, most critically from the National Endowment for the Humanities. A summer seminar at the University of California at Irvine, led by Michael Johnson in 1991, was helpful in the initiation of this project. Some years later a fellowship from the NEH enormously sped my work, as did a sabbatical grant by St. Olaf College. The college also generously funded research trips to Alabama and elsewhere, and the History Department also facilitated the project by various small grants. The Associated Colleges of the Midwest also provided grants for short-term research in Chicago. As for preparation of the book itself, I would like to acknowledge George Skoch for rendering the two maps in the book. I would also like to thank the editors at Louisiana State University Press, especially Sylvia Frank Rodrigue and Nicola Mason, for their kind assistance and advice.

It is common to end acknowledgements of this sort with personal reflections, and there is a passage in my life that probably deserves some note. I am deeply saddened that my mother, Jean Barlettani, is struggling with Alzheimer's disease and will never read this book. She is a native of the South, and in former years she used to struggle through my work and provide pungent commentary. I will always remember and appreciate her effort. But I have a family of my own now, and I am also happy to acknowledge the contribution of my wife, Judy, and my sons, Alex and Nate, for putting up with my repeated absence on research trips and obsession with Mobile. They have all my love.

Abbreviations

ADAH	Alabama Department of Archives and History, Montgomery.
AMA	American Missionary Association Archives, Amistad Research Center, Dillard University, New Orleans.
AP-246	Records of the Division of Appointments, Records Relating to Customs Service Appointments, Records Relating to "Customhouse Nominations," 1849–1910, entry 246.
AP-247	Records of the Division of Appointments, Records Relating to Customs Service Appointments, Applications for Appointments as Customs Service Officers, 1833–1910, entry 247
AP-258	Records of the Division of Appointments, Records Relating to Internal Revenue Service Appointments, Applications for Appointments for Positions as Internal Revenue Collectors and Assessors, 1863–1910, entry 258
LC	Manuscript Division, Library of Congress, Washington, D.C.
M752	Registers and Letters Received by the Commissioner of the Bureau of Refugees, Freedmen and Abandoned Lands, 1865–72, National Archives and Record Service Microfilm M752

M803	Records of the Education Division of the Bureau of Refugees, Freedmen, and Abandoned Lands, 1865–72, National Archives and Record Service Microfilm M803
M809	Records of the Assistant Commissioner for the State of Alabama, National Archives and Record Service Microfilm M809
M810	Records of the Superintendent of Education for the State of Alabama, National Archives and Record Service Microfilm M810
M816	Registers and Signatures of Depositors in Branches of the Freedmen's Savings and Trust Company, 1865–74, National Archives and Record Service Microfilm M816
MAR	*Mobile Advertiser and Register*
MDR	*Mobile Daily Register*
MN	*Mobile Nationalist*
MT	*Mobile Times*
NYT	*New York Times*
OR	*The War of the Rebellion: A Compilation of the Official Records of the Union and Confederate Armies.* 130 vols., Washington, D.C., 1880–1901
RMBACC	Records of the Mayor, Board of Aldermen, and Common Council, RG 3, Mobile Municipal Archives
RG 29	Records of the Bureau of the Census, RG 29, National Archives
RG 36	Records of the U.S. Customs Service, RG 36, National Archives
RG 56	General Records of the Department of the Treasury, RG 56
RG 59	General Records of the Department of State, RG 59, National Archives
RG 105	Records of the Bureau of Refugees, Freedmen, and Abandoned Lands, RG 105, National Archives
RG 393	Records of the U.S. Army Continental Commands, 1821–1920, RG 393, National Archives
SHC	Southern Historical Collection, University of North Carolina, Chapel Hill

Urban Emancipation

Introduction

Ever since the Revisionist tide of the 1960s transformed the study of Reconstruction, historians have been broadly sympathetic to the egalitarian aspirations of the time. Even now, the Republicans generally figure as the era's protagonists, and the idea of the eventual outcome as a crucial defeat for social justice abides. Reconstruction was an "unfinished revolution," to use Eric Foner's phrase, whose overthrow shifted the nation's trajectory toward white supremacy and reaction.[1] Over time historians' attention has turned increasingly toward the social aspects of emancipation, but the political dimensions of the era remain important. Nagging questions remain: Could Reconstruction have succeeded? How might things have been different?

External factors in Reconstruction's collapse were clearly important, among them Ku Klux Klan terrorism and the pervasive hold of racism on the national psyche, to name just two of many. The odds were daunting, but perhaps success was possible, and so historians have often explored the causes for defeat that were within the Reconstruction supporters' control. Unity was an obvious, imperative necessity for the beleaguered movement, but fratricidal infighting undermined the Republicans' hold on power. Many scholars decry the "debilitating factionalism" that "permeated and

1. Eric Foner, *Reconstruction: America's Unfinished Revolution, 1863–1877* (New York, 1988).

bedeviled" the Republican biracial coalition.² These struggles, which generally broke out over individual and collective rivalries for office and patronage, fractured the heterogeneous alliance along the lines of social division.³ This tendency immensely lengthened the odds against the success of Reconstruction, and in states like Tennessee and Virginia, Republican splits directly ushered in conservative rule. Almost everywhere internal struggles hastened the overthrow of Reconstruction.

Factionalism was a serious problem, and the resulting disputes often followed one particularly destructive pattern. The scalawag vs. carpetbagger leadership rivalry has become almost a stereotype, so pervasive is it in the literature. In state after state, as Michael Perman has noted, Republican factionalism pitted a native Southern-dominated moderate bloc, wary of too close an identification with civil rights, against a more militant opposition, the Radicals.⁴ This latter group was generally led by Yankee newcomers, the notorious carpetbaggers of Reconstruction lore, and drew support from the African American mass following. The prevailing version runs that as the black populace gained experience, and as their leaders became increasingly vocal, their numbers prevailed and they established Radical predominance. As part of the same process, African Americans demonstrated increasing skill in pushing a racial justice agenda within the Republican party. The trends sapped native white support for Reconstruction, depriving the movement of its tenuous political legitimacy even as it stoked the ferocious opposition White League campaigns of the mid-1870s. All this facilitated the national retreat from the enforcement of Reconstruction laws and policies that finally allowed racist intimidation and violence to prevail.⁵

Being partial to the egalitarian cause, contemporary scholars generally deplore the partisan infighting over patronage and office. There is no obvious consensus, however, in the evaluation of these internecine struggles between the moderate/scalawag and Radical/carpetbagger factions. Indi-

---

2. Ibid., 349; Michael Perman, *The Road to Redemption: Southern Politics, 1869–1879* (Chapel Hill and London, 1984), 25.

3. Perman, *Road to Redemption*, 22–56; Foner, *Reconstruction*, 346–9; Lawrence N. Powell, "The Politics of Livelihood: Carpetbaggers and the Problems of Republican Rule in the South," in *Region, Race, and Reconstruction: Essays in Honor of C. Vann Woodward*, ed. J. Morgan Kousser and James M. McPherson (New York, 1981), 315–49.

4. Perman, *Road to Redemption*, 22–56.

5. For a clear statement of this prevalent position, see Foner, *Reconstruction*, 350–1.

vidual scholars' allocations of blame vary, and many find the Radicals' civil rights advocacy attractive. The Radicals clearly articulated the widespread and legitimate frustration of the black masses at being ignored by their party leadership. Still, most historians conclude that only the moderate approach had the real possibility of maintaining control. As Perman argues, the centrist moderates alone had a strategy for sustaining a majority coalition.[6] In recent decades several sympathetic studies of scalawag leaders have appeared. These studies imply, with varying degrees of directness, that African Americans made a mistake in abjuring the moderates. At worst, they paved the way for racist Redemption themselves.[7]

Such criticisms have substance. In electoral terms the growing Radical influence over the southern Republican parties posed electoral problems. Radical factional predominance almost certainly facilitated Redemption, and African American preferences certainly contributed to what happened. Given that reality, how is it that the black populace disregarded the apparently obvious demands of political self-preservation? Why did they persist in promoting more advanced civil rights demands in the face of gathering ruin? To understand their behavior, one must engage with how African American political actors saw their situation, especially in terms of what was happening within the black community itself. African Americans had real choices to make. But Republican factional conflicts are generally described in the scholarly literature in racial terms as if the Radical tendency evoked unified black support. That depiction oversimplifies a contentious and often overlooked intraracial dynamic.

In most fields of African American history, the importance of internal class divisions has become an abiding concern, but this trend is less apparent in Reconstruction scholarship.[8] Decades ago, in a trailblazing work,

6. Perman, *Road to Redemption,* 35–6, 55–6.

7. Several state studies follow this general line of interpretation. Prominent among them are William C. Harris, *Day of the Carpetbagger: Republican Reconstruction in Mississippi* (Baton Rouge, 1979); Sarah Woolfolk Wiggins, *The Scalawag in Alabama Politics, 1865–1881* (University, Ala., 1977); and Elizabeth S. Nathans, *Losing the Peace: Georgia Republicans and Reconstruction, 1865–1871* (Baton Rouge, 1968). On the general electoral hopelessness of the Radical approach, see Michael Perman, *Road to Redemption,* 22–56.

8. Among the more prominent of these recent works are Keven K. Gaines, *Uplifting the Race: Black Leadership, Politics, and Culture in the Twentieth Century* (Chapel Hill and London, 1996); Robin D. G. Kelley, *Hammer and Hoe: Alabama Communists during the Great Depression* (Chapel Hill and London, 1990); and John Dittmer, *Local People: The Struggle for Civil Rights in Mississippi* (Urbana, 1994).

Thomas Holt examined African American leadership in South Carolina, stressing the importance of caste background within the political elite in explaining legislative behavior.[9] Few other scholars of Reconstruction have pursued this insight.[10] The literature on African American politics mostly concentrates on the black leadership without tying it to the wider factional struggles within the Republican party or with how the black population approached these issues. Perhaps the best way to examine black agency is to explore the social basis of popular politics in a single location. Only this approach allows a full examination of the factional choices made by both individual leaders and their grassroots followers.

Reconstruction factionalism tended to develop first and most intensely in urban centers. Political interest tended to be liveliest in larger cities, where patronage jobs were concentrated and Republican activists gathered. Though urban developments were not altogether representative of the countryside, they were undeniably crucial in the partisan evolution of the region. These urban places thus illuminate the progression toward stronger civil rights demands and more Radical leadership. If one wants to understand the evolution of popular politics at the grassroots level, it makes sense to look specifically at such areas, where internal controversy was most visible. The subject of this study is emancipation and its aftermath in Alabama's port city, Mobile. It was the Confederacy's fourth largest city, but Mobile's postwar evolution has secured little attention from historians and the activities of its black population almost none.[11] In many respects the city's political evolution followed the typical regionwide pattern of Republican factional development. Here moderate whites, mostly scalawags respectably rooted in local life, pursued a legitimist strategy of providing responsible civic leadership to their entire community. These leaders simultaneously made an aggressive bid for the support of the African American leadership and, through them, the black masses. They had some success,

9. Thomas Holt, *Black over White: Negro Political Leadership in South Carolina during Reconstruction* (Urbana, 1977).

10. The work of the late Armstead L. Robinson comes to mind. See his "Beyond the Realm of Social Consensus: New Meanings of Reconstruction for American History," *Journal of American History* 68 (1981): 276–97.

11. Virtually the only modern study of the city after the Civil War is contained in Don H. Doyle, *New Men, New Cities, New South: Atlanta, Nashville, Charleston, Mobile, 1860–1910* (Chapel Hill, 1990). Doyle's primary focus, however, is on the evolution of business leadership, and his treatment of black politics is quite brief.

but over time they were opposed by a more militant local grouping led by white northern newcomers. These carpetbagger Radicals contested for the control of government patronage positions and elective office. The result was an intense conflict on the streets of the city, a struggle conducted to a striking extent between contending groups of black Republican activists. This rivalry structured the evolution of popular politics during the crucial years of Republican power.

At first examination, black politics in Mobile looks anarchic, a welter of cliques and personal rivalries, but the underlying pattern is fairly consistent. As was the case in all southern cities, an influx of rural migrants after emancipation set the stage for turmoil. Once military Reconstruction decreed equal suffrage, two black factions rapidly emerged in Mobile. On civil rights issues, both groups could be quite aggressive, but their leadership profiles were different, and each group appealed to separate constituencies. The moderate group coalesced first, sponsored by powerful scalawag allies; these black activists were more prosperous and established, asserting political leadership early in the Reconstruction process. They formulated equality in terms of individual opportunity, prizing respectability in themselves and their white comrades. Their more militant challengers, however, were less rooted in Mobile and more willing to appeal to popular discontent, especially among the newly arrived rural migrants. They paid less concern to electoral viability before the wider public, occasionally articulating class-based or black-nationalist formulations stressing collective empowerment. Obvious depictions of the split as one between African American pragmatists and ideologues, though, would be misleading. Leaders from both groups were pragmatic: one faction attended to the partisan needs of the Republican coalition, while the other was more mindful of the immediate privation of the city's poor newcomers.

If Mobile's experience is any measure, emancipation and enfranchisement sharpened existing social divisions in urban African American populations. In the city black Republican leaders seldom met violence at the hands of their Democratic opponents, but they did square off against their factional rivals time and time again. The range of social background within the leadership, their differences in outlook and prewar origin, made racial unity difficult to maintain so long as Reconstruction seemed viable. Conflict within the black community propelled the escalating demands and Radical supremacy that complicated Republican rule. Here, then, is one answer to the original question of whether Reconstruction could have turned out differently—basically, no. Pervasive factionalism was endemic, largely because intraracial conflict in cities like Mobile propelled it. Socially charged leadership contests yielded stronger and stronger civil rights demands, whatever the wider political costs.

The pattern described here has ramifications in terms of the wider literature. For example, Foner's *Reconstruction* is the best regarded overview of the topic, still the touchstone of scholarship over a decade after its appearance. In this work Foner offers an optimistic depiction of what Reconstruction might have achieved had the politics of race not triumphed over the biracial lower-class alliance sustaining it. As W. E. B. Du Bois similarly argued decades earlier, class grievances clearly drove some whites toward the Reconstruction cause, but class was an urgent reality within the African American population too, and it was a particularly pressing source of social differentiation within the swelling urban centers. Assuming the experience of Mobile is remotely representative, the divisions within the black community were so urgent that factional conflict could not be contained, at least so long as any realistic prospect of success existed. Given how intensely divided Mobile's black population demonstrably was, it becomes more difficult to envision Reconstruction succeeding in other urban centers elsewhere.[12]

Only crushing defeat altered this electorally troublesome dynamic, which is perhaps the other important point raised by this study. In the early 1870s, Democrats demonstrated a decisive majority appeal at the local level, sweeping Reconstruction proponents out of civic office and establishing white supremacy as municipal policy. These sobering reverses brought reappraisal. Activists continued to jostle for jobs and position, but their supporters showed an overriding concern with political survival. The African American electorate forced a pragmatic unity upon their long quarrelling leadership, at least on local issues. Republicans thereafter proved adept at exploiting economic divisions among white conservatives. Elections remained closely contested for the next decade and more, and the African American minority repeatedly upended the Democrats through opportunistic support of white dissident movements. In other communities after Re-

---

12. Foner, *Reconstruction*; W. E. B. Du Bois, *Black Reconstruction in America: An Essay toward a History of the Part which Black Folk Played in the Attempt to Reconstruct Democracy in America, 1860–1880* (1935; reprint, New York, 1972). See also the introduction to Eric Foner, *Nothing but Freedom: Emancipation and Its Legacy* (New York, 1983).

demption, insurgent political successes generated racial bloodbaths in places like Danville, Virginia, under Readjuster rule and Wilmington, North Carolina, under the Populists. In Mobile, by contrast, a more circumspect challenge nudged the civic establishment toward a rhetoric of tolerance. As the New South emerged, relative civility returned to public discourse. By the 1880s, even black suffrage became a seemingly normal part of political life, tolerated if grudgingly by the white power structure. Thus if the city's factional politics were self-destructive during the heyday of Republican rule, Redemption's aftermath was surprisingly benign. By and large, scholars have been drawn to the bracing Reconstruction challenge to white supremacy rather than its aftermath, a time of diminishing possibilities. Still, it was in the hard choices of the post-Reconstruction era that Mobile's African American populace demonstrated a more subtle sort of political realism.

There are of course various studies of southern cities covering the Reconstruction era, but most move quickly over the era of direct black participation as an anomaly without lasting influence in the trajectory of regional urban development.[13] Scholars of the Civil War and Reconstruction, though, have examined the issue of race in various communities, but the central focus of this work on grassroots activists and their lives is unique. Precisely because factional disarray was pervasive in Mobile, internal tensions became evident, permitting meaningful examination of African American politicking and what it meant. It is difficult to gauge how representative Mobile's experience was, for sustained analysis of black urban politics has seldom been undertaken. Nevertheless, Howard N. Rabinowitz's classic *Race Relations in the Urban South* suggests analogous factional struggles elsewhere.[14] A recent study of urban black life similarly notes the baffling complexity of Charleston's ferocious factional politics.[15]

13. For an example, see David R. Goldfield, *Cotton Fields and Skyscrapers: Southern City and Region* (Baton Rouge and London, 1982), 80–5. This overview of southern urban history barely mentions Reconstruction. For a less pronounced instance, see the treatment in Doyle, *New Men, New Cities, New South.*

14. Howard N. Rabinowitz, *Race Relations in the Urban South, 1865–1890* (New York, 1978), 282–9. While Rabinowitz's book primarily examines the emergence of segregation in the post–Civil War South, he notes in passing African American political behavior and grievances strikingly similar to those evident in Mobile.

15. Wilbert L. Jenkins, *Seizing the New Day: African Americans in Post–Civil War Charleston* (Bloomington, 1998).

Without making too bold a claim of typicality, what happened in Mobile repays one's consideration, for the same urban social processes were under way elsewhere. At the highest level of abstraction, moreover, this study is not about a single locality. Great issues were at stake after emancipation and enfranchisement. African Americans everywhere confronted the legacy of slavery and the meaning of liberty and citizenship. How the first free generation exercised their agency is crucial to understanding the process of emancipation.

1

An Influx of "Ignorant Country Darkies"
War and Emancipation in Mobile

One might conceptualize the emergence of mass Reconstruction politics in Mobile as occurring at the intersection of several broad forces. Of course, the most important of these was the response of the African American population to the crisis of war and emancipation. Mobile's residents of African descent ranged in background from privileged free blacks to a host of newly arrived freedpeople from the countryside and every condition in between. In their push for effective freedom, this diverse population encountered the contrary priorities of both the U.S. Army and the civilian authorities, who sought to restrain the inconvenient zeal of the black population for equality. In their struggles, though, African Americans also found scattered white allies who would be important as Reconstruction proceeded. These realities, together, established the context for popular activism on the streets of the city.

This study has an overarching theme: the centrality of African American internal divisions for understanding grassroots Reconstruction, both in this one city and by extension more broadly. African American political factionalism was a pervasive urban reality, one deeply rooted in the city's history. Emancipation lumped together as a racially identified group people whose experiences were thoroughly dissimilar, effacing previous distinctions of caste and color. The origins of Reconstruction's political disunity thus extend into the antebellum decades, and in social terms it makes little sense to talk about a single population, so diverse were the backgrounds of people of African descent. Divisions among political activists reflected these differences, which echoed broadly through their popular following as well. When freedpeople were thrust onto the political stage, these realities largely determined the shape of the popular movement in support of Reconstruction.

As Alabama's one large city in a predominantly rural state, Mobile provided a distinctive context for the emergence of black popular politics. In 1860 the city was Alabama's commercial center, socially and politically dominated by its merchant elite. Mobile had little industrial activity, but it boasted the third largest value of exports of any city in the United States.[1] Even under slavery, African Americans in this leading cotton port demonstrated pronounced diversity. Out of a total population of about 29,000 in the city of Mobile, some 8,400 were African American. Of these, over 800 were free people of color, with nearly 400 more living in the surrounding countryside. Mobile County possessed nearly half the state's free black population in 1860, thus the city's free people of color were a sizable presence. After the war they would provide a disproportionate share of Mobile's black political leadership, offering their distinctive experiences and attributes to their formerly enslaved fellows after emancipation.[2]

Among free African Americans before the war, the most distinctive portion was the Creole population, as it was described in Mobile parlance.[3] This group would become the most contentious element in postwar Mobile's black political scene. Afro-Creole numbers are variously estimated, some imprecision being evident in ascription of the status, but there must have been hundreds in the vicinity, representing perhaps one-third of all the free people of color. The Creoles claimed a mixture of French or Spanish and African ancestry, tracing their forebears back into the colonial era. The descendants of liaisons between masters and their slaves, the Creoles' tradi-

1. Alan Smith Thompson, "Mobile, Alabama, 1850–1861: Economic, Political, Physical, and Population Characteristics," (Ph.D. diss., University of Alabama, 1979), 105–6; Doyle, *New Men, New Cities, New South,* 63–5.

2. U.S. Bureau of the Census, *Population, Eighth Census* (Washington, D.C., 1864), 8; U.S. Bureau of the Census, *Compendium of the Ninth Census* (Washington, D.C., 1872), 1:81; U.S. Bureau of the Census, *Preliminary Report on the Eighth Census* (Washington, D.C., 1860), 245.

3. *MN,* April 26, 1866. Throughout the South, the term "Creole" was frequently used in reference to whites of French or Spanish descent in the Louisiana Territory. In Mobile, however, the Afro-Creole community appropriated the term to themselves. Local usage of "Creole" designated some African ancestry, to the frequent comment of confused visitors.

tional status reflected the Latin cultural acceptance of interracial relationships; the Creoles often maintained the Catholic religion and linguistic heritage of their European ancestry. Light-skinned and often prosperous, they were generally assigned as a third racial category, as was the case in Louisiana and the Caribbean region more broadly. Creoles enjoyed a distinctive legal status, dating from the Louisiana Purchase and Adams-Onis Treaty of the early nineteenth century; those who could claim descent from French or Spanish settlers were to enjoy basic civil rights. As the only segment of the (acknowledged) African-descent population to enjoy any significant privileges, their loyalties were necessarily complicated.[4]

The Afro-Creole population maintained a distinct social position into the nineteenth century, as American cultural influence overran the gulf region. For some, their economic success was such that the overriding goal was to maintain their now anomalous status. In northern Mobile County, along the river, several long-established families owned plantations and slaves, most prominently the Chastang, Dubroca, and Collins clans.[5] Seldom did the offspring of these planter families show interest in Republican politics after the war. Other Creoles, however, had a different social profile, and many were drawn to the city in search of economic opportunity. Such less established individuals faced a more fluid situation in negotiating their economic and social status. As with plantation societies elsewhere, free people of color found an urban niche in Mobile's slave economy and often prospered. In the case of the Creoles, these advantages were compounded by the favorable legal status of the "treaty population," which approached

---

4. Christopher Andrew Nordmann, "Free Negroes in Mobile County, Alabama," (Ph.D. diss., University of Alabama, 1990), 63; Lois Virginia Mecham Gould, "'In Full Enjoyment of Their Liberty': The Free Women of Color of the Gulf Ports of New Orleans, Mobile, and Pensacola, 1769–1860" (Ph.D. diss., Emory University, 1991). Christopher Nordmann, the scholar whose dissertation most exhaustively examines this topic, was kind enough to share his research with the author. He counts some 295 adult free-black males in Mobile County, with two-thirds living in the city. Of these, Nordmann finds some 110 to have had Spanish or French surnames, which should provide some notion of the Creoles' probable numbers in the vicinity. A majority of these men lived in the city itself. Nordmann to author, February 13, 2001.

5. Nordmann, "Free Negroes in Mobile County," 151; Marilyn Mannhard, "The Free People of Color in Antebellum Mobile County, Alabama" (master's thesis, University of South Alabama, 1982), 78. On a lesser scale, these families' status seems analogous to the rural Louisiana Afro-Creole enclave described in Gary B. Mills, *The Forgotten People: Cane River's Creoles of Color* (Baton Rouge and London, 1977).

civil equality in all respects save suffrage. As one postwar Radical observed, the Creoles "always enjoyed certain privileges which were denied to the rest of the colored race. . . . [T]hey could stay out as late as they pleased at night, could smoke cigars on the streets, could testify in courts of justice." They were also the only persons of African descent who could legally sell liquor.[6] These exemptions were evident throughout state and local laws. In 1848, for example, the legislature passed a bill banning free blacks and unsupervised slaves from the trade of cotton sampling, but in response to local protest, the lawmakers later exempted Mobile County Creoles explicitly.[7] By the 1850s, the city's Creoles actually enjoyed government-supported schools. Their public presence was augmented by the sponsorship of powerful whites in the community, especially established Catholics, who viewed them as a sort of quaint carryover of Mobile's Latin heritage. The Creoles' toleration also humanized the harshness of the racial order so long as their loyalty was unambiguously demonstrated.[8]

The Creole leadership sought public acceptance, manifesting their solidarity with the white citizenry, though they perceived racial slights readily enough. Their public persona combined community spirit with social exclusiveness. The Creole Fire Company dated from the 1820s, being one of the first founded in the city. It was represented on the city firemen's association, admittedly by a white proxy, but the members insisted on separate public activities.[9] Every April the company held a large procession in which city dignitaries toasted the members' contribution to the community. By the late-1850s, a more exclusive Creole Social Club formed, limited to forty members. One of the younger officers of this club, Ovid Gregory, would become a Republican legislator, and his social profile perhaps represents the aspirations of his fellows. A native of Mobile County, Gregory's parents were born free. He spoke "three different languages, English, French and Spanish," and was considered well educated.[10] He was also well traveled,

---

6. *MN,* April 26, 1866; Nordmann, "Free Negroes in Mobile County," 106–7.

7. Nordmann, "Free Negroes in Mobile County," 74. According to the census, free blacks numerically dominated the trade by 1860. These employees presumably would have been Creoles rather than non-Creole free blacks, given the legal ban. See Thompson, "Mobile," 243.

8. Harriet E. Amos, *Cotton City: Urban Development in Antebellum Mobile* (University, Ala., 1985), 104, 185; Gould, "In Full Enjoyment," 268.

9. *MN,* May 3, 1866.

10. *Montgomery Daily State Sentinel,* November 22, 1867.

having visited Mexico, Latin America, and the western United States. If not rich, he certainly enjoyed social advantages denied most of the free black population, not to mention the slaves themselves. While some studies have found egalitarian tendencies in the Afro-Creole community of Louisiana based on cultural adherence to French political radicalism and literary romanticism, in Mobile's small Creole community, the evidence of this is sparse.[11] Mobile's Creoles had few incentives to associate themselves with the rest of the African American population, and there is only a limited suggestion of psychological identification with their enslaved brethren. Creoles were occasionally arrested for socializing with slaves, and the Creole Fire Company actually considered fining members for undue fraternization.[12] One Creole politician, Philip Joseph, later claimed that his mother had liberated hundreds of slaves in Cuba, having inherited them from her white father. In Mobile, however, Joseph's relations were among the wealthiest Creoles, and they owned slaves and made few waves. During Reconstruction, political rivals accused Joseph of spying for the Confederacy and poisoning black prisoners of war, charges that, however unlikely, suggest something about the repute of such Creoles among the freedpeople. It is difficult to find evidence among Creoles of even private misgivings over slavery, these sentiments being dangerous under the circumstances.[13]

As the Civil War approached, the Creoles confronted increasing challenges. The arrival of large numbers of Irish and German immigrants brought competition for positions as skilled tradesmen. In the 1850s, immigrants represented much of Mobile's adult male population. Their arrival provoked a nativist backlash that promoted racist legislation against African Americans as well.[14] The treaty population escaped many of these laws, but the political climate deteriorated as the sectional crisis placed their loyalties under more scrutiny. In 1861, for example, the Creole Social Club suspended operations for the duration of the war, a precaution reflecting the consciousness that they were under suspicion. After Fort Sumter, Mobile's organized Creole community boldly proclaimed southern loyalties, and to the last days of the war, Creole fairs were held to benefit Confeder-

---

11. Caryn Cossé Bell, *Revolution, Romanticism, and the Afro-Creole Protest Tradition in Louisiana* (Baton Rouge and London, 1997).

12. Amos, *Cotton City,* 101.

13. *MDR,* February 21, 1907; *Livingston (Ala.) Journal,* October 18, 1872.

14. Alan S. Thompson, "Southern Rights and Nativism as Issues in Mobile Politics, 1850–1861," *Alabama Review* 35 (April 1982): 129; Thompson, "Mobile," 170–1, 326.

ate soldiers.[15] White notables repeatedly tried to raise a Creole battalion for the army, assuring Richmond that Creoles were "mostly property-owners, owning slaves," who were "as true to the South as the pure white race." Confederate general Dabney H. Maury, commanding the city's defenses, pointed out that Mobile's Creoles did not stand "on the footing of negroes" and were anxious to serve.[16] Confederate authorities in Richmond turned them down, but Alabama did sanction a Creole unit for local police purposes. The actual state of Creole loyalties is perhaps not clear; the organization was denounced in the press for insufficient drill, so the recruits may not have served with much enthusiasm. Even so, during the final siege of Mobile, all male Creoles were ordered to report for local defense, along with other free blacks. The Native Guard, comprised of Creoles, actually served in the fortifications before the city, risking their lives in defense of the old order.[17]

Emancipation eliminated the Creoles' privileged legal situation, but their ambiguous racial status would make them problematic allies for the multitudes of freedpeople. During Reconstruction, Creole leaders often emerged on the losing end of Republican popular politics, which suggests some estrangement from the black population. But the rest of the antebellum free black population had a different social profile, for nontreaty free blacks had been the scapegoats of prewar politics. By state law, these less privileged free people of color were barred from all formal education, much less public schools. Under slavery, non-Creole free blacks were also excluded from various occupations.[18] Black sailors could not even enter Mobile under state law, having to remain on board ship three miles out in the bay. Mobile's municipal legislation was even more rigorous, as reflected in the city code of 1859. All free blacks had to register a personal description and a place of residence each year. They also had to put up a good-behavior bond on pain of up to four months in jail. No free black could be on the streets after ten in the evening without permission of city officials, and even

---

15. Records of the Creole Social Club, October 1861–July 1865, The Museum of Mobile; *MAR,* February 5, 8, 1865.

16. *OR,* ser. 4, 1:1087–88, 2:941.

17. *Mobile Tribune,* July 12, 1863; *MAR,* March 30, 1865; Arthur W. Bergeron Jr., *Confederate Mobile* (Jackson, Miss., 1991), 105–6; Mobley, "Siege of Mobile," 262.

18. Peter Kolchin, *First Freedom: The Responses of Alabama's Blacks to Emancipation and Reconstruction* (Westport, Conn., 1971), 79; Nordmann, "Free Negroes of Mobile," 106–7.

then no later than midnight. No free black could hold a dance or ball at night under any circumstances or attend such an illicit gathering. There were also restrictions on contact with slaves, however difficult these would have been to enforce in practice. The evident assumption was that these free blacks, unlike their Creole peers, represented a threat to the slave system.[19]

All free African Americans remained socially distinct from their enslaved fellows, most tangibly in physical appearance. Around 80 percent of slaves in the city were described as "black" rather than "mulatto" in the 1860 census, but mixed ancestry predominated among their free counterparts. A full 88 percent of free people of color were listed as "mulatto," a figure that would incorporate Creoles as well as other free African Americans.[20] Phenotypic differences reinforced the other forms of social hierarchy strongly if not uniformly. Light skin color became the visible manifestation of an interconnected network of caste, class, and educational advantages. These ethnic patterns notwithstanding, the circumscribed legal status of non-Creole free blacks encouraged relatively intimate ties to their enslaved brethren. Material circumstances heightened this identification, as racial status was reflected in terms of property.[21] The upper end of the wealth scale was dominated by known Creole families along with the apparent mistresses of rich whites and their offspring. By contrast, many other male free blacks were common laborers, with most of the employed women doing similar tasks as well. Occupational patterns, then, placed the non-treaty free population in closer association with the bulk of the slaves. Perhaps this was by choice, especially among the minority who faced social discrimination as darker-skinned people. They lacked the network of exclusive institutions that exemplified the Creole community.[22]

Non-Creole free blacks become the obvious source of leadership for the freedpeople. Ex-slaves had some cause to view the Creoles as racist and elitist, but they had more reason to trust the remainder of the free blacks, many of whom were themselves once slaves. Religious loyalties encouraged

---

19. Alexander McKinstry, comp., *The Code of Ordinances of the City of Mobile, Alabama* (Mobile, 1859), 17, 119–20.

20. Thompson, "Mobile," 365–7.

21. Population Schedules, Mobile County, Ala., Manuscript U.S. Census for 1860 (M653), RG 29, reel 17. Examination of the census reveals that seventy-five of the eighty wealthiest free African American families were described as led by mulattoes rather than by blacks.

22. Mannhard, "Free People of Color," 75–6.

such attitudes, for the Creoles' traditional status was bound up with Catholicism, a reflection of their Latin heritage. The other free blacks, by contrast, chose Baptist or Methodist churches, a preference they shared with the mass of slaves. As antebellum black congregations formed under white sponsorship, the Protestant free-black community did not aspire to separate religious institutions. Their numbers were too small even had they been so inclined. Free black men instead assumed prominent roles in the black Protestant congregations dominated numerically by their enslaved brethren. Several of these individuals went from antebellum church leadership to postwar political activism. For example, the postwar officeholder Jacob Anderson helped establish the Franklin Street Colored Church.[23] A semiliterate carpenter before the war, he bought his freedom and then aided similar self-purchases by his friends, hoping that they could go to Liberia together. Emigration sentiment among these free blacks doubtless reflected a sense of racial persecution reinforced by religious enthusiasm for the redemption of the homeland. Several future Republican activists involved themselves in African missionary work. The identification with African heritage and emigration among these free black activists was avoided by the Creoles, none of whom were prominent in the effort.[24]

For some free future politicians, the evidence suggests they held strong emotional ties to their enslaved brethren. John Carraway, for example, would become the leading black politician of the late-1860s, an eventual city official and Republican state representative. He was the son of a North Carolina planter and slave mother. Carraway was freed in his father's will but fled Mobile in fear of a legal dispute with his white relations. He left his still-enslaved mother behind in the early 1850s to become a tailor, then a sailor, and eventually an equal-rights activist in New York.[25] When the war broke out, he volunteered for Col. Robert Gould Shaw's famous Fifty-fourth Massachusetts Regiment, though ill-health forced his resignation.[26]

23. John A. Calametti Jr., "The Catholic Church in Mobile during Reconstruction, 1865–1877" (master's thesis, University of South Alabama, 1993), 16; Nordmann, "Free Negroes in Mobile County," 166.

24. Carter G. Woodson, *The Mind of the Negro as Reflected in Letters Written during the Crisis* (1926; reprint, New York, 1969), 53–5; Mannhard, "Free People of Color," 41.

25. *MN*, March 23, May 31, 1866, Sept. 12, 1867; *Montgomery Daily State Sentinel*, November 22, 1867.

26. For Carraway's service record, see Records of the Fifty-fourth Massachusetts Infantry Regiment, 1863–1865 (M1659), Records of the Adjutant General's Office, RG 94, National Archives, reel 2.

He made a musical contribution to the war effort, the specifics of which are murky; a contemporary biographical sketch awards him authorship of the politically astute anthem "Colored Volunteers."[27] The song told African Americans to "never mind the past / we've had a hard road to travel but our time is come at last." It urged blacks to ignore Pres. Abraham Lincoln's half-hearted emancipation policies and seize the moment, for only black military prowess could save the nation and kill slavery forever. Whether or not Carraway wrote the song, this pragmatic advice to utilize even imperfect white allies was thoroughly representative of him. John Carraway's personal odyssey was not typical of the enslaved population, but it does suggest that his unusual preparation for leadership was joined with genuine personal engagement with the plight of the freedpeople. He also demonstrated a testy resentment of the social pretensions of the Creole elite and distaste for their Catholic faith, which he regarded as socially retrograde.[28] Less privileged free blacks like Carraway commonly distrusted the Creoles for their accommodation to the status quo.

During the Civil War, Mobile's civil authorities demonstrated little confidence in the Confederate loyalties of these non-Creole free people of color. With the secession crisis, there were aggressive moves to expel the free

27. The extent of Carraway's patriotic songwriting is unclear. One source says he wrote a work called "No Slave beneath this Starry Flag." But a newspaper biographic sketch, presumably written with his cooperation, allocates him primary authorship of the famous song "Colored Volunteers." One version of the song itself refers to "the gallant company A" of the Fifty-fourth, which was Carraway's company. The political sophistication of the verses also points to him, though musical historians generally list the author as "anonymous" or credit others. See *MN,* September 26, 1867; *Montgomery State Sentinel,* November 27, 1867; Irwin Silber, comp. and ed., *Songs of the Civil War* (New York, 1960), 293–6; Ira Berlin, Joseph P. Reidy, and Leslie S. Rowland, eds., *Freedom's Soldiers: The Black Military Experience in the Civil War* (Cambridge and New York, 1998), 55; Richard Bailey, *Neither Carpetbaggers nor Scalawags: Black Officeholders during the Reconstruction of Alabama, 1867–1878* (Montgomery, 1991), 9; and Eric Foner, *Freedom's Lawmakers: A Directory of Black Officeholders during Reconstruction,* rev. ed.(Baton Rouge and London, 1996), 41.

28. *MN,* February 6, 1868. After Military Reconstruction began, Carraway would serve in the first Republican legislature along with the Creole leader Ovid Gregory. Despite being political allies, the two men did not get along, engaging in prolonged mutual recrimination. At one point, Gregory denounced racial segregation in schools. In response, Carraway pointedly remarked the "inconsistency of his position." It seems that Gregory had previously "headed a committee to send a member to the old legislature to make a law to prevent the going together of colored children and his race the (Creoles)." Carraway was eventually called to order for his personal remarks. *Montgomery Advertiser,* October 3, 1868.

black population to the point that several individuals voluntarily reenslaved themselves to stay with loved ones or simply out of a reluctance to leave.[29] Unlike the Creoles, no one suggested enrolling other free black volunteers in the army, that is until the end of the war, when they were rounded up wholesale for the fortifications. The city council voted to raise a special tax on free blacks living in the city with the evident intention of driving them elsewhere. Even parties and ostentatious dress became subject for anxious public criticism. Authorities stepped up prosecution of free blacks for consorting with slaves, fearing abolitionist designs. These concerns were not necessarily misplaced, especially as Yankee victory loomed. Late in the war, for example, a free man of color named Sylvester received five years in jail for helping slaves escape to Union lines, an effort undertaken with an enslaved co-conspirator. Likewise the free barber Major Lankford apparently was tried for "enticing slaves to leave masters and harboring runaways."[30] Lankford's wartime actions proceeded directly to postwar militancy, for during the early years of black suffrage, he was a constant presence on the streets. He would lead those Republicans most inclined toward direct physical confrontation with white authority.

Important as the free people of color were in terms of postwar leadership, they comprised only a fraction of the overall black population. The bulk of Mobile's African-American residents, about nine-tenths, were enslaved. Their security remained an abiding concern of city leaders, though as one might expect, urban masters generally possessed modest holdings of human property. The average slaveholder owned five slaves, the bulk of slaves living in holdings of less than ten. Slavery nonetheless represented a significant economic presence in the city, with the value of slaves comprising around one-fourth of that of real estate. Antebellum Mobile had little industry, which meant that the slave population lacked the occupational range evident in some other urban centers.[31] The women were mainly do-

29. See Petitions to Become Slaves, Records of the Probate Court of Mobile County, Mobile County Courthouse.

30. *Mobile Evening News,* January 29, 1864; MAR, February 6, 13, 22, 1865; MAR, March 1, 3, 1865, quoted in Joe A. Mobley, "The Siege of Mobile, August 1864–April 1865," *Alabama Historical Quarterly* 38 (winter 1976): 264. The article text misidentifies Lankford as white.

31. Thompson, "Mobile," 306–9, 331; Barbara Joan Davis, "A Comparative Analysis of the Economic Structure of Mobile County, Alabama, before and after the Civil War, 1860 and 1870" (master's thesis, University of Alabama, 1963), 7–8.

mestics, while the men were largely unskilled laborers servicing the cotton trade, but both sexes at least gained experience in the urban environment, which would serve them well after emancipation. As one Confederate officer observed, in Mobile his servant Henry learned "the habits and airs of a town darkee very fast." Moreover, a substantial number of slaves functioned quite independently long before the war. In the 1850s the city government estimated that a thousand slaves lived away from their masters. Officials discouraged this practice, attempting to register such slaves, but by all accounts these provisions were widely evaded when masters found them inconvenient. Newspaper reports suggest that because it was difficult for masters to free people in the face of restrictive legislation, a sort of nominal slavery was common. Thus, even within the enslaved population, gradations existed in status and background that would be significant as Reconstruction unfolded.[32]

City officials obsessively safeguarded the peculiar institution. Slave access to alcohol was strictly limited, though without much success if the court records are any indication. Legislation directed at slaves was severe and often petty, outlawing everything from slaves owning dogs and cows to smoking in the streets. The city code prohibited them from renting out their own time on pain of twenty lashes. Those slaves who were permitted to work by the day had to wear a metal tag issued by the city. The evident concern was that urban slaves had learned dangerously much, but even those newly arrived from the countryside were fully capable of forming subversive ideas. Allen Alexander, a domestic servant, offered one striking illustration. His master once saw Alexander speaking to poorer whites and forbade him from doing it again. "Before the war," Alexander recalled, "a poor white man was not looked upon as being as good as a nigger." Alexander drew the obvious political conclusion, that the system oppressed both slaves and nonslaveholding whites, and after emancipation he emerged as a combative Radical activist. Other slaves could not have

32. S. Croom to "Mother," Sept. 7, 1862, Velma and Stevens J. Croom Correspondence, University of South Alabama Archives, Mobile; Gould, "In Full Enjoyment," 137–8; McKinstry, *Code of Ordinances,* 171–3; Thompson, "Mobile," 315, 318; Nordmann, "Free Negroes in Mobile County," 54, 88; Amos, *Cotton City,* 89; Ira Berlin, *Slaves without Masters: The Free Negro in the Antebellum South* (New York, 1974), 148; *Mobile Army Argus and Crisis,* December 3, 1864.

missed the wider point, that racial oppression was as much a matter of state power as the force individual masters could employ.[33]

The outbreak of the Civil War promised deliverance, but it only worsened slaves' circumstances in the short term. The number of runaways jailed by local officials declined sharply during the secession crisis and the early war years, which likely reflected heightened vigilance in a militarized society.[34] City officials and community sentiment called for stern measures, including an augmented citizens' patrol and further proposals for restrictions on slaves living separately.[35] In 1863, for example, one newspaper correspondent called for action against ostentatious religious festivals on the ground that they would make poorer white residents jealous. Besides, "the negro to be useful to himself and his master must be kept in his place—nothing could be plainer than that." The Mobile Committee of Safety actually petitioned the governor to prevent publication of the Emancipation Proclamation. Even with the increased scrutiny, bread riots, invasion scares, and the tumult of war destabilized the system. For example, the slave Lawrence S. Berry was owned by a prominent Alabama jurist. Early in the war he was sent to the Confederate salt works many miles upriver in Clarke County, working under conditions widely reported as severe. He stayed for three years, and his difficult service presumably encouraged his pronounced postwar militancy and also fitted a more worldly Berry for later political agitation in the interior.[36]

This man's experience, repeated a thousandfold, tattered slavery's bonds. In February 1865 about 900 impressed blacks were working on the fortifications at Mobile, with 263 absent without leave. Anecdotal reports suggest that some hid in the city, while many others made it to the Union lines. Even Confederate officials admitted the laborers were poorly fed and

---

33. Amos, *Cotton City*, 144; McKinstry, *Code of Ordinances*, 171–3; MN, July 28, 1869; U.S. Congress, House, *Affairs in Alabama*, 43d Cong., 2d sess., H. Rept. 262, 345.

34. By my count, in 1859 some eighty-one slaves were jailed as runaways in the county jail, but in 1860 the number was forty-eight, and in 1861 the figure declined further to forty-two. During the secession winter, especially, the number dropped. See Record Book of Run Away Slaves, 1857–65, Records of the Probate Court of Mobile County, Mobile County Courthouse.

35. Board of Common Council, Minutes, December 17, 1861, February 4, 1862, Mobile Municipal Archives, reel 17.

36. *Mobile Tribune*, July 3, 1863; Executive Committee of the Mobile Committee of Safety, Minutes, December 20, 1862, Manuscript Division, New York Public Library; *MAR*, October 26, 1862, February 25, 1863; *MDR*, January 19, 1869.

housed, and the final Union offensive on the eastern shore only increased the work demands. As the Yankee threat loomed, slavery's disintegration became increasingly obvious. The number of jailed runaways from outside Mobile spiked sharply, both as a proportion and in absolute numbers, the harbinger of the stream of postwar rural migration into the city.[37] By the war's final days, the Confederates' own actions disrupted slavery thoroughly. In late March 1865 the army ordered all able-bodied male slaves in Mobile sent into the interior on pain of being enrolled as military laborers. In early April owners were told to deliver all remaining slaves, and the press predicted the authorities would "indiscriminately lay hands upon all able-bodied darkies for the objects in view." The male slave population, at least, was uprooted by the war's final phases, which contributed to sweeping postwar changes in urban residence patterns.[38]

The chapters to follow trace the changes emancipation brought to the city's economy and race relations: a brief sketch of crucial postwar social developments will facilitate the subsequent discussion. With peace, dramatic transformations followed in just about every aspect of city life, while emancipation revolutionized the social geography of urban Mobile. The city's eastern edge lay along the Mobile River, with the commercial district and businessmen's wealthy homes downtown nearby the water. While antebellum domestics lived everywhere, free blacks had always concentrated in the outlying wards, a pattern that intensified with emancipation. Mobile, like virtually every other southern city, confronted a huge influx of African American migrants, and as was the case elsewhere, residential segregation increasingly characterized the city. Prodded by overcrowding, ex-slaves left the downtown, while African American populations skyrocketed on the city's periphery, especially inland, or west, of Broad Street. The Seventh Ward, in the northwest, more than doubled its black population and soon possessed an African American majority. The black population of the city increased from 8,400 in 1860 to 12,400 in 1866, contributing to the city's postwar total population peak of nearly 41,000 in the latter year. As Mobile's ex-slaves moved to the cheap housing going up on the edge of town,

---

37. The number of jailed runaways from outside Mobile County went from nineteen in 1862, to thirty-seven in 1863, to sixty-four in 1864. In early 1865 the rate was even higher. See Record Book of Run Away Slaves, 1857–65, Records of the Probate Court of Mobile County, Mobile County Courthouse.

38. OR, ser. 1, 49(1):1055–6; Bergeron, *Confederate Mobile,* 110–4; MAR, April 7, 1865.

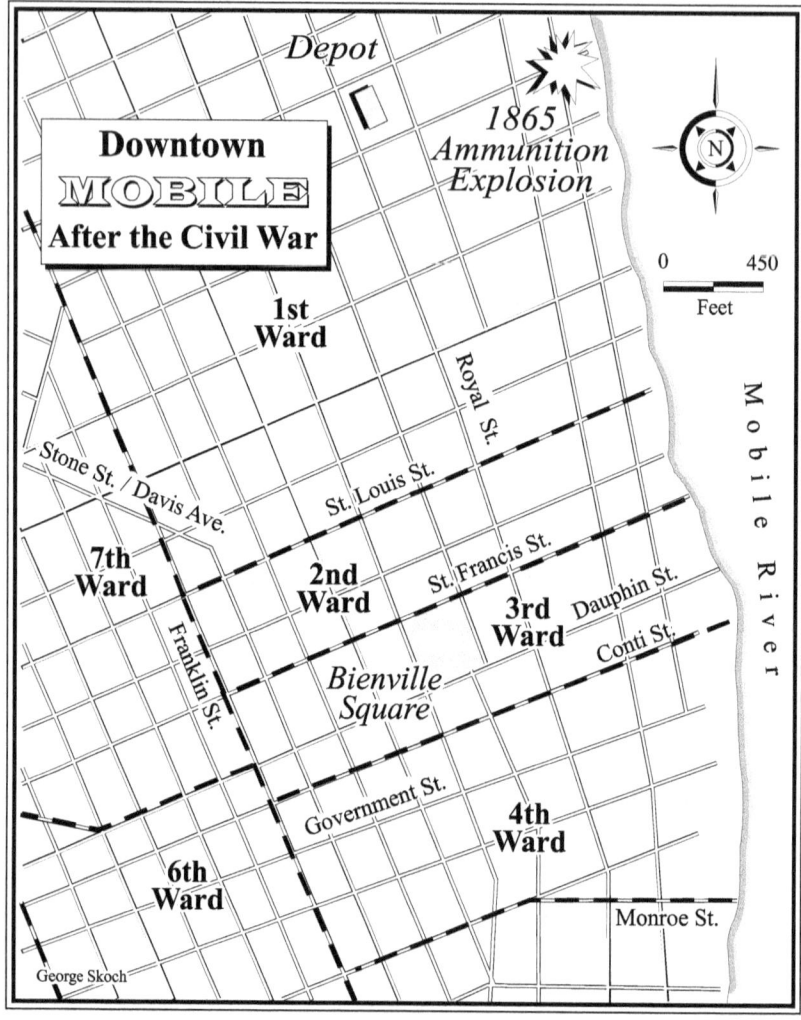

they were joined by new black residents, often politicized former soldiers and successive waves of refugees from the countryside.[39]

The new migrants became the engine driving Mobile's political development. The flow of poverty-stricken rural refugees exacerbated intraracial class divisions, overshadowing other older social divides. In 1866 the city

39. Thompson, "Mobile," 206; Rabinowitz, *Race Relations in the Urban South*, 97–124; *MAR,* Sept. 6, 1866.

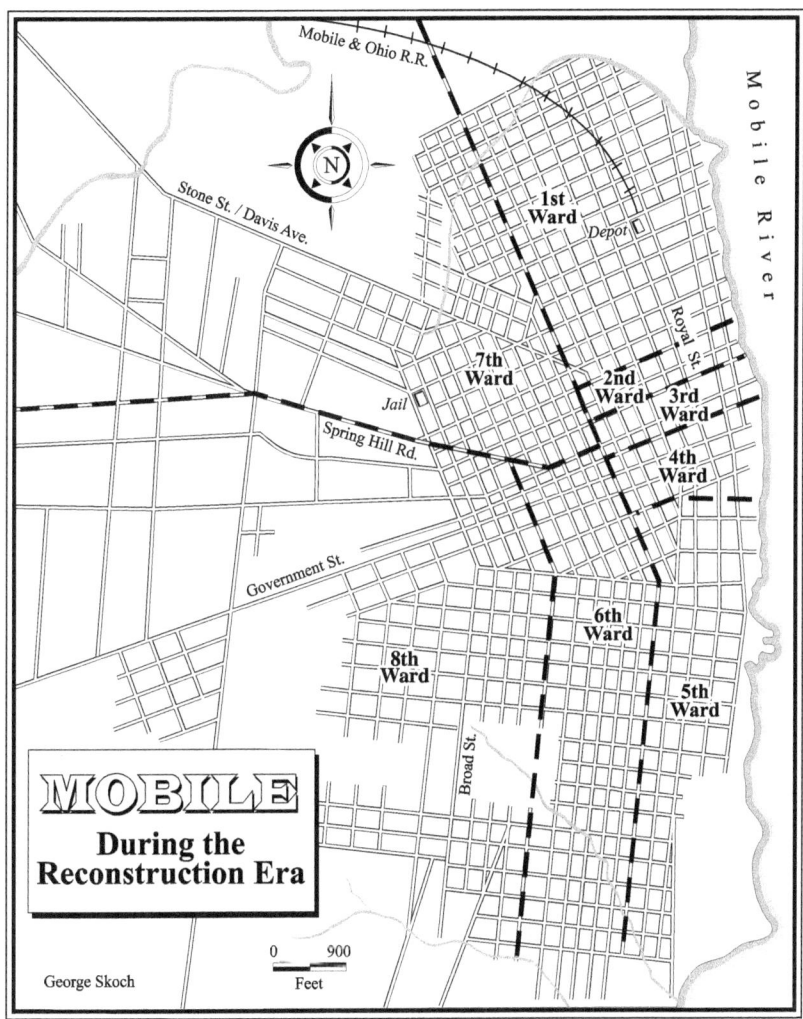

census taker observed a dramatic range of social conditions among African Americans. He conceded that a third of that population were doing well and were thrifty and prosperous, having often purchased newly constructed homes. Simple arithmetic suggests that most of these several thousand fortunate residents must have been former slaves, likely those already established in the community. The remainder of the African American population, however, appeared to be "literally worthless" to the city officer. This class would "work only by the job or day's work, and can hardly be said to have any permanent or fixed place of residence." The census taker found this population clustered together in revolting and disease-ridden conditions. Seduced by the allure of urban life, these people refused "to go back to the plantations of the interior" however wretched they were in Mobile. The clear implication was that these were recent rural migrants, and the investigator concluded that the chain gang was the most effective remedy.[40]

In subsequent years the African American influx continued, reaching 13,900 in 1870, a 65 percent increase in a decade. "Soon after the war," one newspaper recalled, the city was "infested by large gangs of negroes from the country" whose ranks were "constantly recruited from the same source." By contrast, the white population plummeted from 28,500 in 1866 to a reported 18,100 in 1870.[41] Ten thousand whites fled postwar economic stringency, while rural repression sent a continuing stream of freedpeople into Mobile. One desperate father in the countryside manifested the human cost of this in-migration, asking for the police to detain his runaway fifteen-year-old son, last seen as a vagabond about the city. Such new residents only dampened prospects for the legions of unskilled laborers already there. A local freedwoman denounced the "ignorant country darkies" coming to Mobile.[42] These migrants knew nothing and were "only fit" to be slaves, the woman reportedly told her ex-mistress. The city's troubled economy could generate few jobs for the poorer newcomers settling in the expanding northern and western suburbs. Mobile lacked industry and was physically isolated from the inland plantation belt, so the decline of the city's cotton trade left the new residents few job alternatives. These underemployed—and often stranded—multitudes became a central feature of postwar Mobile's life.

Enfranchisement ensured that this restive social constituency would not be ignored, but their privation would complicate Reconstruction politics, particularly the effort to stabilize Republican rule. Basically, the influx of rural population generated a fertile mass of discontent that roiled black

40. *MAR*, Sept. 7, 1866.
41. *MDR*, January 19, 1869; U.S. Bureau of the Census, *Ninth Census* (Washington, D.C., 1872), 1:81. The census figure probably understates the white population due to seasonal migration patterns, whites being more able to leave the city during the unhealthy summer.
42. W. H. Jones to C. A. R. Dimon, January 2, 1867, Mobile City Police Records, W. S. Hoole Special Collections, University of Alabama; Kate Cumming, *Gleanings from Southland: Sketches of Life* (Birmingham, 1895), 267.

politics at moments of confrontation. That social reality combined with normal leadership rivalries for political office to encourage internal factionalism in this crucial urban center. With the grant of suffrage, the most privileged segments of the African American community would assert their leadership based on educational qualifications and social prominence. This fueled ferocious personal resentments that compounded the political task posed by Reconstruction. Leadership challenges came especially from those disposed by background or inclination to speak for the rural migrants gathering in stark agony on the city's outskirts. The newcomers' poverty ensured that insurgents always had a constituency for confrontational measures. Thus the social process of urban emancipation, combined with Mobile's postwar economic decline, promoted endemic factionalism within the African American leadership and the Republican party as a whole.

These social developments lay in the future in early April 1865 as the Civil War entered its final days. With Confederate resistance collapsing, more immediate concerns preoccupied those in positions of power. For the white city leadership, the task at hand was the transfer of the city intact to Union authority; the underlying question was how drastically occupation would challenge the racial order. At Fort Blakely, outside Mobile, the presence of thousands of U.S. Colored Infantry (USCI) raised the race issue in graphic terms. Black troops composed much of the attacking force in the decisive breakthrough on April 9, performing with conspicuous bravery in storming the fort. By all accounts, these soldiers demonstrated extraordinary motivation. The USCI regiments charged with "Remember Fort Pillow" on their lips, this being a reference to the notorious Confederate atrocity against surrendering black troops. Upon breaching the Confederate lines, some UCSI soldiers reportedly were disinclined to take prisoners. Such conduct, if unedifying, at least demonstrated emphatic zeal; after the victory, some embraced and sang "Battle Cry of Freedom" from the battlements, while others fell on their knees in impromptu prayer groups.[43] Reports of the prominent role of African American troops in the battle spread widely within the city. The black population reportedly boasted that the Union

---

43. Noah Andre Trudeau, *Like Men of War: Black Troops in the Civil War, 1862–1865* (Boston and New York, 1998), 396–408; Chester G. Hearn, *Mobile Bay and the Mobile Campaign: The Last Great Battles of the Civil War* (Jefferson, N.C., and London, 1993), 191–201; Michael W. Fitzgerald, "Another Kind of Glory: Black Participation and Its Consequences in the Campaign for Confederate Mobile," *Alabama Review* 54 (fall 2001): 243–73; H. Schofield to Andrews, April 1, 1866, box 7, C. C. Andrews Papers, Minnesota Historical Society.

army could not have won without them, while Rebel sympathizers read the events differently. Kate Cumming, a Confederate nurse, heard that the blacks "acted like demons, and slaughtered our troops on all sides." White Union soldiers had to shoot them before they would desist, but such horrors were best not spoken of, she concluded in disgust. Such exaggerated rumors masked a serious issue: here was the very embodiment of racial transformation at Mobile's doorstep, dramatizing the very issues those in authority least wished to confront.[44]

If black soldiers acted as an egalitarian vanguard, their Union generals proved much less eager to facilitate social change. As Confederate troops withdrew from the city, a riotous scramble for abandoned supplies broke out. Fearing disorder, Mobile's mayor and various dignitaries hurried out to welcome the Yankees into the city. Under the circumstances, Union general E. R. S. Canby and his subordinates chose to cooperate with civil officials. With victory assured, the maintenance of social order seemed conducive to pacification, especially since Canby bypassed Mobile with the bulk of his army. Many soldiers expressed disappointment at not being allowed to enter the city in triumph, but even the occupation force complained that they were under unusually tight rein. One infantryman, camped just outside town, noted that not one house was burned. Rebel sources agreed that the soldiers entered with extraordinary discipline. "Never in the history of any war has any city been occupied by a besieging party with such order," the *New York Herald* concluded. The contrast with events elsewhere was striking. During early April, Yankee invasion wreaked havoc on Selma and Montgomery; in fortunate Mobile, however, Union troops debated the protocol of which units should enter the city first.[45]

In most southern communities, military conquest upended the authority of the former masters, but Mobile's circumstances encouraged a smooth transition from the point of view of the ex-Confederates. General Canby

44. Kate Cumming, *Kate: The Journal of a Confederate Nurse,* ed. Richard Barksdale Harwell (1959; reprint, Baton Rouge, 1987), 306.
45. "Frank" to "Susie," April 30, 1865, in Carl E. Hatch, ed., *Dearest Susie: A Civil War Infantryman's Letters to His Sweetheart* (New York: 1971), 119; *Mobile Morning News,* May 11, 1865; Thad Holt, ed., *Miss Waring's Journal: Being the Diary of Miss Mary Waring of Mobile, during the Final Days of the War between the States* (Chicago, 1964), 16; *New York Herald,* April 30, 1865; E. B. Gary to Andrews, March 5, 1866; and C. H. MacKay to Andrews, March 2, 1866, box 7, Andrews Papers.

preferred to "preserve society intact" so long as the citizens submitted, and perhaps the unsettling racial overtones of Fort Blakely bolstered this inclination. Federal officers thus determined that slavery would expire under conditions that minimized dislocation. For the slaves, of course, the end of slavery was the overriding issue, and the victors received the same euphoric reception they received elsewhere. Most whites stayed indoors, especially the women, but the "apparently overjoyed" slaves occupied the streets. One Rebel woman commented: "You ought to have seen the negroes when the Yanks came in. They were all so delighted that they ran down to see them." Throngs reportedly rushed to greet the arriving Federal ships. Had the black population been more aware of the priorities of the Yankee commanders, they might have been more restrained in their welcome.[46]

Union authorities in the city enforced the government's emancipation policy, but it seemed a matter of limited urgency, a foregone conclusion. Military pacification was the priority as long as Rebel forces remained in the field. Several days after occupying the city on April 12, General Canby ordered the U.S. government's Bureau of Free Labor, operating in occupied Louisiana, to take charge of the freedpeople. Upon his arrival soon thereafter, Col. Thomas Conway found that nearly all the former slaves were still forcibly retained in the yards of their owners. Black leaders seeking advice besieged Conway, and he announced immediate emancipation before assembled black congregations. These statements apparently had some effect, for one white woman complained that his talk "upset all the negroes." To facilitate the colonel's efforts, General Canby issued a manifesto validating Conway's mission and decreeing emancipation as army policy. Still, Canby's order suggested that care would be taken "not to disturb abruptly the connections now existing" with former owners, and all freedmen were advised to remain where they were if well treated. All unemployed African Americans were to report immediately to have their names and residences registered so they could be provided with work. This ambivalence toward the practical consequences of emancipation typified army policy.[47]

46. *Chicago Christian Advocate and Journal,* May 18, 1865; Joseph H. Turner to C. C. Andrews, March 4, 1866, Andrews Papers; *Mobile Morning News,* May 11, 1865; C. Carter Smith Jr. and Sidney Adair Smith, eds., *Mobile, 1861–1865: Notes and a Bibliography* (Chicago, 1964), 43.

47. T. Conway to Col. J. S. Crosby, April 28, 1865, Letters Received, 1865, box 13, Department of the Gulf, RG 393, pt. 1; *New Orleans Black Republican,* April 29, 1865; Kate Oliver to Augusta Rice, May 2, 1865, Nannie Herndon Rice Family Papers, Mississippi State University; *OR,* ser. 1, 49(2):410–1.

Over time, the Bureau of Free Labor and its successor, the Freedmen's Bureau, would protect black liberty more aggressively, but for the moment Conway's agency supported the prevailing military priorities. In Louisiana politics Conway was identified with the moderate Union faction of Gen. Nathaniel Banks and especially with his wartime labor code, which had been criticized by abolitionists as too harsh toward workers. Upon arrival in Mobile, Conway proclaimed the "benefits of the free labor plan, which is such a blessing in Louisiana," declaring his intention to implement it in Alabama. Under the protection of the standardized code, Conway expected the freedpeople to go back to work forthwith. While favoring emancipation, he also believed that freedmen needed encouragement to labor, encouragement that his Mobile subordinate thought included corporal punishment. For Conway, the threat that ex-slaves would turn vagrant was almost as serious as that posed by their former masters' ill will. Furthermore, ex-slaves flocked to the city in alarming numbers: "The exodus of olden times was as nothing compared to this," Conway observed. Within days of Mobile's fall, Union troops reportedly sheltered thousands of African American women and children downtown, many of them the families of Union soldiers. One white woman described a downtown "negro pen" as "shocking to humanity," and indeed the Yankees scarcely knew what to do with the refugees. Thus, between the extension of wartime policies to Mobile and the military's abiding stress on order, stern policies quickly took shape.[48]

For some weeks, military exigency shaped the army's social agenda. Rumors of a Confederate counterattack seemed plausible with most of the Union army marching inland away from the city. In late April army engineers tried to hire laborers for the fortifications, but three days' effort proved futile. Rather than offer higher wages, the officer in charge asked the provost marshal to arrest idle people, and General Canby ordered that five hundred "contrabands" be provided for this duty. All unemployed men applying for food would be employed on the works as well. Yankee officers were well aware of the resulting hardship: one captain noted that "as the men are impressed into the Government service and receive no pay for the

---

48. *New Orleans Black Republican,* April 29, 1865; Geo. Harmount to T. W. Conway, May 15, 1866, Letters Sent, SAC Mobile, vol. 108, entry 142, RG 105; *NYT,* June 6, 1865; Russell E. Belous, ed., "The Diary of Ann Quigley," *Gulf South Historical Review* 4 (spring 1989): 98.

present," they and their families were destitute, wholly dependent on rations. Military orders often were not explicitly discriminatory, but the racial distinctions in practice were evident. A white woman commented that "the negroes are kept in order not a loiterer is to be seen, they keep them all employed & are going to establish work houses for the women." She thought the army intimidated them, and the Confederate nurse Kate Cumming found much the same after her return to the city.[49] Notwithstanding evident pleasure at puncturing northern humanitarian posturing, the general sense of army severity toward black refugees is probably accurate. A sentry actually shot one freedwoman for refusing an order to halt. Even after Alabama's last Confederates surrendered on May 8 and the motive of military necessity passed, rigor intensified. One colonel suggested on May 17 that the army should "arrest all vagrant colored men" and work them on the fortifications at a dollar a day. "Many of them have already been employed and have left and are now strolling about town," he complained. Later that month the commanding general ordered the provost guard to arrest all those without visible means of support except paroled soldiers. Able-bodied men were to be "formed into gangs and worked under guard in cleaning the streets of the city." All those who were not properly residents were to be sent home, presumably into the countryside.[50]

These military precedents encouraged similar efforts of municipal officials, who were happy to have army collaboration in patrolling the streets. For example, that fall the city chain gang, comprising "quite a large number of negroes," was supervised by soldiers under "arrangement with the military authority." In one instance the guard killed one prisoner and wounded another in the act of escaping. These were not the only shootings, for according to an army report, the provost guard killed several blacks late in 1865.[51] Given such severity toward the freedpeople, it is small wonder

49. *OR,* ser. 1 49(2):352, 560–1, 574–5; Capt. Joseph Rankin to Capt. R. G. Custis, May 9, 1865, Letters Received, 1865, box 1, 13th Army Corps, RG 393, pt. 2; Martha V. Schroeder to G. Schroeder, April 1865, H. A. Schroeder Papers, The Museum of Mobile; Cumming, *Kate,* 307.

50. *Mobile News* quoted in *New Orleans Picayune,* May 5, 1865; Capt. John C. Cobb to Capt. R. G. Custis, May 17, 1865, Letters Received, 13th Army Corps, box 1, RG 393, pt. 2; *OR,* ser. 1, 49(2):907.

51. *New Orleans Picayune,* August 8, 1865; *MAR,* October 20, 1865; endorsement on "The Black Population of Mobile" to Secretary of War, October 24, 1865, Letters Received Relating to Military Discipline and Control, ser. 22, Headquarters of the Army, RG 108, NA.

that city leaders seldom demanded the departure of the garrison and army officers frequently endeared themselves to the white locals. For instance, when Provost Marshal Thomas Kinney mustered out, a party of old citizens and merchants presented him a watch. The colonel, a Kentuckian, had rendered himself "particularly popular by the administration of his office."[52] Objective circumstances reinforced this prevailing concern for social discipline, some of them of the army's own making. On May 25 a munitions warehouse exploded, leveling several blocks north of downtown and killing untold numbers of people. The disaster spread havoc and only intensified the fears of social disorder amid the ruins.

In the chaotic aftermath of the explosion, the military arrested people wholesale; at one time, according to a provost guard, 150 individuals were in jail. As the army began policing the city's freedpeople more intensively, the circumstances influenced the attitude of those who patrolled the streets. One soldier found himself stationed in "a pretty hard district of the city, there being many vagrant negroes and women of ill fame, who are very brazen and disgraceful." He disliked these surroundings, but even he found his army colleagues too rigorous toward the freedpeople. It seems his own servant was jailed for being on the streets without his certificate of employment. He was able to liberate the man but could not free the two mulatto women who were arrested along with him.[53] The image of aggressive harassment of employed blacks is substantiated by Freedmen's Agent George Harmount, who complained that the soldiers routinely disregarded his certificates of employment. One of Harmount's colleagues also complained that the provost officers palmed off unpopular decisions in favor of the freedmen to the bureau.[54] Maltreatment at the hands of military guards would be one of the flashpoints of black discontent in the months to come. By one account, the provost marshal actually enforced the antebellum 10:00 p.m. curfew for free blacks. As one black reporter observed, he never saw a "meaner or a more negro-hating class of people than the men who are now on Provost duty here."[55]

The current and former troops of the U.S. Colored Infantry bore the

52. *Mobile News* quoted in *MAR*, Sept. 1, 1865.
53. John W. Schlagle Diary, June 18, 1865, Indiana Historical Society; Lemuel Burke Diary, June 28, July 1, 1865, Illinois State Historical Society.
54. W. A. Poillon to Swayne, August 7, 1865, Unregistered Letters Received, box 2, ser. 9, Records of the Assistant Commissioner for Alabama, RG 105.
55. *New Orleans Tribune*, August 5, July 8, 1865.

brunt of this evolving policy. Substantial numbers passed through the city, many of them having been recruited locally, so they were a destabilizing element, given the prevailing rush to conciliate white opinion. Initially their white volunteer comrades granted them some leeway, but with the arrival of the regulars of the Fifteenth U.S. Infantry in early September, discipline intensified. One German American soldier observed that "the negro soldiers are treated worse than we are. They pull them up by their thumbs; some scream terribly." Another volunteer observed similar treatment of black soldiers by regular-army troops, and he and his white comrades were troubled enough by the brutality to complain. These soldiers actually demolished the guardhouse one night as a protest, threatening the officers if they interfered. This instance of interracial solidarity notwithstanding, the relationship between black and white soldiers was often rough. Bored northern soldiers tended to take out their frustrations on whoever was most convenient. When white soldiers crashed one party uninvited, trouble broke out. As one white sergeant wrote, "Regs. & Negro Soldiers get in a fight. 9 of Nigs. are sent to hosp[ital]," and several were not expected to live.[56]

Affrays between the provost guards and black troops became increasingly common, and the veterans became the initial focus of black resistance more generally.[57] For example, a confrontation occurred immediately after several companies of black troops arrived in the city on the afternoon of September 8. Robert Thompson, an employee of the Provost Marshal's Office, encountered a group of black soldiers and civilians making a "fuss" on Dauphin Street. He ordered them to move along, imprudently displaying the badge of the hated city police force, whereupon a labor detail and other black infantry nearby intervened. The USCI men said they were "soldiers of the United States Army and didn't care a damn" for the city police. Thompson then reasserted his authority as a military employee, but the soldiers cursed him and "everybody as damned rebels." One sergeant then began threatening the whites, stating that there were "colored men enough

56. Frank Wittenberger Diary (translation), Sept. 14, 1865, Historical Society of Wisconsin, Madison; Elisha Stockwell Jr., *Private Elisha Stockwell Jr. Sees the Civil War,* ed. Byron R. Abernathy (Norman, Okla., 1958), 187; Matthew Woodruff, *A Union Soldier in the Land of the Vanquished: The Diary of Sergeant Matthew Woodruff, June–December 1865,* ed. F. N. Boney (University, Ala., 1969), 66.

57. The newspapers describe several such confrontations between black and white Union troops. *MT,* October 5, 10, 1865.

in Mobile to take it now and that they would have it in a week." A throng of soldiers and black civilians began marching toward Government Street, the main thoroughfare. While this transpired, Thompson went into his office, summoned the guard, and reentered the street with his pistol. He called on the assembly to halt and, when they refused, fired into the crowd, which then scattered in all directions. Afterward, several soldiers were tried for inciting insurrection but acquitted, and the military command ordered all other charges dropped.[58] Still, black troops had gone from heroes to a social problem in a matter of months.

The overriding point is crucial: the USCI troops were disruptive precisely because they knew what was going on. The Union authorities offered city officials considerable leeway and even aid in controlling the black population. The very day Union troops took the city, they charged the existing city government with "the maintenance of good order among the citizens." Weeks before Pres. Andrew Johnson outlined his mild Reconstruction plan, Mobile's city council structure resumed functioning without interference. In early May, Union general James C. Veatch concluded that the courts should be reopened because the existing officials were "familiar with the duties, and have the confidence of the citizens." The notion that the restored legal system might not ensure black freedom was not suggested in his long memo on the topic. It appears the Mayor's Court was back in operation on May 14, just over a month after the city surrendered. By the summer of 1865, military provost guards were cooperating extensively with the city police for the enforcement of vagrancy ordinances, regulations that were tailored specifically for the freedpeople.[59]

Given the range of possibilities, Mobile's more prosperous white citizens might have appreciated the circumstances of defeat. Armed conflict bypassed the city itself, and after the battle was over, the army upheld much of the prevailing racial hierarchy. To some extent Mobile's civic leadership did recognize this reality, especially those in positions of responsibility. For the propertied class as a whole, though, other emotions battled with obvious self-interest. The bitterness of the war could not be easily overcome,

58. Wittenberger Diary, Sept. 7, 1865; Ira Berlin, Joseph P. Reidy, and Leslie S. Rowland, eds., *The Black Military Experience,* ser. 2 of *Freedom: A Documentary History of Emancipation* (Cambridge, Mass., 1982), 744–5. See also the case of 1st Sgt. William Barcroft, 86th USCI, MM-2824, Court-Martial Case Files, ser. 15 [H-3], National Archives.

59. *Mobile Morning News,* April 25, 1865; *OR,* ser. 1, 49(2):644–5; "Address of Mayor John Forsyth," August 29, 1865, folder 2, envelope 6, box 13, RMBACC.

regardless of how helpful the occupation force chose to be on racial issues. Perhaps the mild occupation policies left the civilian population less resigned to defeat, or possibly the less than heroic surrender of the city gave civilians something to prove. When it became clear Yankees would not rampage through Mobile, ex-Rebels could express their antinorthern sentiments more freely. Not even the army severity toward the freedpeople was fully appreciated. The changes in African American behavior after emancipation remained an overriding grievance. The fears and resentments of the former slaveholders were intense, and concessions only whetted their appetite for more severe controls.

Few whites viewed emancipation with equanimity. As one man wrote of the gloomy times, "Negroes free, negro schools, negroes everything, everywhere, anywhere, white men nowhere."[60] Given the dimensions of their loss, perhaps this was the natural response, and slaveholding women seemed particularly articulate in their despondency. Weeks after Mobile fell, Kate Oliver urged her Rebel husband to fight on, "what peace could we expect to live here with *free negroes & Yankees*." She reported that many of her neighbors lacked servants, and upper-class women experienced the emancipation of their domestics as traumatic. Ann Quigley commented five days after Mobile fell that "the insolence of servants is intolerable & those who have been treated with the greatest kindness, are the most insolent & ungrateful." After one freedwoman reclaimed her enslaved daughter, Quigley proclaimed the whole African race bereft of gratitude. She concluded that for many whites, "the departure of servants is a happy riddance—for they have become so worthless, so demoralized." Some slaveholding women resolved to do the housework themselves, often expressing a short-lived pride in their self-sufficiency, but it seems that most former owners came to terms relatively quickly. Martha Schroeder, for example, realized that many of her neighbors' domestics had left, and she offered to pay hers. She was relieved by their good behavior in staying put, thanking Yankee intimidation for her luck. Other women were less fortunate; even months later, the novelist Augusta Evans could not secure domestics and was reduced to doing her own cooking. Such upper-class women saw emancipation bring about drastic changes, dependent as they were on their domestics.[61]

60. Alfred Reynolds, May 12, 1865, Henry Lee Reynolds Papers, SHC.
61. Kate Oliver to Starke L. Oliver, [April 25, 1865,] Rice Family Papers; Belous, "Diary of Ann Quigley," 97–8; Martha Schroeder to G. Schroeder, April 1865, Schroeder Papers; Au-

Kate Cumming's postwar travails typified the wider perception. Upon returning home from her Confederate nursing duties, she was shocked to find her sister cooking and her unemployed soldier-brother doing the dishes. No domestics could be had at any price for some time after emancipation, but things were far worse on the streets. Near her house, USCI soldiers serenaded African American women with songs about "what was to be done with the white people," Cumming's apparent depiction of the musical threat to "Hang Jeff Davis from a Sour Apple Tree." According to Cumming, idle ex-slaves promenaded the avenues in gaudy array like children on holiday. It took all the "dignity and strength of mind" she could command to bear with them and their provocative behavior. On one unsettling walk, African Americans refused to clear the sidewalks for her, forcing her to step into the street. After several such instances she was in a fury, which culminated in a violent verbal outburst scattering some black children. Decades later she still marveled that the Yankees afforded no legal redress for such insolence. Clearly, for privileged women like this, the freeing of the domestics was the entering wedge for social disintegration.[62]

As they confronted emancipation, Mobile's white population simultaneously faced the issue of how to interact with the army of occupation and how to square this with their previous Confederate loyalties. A few audacious whites actually welcomed the incoming Union troops, among them Mayor R. H. Slough, who invited the victorious Union generals into his office for cigars. The citizens might understand the expediency of these actions by civic leaders, but private individuals were another matter. Collective political theater ensued on the streets, with elite women orchestrating defiance, encouraged by Victorian expectations of immunity to soldiers' abuse. Laura Pillans, for example, initially would have "scratched out the eyes of any Yankee" who would presume to speak to her. Kate Cumming thought the ladies treated Yankee officers as if invisible. Augusta Evans refused the calls of northern veterans for years, even turning away Federal Judge Richard Busteed, who had favorably reviewed one of her novels.[63] Further down the social scale, contact still raised problems, with one baker's kin being horrified by a relative's "flurting" with Union soldiers.

---

gusta Evans to J. L. M. Curry, October 7, 1865, Augusta Evans Wilson Papers, Alderman Library, University of Virginia.

62. Cumming, *Gleanings from Southland*, 258–9. See also Cumming, *Kate*, 307.

63. Smith and Smith, *Mobile*, 46–7; Cumming, *Kate*, 306; A. J. Evans to Colonel Seaver, January 13, 1867, Wilson Papers.

Those who violated this social proscription fared badly: the renowned socialite Octavia LeVert invited Chief Justice Salmon Chase to her home during his visit in May 1865. She found herself involved in a distasteful exchange in the press over the appropriateness of social contacts with Yankees. LeVert soon moved to the North, having lost caste locally.[64]

However little Mobile's citizens welcomed the Yankee presence as an abstract proposition, city officials could scarcely reject military assistance. For one thing, the Federal troops were soon bored with garrison duty and became restive, frequently drinking or fighting in town. Arresting them posed the risk of conflict between the police and the soldiers, and so military cooperation was essential to prevent riot. Another difficult issue was the question of army relief for the destitute. Incredibly, most rations issued over the summer and fall went to white refugees; here too the concern about drawing blacks into the city and encouraging idleness determined military policy.[65] The approximately three thousand destitute white refugees evoked much less public comment than the influx of freedpeople. Still, the flood of newcomers left the city police facing unprecedented challenges. One evening in July, for example, a crowd of Union and ex-Confederate soldiers looted several whorehouses on Cedar Street only to be dispersed by the provost guard. That same night a crowd of transients broke into a shop and then started robbing people on the street. The *Mobile Tribune* stated that the city police of "less than thirty men" could not resist the "hordes of negroes and Northern whites" who congregated in the ruined warehouses.[66] The paper blamed the disturbances on army force reductions that had weakened the provost guard. "We know of no better plan," concluded the *Tribune*, "than for citizens to take summary measures when marauders, either white or black, are found on their premises." Given a situation of such severity, the cooperation of the Union command in maintaining order was crucial.

In the years to come, Mobile's civic leadership would recognize other issues besides black in-migration looming before them, addressing, for ex-

---

64. Sarah A. Spinks to Mary, June 25, 1865, Gavin Yuille Papers, W. S. Hoole Special Collections, University of Alabama; *Mobile Morning News,* May 13, 1865; Mrs. Semmes to "My Precious Child," October 1, 1865, Raphael Semmes Papers, ADAH; Jay Higginbotham, *Mobile, City by the Bay* (Mobile, 1968), 73–79.

65. Wager Swayne to Howard, Sept. 18, 1865, reel 17; and A. B. Eaton to "All Officers of the Subsistence Dept.," October 6, 1865, M752, RG 105, reel 24.

66. *Mobile Tribune* quoted in *New Orleans Daily Picayune,* July 13, 1865.

ample, the concerns of merchants as the cotton trade deteriorated. In the immediate postwar period, however, the freedpeople's movement into the city was the overriding issue, at least once the novelty of Union occupation wore off. Between 1860 and 1866, Mobile's population grew by more than a third. Over ten thousand new residents descended upon the city. There were few jobs and little housing for the large number of newcomers of both races, but city officials zeroed in on black in-migration as the target of choice. The freedpeople were subject to influx control in ways that whites traditionally were not. White opinion makers thought freedpeople belonged on the farm anyway, and stringent vagrancy legislation and aggressive policing would deter further migration.

The municipal objective became to test how far the army would let civilian officials go in deterring unwelcome new arrivals and in disciplining the black population generally. In July Mayor Slough recommended establishing a house of correction and a work-house system, primarily to deal with the influx of "Negro loafers, idlers and paupers." Such measures would benefit the surrounding countryside by "preventing the Negroes from flocking into the city." The *Mobile Advertiser and Register* agreed with this general approach but thought existing vagrancy policies too costly to act as an effective deterrent. Another newspaper, the *Mobile Times,* suggested that it was high time for the authorities to "take all vagrants and place them at grading and cleaning streets—that is, make a wholesale matter of it." Behind the political motivation of deterring migration was the wider elite sense of grievance toward the conduct of their former slaves. A palpable animus drove city policy, and heavy-handed police measures became the flashpoint of the freedpeople's anger. On racial matters elite Mobilians recognized few limits beyond those posed by external constraint, and military pliancy only encouraged further demands. The extremist consensus of Mobile's dominant political classes guaranteed escalating political and racial confrontation.[67]

As the weight of army policy and civil rule bore more harshly upon the freedpeople, opposition gathered. African Americans (as shall be seen in the next chapter) mobilized to proclaim their dissent before the national public. In this effort they gained the assistance of pockets of white sympathizers,

---

67. Mayor R. H. Slough to Boards of Aldermen and Common Council, July 25, 1865, Board of Common Council, Minutes, Mobile Municipal Archives, reel 17; *MAR,* Sept. 28, 1865; *MT,* October 8, 1865.

both inside and outside the military, who thought the ex-Rebels had gone too far. An interracial group coalesced that foreshadowed the Republican party of Congressional Reconstruction. A cluster of native Union men existed in Mobile, articulate in their discontent but not closely attuned to the needs of the freedpeople. From the point of view of the African Americans, the most useful of their outside allies were the officers of the Freedmen's Bureau and the northern missionaries and educators surrounding them. If bureau personnel often pursued conservative social objectives elsewhere, in Mobile the belligerent defense of their definition of the freedpeople's interest seemed more evident.[68] Outside help came with strings attached, but African Americans were short of friends and needed whatever aid presented itself.

National political developments set the context for the local confrontation. After Lincoln's assassination, his successor, Andrew Johnson, formulated the approach known as Presidential Reconstruction, which took shape by the summer of 1865. This policy's hallmark was a swift restoration of civil rule with minimal preconditions beyond acquiescence in reunion and emancipation. Once the mass of ex-Confederates swore allegiance, new state constitutions would be enacted following these guidelines, and if deemed acceptable, President Johnson would recognize civilian government. Congress, when it assembled, would then hopefully readmit their federal representatives and Reconstruction would be complete. Under Johnson's policies the probability was that ex-Rebels would return to power almost everywhere. In Mobile the implications were alarming for the freedpeople, but the city's few open loyalists were among the most vociferous critics of Presidential Reconstruction. These Unionists were mostly from a segment of Mobile's merchant class. Their improbable emergence as leaders of the Reconstruction cause grew directly out of their wartime experiences.

In the antebellum years, Mobile had an ethnically diverse population, and like many southern cities, it possessed a substantial northern- and foreign-born presence within the business community. Sectional moderation had long dominated Mobile's politics, with Steven A. Douglas actually carrying the city in the 1860 presidential election. It came as a shock when

---

68. William S. McFeely, *Yankee Stepfather: General O. O. Howard and the Freedmen* (New Haven, 1968), 5; Louis S. Gerteis, *From Contraband to Freedman: Federal Policy toward Southern Blacks* (Westport, Conn., 1973), 183–92.

Abraham Lincoln's election brought a popular surge toward the southern-rights cause. Conservative older businessmen found themselves and their misgivings ignored as the state rushed toward secession and war. One Vermont-born merchant manifested his sense of alienation. To escape the events surrounding Fort Sumter, he went fishing, taking one of his slaves, Hannibal, along for company. While on Mobile Bay, he heard the sounds of celebration coming from the city and guessed that it meant war. Despondent as he was, he noticed that Hannibal did not seem that upset, and he dimly perceived that civil war might mean deliverance to his slave. Other unwelcome reflections would follow as the merchant discovered that Unionists and the enslaved were in much the same boat.[69]

Some opposition to the Confederacy or its war measures, of course, extended throughout the city's white population, but most draft evaders or dissidents could hardly afford to call attention to themselves. The profile of the elite Unionists was different. While most business-community opponents of secession fell in line once war broke out, a smaller number remained unreconciled to the new Confederate nation. About two dozen residents, mostly merchants born outside of the South, were old enough to escape conscription and well-established enough to risk a dissident reputation. Few courted martyrdom, but their opinions were known by their friends and relations and widely rumored on the streets. Groups of Union sympathizers met regularly in homes and businesses, with the knowledge of Confederate officials. Elite Unionists, especially the richer ones, generally secured some protection from the authorities in exchange for pledges of discreet behavior. Compared to Union men elsewhere in the South, their treatment was notably mild, as one of their leaders acknowledged. Still, they did suffer official surveillance and a good deal of popular disapproval. Mobile's knot of Union men considered their political ostracism and enforced public silence an ordeal.[70]

That trial was most intense for Gustavus Horton, the city's one uncompromisingly public Unionist. A native of New England, he had been in business in Mobile for decades; though not rich, he had helped found the local

---

69. [William Rix,] *Incidents of Life in a Southern City during the War* (Rutland, Vt., ca. 1880), 5; Michael W. Fitzgerald, "From Unionists to Scalawags: Elite Dissent in Civil War Mobile," *Alabama Review* 55 (spring 2002): 106–21.

70. [Rix,] *Incidents of Life*, 5; Fitzgerald, "From Unionists to Scalawags," 106–21.

public school system and "stood very high socially" before the war.[71] When the Confederacy began to force older men into militia service, Horton refused and was briefly jailed by the home guard.[72] Even so, his social connections got him released, though he would be periodically harassed thereafter, once reportedly for possession of a U.S. flag. Horton's wartime persecution, harsh or not, propelled him toward political activism after the war. There were few consistent Union men like himself, Horton thought, but these were Mobile's proper postwar leaders. Horton and his comrades expected to direct the process of reunion, but President Johnson's policy unfolded differently, stressing conciliation of former foes. The now impoverished Horton, with his occupation as a cotton merchant gone, saw federal treasury jobs go to either ex-Rebels or thieves—the latter being spectacularly the case in Mobile.[73] Horton was embittered because as things stood Union men were as hated as ever. Public opinion had to change, he thought, and in the meantime the "safety of the Negro, as well as protection to Union men" depended on military occupation.[74]

Wartime dissidents generally escaped jail, but many shared Horton's sentiments. Another merchant family, that of the German immigrant Francis Bromberg, took a similar political trajectory during the crisis. The senior Bromberg owned a successful toy store, and during the war he gathered a group of Unionists who "formed a circle of their own." His middle son, Frederick G. Bromberg, would become Gustavus Horton's longtime ally. The younger Bromberg was a tutor at Harvard University when the war broke out, and he sought to serve the Union without bringing retribution upon his family. He repeatedly volunteered to serve in a noncombatant role, even under fire, asking no pay beyond expenses. Upon returning to Mobile after Appomattox, Frederick Bromberg was horrified by the prominence of ex-Confederate leaders. He injudiciously allowed his name to be

---

71. F. G. Bromberg to Carl Schurz, March 15, 1877, box 4, AP-247, RG 56. See also Harriet E. Amos, "Trials of a Unionist: Gustavus Horton, Military Mayor of Mobile during Reconstruction," *Gulf South Historical Review* 4 (fall 1989): 134–51.

72. C. W. Horton to Lewis Parsons, August 1, 1865, [Provisional] Gov. Lewis E. Parsons Papers, ADAH; Horton to S. W. Field, January 31, 1866, box 4, AP-247, RG 56.

73. *Mobile News,* May 31, 1865; Horton to Eliza Horton, June 28, 1865, Gustavus Horton Papers, The Museum of Mobile. See also Richard W. Griffin, "Cotton Frauds and Confiscations in Alabama, 1863–1866," *Alabama Review* 7 (October 1954): 265–77.

74. Horton to S. W. Field, January 31, 1866; *Harper's Weekly,* October 21, 1865, 658.

used on the local advisory board for the Freedmen's Saving Bank branch, and as soon as this became known his teaching prospects vanished, as one Republican source noted.[75]

Gustavus Horton and the Brombergs became the focus of native white Republicanism, and much of Mobile's scalawag leadership emerged from among their circle of Union dissidents and their sons. For example, two of Horton's Unionist friends, Amos Towle and the immigrant William Hurter, were his close postwar collaborators. Hurter had actually moved to Mobile with Horton decades before, which suggests the sort of personal ties that kept these men together. Reconstruction never secured a white popular constituency in Mobile, but this enclave of wartime business-class Unionists was a significant source of individual Republican activists. With Appomattox, wartime Union men momentarily stepped forward to initiate the Reconstruction process, but this public agitation ceased once the outlines of Presidential Reconstruction became clear. Thereafter, the best-connected and richest of the wartime Unionists mostly dropped from sight, and victory ended their estrangement from respectable society. However, the most alienated Union men, and especially those who needed employment, tended to gravitate into politics once black suffrage transformed the scene. At least ten of the two dozen relatively prominent wartime Unionists became Republicans, and several of them would serve as Reconstruction officeholders or federal patronage employees.[76]

For the black population, these newfound Unionist allies possessed obvious appeal. The slave grapevine monitored their political preferences, aided by the Union men's tendency to vent their frustration to their domestics. Some African Americans were favorably impressed with the evidence of elite disaffection. One free black, Frank Starke, heard the rich businessman John M. Brown denounced before the city government as disloyal. Starke subsequently approached Brown for advice on how to evade the forced labor on the fortifications imposed on free blacks. Brown's suggestion that as a city employee Starke was exempt proved technically accurate, though pursuing it got Starke arrested and beaten by Rebel soldiers. Starke's perception of Brown as antislavery was not altogether accurate, but this repu-

---

75. F. G. Bromberg to Carl Schurz, March 15, 1877; F. G. Bromberg to "Dear Sir," Sept. 6, 1861, Letters of Application and Recommendation during the Administration of A. Lincoln and A. Johnson (M650), RG 59, reel 8; *MN,* August 15, 1867.

76. J. W. Sullivan to G. S. Boutwell, July 28, 1870, AP-247, RG 56; Rix, *Incidents of Life,* 28; Fitzgerald, "From Unionists to Scalawags," 106–21.

tation perhaps encouraged the black community to look favorably on him as a Republican and similarly upon his younger brother, Wiley, who would emerge as an postwar activist. Other black leaders had positive wartime experiences with loyalists too, sometimes fairly dramatic ones. At a coffeehouse downtown, John Brown and other Union men congregated to read smuggled northern newspapers and talk about the war. But more was afoot: the proprietor recalled that "Jim Bragg a cab driver, colored man" used to bring U.S. spies "disguised in Confederate uniforms" to the coffeehouse. Espionage was no light enterprise, and having trusted the Union men with his life during the war, James Bragg was willing to collaborate with them politically thereafter. Bragg would become a prominent black spokesman for Frederick Bromberg and his moderate scalawag allies. The point applies more broadly: those African American leaders resident in Mobile the longest tended to be those drawn to the native white leadership. These prewar residents were most knowledgeable about the Unionists' record of hostility to the Confederacy.[77]

Still, wartime loyalty only went so far to endear prosperous Unionist businessmen to the black population. Even if they were generally born outside the South, most of these merchants had owned slaves, and few showed hostility to the peculiar institution. To be sure, men like Gustavus Horton and Frederick Bromberg loathed the Confederacy, and they were well known as early critics of the postwar regime. Both were committed, personally reputable men, and with black suffrage they became the leaders of the moderate faction that dominated Republican politics. However, during the immediate postwar years, they were hesitant allies for the freedpeople, raising civil rights issues cautiously if at all. This made some sense. Horton was an established figure in antebellum Mobile, after all; he had owned slaves, and one of his sons served as an officer in the Confederate army. If he had antislavery sentiments, he kept them well hidden, and his scattered postwar correspondence suggests his racial views were those of his class and circumstance. One admirer observed that he "loved his country intensely, but was no negro-worshipper."[78] If the freedpeople were going to find more respon-

77. "Deposition of Frank Stark"; and "Deposition of Frank Slocovich," case of John Morgan Brown, Case Files for Mobile County, Approved Claims for Alabama (M2062), Southern Claims Commission, National Archives, reel 29.

78. Newspaper clipping of obituary, [1868?,] Horton Papers. The obituary was apparently prompted by a mistaken rumor of his assassination.

sive white allies, then they would have to come from beyond the circle of polite society in Mobile.

Other aid was near at hand, for the war brought hundreds of northerners to the city. Some of these, particularly those in business, adopted protective coloration on racial matters. "Damn the Niggers" was a Yankee "countersign for safe conduct" in the South, one correspondent observed. Still, the resurgence of Rebel sentiment alarmed many newly arrived northerners. Dozens spoke out, often encouraged by professional concerns, like the officers in black units who complained about the treatment of their soldiers. One USCI lieutenant accused the *Mobile News* of slighting the role of black troops at Fort Blakely. A northern correspondent believed such officers prodded their men to demand their rights; he thought they were egalitarian zealots alienated from their peers. The strictures aside, the point was valid. A few of these officers had personal motives, among them Col. G. Yarrington, who married a local African American woman. His military colleagues were outraged, but he later established himself in a second-tier political career as a Republican, an outcome that perhaps reflected his personal choices. In addition to such examples from the army, there were northern lawyers like George F. Harrington and W. W. D. Turner who were willing to speak up for the freedpeople for a fee.[79]

Northern religious and benevolent societies likewise fostered activism. Yankee churches operating in Mobile, like the Northern Methodists, made little headway among the freedpeople, who preferred the African Methodist denominations or locally controlled black Baptist churches. Still, northern missionaries seemed more troubled by the conflict with southern rivals than their lack of success with the ex-slaves. For example, an army chaplains' association was permitted to meet in facilities provided by a local congregation, that is until they were locked out for expressing antislavery sentiments. The other philanthropic efforts centered in Mobile generated similar experiences, given that relief and educational society employees were often abolitionist in background. For example, the antislavery American Missionary Association eventually wound up in control of the major black school. The schoolteachers and missionaries sent south to work for such agencies distinguished themselves as critics of the conservative establishment. Their accounts appealed to the freedpeople and demonstrated the

---

79. *MAR*, March 3, 1866; *New York World*, July 24, 1865; *New Orleans Tribune*, June 10, 1865.

importance of their witness to financial supporters back home. One Yankee teacher wrote that in Mobile, "through the connivance of somebody, churches and negro houses are burned," while women were "set to work cleaning the streets." The army's conciliatory approach to the ex-Confederates infuriated him. Similar letters from Mobile appeared in the denominational press and also in abolitionist papers. William Lloyd Garrison managed to place the city in Georgia, but his *Liberator* effectively publicized Mobile's retrograde politics. Mainstream national publications from the *New York Times* on down reprinted these reports and embellished them.[80]

A stream of visiting dignitaries came to similar conclusions, and their vocal dissent against Andrew Johnson's Reconstruction policies heartened opponents of the local status quo. In May Chief Justice Salmon P. Chase stopped for a formal reception. He used the opportunity to promote his favored reform, universal suffrage, jarring the local dignitaries who scarcely expected such talk. Gen. C. C. Andrews, briefly in command in the city, was persuaded, and he espoused it openly on his return to the North.[81] Chief Justice Chase thought he had a similar effect on Mayor Slough, wholly inaccurately, but he at least managed to impress upon Mobile's residents the contrary tendency of northern political opinion. Other Republican politicians also visited, among them Carl Schurz, who arrived in September on his southern tour. Schurz's published letters broadcast the views of those missionaries and Freedmen's Bureau agents who were most aggravated. He denounced Mobile's mayor for his "southern prejudice against our black soldiers." Schurz dismissed as hogwash the rumors of black insurrection, claiming they were manufactured for political effect.[82]

These varied strands of dissent, from native Unionists to Yankee interlopers, came together as a sort of ad hoc lobby of concerned whites. Their interests and values were in some tension with those of the African American community, but all dissidents had incentive to work together. At the

---

80. *(Boston) Zion's Herald,* Sept. 6, 1865; *The Independent,* August 24, 1865; *Christian Recorder,* December 9, 1865; *Liberator,* December 22, 1865; *NYT* quoted in *Chicago Christian Advocate and Journal,* June 15, 1865.

81. Christopher C. Andrews, *Recollections: 1829–1922* (Cleveland, 1928), 201; undated clipping from *St. Paul Press,* [October 1865,] in autobiography manuscript, Andrews Papers.

82. John Niven et al., eds., *Salmon P. Chase Papers, Volume 1, Journal, 1829–1872* (Kent, Ohio, and London, 1993), 563; C. Schurz to Andrew Johnson, Sept. 15, 1865, Andrew Johnson Papers, LC, reel 18.

center of this network stood the Freedmen's Bureau. By the summer of 1865, the bureau moved to defend basic rights for the freedpeople, both from city officials and from their own army comrades. The literature on the Freedmen's Bureau stresses the social-control agenda, and it is certainly true that the initial freedmen's agency set up under Colonel Conway's guidance promoted labor.[83] Capt. George Harmount, the local agent, supported severe vagrancy policies at first. In April he wrote that "some system should be instituted immediately which will oblige these colored people to obtain employment at wages" because they would not work so long as the government gave them provisions.[84] Harmount issued labor guidelines for the vicinity, modeled on the wartime Louisiana code; it provided for wages of ten dollars a month for both able-bodied men and women plus food, housing, and medical attention. Harmount insisted on approving all contracts, and with this protection in place, he began issuing certificates of employment to African Americans.[85] Any person without employment could then be "easily found and 'pressed'" in case of any sudden demand for labor" or if the "number of idlers and vagrants" became a nuisance. Later, Harmount urged the army to arrest those idling in the streets without a certificate of employment issued by him.[86]

These initial steps toward the freedpeople were harsh, but Harmount soon reconsidered his priorities. His concerns over vagrancy quickly paled in comparison to the oppression blacks faced. He found that Union guards continually disobeyed the order to leave employed people unmolested. Those who were "law abiding and self supporting" should not be forced to labor, he emphasized.[87] If federal soldiers were problematic, Harmount was appalled by the civil officials, now restored to office under Union authority

---

83. On Conway's labor policies, see Michael W. Fitzgerald, "Emancipation and Military Pacification: The Freedmen's Bureau and Social Control in Alabama," in *The Freedmen's Bureau and Reconstruction: Reconsiderations,* ed. Paul A. Cimbala and Randall Miller (New York, 1999), 54–5.

84. G. Harmount to R. G. Curtis, April 28, 1865, Letters Sent, SAC Mobile, vol. 108, entry 142, RG 105; Harmount to Col. C. T. Christianson, May 5, 1865, Letters Received, 1865, box 13, Department of the Gulf, RG 393, pt. 2.

85. *Mobile News,* May 4, 1865.

86. George Harmount to T. W. Conway, May 30, 1865; and George Harmount to B. Porter, June 8, 1865, Letters Sent Sub-Assistant Commissioner at Mobile, vol. 108, entry 142, RG 105.

87. G. Harmount to Col. T. Kinney, July 27, 1865, Letters Sent, SAC Mobile, vol. 108, entry 142, RG 105; George Harmount to T. W. Conway, May 30, 1865.

and reasserting themselves. The city courts would not even accept black testimony until Harmount procured an order from General Andrews resolving the issue, temporarily at least. On one occasion he ordered a search of the city jail for evidence of torture, apparently without success.[88] Bureau agents were actually arrested that summer for interfering with the proceedings of city court, and Mayor R. H. Slough was a constant focus of Harmount's concern.[89] In Mayor's Court the "evident design" was to require so large a peace bond that the accused would have to leave town, guilty or not. The mayor also enforced the antebellum curfew, applying to blacks only. Slough apparently interpreted simple unemployment as willful idleness and, when challenged, refused to release men from the street gang in response to military orders. Perhaps the most striking indication of Slough's attitude was his objection to the freedpeople gathering downtown to celebrate the Fourth of July on the grounds that the crowd would damage the lawn of the city park. His intransigence foreshadowed the violence that would mar the festivities.[90]

Eventually, Mayor Slough overstepped himself by disallowing black testimony in his court. Despite his previous compliance with military orders, he concluded that once Presidential Reconstruction was underway, antebellum legal statutes barring black testimony were again in effect. In one instance a "negro wench" brought charges against a white man for "knocking her over," and the mayor, declining her testimony, dismissed the charges. Northern observers were outraged, which compounded their strong personal dislike of the mayor: one Yankee general predicted Slough would "eat his own words . . . like a spaniel" when challenged. In late July the bureau's assistant commissioner for Alabama, Gen. Wager T. Swayne, prevailed on the provisional governor to remove the mayor, Slough having distinguished himself as the sole civil official in the state to merit such treatment. Slough's successor, *Mobile Advertiser and Register* editor John Forsyth, complied more readily with military orders, though his racial views were similar.[91]

88. *Mobile News* quoted in *New Orleans Times Picayune,* June 11, 1865; *Mobile Daily News,* May 19, 1865.
89. G. Harmount to Capt. W. H. Clapp, August 28, 1865, Letters Sent, SAC Mobile, vol. 108., entry 142, RG 105; W. A. Poillon to Swayne, August 8, 1865, M809, RG 105, reel 9.
90. G. Harmount to R. H. Slough, June 22, July 3, 5, 26, 1865, Letter Sent, SAC Mobile, vol. 108, entry 142, RG 105.
91. Gen. Thomas Kirby Smith to Wager Swayne, August 9, 1865, Letters Received, 1865–

By the summer, Harmount found himself constantly embroiled. Increasingly, such critics of conservative rule under Presidential Reconstruction looked for redress from the Republican majority in Congress. Harmount told his superior, General Swayne, that there was no hope in Mobile unless the bureau's "friends in Washington" came to the rescue. Harmount urged immediate measures "to take lands and buildings and sell and rent them to the colored people. Numbers of them wish to buy land and build on it, to rent land and work it, and to rent houses in the city at living rates." Harmount recommended that his colleague, Capt. W. A. Poillon, confiscate Rebel property immediately before President Johnson could pardon the owners. This private advice would suggest both Harmount's level of alienation from the city's whites and his urgent desire to help the freedpeople. For his part, Captain Poillon had much the same racial views as his associate. In attending court as an observer, he was arrested by civil officials for contempt, an experience that enraged him. Poillon afterward testified that the policy of restoring civil authority had failed because the police were arresting people without the shadow of an excuse. Vindictive hatred was "universal," and blacks would only be accepted as slaves. "Incendiary and lying" reports in the papers of black insurrection plots were "utterly without foundation." Upon his return to the North, Poillon enlightened the press about what he had seen. By the fall, bureau personnel clearly accepted confrontation with the civil authorities.[92]

Perhaps the most dramatic illustration of the bureau's combative attitude was the lengthy struggle over the Mobile Medical College, which the army had turned over to missionaries for a freedmen's school. Though the vacant institution's trustees had initially agreed to the temporary arrangement, they reneged in the fall of 1865. The dean of the college, the renowned ethnologist Josiah Nott, mounted an increasingly public campaign to have the college restored. However, the Yankee missionaries, under Prin-

---

67, Department of Alabama, RG 393, pt. 2; Wager Swayne to Gov. Lewis Parsons, August 11, 1865, M809, RG 105, reel 1.

92. Harmount to Swayne, July 26, 1865, M809, RG 105, reel 5; U.S. Congress, Senate, *Message of the President of the United States, Communicating, in Compliance with a Resolution of the Senate of the 12th Instant, Information in Relation to the States of the Union Lately in Rebellion, Accompanied by a Report of Carl Schurz on the States of South Carolina, Georgia, Alabama, Mississippi, and Louisiana; Also a Report of General Grant, on the Same Subject*, 39th Cong., 1st sess., S. Exec. Doc. 2, 72–3 [hereafter cited as *Report of Carl Schurz*]; *St. Louis Republican* quoted in *MAR*, April 20, 1866.

cipal E. C. Branch, could secure no other location, if only because the fear of arson discouraged rentals. The besieged teachers called on northern allies to come to their aid, and as one freedmen's aid official observed, the case was clearly a test of President Johnson's intentions. As a result, the leaders of the Freedmen's Bureau found themselves in the midst of a major confrontation. Assistant Commissioner Swayne decided to stand firm despite his well-established reputation for cooperating with southern whites. The legalities were murky, but Mobile was already "in a state of quasi-riot," and Swayne rejected further concessions to resurgent Rebel sentiment. Besides, as a practical matter, the building was public property, and the school was relatively safe from fire where it was.[93]

Swayne's superior, Freedmen's Bureau Commissioner O. O. Howard, came to the city to take stock of the situation. By this point, Josiah Nott was beside himself, publicly manifesting the racial intransigence that typified Mobile's elite. A meeting between the two went badly; and Nott proclaimed that he would "rather see the building burned down than have it used for Colored children." Afterward, Nott claimed that the freedpeople were gloating in their continued possession of the building, and he privately concluded that the future looked gloomy until they were "all killed out." Meanwhile, the agency dug in. For the next year, General Howard engaged in a stubborn bureaucratic battle to prevent the restoration or else secure another building. The school finally found other quarters and moved, but the bureau's involvement did not end there. Late in 1867 General Swayne concluded that a permanent presence was necessary in view of the city's lack of interest in black education. He negotiated a joint purchase of a school building, to be called the Emerson Institute, by the bureau and the American Missionary Association. The purchase, reluctantly acceded to by the financially strapped association, was facilitated by the imaginative use of bureau financing. It was Swayne's final act as military commander in the state, completed in his last hours before departure. The following year the bureau insisted on the Emerson Institute's having a central role in the public school system. The record suggests that bureau leaders invested personal ego in the outcome, if only to defy the rebellious whites of Mobile.[94]

93. J. R. Shipherd to "General," October 14, 1865, M809, RG 105, reel 6; Swayne to Parsons, August 11, 1865; Wager Swayne to J. R. Shipherd, Sept. 30, 1865, M752, RG 105, reel 23.

94. Josiah Nott, "The Problem of the Black Races," *De Bow's Review, After the War Series,* March 1866, 267–8; J. C. Nott to E. Squier, December 5, 1865, E. G. Squire Papers, LC; George D. Robinson to C. Cadle, November 5, 1865, M809, RG 105, reel 6; Michael

"See how the damd Military, the nigger troops, the Freedmen's Bureau spit upon us and rub it in." Such was Josiah Nott's verdict, and it is certainly hard to charge Swayne, Howard, and company with insufficient egalitarian zeal in Mobile. The episode similarly politicized E. C. Branch and the Yankee missionaries around him, exacerbating their sense of siege. These men and women formed a social enclave, and several marriages occurred between the mostly teaching female staff and their white Radical allies. This profile was not wholly to their benefit; as time went on, even the teachers' bureau allies found them too insular, wholly isolated as the surrounding hostility lessened. Still, perceived persecution at the hands of ex-Rebels enhanced their legitimacy in the eyes of the freedpeople, some of whom ideally would have preferred black teachers.[95] As African American politics emerged in Mobile, much of it would center on the medical college school, and the missionary teachers would be in the midst of it. By late 1865, an array of white activists clustered around the Freedmen's Bureau with emotional and bureaucratic stake in resisting conservative rule. These would be among the few whites in Mobile committed to Radical Reconstruction, and though they were often sincere, they were also a disruptive presence within the environing black community. The issue of how best to utilize these and other white allies, and what their appropriate role should be, became the crucial internal debates as African American politics took shape.

W. Fitzgerald, "Wager Swayne, the Freedmen's Bureau, and the Politics of Reconstruction in Alabama," *Alabama Review* 48 (July 1995): 215.

95. J. Nott to E. Squire, March 2, 1866, Squire Papers; C. W. Buckley to Rev. E. W. Cravath, August 14, 1867, M810, RG 105, reel 1; *Anglo-African,* Sept. 16, 1865. Missionaries from black denominations visiting the city during this period, for example, called for black instructors.

2

None but Colored Men

The *Mobile Nationalist* and the Dilemmas
of Interracial Activism

The social woes of the arriving freedpeople would fuel mass-based factionalism within the Republican party, but this only emerged over time. Before universal suffrage, during Presidential Reconstruction, popular unrest was evident on the streets, but organized political activity among African Americans was focused more narrowly. Formal agitation commenced as an affair of committed and often privileged activists rather than drawing upon the grassroots energies so evident in later factional disputes. Still, the precursors of later fault lines quickly became evident in terms of both disagreements over strategies of racial advancement and aspirations for individual prominence. From the start, the movement in support of Reconstruction was a startlingly contentious enterprise, which was the harbinger of future developments. Internal strife was pervasive long before African Americans had real power to fight over. One substantive issue in particular divided black activists: the appropriate role of white allies. From the initiation of political activity, the influence of the few favorably disposed Yankees proved more troublesome than any other topic. The dispute found practical expression in battles over direction of a community-owned newspaper, but the wider issue of external control over black political expression proved endemic.

Initial controversy over this pregnant issue emerged days after Union victory, with Gen. E. R. S. Canby's occupation of the city in April 1865. When the Bureau of Free Labor's Thomas Conway arrived to oversee emancipation, he promoted a political agenda shaped by his own recent experiences. In Louisiana, Conway was embroiled in controversy over the policies of his superior, Gen. Nathaniel Banks, and more broadly over President Lincoln's "lenient" wartime Reconstruction plan. In implementing General Banks's draconian labor code, Conway received criticism, especially from the activists associated with the *New Orleans Tribune*.[1] Stung by the negative publicity, Conway blamed his troubles on the "insubordination of Creole negroes of French spirit and slave holding antecedents." These elite malcontents criticized government officials and made "the poor freedmen in the city unhappy at the idea that they do not vote and hold office." Thus, as Conway arrived in Alabama to oversee emancipation, he relied on his experience with Afro-Creole critics back in New Orleans, despite the fact that Mobile's Creoles sought no similar role as civil rights vanguard. In emphatic terms Conway urged his African American audiences to trust white Yankee soldiers and missionaries as the appropriate friends of freedom. He called on blacks to withdraw from the treason-tainted Southern Methodists and affiliate instead with northern denominations like the Methodist Episcopal Church. Conway even hawked subscriptions to his own faction's short-lived newspaper, the *Black Republican*, initially claiming hundreds of Mobile readers.[2]

The episode was emblematic. Conway was the first of many outside advisors urging cultivation of white allies, in the military, in the Republican party, or in the northern churches and benevolent societies. This counsel of necessity always raised delicate issues. A backlash materialized quickly as Conway's Louisiana opponents dispatched emissaries to present their side. One "Avery," a *Tribune* activist from a free black family with Mobile connections, established himself as the opposition spokesman on the scene. At the same time black religious leaders arrived from New Orleans to counteract Conway's religious teaching. Soon, the *Tribune* gloated that virtually the whole freed population had joined one of the African Methodist denominations or else local black Baptist churches.[3] Ideologically, the African

---

1. Bell, *Revolution, Romanticism, and the Afro-Creole Protest Tradition in Louisiana*, 252–8.

2. T. Conway to E. M. Stanton, March 25, 1865, M752, RG 105, reel 14; *New Orleans Black Republican*, May 21, 1865.

3. *New York Anglo-African*, June 10, 1865; *New Orleans Tribune*, May 4, 7, 1865. The Avery in question is either Moses B. Avery or one of his sons. Moses Avery was a prewar free black, originally from Mobile, who became an editor and activist with the *New Orleans Tribune*. Bailey, *Neither Carpetbaggers Nor Scalawags*, 109–10.

Methodist Episcopal (AME) and AME Zion, both northern imports, approached the freedmen in as thorough a spirit of paternal uplift as the white Yankee churches.[4] However, the central role of racial assertiveness, the notion of race-specific institutions as legitimate even after emancipation, were distinctive contributions. As Reginald F. Hildebrand has observed, black Methodist missionaries "emphasized the need for former slaves to free themselves from the control of whites and become equal, independent, fully franchised citizens."[5] This concept so clearly articulated in the religious sphere would resonate in Mobile's popular politics more broadly.

This initial controversy raised enduring issues. Conway encouraged pragmatic accommodation of northern allies, while his *Tribune* critics responded with a language of racial assertiveness, contending that only their fellow African Americans could speak for the masses. The Louisiana Afro-Creoles sought racial integration as an ultimate goal, but their campaign against Conway emphasized contrary rhetoric.[6] Their discourse of self-determination was amplified by that of the black religious denominations. The influence of these ideas long outlived the circumstances of their introduction to Mobile. The result was that from the moment of emancipation, what might be termed incipient "black nationalist" ideas were under discussion, concepts in tension with the interracial Radical Republican formulations that would dominate formal politics. However imperfectly articulated, racial self-determination rhetoric would become the recurrent language of community resistance to the demands of white allies—allies who sought deference far beyond their numbers as surrogates for the loyal North. Factional struggles were superimposed upon this core social and ideological dispute in a variety of incarnations.

Following Conway's eclipse, organizational efforts for some time proceeded primarily from within the African American community rather than from outside initiation. Public political agitation languished for months despite repeated prodding by the *Tribune*. Perhaps in part this was because Mobile's educated Creoles provided less leadership than their politicized counterparts in Union-occupied Louisiana, for unlike the *Tribune* Radicals,

---

4. Clarence E. Walker, *A Rock in a Weary Land: The African Methodist Episcopal Church during the Civil War and Reconstruction* (Baton Rouge, 1982).

5. Reginald F. Hildebrand, *The Times Were Strange and Stirring: Methodist Preachers and the Crisis of Emancipation* (Durham, 1995), 33.

6. Bell, *Revolution, Romanticism, and the Afro-Creole Protest Tradition in Louisiana*, 264, 272.

Mobile's Creole organizations still hoped their privileged position might survive emancipation.[7] Moreover, given the recent emergence of independent black religious denominations, other forms of community building likely took precedence. Educational efforts began instantly, developing in unison with the African American churches. For example, less than one month after the city fell, the "State Street M.E. Colored Church" opened a school with the assistance of a northern aid society. Ten days later over five hundred students were in attendance, gathered from churches throughout the city.[8] E. C. Branch was one of the instructors, and this was the school that would soon be moved into the disputed Mobile Medical College. Other schools quickly opened under black church auspices. However, the response of the wider community was frosty, and at least two schools were soon destroyed by arson.[9]

The threat of violence probably deterred open political agitation, but less confrontational mobilization efforts proceeded swiftly. The community spirit of the freedpeople of Mobile was pervasive, as Gen. Wager Swayne of the Freedmen's Bureau emphasized. They gave "zealous support" to schools and churches and established an "Association to provide work for the unemployed."[10] Community organizations proliferated, especially collective benefit or group insurance societies, along with church benevolent associations. From the Daughters of Zion or the Evening Star Virgin Sons and Daughters to occupational associations like the Mechanics' and Draymen's Association, these groups were little noticed by the outside world, but they were a major focus of initial community activities. Within months, eleven fraternal organizations held accounts at the new Freedmen's Bank in Mobile. While not explicitly political, these organizations' very existence facilitated popular discussion and mobilization. They were strikingly democratic and even plebian in leadership. Illiterates frequently served as officers, as did women, which would suggest a broad base of participation. Unlike the organizations in the political and educational spheres, which

---

7. Petition of Creoles, October 11, 1865, Creole Fire Company Papers, The Museum of Mobile.

8. E. C. Branch, "Report of Schools of AFAC," January 15, 1866, enclosed in Wager Swayne to Howard, February 10, 1866; and E. C. Branch to Howard, December 4, 1865, M752, RG 105, reel 19.

9. Swayne to J. R. Shipherd, September 30, 1865, enclosed in Shipherd to A. Johnson, October 14, 1865, M752, RG 105, reel 23.

10. Wager Swayne to Howard, July 24, 1865, M752, RG 105, reel 1.

often involved interracial participation and solicitation of northern allies, these groups were all black and internally directed. Here too was the prevailing pattern reflected in the churches: the popular constituency trusted race-specific institutions and saw them as legitimate, even if this was in tension with the colorblind Radical Republican ideology.[11]

While the process of church, school, and community organization proceeded apace, harsh military and civil policies toward the freedpeople provoked a sense of crisis. The political developments demanded a public response. Activists seized on the Fourth of July as opportune, hoping that the holiday would ensure the protection of the U.S. military and thus facilitate entry into public space. A *New Orleans Tribune* correspondent on the scene betrayed little awareness that trouble was in prospect. Mayor R. H. Slough, however, might have given them some clue of the danger; he tried to deprive them of the use of the city's central Bienville Square on the pretext of protecting the public lawn. On the holiday, thousands of black men and women gathered along with a significant number of white onlookers. Two U.S. Colored Infantry (USCI) regiments led a procession from the medical college down Royal Street. Following them were other participants "assorted as to trades and callings" marching four abreast. Replicas of saws, hammers, and other "implements of trades" were carried aloft. The various benevolent societies marched as well, which manifested the political purpose implicit in the community groups. At the rally, African American speakers hailed the death of slavery, and afterward the gathering disbanded and marched back to the medical college for a picnic. A self-described southern conservative commended their good behavior: "I sympathized with their great joy, and I could but do justice to the moderation of its fruition." Unfortunately, other whites saw the matter differently, even some within the Yankee military.[12]

Confrontations occurred between the white soldiers present and the black soldiers escorting the crowd, though as usual the partisanship of the press obscures precisely what transpired. By several accounts, some white troops took offense at the appropriation of the flag by the blacks and began harassing people. The *New Orleans Tribune* correspondent asserted that most of the insults and injuries to freedmen came from white troops.[13] The

11. *New Orleans Tribune,* July 8, 1865.
12. Ibid., July 6, 1865; *New Orleans Picayune,* July 9, 1865.
13. *New Orleans Tribune* quoted in *The Liberator,* July 21, 1865; Clayton to "Brothers," July 9, 1865, *A Damned Iowa Greyhound: The Civil War Letters of William Henry Harrison*

local papers even claimed there were "some heads broken" by the Yankees. Racist resentments clearly motivated the affray: one soldier thought the freedmen were throwing their weight about downtown, and he was outraged that whites had to cede them the central square. In another soldier's retelling, the blacks were "a litle biger than anybody else that day they had several fights with the soldyers on account of being somewhat saucy threw the day."[14] By several accounts, soldiers and other whites threatened a general row in the evening, which induced the freedpeople to curtail their planned festivities. Whatever the misdeeds of the occupying soldiers, they paled in comparison to those of some of the civilian population and especially the city police. "Within my own knowledge," one general observed, "colored girls seized upon the streets had to take their choice between submitting to outrage on the part of the policemen or incarceration in the guard-house."[15] The city's conservative press printed "blackguard articles," as the bureau's George Harmount termed them, blaming the freedpeople for the trouble. The evidence suggests that these reports were fabrications; the celebrants certainly were not expecting a confrontation in the midst of their patriotic ceremonials. Even the *New York World*, no friend of African Americans, concluded the local press embellished tales of black mayhem. The aforementioned southern columnist was clearer: he had never witnessed "a more quiet, well behaved and orderly crowd."[16]

The Fourth of July disturbances generated a surge of popular outrage. One agitated *Tribune* correspondent predicted "the scenes of San Domingo will certainly be re-enacted here. We are ready to strike for liberty or death, justice or blood." Racial confrontations in the streets escalated, mostly in the form of spontaneous fights or crowd actions. Prodded by the growing militancy, a group of the more established and literate African Americans tried to channel the discontent into a more structured response. Official violence demanded emphatic protest, and while individuals had been talking about some kind of political organization, the impulse toward concrete ac-

---

Clayton, ed. Donald C. Elder Jr. (Iowa City, 1998), 173; Cumming, *Gleanings from Southland,* 266.

14. *Mobile Tribune,* July 11, 1865; John W. Schlagle Diary, July 4, 1865, Indiana Historical Society; E. B. Platt to "Father and Mother," July 11, 1865, Eldridge B. Platt Papers, SHC.

15. *New Orleans Tribune* quoted in *The Liberator,* July 21, 1865; Gen. Thomas Smith to Schurz, September 14, 1865, in U.S. Senate, *Report of Carl Schurz,* 58.

16. G. Harmount to T. W. Conway, July 10, 1865, Letters Sent, SAC Mobile, vol. 108, RG 105; *New York World,* July 24, 1865; *New Orleans Picayune,* July 9, 1865.

tion now intensified. Ambitious demands were in prospect, as another *Tribune* correspondent observed, "we want a military Mayor, and a change in the police department," adding that "we need a newspaper of our own . . . that our grievances can be published to the world." As formal activities took shape, a cohort of Yankee sympathizers joined in as well. The medical college school became the focus of well-attended community meetings, the location facilitating involvement by the white teaching staff. To a striking extent, the debates revolved around the appropriate role of such white allies, especially those in the Freedmen's Bureau. The issues earlier raised by Thomas Conway and his Afro-Creole critics reasserted themselves, this time in renewed conflict over goals and strategy.[17]

The dominant impulse among activists was to bring Mobile's black community into working alliance with the Republican mainstream in Congress and more broadly with northern sentiment. This strategy suggested a prominent role for supportive Yankees present in Mobile, who were the obvious vehicle to the loyal press and public. These white allies presented themselves as qualified for immediate leadership, and this assertion of pre-eminence undergirded debate. For example, at the initial meetings, some speakers suggested the immediate creation of an autonomous political entity to be called the Loyal League, but the idea ran into controversy. One black leader, Joshua Davis, objected to the name on the grounds that "it would displease Mr. Conway and other friends." Davis wanted to avoid any implication of exclusiveness through an incautious choice of name, insisting that "our action instead should be catholic and universal." Conway, now with the Freedmen's Bureau, remained a useful contact, and the fear such allies would be somehow unsettled was the underlying concern. A *Tribune* reporter held these tactical concerns up for derision: he dismissed as a "joke" the notion of a black man being opposed to a league "for fear of displeasing a white man."[18]

Joshua Davis insisted that the obvious objective was a loyal newspaper to "advocate the cause of the colored man," and his politic approach prevailed.[19] Though the newspaper proposal had uplift overtones, given widespread illiteracy, the notion also made sense as a bid for northern support. As one black leader explained to Massachusetts senator Charles Sumner,

17. *New Orleans Tribune,* August 5, July 8, 1865.
18. Ibid., July 18, August 3, 1865.
19. Ibid., August 3, 1865.

this was the only effective method for demanding their rights. When the African American minister Charles Leavens called one meeting to order, discussion centered around the newspaper idea, and again outside influences proved divisive. Yankee missionaries took a prominent role, among them "E. C. Branch (white)," as the *Tribune* tendentiously termed him, who perhaps hoped to secure publicity for his beleaguered teachers in the medical college. Branch had approached military officers, presumably in the bureau, on the subject of a newspaper. He thought he had their support, but Branch suggested that still "it would be safest to have a white editor for the present." When this counsel of expediency awakened controversy, Chairman Leavens endorsed Branch's notion. The *Tribune* correspondent expressed irritation that Branch could find black spokesmen willing to privilege white participation. The offensive implication was that "we still must look up to some white man to lead us."[20]

The white man put forth by Branch was John Silsby, his fellow missionary. Silsby took the lead in the newspaper planning efforts and, not surprisingly, his prominent role sparked still more discussion. While proposing a scheme for structuring the enterprise, he drew a hostile question from Avery of the *Tribune,* who asked rhetorically "if this was to be the colored man's paper." Avery pleaded for a black editor because "none but colored men" could truly sympathize with the race. Joshua Davis criticized these remarks, and when Avery attempted to respond, the chairman ruled him out of order. John Silsby then accused the reporter of trying to exclude loyal whites, and Avery denied it only to be ruled out of order yet again. At that, he walked out of the local movement for good. Avery had argued that "the time had come for colored men to think and act for themselves," but for the moment, at least, activist sentiment determined otherwise. Subsequent meetings openly praised Yankee allies, especially in the Freedmen's Bureau, which had come in for criticism.[21] Colonel Harmount was invited to address one gathering, and this conciliatory approach assured bureau cooperation. General Swayne privately promised a personal contribution.

20. A. Saxon et al. to Sumner, October 25, 1865, *The Papers of Charles Sumner,* ed. Beverly Wilson Palmer (London, 1987; Alexandria, Va., 1988, microfilm), reel 34, no. 442; *New Orleans Tribune,* July 18, 1865.

21. *New Orleans Tribune,* July 18, October 24, 1865; *Christian Recorder,* October 24, 1865.

The bureau arguably co-opted the activists, though mutual conciliation might be the more accurate reading.[22]

Mobile's black leadership concluded that the egalitarian cause was stronger in alliance with the teachers, missionaries, and the bureau. In this context of solicitation of white allies, the activists turned to Reverend Silsby as the newspaper's first editor. The choice made some sense. Silsby had useful connections in the northern abolitionist and freedmen's aid societies and was well respected by Swayne and the bureau. Silsby's subsequent teaching career indicated real commitment to the cause of black education, and his later prominent role in Republican party politics in Selma suggested broader reform interests and established his personal probity. Still, he had certain limitations, not the least of which was the lack of journalistic experience. Silsby's enthusiasm for the Congregational church also complicated relations with the adherents of the independent black denominations. A crucial problem with Silsby, though, was one he shared with other Yankee activists drawn to the movement: he expected a "white" standard of living. As a family man nearly fifty years old, Silsby resigned his commission as a teacher with some reluctance on fiscal grounds. He had to make the new newspaper repay his labor, which posed sensitive issues with the freedpeople who would raise his undisclosed salary.[23]

Financial matters weighed on John Silsby's mind in other respects, for the new editor proposed setting up the newspaper enterprise as a joint-stock corporation. Shares in the "Loyal Newspaper Society" would sell for five dollars apiece to the public and confer voting rights. Major decisions would be made at mass meetings of shareholders, while a board of directors or trustees would oversee the editor. This structure was probably necessitated by the limited capital available. None of the paper's activists had great personal wealth, and no way existed to tap community resources without widespread participation. The estimated cost was eight thousand dollars for one year, which observers believed made it financially dicey.[24]

---

22. *New Orleans Tribune,* July 30, 1865; Swayne to E. C. Branch, December 1, 1865, M809, RG 105, reel 1.

23. Silsby to George Whipple, November 2, 1865, Alabama, AMA, reel 1; Jennifer Kaye Spiers, "Educating Blacks in Reconstruction Alabama: John Silsby, the American Missionary Association, and the Freedmen's Bureau" (Ph.D. diss., Auburn University, 1991), 17–54.

24. Roy to Badger, November 30, 1865, reel 2, American Home Missionary Society Papers, LC.

Silsby's scheme nonetheless worked surprisingly well: several hundred people must have become shareholders, with many of them reportedly purchasing small blocs of stock. While Silsby's blueprint successfully raised the initial money for the *Nationalist,* as the paper was called, the plan had significant structural implications. Most contemporary black-owned newspapers, such as the *New Orleans Tribune,* had single proprietors or perhaps a few partners; they aimed at making a profit, as did Reconstruction Republican papers in general. The *Nationalist* was different, a movement enterprise from its inception, and its democratic ownership structure guaranteed it would become the focus of struggle as Reconstruction proceeded. The paper was essentially a race-based institution like the churches and fraternal orders, but as a political organ it necessarily operated in the public sphere, articulating a Radical Republican ideology that challenged the legitimacy of racial distinctions. As a community enterprise it exemplified racial solidarity, but it also addressed a national audience in a language of egalitarianism. This dual character posed political questions that encouraged dissention throughout the paper's existence.

The composition of the directors also suggests other internal tensions that would characterize Mobile's African American politics more broadly. So far as can be determined, none of the trustees participated in the postwar migration into the city from the countryside, nor were any common laborers. The seventeen men who served over the next year were predominantly small businessmen, grocers, peddlers, tailors, and the like serving a black clientele. Between them they provided much of the paper's sparse advertising revenue. As a group they were literate, middle-aged tradesmen; several held significant property and at least five were free before the war. Commercial motivations for participation may have been significant, but for about half of them their *Nationalist* involvement would be their entrée to political activism, with John Carraway and James Bragg becoming the most prominent as Republican leaders. The trustees provided much of the African American leadership of the moderate group that initially dominated Reconstruction politics, acting in collaboration with the city's small cohort of wartime Unionist scalawags. Indeed, the *Nationalist* and its editors would become the mainstay of that faction, its voice among the African American popular following.

It was perhaps to be expected that poorer newcomers would have little involvement among the *Nationalist* trustees. More anomalous, perhaps, is the absence of Mobile's well-established Afro-Creoles, given their education, financial resources, and later prominence in Republican politics. Of the *Nationalist* directors, only James A. Summerville might have had Creole background, and even he was not prominent in the city's Creole organizations. This is consistent with the antebellum pattern of Mobile's Creoles being slow to identify with the mass of the black population. The *Nationalist* trustees, by contrast, were wholly invested in African American community organizations, especially the Protestant churches. Of the trustees, two actually preached, while seven more served as lay officials. It was this group, rooted in black religious associations, that would mediate between the African American stockholders and the newspaper's Yankee staff. As criticism rose over the conduct of the paper, the initial race-tinged polarization repeatedly reemerged.

Whatever governance issues the structure of the paper caused, the directors raised enough money to dispatch E. C. Branch northward to purchase a printing press. Had activists been inclined to let the initial enthusiasm wane, the actions of the city's conservative whites deterred it. In early September 1865 came the disturbance involving black soldiers and city police, an episode publicized in lurid terms by Henry St. Paul's uninhibited *Mobile News*. At the same time, the new African American churches found themselves under attack. Before the war, several dependent black congregations had been "permitted & to some extent encouraged" to operate. At least two had purchased buildings, vesting the title with white trustees due to legal restrictions. When Mobile fell, the Union military handed over the churches to their congregations. But with the mass departure of blacks from the southern denominations, the white trustees asserted their legal title. They were motivated by hostility to the independent Methodist organizations, one black petition observed, and for the destitute congregations, possession of these properties was important. The restoration of civil law under conservative rule threatened dispossession for the State Street and Zion Methodist Churches, property worth in excess of twenty thousand dollars.[25]

A bitter impasse occurred at the Zion Church, where eight hundred members faced a demand to vacate the building backed by civil authorities. Public resolutions denounced the "unprecedented and audacious robbery."[26] Subsequent conflict mostly centered on Zion's preacher, Ferdinand

---

25. Charles Lee et al. to Congress, [January 8, 1866,] M809, RG 105, reel 8.
26. Charles Lee et al. to Congress, January 1866, reel 8; and A. Saxon et al. to Swayne, August 2, 1865, M809, RG 105, reel 18.

Smith. The minister had been recently prosecuted before Mayor Slough on some charge and denied the right to testify on the basis of his race. In September, at the time of the trouble involving USCI soldiers, rumors circulated that Reverend Smith was "calling upon the negroes to dip their hands in the blood of the whites." Whatever he actually said, some of his church colleagues apparently thought his statements unwise.[27] The *Mobile News* reported Smith's preaching in sensational terms, whereupon the author of the offending article received threats from the black congregation. The affronted journalist thereupon assaulted Reverend Smith, threatening to kill him, and by one account the man also led a sack of Smith's grocery store.[28] As for the freedpeople, the *News* reported that a mob accompanied by a white teacher broke into a fire station, the offending correspondent reportedly being the chief of the fire company.[29] The military subsequently found the *News* reports so exaggerated that they threatened to close the paper. Something dramatic must have happened on Mobile's tense streets, but the actual details of this tangled episode are beyond recovery.

By contrast, Reverend Smith's subsequent legal troubles were distressingly concrete. He was arrested for fraud in connection with his grocery store. It seems that Smith had gone four hundred dollars into debt for merchandise, and during the church controversy, an unpaid creditor accused him of lying about his financial condition. The courts dispatched Smith to the penitentiary for a long sentence. According to his lawyer, George F. Harrington, the white church trustees wanted to get him out of the way, which Smith's subsequent gubernatorial pardon rather substantiates.[30] With Smith incapacitated, in early November the white trustees assumed possession of the disputed church property, but even this did not end the controversy. When a white preacher began to speak, some of the congregation threatened him. The police were called in, but the freedmen "refused to give up the keys of the church, alleging that they were lost." The *Mobile*

27. Carl Schurz to Johnson, September 15, 1865, Andrew Johnson Papers, LC; *MN,* May 19, 1866.

28. *New Orleans Tribune,* November 4, 1865. The assault and the grocery raid may have been the same incident. The reporter, Frank James, was fined for the assault, which, given the biases of the legal system, strongly suggests guilt.

29. *MAR,* September 8, 1865.

30. G. F. Harrington to Maj. J. D. Wilkins, provost marshal, District of Alabama, December 24, 1865, Letters Received, ser. 2323, District of Montgomery, RG 393, pt. 2; *Manhattan (Kans.) Nationalist,* April 14, 1871.

News, now renamed the *Times,* fingered one of the medical college teachers as the inspiration of all the trouble. The paper concluded that it was "about time these 'white trash' were made to leave our city, as their teachings and company demoralize the negroes they associate with."[31]

The episode had a revealing, if scarcely credible, sequel as related in the *Mobile Times.* One of Reverend Smith's Zion Church allies, a sometime preacher named Sam Gaillard, was working as a carpenter a few days after the first confrontation. A white man came to the door and asked for the proprietor, offensively referring to the freedmen present as "boys." The elderly Gaillard replied that "there ain't no boys here, we're all grown men." An altercation ensued in which Gaillard reportedly threatened the man with an ax, after which he was arrested. He was sentenced to four months hard labor, to make an example of him according to the *Times.* When ordered out to work on the chain gang, Gaillard refused on the grounds he was a preacher. Threatened at gunpoint, he responded, "Shoot me, d——m you! I can die, but I won't work." The guards gunned him down on the spot. Afterward, the paper anticipated that his punishment would have "a salutary effect on the negroes."[32] With equal sensitivity, Josiah Nott added that troublemaking black preachers like Smith and Gaillard were the worst citizens in Mobile. This bloodletting aside, the church issue was soon moot anyway. The Confederate former preacher reportedly threatened arson, and when the military again restored the Zion Church to the congregation, the uninsurable building was torched.[33]

The string of ugly incidents sustained activism within the black community, while the biased press coverage dramatized the need for a black-owned newspaper. Several of the prominent figures in the dispute over the Methodist property led the *Nationalist* drive as well.[34] Moreover, in November 1865, local activists, some associated with the newspaper, summoned the first statewide African American convention. Fifty-six delegates from across central and southern Alabama gathered, "most of them minis-

31. *MT,* November 4, 1865.
32. Ibid., November 8, 7, 1865.
33. J. C. Nott, "The Problem of the Black Races," *De Bow's Review, After the War Series,* March 1866, 267; L. S. Berry to James Gillette, June 10, 1868, Letters Received, Sub-Assistant Commissioner, Mobile, RG 105.
34. One of the AME Zion committees negotiating for the property included James Thomas, E. D. Taylor, Richard Butler, and Washington Dick; several of these men would be prominent among the *Nationalist* trustees. *MN,* December 28, 1865.

ters of the Gospel and all of them God-fearing men." The evident expectation was that the meeting would showcase the paper and facilitate its regional distribution. Published resolutions for local consumption were moderate. The resolutions urged the freedpeople to labor and obey the law, and they denied the rumors of any sort of insurrection. Statements of a different order, however, were dispatched to Republicans in Washington. These cast the status of freedmen in starker terms, demanding the suffrage as the only remedy possible. The disclosure of these statements in the local press assured the Radical paper a lively reception.[35]

The *Nationalist*'s premiere issue finally appeared in mid-December 1865, containing news of the freedmen's convention. Editor Silsby was able to produce an attractive four-page sheet, and its debut was well timed, with Congress convening and national attention riveted on Presidential Reconstruction. Unfortunately, the new paper had little advertising, and the few businessmen who supported it were "threatened with the loss of all trade."[36] Salespeople were harassed on the streets, and distributors in the Alabama interior were mobbed, as traveling agent L. S. Berry discovered. But Mobile's conservative press mostly ignored the new paper. Silsby found production an ordeal, afflicting him with "the *Nationalist* on the brain." Issuing it weekly as promised was beyond him, and he scaled back publication to twice monthly. Silsby soon brought in a skilled printer, Albert A. Griffin of Chicago, along with another associate, James Shaw. This help did not come cheap, for Shaw's pay was 50 percent above the prevailing wage back home. Editor Silsby apparently missed the possibility that this concentration of well-paid Yankee employees might irritate his trustees.[37]

In every respect save profit, the newspaper proved immediately effective. It provided a political voice for Alabama freedpeople, counteracting the local press blackout of inconvenient news. The Freedmen's Bureau agent in Mobile termed it a success, adding that it was "the only paper published here that can be used as an organ of the Bureau." Agents occasionally served as correspondents, and E. C. Branch prevailed on Gen. O. O. Howard himself for aid.[38] By late March, the paper's editor claimed twelve hun-

35. *MN*, December 14, 28, 1865, January 19, 1866.
36. J. Silsby to C. W. Buckley, December 23, 1865, reel 3, M810, RG 105; *MN*, March 29, 1866.
37. Silsby to Buckley, December 23, 1865; *Aurora (Ill.) Beacon News*, July 31, 1915.
38. G. D. Robinson to C. Cadle, February 5, 1866, M809, RG 105, reel 18; J. Silsby to C. W. Buckley, February 14, 1866, M810, RG 105, reel 3; Branch to Howard, February 22, 1866, O. O. Howard Papers, Bowdoin College Library.

dred subscribers, and while this was dwarfed by Mobile's conservative newspapers, this figure still would represent one of the larger circulations in the state.[39] The paper provided a forum on statewide events, and as a Radical voice from the Deep South, its articles were reprinted in the crucial northern press. The paper directly influenced policy debates. For example, in January 1866 General Swayne "learned through the *Nationalist*" that black draymen were prevented from working by discriminatory municipal fees. He told the Mobile bureau agent to seek redress, implying that his subordinate might have kept him better informed. The agent, chastened, admitted the *Nationalist* account was accurate.[40]

Despite the *Nationalist*'s obvious accomplishments during his tenure as editor, John Silsby only lasted three months in the position. The specifics of his departure are unclear, but Silsby's idiosyncratic priorities probably contributed to his troubles, moral uplift being one of his paper's distinguishing features. As a teacher Silsby wanted to "make the newspaper a most important means of promoting the educational work."[41] Likewise the longtime missionary Silsby also denounced "that old tyrant King Alcohol, the worst of slave holders." He even repeatedly warned his readers against profanity. Salutary advice, perhaps, but such preachments may well not have been what *Nationalist* supporters expected for their pains. Silsby, however, saw his editorial policies as high principle: "I hold that no paper has a right to ignore the great central truth that the Kingdom of Heaven is paramount and that all other interests center around that." As religious as his directors were, Silsby's emphasis on personal moral responsibility likely seemed excessive, given the range of external oppression African Americans encountered. Sectarian rivalries also may have limited enthusiasm for Silsby's preaching.[42]

The overt issue in Silsby's rapid departure as editor was financial—at least that was the public version—and monetary issues certainly exacerbated other tensions. In taking the position as editor, Silsby had feared the paper would tax the freedmen's means. He repeatedly asked the American Missionary Association to contribute toward his salary. Failing that, he

39. A. Griffin to M. E. Strieby, March 29, 1866, Alabama, AMA, reel 1.
40. O. Kinsman to G. D. Robinson, January 20, 1866, M809, RG 105, reel 1; G. D. Robinson to C. Cadle, January 23, 1866, Letters Sent, SAC, Mobile, vol. 108, RG 105.
41. Silsby to Whipple, December 2, 1865, Alabama, AMA, reel 1.
42. *The American Missionary,* July 1867, 164–5; *MN,* February 1, 1866; J. Silsby to "Dear Brother," November 5, 1866, Alabama, AMA, reel 1.

suggested to General Swayne that he might support himself by teaching part time; he hoped the bureau would subsidize his editorial writing while he handed over management to his foreman.[43] In mid-March the *Nationalist* announced Silsby's relocation to Montgomery to establish a branch office. As Silsby explained, "the foreman in the office of the *Nationalist* has taken the work of editing in hand, as we thus diminish the expense of the concern. I fear the enterprise cannot be sustained unless aid can be had from the north."[44] Silsby left, mustering what dignity he could, but he was peeved over the circumstances. One black colleague later recalled that Silsby had been forced out by unfair means and that Albert Griffin, his successor, had a hand in his ouster. Strikingly, in his departing editorial, Silsby warned against internal dissention, welcoming an opportunity to serve the cause in some less perplexing venue. In his correspondence Silsby was more explicit: the freedpeople lacked "the experience and mutual confidence which are needed in successful cooperation." This failing he blamed on the heritage of slavery, though whether he meant a distrust of whites or of each other is unclear, perhaps both. Whatever the intent, Silsby predicted difficult times in the future, and his successor would occupy an equally troublesome tenure as editor. The external political omens, though, began to brighten markedly.[45]

While the *Nationalist* was getting under way, the local conservative power structure's priorities evolved to the freedpeople's advantage. Racial persecution relented in response to a variety of forces. Nationally, Congress's rejection of the southern representatives in late 1865 and the growing controversy between President Johnson and Congress over civil rights suggested increased scrutiny of southern conduct. The appearance of the *Nationalist,* however unwelcome, augmented the threat of negative publicity. Similarly, the state's governor elected under Presidential Reconstruction, the Whiggish Robert M. Patton, provided strong moderate leadership. Governor Patton avoided confrontation on racial matters in favor of pro-

---

43. E. C. Branch, "Report of Schools of AFAC," January 15, 1866, enclosed in W. Swayne to O. O. Howard, February 10, 1866, M752, RG 105, reel 19; J. Silsby to George Whipple, November 2, 1865, Alabama, AMA, reel 1; Silsby to Swayne, February 27, 1866, M809, RG 105, reel 9.

44. Silsby to "My Dear Bro," March 23, 1866, Alabama, AMA, reel 1.

45. *MDR,* January 19, 1869; *MN,* March 29, 1866; Silsby to "My Dear Bro.," March 1866, Alabama, AMA, reel 1.

moting economic development, especially railroads.⁴⁶ In this context, arson, race riots, and strident rhetoric looked increasingly ill timed. Furthermore, once the initial shock of emancipation wore off, other concerns emerged relating to the economic future of the city, issues less tied to race relations. Mobile's chastened city political leadership responded to these wider political developments as well as the disorder suggested by the series of riots elsewhere. By 1866, a new city administration sought accommodation with federal officials and even to some extent with the freedpeople themselves.⁴⁷

The fate of the cotton trade became an urgent preoccupation, quite rational in view of the city's financial history. Over time, the city's traditional economic priorities reasserted themselves. As one British observer commented during the prewar boom, Mobilians "buy cotton, sell cotton, think cotton, eat cotton, drink cotton, and dream cotton. They marry cotton wives, and unto them are born cotton children."⁴⁸ Here was a concern to rival the elite's obsession with the freedpeople's in-migration. Before the Civil War, Mobile's geographic position at the mouth of Alabama's major rivers guaranteed it predominance over the interior's trade. Most Alabama cotton passed through Mobile's docks, and the community also handled the financing of the trade. Mobile's factors served as business agents and provided credit and information for the great planters of the interior. As Alabama's largest city, Mobile functioned as a social center for visiting planters, and it was known for ostentatious homes and lavish entertainment. Merchants dominated the community socially and politically, and the 1850s had been the city's best decade ever, capped by the completion of the Mobile and Ohio Railroad on the eve of the Civil War. As one visitor summed up Mobile's antebellum history, cotton was king beyond question: "She has looked to nothing else, talked of nothing else and leaned on nothing else. In producing, handling, selling, storing, compressing, insuring and shipping cotton you find almost the entire business of the city." With little other significant economic activity, any change in the flow of trade threatened ruin.⁴⁹

The war brought crisis for Mobile's economy, with a host of changes

---

46. On Patton's close cooperation with General Swayne of the Freedmen's Bureau, see Fitzgerald, "Wager Swayne," 188–218.
47. Doyle, *New Men, New Cities, New South,* 59–71, 76–86.
48. Hiram Fuller, visiting Mobile in 1858, quoted in Amos, *Cotton City,* xiii.
49. *NYT,* December 15, 1868.

sapping the city's lifeblood. The wartime blockade interrupted the city's cotton trade, and obstructions built to deter the Yankee navy permanently damaged the channel. As a result, larger ships had to unload goods in the bay well below the city, resulting in lighterage fees and higher labor costs than rival ports.[50] The May 1865 ammunition explosion also demolished the warehouse district north of downtown just as commerce resumed. These problems only exacerbated short-term disruptions in the cotton trade as the army seized cotton pledged to the Confederate government.[51] A corrupt commerce in laundered cotton, so to speak, developed among federal treasury and army officials. In addition, there was the financial prostration of the planters, the factors' largest customers. For example, late in 1865 one merchant dispatched his brother into the interior to collect thirty thousand dollars in antebellum debts. After some weeks, the agent abandoned the effort, having accumulated all of ninety dollars in payments. Finding that there was "no earthly hope or prospect of collecting anything," the merchant tried to reason with his northern creditors, offering to settle with them at a large discount; they just laughed at him. Clearly, reestablishing business in postwar Mobile was not going to be easy.[52]

For some time, the business community assumed the postwar cotton trade would return to normal. One merchant anticipated prosperity would return "were it not for the miserable Yankees," who threw "every obstruction in the way of business." Immediate disruptions disguised the long-term erosion of the city's economic role. Postwar expansion of railroads would undermine Mobile's monopoly on river commerce, and it became easier for planters, with access to price information though newspapers and telegraphs, to ship cotton directly to the best market. This compromised the factorage system, for planters could increasingly dispense with agents' marketing expertise. As a result, interior railroad towns like Selma and Montgomery stripped away Mobile's business. The official figures are dramatic: in 1860, cotton receipts peaked at about 850,000 bales; the figure in 1867 was 240,000. Mobile's cotton supply eventually stabilized at about half the prewar level. Many of the bales that continued to pass through the city had been purchased in the interior and now were being transshipped elsewhere, cutting Mobile's middlemen out of the flow of profit. Furthermore, share-

50. *MAR,* December 27, 1865.
51. Griffin, "Cotton Frauds," 265–76.
52. Unidentified to "Dear Uncle," February 17, 1866, Henry Lee Reynolds Papers, SHC.

cropping decentralized the market in goods and provisions, undermining the large purchases planters used to make. These changes provided opportunities for small-scale merchants and entrepreneurs, but they hurt the established factors of Mobile.[53]

For some months after surrender, a burst of pent-up consumer demand obscured what was actually happening. By 1866, though, opinion leaders were beginning to grasp that things had changed, their attention concentrated by a wretched fall business season.[54] Editorials noted that "business is very dull for this season of the year" and that merchants were talking about leaving town. For an editor so devoted to civic puffery as John Forsyth of the *Mobile Advertiser and Register,* these were arresting observations. Finally alarmed, leading merchants concluded that "Mobile should be up and doing, if it be desired to retain her trade." The existing chamber of commerce had lapsed into inactivity, but a new force emerged on the scene, a board of trade comprising nearly four hundred merchants.[55] Led by the board, businessmen reappraised the city's economic practices, debating an array of economic proposals. Some thought the priority was to clear the shipping channel, others thought labor costs too high because of Mobile's elevated cost of living. The *Mobile Times* thought the levies of the privately owned docks were driving away trade, and it suggested seizing the waterfront under long-forgotten legal precedents. Railroads, as might be expected, were a major focus of interest. Some feared the completion of the rail connection to New Orleans would hurt business further and suggested schemes of obstructing it. The major positive proposal, however, was a railroad into northern Alabama; if the cotton trade was in decline, surely the untapped mineral wealth around modern Birmingham presented new opportunities. This line, the Mobile and Alabama Grand Trunk, was conceived in the board of trade, and it probably enjoyed more support than any other postwar proposal. As the *Advertiser and Register* proclaimed, the railroad would overshadow everything previously attempted.[56]

53. J. Mordecai to "Uncle," October 9, 1865, Mordecai Family Papers, SHC; Mobile Board of Trade, "Twelfth Annual Report of the Mobile Board of Trade for the Year Ending November 1, 1880," (Mobile, 1881), 20.

54. William P. Hamilton to "Dear Aunt," April 22, 1867, Bullock and Hamilton Family Papers, SHC; *Montgomery Advertiser,* February 6, 1866; *MT,* May 25, 1866.

55. *MAR,* February 6, October 17, 19, 27, 1866; *MT,* December 3, 27, 1867; *Mobile Register,* April 13, 1869.

56. *MAR,* March 11, October 17, 1866.

John Forsyth, longtime editor and recent mayor, emerged as the city's most articulate advocate of aggressive municipal programs. He was the dean of Alabama Democratic journalism, whose racial extremism and ferocious partisanship made him prominent in national politics (though his crucial role in Mobile economic development has attracted little attention from historians).[57] For years, his editorials promoted ambitious civic initiatives, both public and private, almost indiscriminately. Even before the scope of the crisis became evident, Acting Mayor Forsyth warned against excess frugality. He assured city legislators that the city debt was manageable; it should not serve as a "scare-crow" to impede "economic progress and needful improvement."[58] An editorial added that "no city in America is so lightly taxed," and so the unpaved streets and ragged appearance of Mobile were beyond excuse. By 1866, this became Forsyth's constant refrain. As the *Advertiser and Register* pointed out in June, "we have indulged in a long urban slumber, pending which we have been outstripped by every other city, far and near." Forsyth meant to rectify the situation, dismissing those who disagreed as barnacles.[59]

If the city's economic crisis troubled the merchant elite, the effect on the freedpeople was considerably more immediate. The lack of jobs and the large pool of underemployed workers kept unskilled wages down, but freedpeople from the countryside kept coming anyway, long after the white population began heading elsewhere. Even the conservative press noticed the resulting glut of unskilled labor. Black homeless congregated "around the wharves and other public places, and the miserable creatures spread their pallets wherever night overtakes them." In one instance a watchman encountered an ailing freedman and allowed him to sleep on board ship, but the man died of exposure anyway. In July the newspapers commented on the freedpeople leaving downtown every night to sleep under trees in the suburbs.[60] For those without shelter, even Mobile's mild winters were

---

57. One recent biographic sketch of Forsyth as editor of the *Mobile Advertiser and Register* only touches on his promotion of economic development, omitting the catastrophic outcome and the conflict of interest so evident in his career. See Carl R. Osthaus, *Partisans of the Southern Press: Editorial Spokesmen of the Nineteenth Century* (Lexington, Ky., 1994), 118–48. See also Lonnie Alexander Burnett, "The Pen Makes a Good Sword: John Forsyth and the *Mobile Register*" (Ph.D. diss., University of Southern Mississippi, 2000).

58. John Forsyth, "Inaugural Speech," August 29, 1865, folder 2, envelope 6, box 13, RMBACC.

59. *MAR,* October, 13, 1865, June 17, 1866.

60. Ibid., January 4, August 29, 30, 1866.

difficult, and as the *Advertiser and Register* observed, disease mowed them down.[61] A reactionary homily generally followed such reports, pointing out how much better things had been before emancipation, while any thought of humanitarian intervention was stilled by the fear of attracting yet more homeless. Still, the local press was surprisingly candid on the human agony, and the extent of the privation must have been fearful. In one conservative newcomer's words, "at the present rate of mortality amongst the Negroes they will be exterminated in a few years."[62]

Economic decline worked dire hardship, but it simultaneously opened political possibilities for African Americans. At the simplest level, the power structure increasingly had something besides race to obsess about. The black contribution to Mobile's economic decline was clearly peripheral, and indeed, the influx of freedpeople reduced wages and helped businessmen ward off trade unionism. After the war a brief flurry of organized-labor activity occurred among white tradesmen, carpenters, bricklayers, and the like.[63] There was public discussion of the eight-hour movement and other reforms, but this activity proved short-lived, and most groups passed resolutions and then dissolved. Only a few skilled trades, such as the screwmen intricately loading cotton into ships, were able to organize; they struck effectively on occasion, blacklisting those who undermined the wage scale. The Baymen's Association parlayed a racial monopoly of this crucial skill into a six-dollar-a-day wage.[64] In the less skilled trades, interracial unions were essential in practice but impossible given the racial climate.[65] Thus, instead of white workers uniting to form effective unions, they lost ground in the postwar workforce. St. Paul's *Times* made the scope of the problem manifest. Despite its self-appointed advocacy of white workers, immigrants, and Catholics, the paper pointed out that "the white laboring population is not willing to work for the wages which are given to negroes, except in the case of draymen or mechanics." Businesses often preferred whites, but employers had to look for the cheapest labor wherever it could

    61. Ibid., January 11, 1866.
    62. C. M. France to C. B. France, February 18, 1866, Charles B. France Papers, State Historical Society of Missouri.
    63. *MAR,* March 23, 1866.
    64. *MT,* December 3, 1867; *MAR,* April 24, 1866; *MAR,* June 20, 1878; *Mobile Tribune,* December 16, 1874.
    65. On the explicitly white-only character of the formal union movement, see *MT,* March 23, 1866.

be found. Perhaps the answer, the paper observed, was for poor whites to take the jobs the freedpeople were deserting in the countryside. The advice could hardly have provided much comfort.[66]

White workers had recourse to the vote, and they defended their interests through the political process. For example, white draymen induced the city to restrict black competition by imposing a five-hundred-dollar bond.[67] White laborers also demanded racial preferences in city employment policies. As one worker explained, if the city let out street work to contractors, "scarcely one dollar" would go to whites because blacks would work for less. In most private employment, though, nothing could stop the freedpeople from securing employment by undercutting wages. Albert Griffin talked to painters who complained that blacks had ruined their business because they worked for half the white wage. On the waterfront black men vastly predominated as unskilled dockworkers. At the municipal market whites rented almost all the stalls, but most of the actual marketing was "done by colored people." An analogous process occurred in rental housing, where freedpeople were outbidding poorer whites for homes and land on which to build them. Landowners constructed cheap housing in the suburbs, facilitated by an expanding horse-drawn streetcar network, and the northwestern Seventh Ward became predominantly African American. If white workers saw the freedpeople muscling them out of jobs and neighborhoods, some businessmen and property owners acknowledged them as a source of profit.[68]

The experience of the hardware merchant William C. Reynolds illustrates these wider tendencies. As conservative politically as any of his peers, he nonetheless depicted blacks around him in pragmatic terms. Reynolds wrote of the efficient laborers who built his shelves at ten dollars a week and expressed pleasure when the former family slave John inquired about a job. Reynolds rented workshop and living space to a Creole named Gomez and his little son, the latter "quite a good tinner." Gomez prospered, hiring four employees; Reynolds used Gomez and another Creole to repair his roof. In January 1866 Reynolds hired two African Americans for his firm, adding, "I suppose I will have to make clerks of them." He even

66. *MT,* January 17, 1868.
67. Ibid., January 3, 1866; J. D. Robinson to C. Cadle, January 22, 1866, M809, RG 105, reel 9.
68. *MT,* May 24, 1866; *MN,* September 5, 1867, May 31, 1866.

rented a home to the family of "a very nice colored man, yellow complexion." This carpenter had built shelves for Reynolds at five dollars a day, an excellent wage for a skilled workman. Such appreciative commentary could not have been motivated by optimism, for the merchant was losing money and irritated by the whites around him. Given the wider context, the racial commentary of this man of commerce was notably upbeat.[69]

This circumspect pragmatism on racial issues, it seems, became more widely shared over time. By 1866, a city census taker could publicly declare that fully a third of the black population were employed, law abiding, and respectable. At this time a less confrontational style of political leadership toward some blacks emerged, personified by Mayor J. M. Withers. In December 1865 Mobile's white electorate headed to the polls to replace the appointed caretaker government of Mayor John Forsyth. In a close election, reportedly featuring widespread vote buying and illegal voting by soldiers, Withers, a former mayor, defeated the lawyer Cleveland F. Moulton. The outcome was anomalous; Moulton's ticket for the City Council and Board of Aldermen mostly won. The circumstances encouraged Mayor Withers to act independently, and having lived in the city very little for the preceding several years, perhaps he was less deferential to local opinion anyway. Furthermore, as a former Confederate general, Withers spent several weeks waiting for a presidential pardon before assuming office. His stay in Washington likely reinforced his sense of national currents and encouraged a cautious approach to the civil rights issue.[70]

Mayor Withers's relative enlightenment may have had a less benign origin: early missteps on the race issue surely soured him on confrontation. Upon assuming office, he shared the prevailing animus against the rural migrants. While conducting Mayor's Court, Withers called for police action against the "extraordinarily large number of vagrants," estimating their number at five thousand. This inflated figure—nearly half the black population—must have included jobless people with some housing, which suggests a certain lack of discrimination. Withers intended to return this host to the countryside, asserting that the steamboat companies that brought them should bear the cost. The merchant William Reynolds noted that

69. W. C. Reynolds to H. L. Reynolds, November 21, December 6, 1865, January 6, October 4, 1866, Reynolds Papers.
70. *MAR,* September 7, 1866; Swayne to Howard, January 24, 1866, M809, RG 105, reel 1.

"about 50 negroes come up before the Mayor almost every morning on the score of vagrancy, and are generally remanded to the guard house until they make a contract with somebody to work."[71] The demand for labor being "tremendous," the prisoners were gone by noon, with most apparently bound for the plantations. Unfortunately for Mayor Withers, the wholesale rousting of the poor drew the intervention of the Freedmen's Bureau. The bureau sent a lawyer to monitor Mayor's Court proceedings and also established Freedmen's Courts to ensure judicial access. Afterward, Withers recognized he had blundered, and he announced that in cases where supposed vagrants claimed to have jobs, their stories were to be investigated prior to deportation.[72] Withers had to satisfy himself with institutionalizing a civic chain gang and implementing the new city charter, which lengthened the antebellum penalty for vagrancy to six months.[73]

Chastened by this experience, Mayor Withers thenceforth conciliated the army and especially General Swayne of the Freedmen's Bureau. For instance, when the bureau instituted the Freedmen's Courts, the former mayor, John Forsyth, denounced this action in his *Advertiser and Register*.[74] Stung personally, Swayne sought Withers's opinion: the mayor told him that he had not raised the issue "because he saw the necessity, and determined not to complain until a conflict arose." This unaccustomed discretion made a favorable impression, and thereafter the army carefully selected Freedmen's Court officers who would not offend white opinion. Mayor Withers and Swayne collaborated closely thereafter. Withers actually volunteered to help General Swayne with the medical college imbroglio, offering to try to find the freedmen's school other premises.[75] Withers pledged to protect the relocated school, and he soon had the opportunity to act on this promise. A rumor spread that the school would move into a building then owned by Reverend Smith's former congregation, and in early March his African Methodists were burned out of yet another build-

71. *MT,* January 13, 1866; William Reynolds to H. L. Reynolds, January 27, 1866, Reynolds Papers.
72. *MN,* January 18, 1866; *MAR,* February 6, June 17, November 10, 1866.
73. *Mobile Register,* July 3, 1865; Reuben A. Lewis, comp., *The Charter and Code of Ordinances of the City of Mobile* (Mobile, 1866), 17.
74. *MAR,* February 10, 1866.
75. Swayne to Forsyth, February 12, 1866; Swayne to Howard, January 24, 1866; and Swayne to G. D. Robinson, February 22, 1866, M809, RG 105, reel 1.

ing.[76] Declaring it unquestionably the act of incendiaries, Withers announced a one-thousand-dollar reward for the perpetrators of this or other such crimes. He also denounced the "cowardly and infamous" men who disgraced their community. It may not seem controversial for a mayor to oppose arson as public policy, but in postwar Mobile it required a degree of courage. The *Times* actually denounced the mayor for his unproven claim that whites were responsible. The fire was actually set, the paper speculated, "to cast blame on a highly respectable community, without any foundation whatever." For good measure, the paper concluded that the previous fire in Reverend Smith's church had been set by his own parishioners. Incredulous army officials afterward described Henry St. Paul, editor of the *Times,* as "a half breed Frenchman with no common sense," but his extremism only highlights the relative sobriety of the mayor.[77]

Mayor Withers asserted the principle of fair treatment before the law, occasionally with some unction. According to the *Advertiser and Register,* the mayor had "more than once announced his determination" to penalize harshly those who "abuse negroes without provocation." He had plenty of white offenders upon whom to demonstrate his convictions. In April city leaders participated in the anniversary festivities of the Creole Fire Company, whose brass band performed "Dixie" for an interracial crowd. The *Nationalist* derided the Creoles' conciliatory behavior as abject, but the established Creole leadership did elicit official recognition of their community stature from municipal officials. The white fire companies attended in force, and even St. Paul praised them. Various dignitaries toasted the Creoles for their southern patriotism. Unfortunately for the show of interracial amity, scores of young bloods roved through the crowd to "knock down Negroes" watching the torchlight procession. One black bystander fought back and was killed, which highlighted the pressure for an official response. In this instance Mayor Withers fined one apparently wealthy perpetrator fifty dollars.[78]

As one might expect, the mayor's verdict hardly seemed sufficient to the

---

76. *MN,* May 10, 1866; J. Silsby to Swayne, February 27, 1866, reel 9; and [C. Cadle] to Swayne, March 1, 1866, M809, RG 105, reel 1.

77. *MAR,* March 15, 1866; *MT,* March 3, 1866; Gen. C. Woods to U. S. Grant, April 6, 1866, Ulysses S. Grant, *Grant The Papers of Ulysses S. Grant,* ed. John Y. Simon, 24 vols. (Carbondale and Edwardsville, Ill., 1967–), 16:73.

78. *MAR,* April 28, 29, 1866; *MN,* May 3, 1866; *MT,* April 29, 1866.

freedpeople, however much of an improvement over previous official conduct. Nor were the Creoles readily mollified after the disruption of their traditional activities. One offending white formally apologized for his actions, offering to treat the Creole Fire Company's membership to drinks, but the members indignantly declined his offer. Thereafter, a dispute broke out in the fire company over the conservative policies of their leadership, which had continued the antebellum tradition of choosing white official spokesmen. Pres. T. S. Bidgood offered his resignation, warning that if his company disbanded, "the distinguished position you have earned as Creoles will be totally lost, and all marks of distinction will be obliterated." Bidgood was eventually restored to office, but several members were expelled soon thereafter, among them future Republican activists Constantine Perez and John Trenier Jr. The struggle seems to have taken on the overtones of generational revolt, with younger members abandoning their old-regime loyalties and transferring racial allegiance to the freedpeople. Despite the departure of some of these militants, the organization itself became more assertive, demanding the right to elect nonwhites to represent them in the city firemen's association. The Creole Fire Company would fly the Yankee flag at the next annual procession.[79]

While the prosperous Creoles were the object of Mayor Withers's special attention, he tried to build bridges to the black community more generally. In particular, the mayor reined in police brutality. He fired an officer who had blackjacked a USCI soldier in the course of arresting him; the officer was fined fifty dollars for good measure. In another instance, a policeman manhandled an unoffending child in order to get him to reveal a suspect; Withers fired the officer, fining him as well. Perhaps such examples inhibited police abuse, and the crime statistics suggest the possibility of increasing caution. Despite obsessive press attention to black crime, African Americans were not overrepresented in published arrest figures. In February and again in April 1866, for example, about twice as many whites were arrested as blacks.[80] The pattern becomes more pronounced if one disregards unprosecuted cases and minor infractions. Perhaps the police restraint simply reflected the belated recognition that the freedpeople were surprisingly law abiding, given their impoverished circumstances. None of

79. Minutes, May 12, August 6, September 6, 1866, Creole Fire Company Papers; *Mobile Register,* April 28, 1870.
80. *MAR,* March 9, 23, May 3, 9, 1866.

these changes openly impressed the black leadership of the city, for praise could be used to legitimize conservative rule. Moreover, Withers's vagrancy policies remained in conflict with the interests of the newer migrants, at least, and black women were assigned to the chain gang as washerwomen, which was resented as a grave affront. Still, the activists associated with the *Nationalist* tacitly acknowledged an improving racial climate. The paper noted the mayor's "reputation for impartiality." One letter, by "Colored Volunteer," demanded suffrage but added that enfranchisement might wait if all whites were as sober as Gen. Robert E. Lee—or Mayor Withers.[81]

Relatively enlightened municipal leadership inspired a mixed African American response, logically enough since the point of official policy was to distinguish between respectable black Mobilians and the wretched poor. The evidence suggests an internal bifurcation, with more established, prosperous, and politically engaged elements of the black community seeking a modus vivendi with city officials. On occasion, the activists around the black newspaper even called on civic authorities for help with unruly elements. In May, for example, disorder broke out among recently discharged black soldiers, many from out of town and without means. An obscure African American claims agent advertised for a meeting at the St. Louis Street Baptist Church, offering to secure their military bounties for a fee. The *Nationalist*'s editor, and some of his activist comrades, feared the agent was irresponsible; they preferred entrusting Yankee lawyer George F. Harrington's firm with the bounty money. The USCI veterans were always a volatile element, and the racial angle of the dispute possibly enflamed feelings. A fight broke out at the church, which reportedly included gunplay.[82] Police swept in to be greeted by thrown bricks, but they made nine arrests with "*the aid of the citizen negroes,*" as the conservative press noted.

Precisely who these citizen Negroes were is unclear, but the concern of some of the more established African Americans residents for social order was evident. Throughout this period everyone understood that the threat of a popular outbreak was real. A rational fear existed that some freedpeople, especially the new migrants, might initiate a conflict, with potentially catastrophic results. For example, after the New Orleans race riot on July 30, 1866, rumors spread of possible street action against Mobile's hated chain

---

81. *MAR,* July 25, 1866; *MN,* August 2, September 6, 1866. On the favorable reference to Withers, the name of the submission might suggest John Carraway as author.

82. *MT,* May 15, 16, 1866.

gang. Doubtless intimidated by the recent slaughter, the *Nationalist*'s editors urged readers to remain calm and not to provoke conflict.[83] According to the conservative press, an unspecified delegation of the African American "better class" called on the mayor to "place themselves on record as good law abiding citizens." These "old Mobile negroes" reportedly offered their assistance in repressing any riots caused by "either Yankee agitators or New Orleans negroes." This tantalizing evidence of class and other internal divisions is susceptible of various interpretations, but the evident fact is that the mayor was seen as someone worth approaching with such an offer of cooperation.[84] Under J. M. Withers, there was some prospect that the requests of at least a portion of the black community would be heard with some respect.

Mayor Withers's policies suggested opportunities in quite another political direction as well; his actions foreshadowed elite discord over emerging postwar economic issues. The city's white leadership bitterly debated economic development for the next decade. This was never a priority for the black community, but the political implication was straightforward: if the white leadership divided over an issue that the freedpeople cared little about, black leaders might exact concessions. Lacking the franchise, the freedpeople had no voice in the development debates, but Withers's determined opposition to expenditures suggested the dissention to come. The mayor's motivations are not clear; perhaps he was simply cautious by temperament, as his conduct toward the freedpeople suggested. During Withers's first term as mayor, in the mid-1850s, the city had experienced drastic fiscal problems over railroad subsidies, and perhaps this experience troubled him. Furthermore, his recent renegotiation of overdue debt payments with Wall Street impressed him with the gravity of the situation. It appears that he repeatedly vetoed his own pay increase, surely testimony of serious intent. Withers favored retrenchment as did a few likeminded allies, such as the president of the Board of Aldermen, Caleb Price. None of these municipal expenditures, however, amounted to much compared to the vast subsidies under contemplation.[85]

The city charter gave the mayor absolute veto power over bond issues,

---

83. *MT,* May 15, 1866; *MAR,* August 11, 1866; *MN,* August 16, 1866.
84. *MAR,* August 18, 1866; *MT,* August 18, 1866; *MN,* August 9, 1866.
85. Amos, *Cotton City,* 206–7, 229–32; Ordinances of March 16 and December 6, 1866, folder 1, envelope 3, box 12, RMBACC; *MAR,* April 11, August 8, October 12, 1866.

so Withers's opposition forestalled serious consideration of subsidy measures.⁸⁶ At the moment, none of the proposals were practical anyway because the unsettled national political convulsions deterred fresh outside investment. The development issue would reemerge with a vengeance once Reconstruction installed governments supportive of promotion measures. Mayor Withers anticipated the series of municipal officials during Reconstruction, Democratic and Republican, who opposed the economic subsidies promoted by the business community. The merchant leadership, conservative as they were, could hardly afford to focus solely on partisan issues or racial resentments given their economic needs. This would be the financial context within which the African Americans electorate would pursue freedom and civil rights, once black suffrage transformed the political scene.

Economic woes on a less grandiose order occupied the editors of the *Mobile Nationalist*. The civic-development issue made little impression at the newspaper, but Albert Griffin had his own fiscal and factional problems. The incoming editor, however, had more experience upon which to draw than his deposed predecessor, John Silsby. Despite his relative youth, being about thirty, Griffin's egalitarian credentials were in order. The son of an editor, he had been driven from Macon, Georgia, by a mob for holding interracial religious meetings, reportedly with antislavery overtones. Soon thereafter he headed for Manhattan, Kansas, where he became active with the Free State forces. During the Civil War, Griffin relocated to Chicago, where he was elected vice president of his typographical union. It was from there that he and a subordinate, James Shaw, went to the *Nationalist* in January 1866. Shaw noted Griffin's "moral earnestness," but he also recalled that the paper paid well—at least when it actually paid. Given his background, Griffin knew the dangers, remarking that it was only the army that made it possible for him to stay. He would soon be the most hated man in Mobile, and the one white political figure with both personal influence and bitter enemies in the black community.⁸⁷

The *Nationalist* was created under missionary auspices, but Griffin had different priorities and quickly modified Silsby's divisive Christian empha-

86. Lewis, *Charter and Code of Ordinances,* 40–1.
87. Kimberly Bess Cantrell, "A Voice for the Freedmen: The *Mobile Nationalist,* 1865–1869" (master's thesis, Auburn University, 1989), 15–7; John Richard Dennett, *The South as It Is, 1865–1866* (1866; reprint, New York, 1965), 300–1.

ses. As James Shaw recalled, "the *Nationalist* was transformed from a teacher of ethics, morals and manners. It became a republican paper." Griffin pragmatically addressed black interests; for example, he supported preferential hiring for qualified black teachers. He was particularly respectful of the independent black churches. In one instance Griffin engaged in a debate with a national religious publication, urging the Northern Methodists to cede the field to the African Methodist denominations. Continued missionary activity, he advised, would simply push the freedpeople into the arms of the southern white churches, who had recently modified their policy of intransigent hostility.[88] For Griffin, political unity and alliance with the Republican North were the overriding concerns. None saw this more clearly than Silsby, who complained privately that "the present editor has made a purely secular paper."[89]

Griffin's bold egalitarianism and political emphasis proved popular with his local audience and with external constituencies too. He reached a national public in the language of Radical Republicanism. "The essential feature of Republicanism is that every man has exactly the same rights, privileges and immunities as every other man," Griffin proclaimed.[90] The paper's editorials revolved around this core principle, from attacks on the chain gang and "whites-only" streetcars to denunciations of Creole caste prejudice. From the first, Griffin emphasized that Radicalism was not a racial ideology but a universal vision of human liberty. Beyond this, perhaps his most controversial emphasis was on the urgency of self-defense, which was somewhat inconsistent with his general desire to restrain popular militancy. Griffin urged freedpeople to obey the law and sometimes counseled patience, but he also endorsed legitimate self-defense. After the disturbances at the Creole celebration, he recommended that freedmen "kill those who attack them," then they would be left alone. The Memphis riot elicited the suggestion that freedpeople go armed.[91] After one riot, the army actually closed down the paper for advising that one shoot only to hit, and he later advised shooting prowling Klansmen on sight. Griffin's combative prose was probably encouraged by his sense of personal danger, and one suspects that his advice fell on a receptive popular audience.[92]

88. *Aurora (Ill.) Beacon-News,* July 31, 1915; *MN,* July 12, 1866; *Northwestern Christian Advocate* quoted in *Christian Recorder,* August 4, 1866.
89. J. Silsby to "Dear Brother," November 5, 1866, Alabama, AMA, reel 1.
90. *MN,* June 28, 1866.
91. Ibid., May 3, 17, 1866.
92. Ibid., April 26, May 17, June 28, 1866, May 30, 1867, May 2, 1868.

Griffin's editorial policies served to distinguish his priorities from that of his troubled predecessor. Beyond solidifying the support of his readership, his immediate priority was fundraising, which he attacked with zeal. The editor offered to do all sorts of printing jobs, and he also announced a subscription drive with "the most magnificent prize scheme ever offered by a Southern newspaper," offering participants everything from a cabinet organ to engravings of Abraham Lincoln. Various *Nationalist* auxiliaries, men's and women's, also hosted fundraisers. For his part, Griffin tried to market the newspaper nationwide as "the grand, political and commercial organ of the colored people of the South." He appealed to the northern public and advertisers for support, reportedly downplaying local news in favor of topics of wider interest. The results of these efforts, however, were mixed. Griffin reported in June 1866 that the subscription list was increasing but that "the receipts are not so large as they should be." With Griffin reportedly receiving forty-five dollars per week, the newspaper's costs were substantial.[93]

Unfortunately for Griffin, his efforts to increase revenue exacerbated the paper's factional difficulties. Lawrence S. Berry, the paper's traveling agent, emerged as Griffin's strongest critic over fiscal issues, and he would subsequently become a political rival as well, the most prominent black militant or Radical in early Reconstruction politics.[94] So far as can be determined, Berry's background was different from that of most of the *Nationalist* activists. He had been a slave in Montgomery and been moved to Mobile in the early 1850s; during the war, his master sent him to the Confederate salt works in the interior. With emancipation he joined the general exodus downriver to Mobile.[95] Berry's absence from the newspaper's board of directors would suggest a lack of means, but he was literate. He is known to have been an AME Zion lay leader, and his denunciations of Griffin raised divisive racial issues, though Berry and the editor originally fell out over promotion strategy for the paper. When he became traveling agent in January 1866, Berry thought quantities of newspapers ought to be sent out on consignment. Griffin believed the practice would not pay, and upon becoming editor, he stopped sending the newspapers. The change in policy and

93. Ibid., June 7, 1866.
94. Foner, *Freedom's Lawmakers*, 18.
95. *MAR*, January 19, 1869. A brief autobiographic sketch by Berry strongly suggests he was a slave until near the very end of the war.

the consequent phasing out of his job troubled Berry, who later claimed he had not been paid.[96] Rumors spread that the white editor had impugned the honesty of the local distributors, who were all African American, and an outraged Griffin called on Berry for a denial of these tales. Not surprisingly, Griffin found another general agent, simultaneously decreasing Berry's prominence in the paper's columns.[97]

Given the troublesome racial implications of the dispute, the editor needed a credible black spokesman. Griffin's protégé, John Carraway, the former slave who had fled Alabama after being freed by his white father, swiftly became Mobile's leading African American political figure after his return.[98] As Griffin's general agent, Carraway tried to calm the waters, but his first venture into prominence demonstrated how turbulent they were. One of his editorials denounced visiting ministers for profiteering at the expense of black congregations.[99] At the mass meeting in May, Carraway said something still more injudicious; the specifics are unclear, but "highly objectionable" remarks were attributed to him.[100] Carraway subsequently offered his resignation, and Berry briefly was restored to the position. Upon reflection, the *Nationalist* board rejected Carraway's resignation, and he again resumed the position as general agent. The job would change hands yet again, with the rivalry between the two men suggesting continuing factional struggles over Griffin's leadership as well.

There was an ideological dimension to these personal controversies. They touched on the intent of the newspaper enterprise and recalled the earlier debates about Yankee influence over the movement. Griffin, as a northern outsider, felt some scrutiny from the community, though political constraints discouraged open discussion of the issue. On one occasion he reminded readers that the paper was black owned, adding that contributors would not "be building up a white man's enterprise." Given his circumstances, however, Griffin could hardly emphasize the racial character of his paper with comfort, and his eleven-point statement of principles did not mention it. One editorial suggested that it would have been better had the paper been founded on a "purely political basis," though he admitted its race-based nature had been necessary. Radical Republican ideology de-

---

96. *MAR,* January 19, 1869.
97. *MN,* January 11, April 12, 19, 26, May 10, June 26, 1866.
98. Ibid., September 12, 1867.
99. Ibid., May 31, April 19, March 22, 1866.
100. Ibid., May 17, 24, 1866.

manded a colorblind polity, which implicitly legitimized Griffin's role as editor. However, for his African American colleagues, rooted as they were in black community organizations and churches, part of the appeal of the paper was precisely that it was racially identified. Berry wrote of "colored newspaper enterprises" and described the *Nationalist* as "a newspaper for colored people."[101] Such talk circulated naturally among the *Nationalist* speakers. In Montgomery local agent Holland Thompson boasted that the paper was "owned by a black man in Mobile," admittedly taking some license. Even John Carraway referred to "our" paper as opposed to the "white papers." As criticism of Griffin mounted, the language of racial self-determination grew more insistent.[102]

The editor's position became increasingly troublesome, and for all his efforts, the financial outlook remained bleak. As Griffin wrote privately, "our expenses are very heavy and advertising patronage very light, as the people here will not let their business men advertise with us." Physical interference with distributors and the mails also restricted revenue, and the limited wealth and literacy of the African American population also hurt. John Carraway's plea that illiterates should subscribe as a down payment on their children's futures itself testified to the practical difficulties. Griffin tried everything: he lowered the subscription price, then abandoned the experiment some months later because it did not work. Rival papers publicly claimed the *Nationalist* was on its last legs, predicting the editor would soon be indicted for sedition as well.[103] The unraveling of Griffin's expansive fiscal promises weakened his position, and by the summer, he was under assault from all directions. There were rumors in June of a hostile takeover of the Loyal Newspaper Society by Montgomery shareholders, about the time of Griffin's confrontation with Berry. There were also complaints that in his zeal to reach a national audience, he was ignoring local human-interest stories. The obvious disarray eventually prompted John Silsby to ask the missionary association to send him back to Mobile so he could resume his editorial duties. Still irritated by the secular tone of the paper, he proposed to restore its original character "as an auxiliary to every good work here."[104]

101. Ibid., June 7, 21, 1866.
102. Ibid., January 25, April 19, 1866.
103. A. Griffin to M. E. Strieby, March 29, 1866, Alabama, AMA, reel 1; *Montgomery Advertiser,* April 4, 1866; *MN,* May 30, August 23, 1866.
104. *MN,* April 12, 19, June 21, 1866; J. Silsby to George Whipple, December 2, 1865, Alabama, AMA, reel 1.

By late July, Griffin had reached a personal impasse. In an editorial entitled "Discouragements," he unburdened himself: "It is really disheartening when one knows himself to have been prompted by pure motives to find that selfish, or even base designs have been attributed to him." Even Christ was maligned, he observed revealingly, adding that good people would withdraw from public business if unappreciated. Perhaps alluding to his financial projections, he observed that if an adviser sometimes gave bad advice, it did not follow that he was a fool. The editor made these defensive comments because various enterprises that deserved united support were "suffering serious injury" at the hands of professed friends. For the future, he urged everyone to "drop personalities" and concentrate on the general welfare. With that, the editor announced his departure to Kansas and the North for a speaking tour. Griffin left matters in Mobile to sort themselves out for the next sixteen weeks while his leading critic, Lawrence Berry, resumed his old position as general agent.[105]

At this point, fortuitously, the national political convulsions intersected with the fate of Griffin and the *Mobile Nationalist*. Throughout 1866, President Johnson and the Republican Congress were engaged in a bitter contest over southern Reconstruction policy. The president vetoed a Freedmen's Bureau extension and numerous civil rights statutes, while Congress refused to recognize his southern governments or permit southern congressmen to assume their seats. A stalemate resulted, the resolution of which would be up to the northern electorate in the fall 1866 elections. If the Republicans emerged victorious in the midterm canvass, big changes were likely in federal southern policy. This had immediate ramifications for the loyal southern press: federal printing subsidies were probable if Congress assumed control of Reconstruction. Griffin realized this prospect of outside salvation was immanent, and during the fall campaign, he acquired some prominence on the northern lecture circuit. At the Southern Loyalist Convention in September, he opposed expedient Republican efforts to downplay the black-suffrage issue. He also helped organize a southern Republican association to lobby Congress. By October, Griffin predicted Republican victory and called on his Mobile comrades to prepare to exercise the franchise responsibly. Demonstrating foresight, Griffin opposed the Fourteenth Amendment because that measure would leave former Rebels

---

105. *MN*, July 26, 1866.

in power, and he rejoiced when southern rejection forced Congress's hand on black suffrage.[106]

By the time Griffin returned to Mobile late in the year, the national portents were excellent, given the Republicans' sweeping electoral triumph. However, this did the paper's immediate prospects little good. The *Nationalist* office narrowly escaped an apparent arson attempt. James Thomas, president of the trustees, complained of continuing factionalism: the paper had enemies "even among the people whose interests it so fearlessly defended."[107] Another observer concluded that the *Nationalist* was rapidly sinking. Griffin seized on desperate short-term measures and in January 1867 asked the *Nationalist* directors to borrow one thousand dollars from Mobile's Colored Orphan Asylum. The board authorized the loan reluctantly, and one member, Jacob Anderson, openly opposed it. Only the prospect of aid from Washington kept the imperiled enterprise alive.

The editor again left for the capitol, happy to find that politicians there knew of him and respected his work. Griffin lobbied for legislation directing federal advertising toward the loyal southern press. There seemed no doubt of it passing, he wrote privately, and it would enable the *Nationalist* to appear as a daily and *"pay a splendid profit."* Griffin had no intention of having these changes work to his personal disadvantage, and having been buffeted by months of factional controversy, he realized that this prospective financial boon endangered his position. Once the paper began to pay, "every stockholder will be wanting to be president, director, or something else." In response, Griffin privately directed his allies to buy up as many shares as possible. He worried particularly about the "dollar stockholders," which suggested he saw the paper's grassroots supporters as a major threat to his control.[108]

Griffin anticipated that implementation of Congressional Reconstruction would make restructuring the paper financially advantageous. The riotous next few weeks (see chapter 3) must have reinforced his desire for control on political grounds as well. Soon after his return to Mobile, major changes occurred in the paper's character. According to Carraway's recollection, Griffin moved "to cut the board of fifteen colored directors down to five; he and his foreman were to be part of that five." In April the paper

106. Ibid., December 27, October 25, 1866.
107. Ibid., November 31, December 6, 1866, January 10, 1867.
108. Ibid., February 21, 1867.

announced an "entire reorganization" of the Loyal Newspaper Society after its mass meeting. Griffin became president and Shaw became secretary, becoming for the first time members of the governing body. Berry, Carraway, and Jacob Anderson of the old board also became directors, so African Americans still retained the majority. The shareholders ordered the paper to appear as a daily, as Griffin repeatedly promised he would do. These changes coincided with a shift in editorial philosophy as well. Up to this time, the *Nationalist* had been looked upon as a "class paper," but henceforth it would be "simply a Republican paper—knowing no North, no South, no black, no white."[109]

These changes were a logical extension of Griffin's editorial policies, but they raised misgivings that the paper had slipped from community control. L. S. Berry would acidly describe the *Nationalist* as "formerly the colored people's paper," and John Carraway claimed he opposed the restructuring. These assertions only occurred in retrospect, and at the time the changes slid through without public controversy. Why? Perhaps Griffin simply bought up enough shares, but more likely the financial crisis dramatized the need for restructuring. More broadly, Radical Republicanism demanded the abolition of racial distinctions in public life, and it was difficult at the moment to argue that freedpeople needed control of their own institutions. In Griffin's words, with equal suffrage there were "no 'freedmen' now, all are freemen—and intend to remain so."[110] Skepticism toward the white editor, however merited, inevitably took on racial overtones, which let Griffin identify his tenure with the wider goal of racial equality. He also infused this utopian vision with the promise of material benefits. Government printing contracts were now in prospect, and these were "very lucrative," as another Republican editor pointed out.[111] But being a race paper might preclude public advertising, or at least this was what Griffin contended. What better way to demonstrate the *Nationalist*'s nonracial character than to appoint white directors?

Thus, at the crucial moment of black enfranchisement, Albert Griffin ironically solidified control over the major political voice of Alabama's

109. *Selma Times and Messenger,* February 14, 1869; *MN,* April 18, 1867.
110. *Mobile Register,* January 19, 1869; *Selma Times and Messenger,* February 14, 1869; *MN,* April 14, 1867.
111. Jean-Charles Houzeau, *My Passage at the* New Orleans Tribune: *A Memoir of the Civil War Era,* ed. David C. Rankin, trans. Gerald F. Renault (Baton Rouge and London, 1984), 139.

black population. In this instance the language of racial egalitarianism legitimized the influence of white allies, with the editor acting in large part to restrain the freedpeople. The precise same thing would occur in the electoral sphere, within the Republican party as a whole, and Griffin's augmented power allowed him a leadership role here too. In the spring of 1867, the editor joined with moderate Republicans to check the radical tendencies of the energized black populace. The *Nationalist*'s columns facilitated a purge of those Republican leaders the editor thought dangerous or too aggressive. The intervention of Griffin and his white allies would open glaring rifts between black activists, between those favored and disfavored by the emerging white Republican leadership. The resulting factionalism, mirroring lines of internal social division, would become the underlying reality in African American politics as the day of universal suffrage dawned.

3

The Most Influential People

Suffrage, Class, and Factionalism

Popular agitation swept Mobile the moment Congress overthrew Presidential Reconstruction and decreed universal suffrage. Shocked conservatives saw only a monolithic Radical threat to social order, but they misperceived what was happening: overwhelming black support for Reconstruction at the polls masked a rapidly fragmenting insurgency. As the *Mobile Nationalist*'s contentious history suggests on a limited scale, tension within an interracial Republican leadership was predictable, a direct result of outside influence over black community priorities. More surprising, perhaps, was the strife among the African American activists, which gradually took on the form of a permanent factional polarization. Individual rivalries quickly became embittered, amplified by differences in background dating back to emancipation and beyond. These leadership cleavages were intractable because they echoed those of the black community more broadly, especially the division between established residents and destitute newcomers from the rural hinterland. This dynamic propelled African American political development in the years ahead.

Even before black suffrage, political activities quickened in the face of utopian hopes becoming reality. The actual enactment of Military Reconstruction in early March 1867 encouraged a surge of community agitation.[1]

---

1. Anonymous to American Missionary Association, December 10, 1866, Alabama, AMA, reel 7; G. Tracy to C. W. Buckley, March 2, 1867, M810, RG 105, reel 3; *MN*, January 10, 1867.

Not surprisingly, *Nationalist* activists led the way, but the striking development was the emergence of militant white Radicals. Enfranchisement promised both political change and personal advancement, drawing fresh recruits, and in the early meetings the leading white activists were northern lawyers George F. Harrington and W. W. D. Turner. Both had previously represented black clients and served as claims agents for U.S. Colored Infantry veterans, but neither had been involved with the *Nationalist* or publicly prominent as Radicals. By virtue of their education and political experience, they were strategically placed, and they utilized most of the platform time explaining the political duties of the new electorate.[2] With editor Albert Griffin away lobbying in Washington, and while Mobile's native Union men hesitated, Harrington and Turner distinguished themselves for bold advocacy of egalitarian demands. These Yankee lawyers, ironically, served as midwives for a style of popular politics that promoted aggressive black leadership. At the March 4 meeting, Harrington and Turner moved for the creation of a Union League, this being the name for the secret Republican clubs that were then spreading throughout the South. The freedpeople responded with enthusiasm, and the initial planning session was "crowded to overflowing, hundreds outside being unable to gain admittance." On March 21 the *Nationalist* claimed twenty-five hundred members for the league. This would have been over half the adult male black population, which clearly meant political agitation touched a wide portion of the community. The outpouring of support would change the movement in unanticipated and dangerous ways.[3]

During this initial phase, league meetings occurred several times per week, and they generated considerable momentum. For example, C. A. Woodward, cashier of the Freedmen's Bank branch, turned the rhetoric of racial uplift toward financial ends. Turner and Harrington were the claims agents for four hundred black veterans, so Woodward's collaboration with their political efforts had a certain fiscal logic.[4] After one Turner speech, Woodward read a circular promoting the bank and was rewarded with considerable new business. After another meeting, Woodward reported "twenty-one new depositors since yesterday morning." Obviously, Radical agitation encouraged some of Mobile's new citizens to take charge of their financial futures. For the laboring population more broadly, the effect was

---

2. *MN,* March 14, 1867.
3. *MN,* March 14, 21, 1867.
4. C. A. Woodward to John Alvord, April 9, 1867, M803, RG 105, reel 14.

equally immediate but more unsettling. Dramatic confrontations, among the most convulsive of the city's history, ensued on the streets. The radical political rhetoric of the meetings acted as a catalyst, prodding the long-frustrated populace toward direct action.[5]

The freedpeople now took the initiative in the city's public places, encouraged by similar events in other ports. The initial focus was the workplace, though the mobilization was unconnected with the established white union movement. "Discontent among Negro Laborers," as the *Mobile Advertiser and Register* characterized it, had been growing since mid-March, and the unrest was intense among dockworkers and day laborers. On Saturday, March 30, several hundred workers gathered at the foot of Government Street. They presented a riotous appearance, the *Selma Messenger* thought, and the protesters complained of various grievances, including violent treatment of steamboat hands. The main issue was pay for dockworkers: the strikers demanded an increase from twenty-five to fifty cents per hour, which was paid in New Orleans. The crowd reportedly prevented replacement laborers from working, perhaps roughly, though no whites were involved in the action. The police arrested one of the strike leaders, who afterward pressed charges for assault and false imprisonment, which might suggest that Yankee legal advice was at hand. For the moment, the police repressed the strike, but a more confrontational labor dispute ensued that same day.

At Jewett's Sawmill, a group of employees demanded an increase from one dollar to one dollar fifty cents a day, this being a relatively low wage. A sawyer named Wylie Brown urged the workers to walk off the job, but he soon was arrested for disorderly conduct, apparently at the employer's instigation. As L. S. Berry recalled, the freedman was knocked down and "hauled through the public streets like a hog." An excited crowd followed behind debating whether to intervene. After Brown was lodged in jail, an impromptu meeting occurred throughout the afternoon featuring strong rhetoric. One black from New Orleans, perhaps drunk, wandered around with a sword, urging resistance. Harrington and Turner suggested it might be well to arrest him, indicating that even these white Radicals were alarmed by the possibility of an outbreak of violence.[6] The following Mon-

5. C. A. Woodward to John Alvord, March 16, 26, 1867, M803, RG 105, reel 14; *MN*, April 18, 1867.

6. *Selma Daily Messenger*, April 7, 1867; *MAR*, April 2, 3, 1867; *MN*, April 4, 25, 1867.

day, April 1, strike leader Brown was tried. The courtroom was packed, while "the negroes in the street gathered in throngs and conversed in the most excited manner." After inquiry, the acting mayor ordered Brown released on the ground that no crime had occurred. A triumphant crowd bore him outside amid general celebration, but his release did not quiet the freedmen for long. That same day some two hundred armed men marched down Broad Street to "release the chain-gang who were at work in the Southern part of the city." They eventually abandoned the attempt, but the following day crowds could be seen on various street corners discussing the matter.[7]

Mobile's white residents responded cautiously to these unprecedented events, at least at first. One businessman reported that "we are in the midst of *much* negro politics," but it reassured him that Radical meetings were off in the suburbs. The city fathers, perhaps intimidated by Congressional Reconstruction, voted to remove racial distinctions from the charter in a concession to changed circumstances.[8] The city also hired some African American police, stationing them at black churches, where they received a mixed reception. Even the conservative press was surprisingly temperate. Bad white men rather than the freedpeople caused the troubles, according to the *Advertiser and Register*. One of the "Negro rioters" was overheard saying that their lawyer had told them "that under the Civil Rights Bill they were entitled to fifty cents an hour." Whatever precisely Harrington and Turner were advising, Agent George Tracy of the Freedmen's Bureau agreed it was injudicious. According to him, the freedpeople were told that they would "only get their rights by making a bold stand" and that the "law of Congress is a dead letter unless they spur it into vitality." Still, one might expect lawyers to counsel staying within the law, and the strike leaders seem to have been ordinary laborers rather than political activists. The evidence thus suggests a spontaneous eruption of grassroots resistance encouraged by league rhetoric and the millennial mood of the moment.[9]

Popular unrest, moreover, often won tangible concessions. For example, the disturbances of that spring seem to have caught the attention of Mo-

---

7. *MT,* April 2, 1867; *MAR,* April 6, 21, 1867; *Selma Messenger,* April 3, 1867.

8. William P. Hamilton to "Dear Aunt," April 22, 1867, Bullock and Hamilton Family Papers, SHC; *Selma Messenger,* April 7, 1867.

9. *MAR,* April 2, 6, 9, 1867; Tracy to Swayne, April 17, 1867, M809, RG 105, reel 13; Eric Arneson, *Waterfront Workers of New Orleans: Race, Class, and Politics, 1863–1923* (Oxford, 1991), 28.

bile's conservative local authorities. During the previous year, Mobile County officials charged with poor relief had distributed substantial quantities of food to about one thousand families a month. Of these, about one hundred, or around 10 percent, were freedpeople, a proportion far below their share of the population or their obvious need. Immediately after the spring 1867 disturbances, though, relief policy was transformed. In April county officials distributed food to nearly two hundred fifty black families, a large increase in the proportion from the previous months. In the tumult-filled summer ahead, the proportion of food relief granted African Americans grew, reaching around four hundred families. By late 1867, blacks were receiving most of the food distributed and were actually overrepresented relative to their population. County officials never explained the motive for this dramatic change in policy, but given the timing, the growing social unrest along with the altered political climate would be the obvious answer. For the bulk of the African American populace, the implications were fairly straightforward. Poorer freedpeople might rationally have concluded that direct action could yield positive dividends, and more quickly than through the electoral process, if mass protests indeed resulted in hundreds of families being fed.[10]

If conservative officials responded with discretion to the disturbances, the freedmen's prospective Unionist allies were unnerved, for they had never seen the freedpeople behave so aggressively. Gustavus Horton and Frederick Bromberg, for example, conspicuously avoided the league gatherings. Similar issues troubled Thomas Conway, now visiting Mobile on behalf of the national Union League. As had been the case when he proclaimed emancipation in the city in 1865, Conway feared the emergence of an ultraradical "Colored men's party." Albert Griffin, on his return to Mobile, chose this very time to solidify control over the *Mobile Nationalist* board. Griffin's paper defended the strikers in public, affirming the justice of their demands, but he strongly urged them to avoid provoking violence. The last thing most white Republicans wanted was a campaign of direct action coinciding with the implementation of the Reconstruction acts. Agent Tracy privately regarded the Radical meetings as premature and dangerous. Bureau personnel concluded that something had to be done lest the city explode.[11]

10. Board of Revenue Commissioners, Minutes, May 1, August 1, 1866, February 5, August 6, 1867, February 4, 1868, Mobile County Commission, Mobile Government Plaza.

11. T. W. Conway to C. W. Buckley, May 4, 1867, M810, RG 105, reel 3; J. Silsby to Swayne, April 1, 1867, Wager Swayne Papers, ADAH.

Gen. Wager Swayne was now Freedmen's Bureau and military commander for the state, and he supported the Reconstruction process as did his superior, Gen. John Pope, in Atlanta. Swayne sought a coalition with enough white support to be viable, and he responded aggressively to the trouble in Mobile. He dispatched his chief clerk, John Keffer, secretary of Alabama's Union League, along with John Silsby, the former *Nationalist* editor. Swayne wanted the Mobile league reorganized "because that seemed to be the only way to suppress a riot." Reckless white men were giving terrible advice, both sides were arming, and the general lacked the forces to keep order. Swayne therefore wanted to "organize the black men down there into Union Leagues, and put them under the charge of white men who would give them reasonable counsel." Operating under these instructions, Silsby arrived in the midst of the labor disturbances and concluded that Harrington and Turner had made "ill judged and inflammatory" speeches, though they "had influence only with the less stable portion of the Colored people." Silsby presumably meant the poorer laborers and the recent migrants, and the class overtones of his remarks are suggestive. Keffer exacted a promise from Harrington that the lawyer would mind his tongue, and Keffer also restructured the league so that "Mr. Harrington could no longer take the lead." Two organizations were created: a black council, ironically under the leadership of Gustavus Horton, and a white council under Frederick Bromberg. The logic of the segregated structure was that white recruits would find participation easier in a separate council. Silsby concluded that affairs in the city were now satisfactory, while the *Nationalist* commented on the excellent result of the visit.[12] Swayne's purge placed the Union League in something like receivership; the main vehicle of black politics passed under the direction of the native Unionists, Griffin, and Swayne's bureau. These elements would henceforth lead the dominant moderate, or scalawag, faction in Mobile's Republican politics. The intent of the intervention was clearly control, to use the now more hierarchical league to discipline popular activism. As Thomas Conway advised from the scene, "Let the League be the mainspring [of organizing] . . . , for if you do not you will have trouble from the ignorance of many."[13]

---

12. U.S. Congress, House, *Testimony Taken before the Judiciary Committee, House of Representatives, in the Investigation of the Charges against Hon. Richard Busteed* (Washington, 1869), 167; Silsby to Swayne, April 1, 1867; *MN,* April 4, 1867.

13. T. W. Conway to C. W. Buckley, May 4, 1867. Conway was traveling organizer for the national Union League at the time. See Michael W. Fitzgerald, *The Union League Movement in the Deep South: Politics and Agricultural Change during Reconstruction* (Baton Rouge, 1989), 13–4.

The Republican leadership acted to rein in the militant talk that incited working-class blacks to strikes and direct action. The outside intervention through the league was not subtle, and some African Americans perceived the implications with unease. Harrington himself soon made something of a comeback; he was never driven off Republican platforms, to the frustration of Griffin. Several black activists, moreover, were frankly rebellious. For example, when a statewide gathering of black Republicans met in Mobile in early May, L. S. Berry was on a committee to draft resolutions. The proposed statement concluded that "Republicans of both races [should] hold their party meetings together," a criticism of the separate league councils, but this was edited out of the final resolutions. A subsequent published letter by "York" explained that the creation of the two leagues "gave rise to distrust in the minds of our people." When Turner and Harrington started organizing, only a few white men entered the original Union League. Griffin, Bromberg, and company then decided to set up a "white League for the benefit of all *quasi* Republicans whose prejudices were stronger than their principles." Of seventy members of the new white council, "York" thought perhaps a dozen were genuine Republicans who could be trusted. The acerbic commentary of "York" suggests that activists grasped what was happening and that some found the trend toward control by white moderates disturbing.[14]

Despite such misgivings, most black activists apparently acquiesced to the restructuring of the local movement. As "York" himself admitted, the league had gotten "control of some of our good colored men," and the black council under Horton's leadership grew quickly. By summer, Bureau Agent Tracy concluded that the turbulent and impulsive black leaders were losing ground. The evil consequences of bad advice, he thought, were now recognized by the more thoughtful and well-meaning freedpeople.[15] If anything politically characterized the black leaders in the moderate faction, it was their lack of enthusiasm for direct action, and the recent labor turmoil and the threat of riot might legitimately have given them pause. For example, John Carraway criticized W. W. D. Turner for provoking street confrontations, recommending recourse to the military authorities and the ballot box instead. Other community activists similarly discouraged pro-

14. *MN,* May 9, 1867; *Montgomery State Sentinel,* June 26, July 2, 1867.
15. *Montgomery State Sentinel,* July 2, 1867; F. Bromberg to Keffer, April 27, 1867, Swayne Papers; G. H. Tracy to O. D. Kinsman, June 20, 1867, M809, RG 105, reel 13.

vocative actions in the weeks ahead. One black correspondent for the *Nationalist* actually minimized popular involvement in the labor disturbances. The strike leaders, he claimed, were *agents provocateurs;* they were used by the police to demonstrate that "the negroes of Mobile were not a law abiding people." This thoroughly unlikely allegation suggests the discomfort some leaders felt toward the recent disorder.[16]

If this edgy response to the strike was typical, the relatively established social backgrounds of the prominent political activists likely encouraged it. Among the former *Nationalist* trustees, for example, small businessmen predominated and common laborers were rare. The initial cohort of black political spokesmen were likewise drawn from those whose basic complaint was racial discrimination rather than economic misery; at least, these were the individuals whom the dominant faction of white Republicans recognized and promoted as leaders. Such activists might well be comfortable with a more focused movement, concentrating on political Reconstruction and welcoming established white allies. Furthermore, the newer recruits to the Republican leadership were often even more well heeled. In the coming months, two young Afro-Creoles emerged as Republican spokesmen, having been inactive before politics became a viable profession. Ovid Gregory was an officer in the Creole Social Club, a position he soon resigned, while Philip Joseph was the son of a wealthy and slaveholding Creole family. By his own account, Joseph had been raised to a life of ease, but the war undermined his prospects and forced him to seek employment. Along with several other Creole comrades, these men now committed themselves to the Republican cause, but the proletarian tumult on the wharves would be foreign to their backgrounds. These were just the sort of race spokesmen Griffin, Horton and their moderate colleagues welcomed.[17]

Distrust of direct-action tactics united the ranking white leadership and their black allies, but other freedmen drew their own lessons from the previous disturbances, concluding that they could dramatize social grievances and force immediate redress. The Republican leaders controlling the Union Leagues could shape the formal political agenda, but they could not dominate the streets. Attention now turned to the city's horse-drawn streetcar

---

16. *MN*, August 22, April 11, 1867.
17. Christopher Andrew Nordmann, "Free Negroes in Mobile County," 115–6; U.S. Congress, Senate, *Report and Testimony of the Select Committee of the United States Senate to Investigate the Causes of the Removal of the Negroes from the Southern States to the Northern States,* 46th Cong., 2d sess., S. Rept. 693, 412–3.

system connecting the largely black suburbs with the downtown waterfront. The streetcar companies routinely made black riders stand on the outside platforms, and in April a black woman attempting to sit on the inside of the car was ejected, reportedly with unnecessary vigor. Several more attempts ensued, causing "considerable excitement and gatherings of crowds on the street." W. W. D. Turner and L. S. Berry then prevailed upon George Tracy for help, but the agent recommended taking the matter to court. Lawyer Turner agreed, but the apparent result was a near riot. On April 14 an African American named Roderick B. Thomas entered the car on Government Street. Mayor J. M. Withers, happening on the scene, instructed the driver to disconnect the horses. Thomas eventually left the car to talk with bystanders, whereupon white customers quickly tried to get the car moving. When Thomas attempted to reboard, one white threatened to blow his brains out and another struck him and threw him from the car. Freedpeople came to his aid, and a full-scale melee developed with brickbats flying.[18] The police arrested Thomas and four other people.[19] These pressure tactics had some effect; in Montgomery, General Swayne determined that some sort of concession to black discontent was essential, and he banned the chain gang by military edict.[20] Albert Griffin pushed for more, informing the general that the "colored people are very impatiently waiting for an order from you settling the car question." Swayne was apparently willing, but his superior, General Pope, thought discrimination by private parties best left to the courts.[21] Some of the streetcar lines established segregated "Star Cars" for black use, but the basic issue remained unresolved and served as a flashpoint for popular anger in the coming years.[22]

Had the Republican leaders missed the dangerous implications of the streetcar confrontations, events a few nights later underscored the point. After a Union League evening meeting in the outskirts, members discharged

18. *MAR,* April 17, 1867; G. H. Tracy to Swayne, April 15, 17, 24, 1867, M809, RG 105, reel 13.

19. Joseph Edgar Brent, "No Surrender: Mobile, Alabama, during Presidential Reconstruction, 1865–1867" (master's thesis, University of South Alabama, 1988), 64–5.

20. *MN,* April 18, 1867.

21. A. Griffin to Swayne, April 22, 1867, Swayne Papers; Horton to Dimon, June 15, 1867, Mobile City Police Records, W. S. Hoole Special Collections, University of Alabama; Gregory to Swayne, July 3, 1867, Letters Received, box 1, District of Alabama, RG 393, pt.2.

22. *MAR,* April 21, 1867; *Louisville Courier* quoted in *Montgomery Mail,* May 10, 1867.

firearms in a show of bravado. The white Unionist leaders were deeply embarrassed. Frederick Bromberg forwarded to Swayne the league's subsequent resolutions opposing martial display, assuring him that no more such rallies would be held.[23] Meanwhile, a *Nationalist* editorial advised readers to "Keep Cool" and give whites time to "get used to the situation." Heading off provocative behavior became the obsession of moderate Republican leaders. All through the spring, the *Nationalist* preached restraint, denouncing Harrington and Turner as dangerous opportunists. Editor Griffin's most pointed advice, though, was to the black leadership, urging them to defer to their more trustworthy white colleagues. African Americans were "not yet sufficiently educated and accustomed to public affairs" to run the "government machine" without help. Mindful of his troubles at the *Nationalist,* Griffin warned against "Colored people, with strong positive minds, who are either suspicious of all white men, or who wish their people to put them into offices which they know some white man is better qualified to fill." Such leaders would raise extreme demands, then denounce their white allies when compliance proved impossible. Griffin's enhanced personal control over the *Nationalist* made it the vehicle of his moderate allies, and he marginalized those activists who favored direct action or more forthright promotion of black leadership.[24]

While Republican leaders attempted to stabilize the situation by looking toward peaceful implementation of black suffrage, the conservative opposition grappled with the new political realities. Universal suffrage forced unprecedented choices upon them too, and some conservatives wanted to appeal to blacks. John Forsyth and other Democratic leaders orchestrated an appeal to the new electorate, scheduling a large interracial rally downtown. The proposed speakers included Federal Judge Richard Busteed and others with Union backgrounds, and Forsyth approached various black and Creole leaders, such as Ovid Gregory, to negotiate terms for their participation. According to the *Nationalist,* some white Radicals proposed attending the meeting and offering resolutions of their own, but "the leading colored men all opposed the idea," again advocating restraint in the face of possible violence. As it happened, the rally came off peacefully, with several thousand whites and perhaps three hundred freedpeople in attendance.

23. C. A. R. Dimon to Swayne, April 18, 1867, Swayne Papers; *MN,* April 25, 1867; *MAR,* April 19, 1867; F. Bromberg to Swayne, April 27, 1867, Swayne Papers.
24. *MN,* April 18, May 30, June 6, 1867.

Two Creoles addressed the crowd, but this "novelty" was "interrupted with jocular remarks" by whites, according to a conservative source.[25] The freedpeople listened more politely, but the performance persuaded few. The recognition that conservatives could not influence the freedmen, combined with the white resentment at the events of the previous weeks, set the stage for public violence in May. The immediate emotional spark was provided by an inflammatory and unfortunately timed rape case, one of relatively few to occur in the vicinity. Several miles south of Mobile at Dog River, four intruders broke into the home of the Peters family. According to a Freedmen's Bureau investigation, the intruders robbed the family of over a thousand dollars at gunpoint, beating them and raping the mother and a twelve-year-old daughter. An army doctor's examination found physical evidence consistent with the survivors' testimony. The victims described the assailants as black males, though they had difficulty identifying the perpetrators.[26]

News of the episode broke just as the Republican statewide freedmen's convention gathered in Mobile, and the case generated a spasm of violent press rhetoric. Henry St. Paul's *Mobile Times,* for example, directly blamed the Republican troublemakers for the attack, despite the total absence of any explicit connection. "How long will the vile agitators, who plot mischief and murder, be protected from well deserved punishment . . . ?" The *Advertiser and Register* was more restrained, withholding news of the event at police request, but even that paper threatened "fearful vengeance" upon incendiaries for the "first drop of blood that flows from their teachings."[27] The *Mobile Tribune* concluded it was the white Radicals in the city who instigated the deed. For a week, Albert Griffin observed, editorials incited murder. Griffin reprinted the texts, noting uncomfortably that the articles endangered *all* Union men, not just the irresponsible ones. Such fears were widely shared in private. One white leaguer wrote Swayne that after the articles appeared, the streets were dangerous, and it would have taken little more for whites to mob "all prominently obnoxious" Republicans.[28]

Into this vortex strode Congressman William D. Kelley, a Radical Re-

25. *Grove Hill (Ala.) Democrat,* April 25, 1867; *MN,* April 18, 1867; *Louisville Courier* quoted in *Montgomery Mail,* May 10, 1867; *MAR,* April 20, 1867.

26. *MAR,* July 11, 1867; *MT,* May 2, 1867; A. J. Gray to George Tracy, May 19, 1867, with enclosures, M752, RG 105, reel 43.

27. *MN,* May 9, 1867; *MAR,* May 5, 1867.

28. J. R. Eastburn to Swayne, May 6, 1867, M809, RG 105, reel 10.

publican from Pennsylvania, to give a public address. On the evening of May 14, 1867, Republicans gathered at the downtown corner of Government and Royal. The freedpeople came well armed, while Mayor Withers and the city fathers made themselves scarce. As Kelley spoke, a group of white hecklers approached the speaker's stand, hurling coarse jibes and crying "pull him down."[29] Kelley, perhaps unwisely, referred to the army regulars stationed nearby as his guarantee of free speech. The police chief then tried to arrest a heckler and a scuffle broke out. Someone fired, and bullets were directed at the speakers' stand by whites while the freedpeople fired hundreds of shots in the air seeking to deter the attackers. The crowd fled in all directions. Afterward, armed freedmen dominated the streets, patrolling the suburbs for hours, while the police tried to induce them to return home. One white claimed that the killing was all done at some distance from the rally by "bands of negroes attacking single white men." The statement is inaccurate, but there are accounts of retaliation by bodies of freedmen.[30] Overall, it appears that one white and one black died in the Kelley riot, with many more wounded. The bureau's George Tracy concluded that "the riot was undoubtedly commenced by whites," and this seems to have been the dominant opinion, though some also blamed Kelley for his maladroit comments.[31] Even the *Advertiser and Register* admitted that the freedpeople had not been looking for trouble.[32] An army investigation of the violence concluded that the hecklers tried to prevent the speech, though the bloodshed perhaps was not premeditated, nor was it a police riot along the lines of Memphis or New Orleans.[33] Ironically, the only paper suppressed was the *Nationalist* for printing an editorial by a freedman advising people not to fire in the air in future. Griffin's comment that "throwing away" ammunition only deprived one of the means of self-defense struck a military official as inflammatory and resulted in the temporary closure.[34]

29. *Congressional Globe,* July 12, 1867, appendix, 9.
30. "W. P. H." to "Dear Aunt," May 28, 1867, Bullock and Hamilton Family Papers; *MAR,* May 16, 18, 28, 1867; *Mobile Tribune* quoted in *New Orleans Picayune,* May 16, 17, 1867.
31. George Tracy to Swayne, May 15, 1867, M752, RG 105, reel 41; Whitelaw Reid to Salmon P. Chase, May 28, 1867, Salmon P. Chase Papers, LC.
32. *MAR,* May 16, 1867.
33. O. L. Shipherd to D. H. Williams, May 17, 1867, enclosed in D. H. Williams to O. O. Howard, May 21, 1867, M752, RG 105, reel 41.
34. *MN,* May 30, 1867.

The Mobile riot briefly became the focus of national attention, and it prompted drastic changes in municipal governance. If the subsequent investigation revealed no sign of large-scale conspiracy, the bureau's Swayne blamed Mayor Withers for the limited police presence. Preventing the riot may well have been beyond his control, but the mayor was taken by surprise, and the violence thus provided some plausible basis for military intervention. It also served as pretext for Swayne to put loyalists into the city government, specifically those of his favored faction. At his recommendation, General Pope, commanding the Third Military District, ordered the removal of Mayor Withers from office along with the governing boards. Pope immediately appointed a new mayor and other officials and set about selecting individuals for the city boards as well. Thus the Unionist leader Gustavus Horton became mayor of Mobile, and Republicans obtained a significant presence in the city government. The ironic outcome of the riot was to place Republicans in power in a city in which their lives were in danger, but it also presented an unprecedented opportunity for the newly enfranchised African Americans to exercise real influence.[35]

As disliked as he was by his white fellow townspeople, Mayor Horton brought certain strengths to his new position. His stubborn Unionism and personal probity were generally recognized if not admired. He was seen as fiscally responsible, while his age and business connections inhibited actual violence, though threats were common. Even the rabid *Times* initially granted him some benefit of the doubt as interim mayor.[36] But he strongly backed the Reconstruction process, and as head of the Union League, he was in immediate touch with his African American following. The popular ferment of the spring had caught his attention, and Horton grasped that only major policy concessions could hold the loyalty of the black community and check unbridled popular radicalism. Over the coming months Mayor Horton delivered significant change, especially on the sensitive issue of law enforcement. With the city charter granting the mayor exclusive control over the police, he was in a strong position to implement new policies.

The immediate task before Mayor Horton and Generals Swayne and Pope was to reconstitute the city boards and get civic government running again. With the mayor's position and other ranking city offices firmly in loyal hands, Swayne preferred bipartisan governing boards. Respectable

35. Amos, "Trials of a Unionist," 134–51.
36. *MN*, May 30, 1867.

businessmen might thereby be drawn into collaboration with Reconstruction. At Swayne's suggestion, General Pope appointed all-white city boards, but local notables were not eager to assume these unpaid positions, and one military appointee after another demurred, with press encouragement. Finally, Swayne lost his patience.[37] As future Democratic mayor G. M. Parker observed: "Swayne said he would appoint niggers and [we] thought it better to submit. No use kicking in existing circumstances."[38] Swayne's intervention, however effective, brought him difficulty with his superior, for General Pope thought black officeholding premature. At this juncture, the black leadership came to Swayne's aid with a startling declaration disavowing all desire for office. "The welfare of the city, and the condition of her finances," required that the next appointee be a businessman, they thought. Strikingly, the signers recommended the aforementioned G. M. Parker for the Mobile City Council, perhaps unaware of his full racial animus. For the moment, the freedpeople would "waive cheerfully their claims as a class" in order to demonstrate their benign intent to their "white fellow-citizens." The thirteen signers included prominent spokesmen like Ovid Gregory and Joshua Davis and even the more militant like L. S. Berry and the future popular firebrand Allen Alexander. For this striking pronouncement, the delighted Griffin praised them in the *Nationalist,* and the declaration even won favorable notice in the conservative press.[39]

Coming at a time when African Americans universally demanded participation in public discourse, this statement was indeed a dramatic renunciation. The recent riot probably encouraged it, along with a favorable assessment of Swayne and his local protégés. The first statewide Republican convention in early June provided evidence of these allies' helpfulness as Mobile's black representatives gained considerable leverage on a matter of local concern. The main controversy at the convention centered on the exclusion of District Judge Richard Busteed. Because the judge had ample federal patronage to bestow on Republican activists and newspapers, many party leaders viewed him as a desirable accession to the cause, and he was already spoken of as a candidate for the U.S. Senate. However, Busteed was probably the most corrupt public official in Alabama's history, and more

---

37. *MAR,* June 3, 9, 11, 1867; *MT,* June 6, 13, 1867.

38. G. M. Parker to Frank Parker, June 15, 1867, G. M. Parker Papers, The Museum of Mobile.

39. *MT,* June 14, 15, 1867; Swayne to Pope, June 15, 1867, box 1, Records of the Third Military District, RG 393; *MN,* June 20, 1867.

to the point, he had opposed equal suffrage until recently. He had privately "insulted" Mobile's black activists and "abused Congress and the reconstruction acts." Thus, when several white delegates invited Busteed to attend the convention, Ovid Gregory and John Carraway objected.[40] The subsequent debate grew quite heated. The core issue was how much support for civil rights would freedpeople insist on in prospective party leaders. Carraway and Gregory prevailed upon the aid of powerful white allies and carried their point. Swayne refrained from defending Busteed, to the judge's personal fury. Mayor Horton had already denounced Busteed in a published letter, an indignity the judge would soon have opportunity to repay.[41] For Albert Griffin, the choice was a painful one because he had just been nominated as federal registrar in bankruptcy, with the appointment in the hands of Judge Busteed. Griffin estimated the post would initially be worth a fabulous ten thousand dollars a year or more. As Griffin admitted, he "did desire the position very much" and yearned to keep silent. Still, he joined in the public attack on the judge and forfeited the position because the legitimate demands of his African American comrades were not to be trifled with.[42]

Mobile's black political activists understood the need for allies, but their loyalty to Swayne's favored moderate faction was conditional. The new mayor understood this, and as Horton pulled together an administration, he moved quickly on the patronage issue. He replaced eighteen street laborers, mostly Irish, with African Americans. The activist L. S. Berry was asked to suggest appropriate choices.[43] These manual-labor jobs were not sufficiently attractive to generate widespread resentment, but the police force was another matter. This administrative bureaucracy would illustrate the difficulties of implementing equality in practice, for the police would be the crucial source of jobs subject to the mayor's sole control. Changes there could be done without spending money while being relatively consistent with existing political practice. Enough of these positions might go to African Americans to persuade them that their interests were being advanced.

---

40. Charles Fairman, *Reconstruction and Reunion, 1864–1888*, vol. 6 of *History of the Supreme Court of the United States* (New York, 1971), 828–32; U.S. Congress, House, *Investigation of the Charges against Hon. Richard Busteed*, 208; MT, June 6, 1867.

41. U.S. Congress, House, *Investigation of the Charges against Hon. Richard Busteed*, 164, 264.

42. MN, June 13, 1867.

43. MAR, July 4, 1867; memo, July 3, 1867, Mobile City Police Records.

The *Advertiser and Register* speculated that the hope was that black leaders would be satisfied with these lesser posts, leaving the higher positions for Horton and his allies. The mayor clearly intended to use the city jobs to build a following of white supporters and satisfy the freedpeople as well.[44]

Horton's police chief, Col. C. A. R. Dimon, a military appointee of General Pope, initially cooperated with the mayor.[45] Dimon sought an increase in the size of the force in the aftermath of the Kelley riot. In particular, he thought the suburbs required an increased police presence because "fully 1/4 of the city is now without suitable protection day or night."[46] After the municipal boards turned down his request for more men, he established a citizen's patrol for the western outskirts. Dimon's initiatives were largely intended to dampen exuberant Radical political activity, the law enforcement analogue of the mayor's struggle against Harrington and Turner. Reports circulated that armed leaguelike groups were drilling outside town. The militant James B. Gibbs reportedly led a marching club in the suburbs, and such shadowy militias sprang into action during civil conflict in subsequent years. The conservative *Times* claimed these groups were comprised of members of the "colored (principally black) population," while the "men of mixed blood" held aloof.[47] The account suggests caste- and class-based political differences, with the lighter-skinned freedpeople—disproportionately the longer-term residents in the city—resisting the confrontational inclinations of the mass of African Americans.[48] Whatever the reality of this, the alarmed Dimon banned outdoor drilling by secret organizations, running into problems with the military for his zeal in seizing the freedmen's arms.[49]

Patronage in law enforcement also became a continuing concern. Hor-

---

44. MAR, August 11, 1867. On the general context for black police during Reconstruction, see W. Marvin Dulaney, *Black Police in America* (Bloomington and Indianapolis, 1996), 8–18; and Dennis C. Rousey, *Policing the Southern City: New Orleans, 1805–1889* (Baton Rouge, 1996), 126–58

45. D. Alexander Brown, *The Galvanized Yankees* (Urbana, 1963), 71–94.

46. G. Horton to Boards of Aldermen and Common Council, August 30, 1867, folder 2, envelope 5, box 12, RMBACC; Dimon to Horton, May 27, 1867, Mobile City Police Records.

47. *MAR*, July 25, 1867; *MT* quoted in *Grove Hill Democrat*, July 18, 1867; *MN*, September 26, 1867.

48. *MN*, July 13, 1867. The *Nationalist* ran two letters denying that any substantial divisions existed between light-skinned and dark-skinned blacks, a response that rather confirms that such talk circulated freely.

49. Dimon to [Horton?], May 30, July 13, 1867, Mobile City Police Records.

ton and Dimon faced numerous applications for police jobs, nearly two hundred in the month after the riot. Dimon's initial policy was to remove the more recalcitrant officers immediately, replacing them with white Republicans. The chief hoped to draw most of the officers into a political alliance, thereby providing support for the mayor and continuity in the force. As Dimon later observed, "I was gradually getting my men in a state of discipline and anxious to join the 'L. L.' "—this being a reference to the white Union (Loyal) League.[50] In practice, Dimon's effort to retain much of the existing force meant the exclusion of blacks for the time being. For Mayor Horton, however, such a policy was not politically inviting, for General Swayne himself had urged the hiring of black police. In late June, a petition signed by L. S. Berry, Allen Alexander, Major W. Lankford, and other restive black leaders made their expectations manifest. Municipal employment represented a civil rights issue fraught with personal ramifications for activists. "We are very poor," they observed, and their politics had deprived them of employment. In Lankford's case this was literally accurate; hundreds of dollars in punitive taxes had all but driven his barbershop under, leaving him, his wife, and their seven children without means. The *Advertiser and Register* depicted the petitioners' motives in terms of occupational mobility: black activists were willing enough "to preach, or practice law, to teach school, or to sell dry goods, but unfortunately nobody is willing to employ them for these pursuits." Whatever the truth of this, a few symbolic appointments would not do: the petitioners thought half the positions could go to blacks without detriment to the public interest, which would place sixty thousand dollars annually in the hands of the black community. Besides, the policy of some Republican leaders "to pander to a conservative element at the expense of our legal rights" they considered neither wise nor just.[51]

Mayor Horton agreed that black appointments were "*right* as well as *politic*," but unrelenting pressure forced his hand. As Dimon reported, "Mr Horton was arraigned before the 'L L L' by Harrington Turner & co for certain of his decisions which he had made in Mayor's Court and they also

---

50. Tabulated from Mobile City Police Records, May–June 1867; C. A. R. Dimon to General Pope, August 18, 1867, box 3, Records of the Third Military District, Office of Civil Affairs, 1867–1868, RG 393, pt.1.

51. G. Horton to Swayne, June 1, 1867, Swayne Papers; Lankford et al. to Swayne, June 14, 1867, ser. 9, box 7, Unregistered Letters Received, Letters Received by the Assistant Commissioner for Alabama, RG 105; *MAR*, July 4, 1867.

demanded the appointment of Mr [Ovid] Gregory as Asst. Chief."[52] On July 1 Horton ordered Dimon to hire five black officers, among them Allen Alexander, to be stationed on the outskirts of the city. In August the mayor appointed fourteen more, and he also chose the Creole leader Ovid Gregory as one of four assistant chiefs.[53] Dimon thought these policies injudicious, but his emphatic protests to Pope and Swayne were overruled, and a brace of white resignations from the force ensued. Officer John O'Connell, for example, quit on the grounds that "although necessity may compel me to acknowledge a negro my equal I never will admit that he is my superior."[54] The vacancies allowed Mayor Horton the changes he wanted, but each appointment only raised expectations further. "Every colored man who has not been appointed seemed to feel himself more or less aggrieved," the *Advertiser and Register* claimed.[55] Gregory agreed, citing the choice of one appointee who already had a city job as causing "dissatisfaction among those who [had] an eye to these positions." These personnel decisions raised issues of social privilege, exacerbated by the prominence of Creoles like Gregory and former free men of color in the appointments. One paper claimed that the new policemen were "not the poor and needy blacks, but the blacks of substance," especially league activists. Disaffected black job-seekers tried to call a protest meeting in August, but ministers reportedly advised people not to attend from their pulpits, so the divisive gathering never came off. Even if Republicans contained discussion for the moment, such class- and color-tinged patronage issues would remain a continuing concern.[56]

Once African Americans and white Republicans were hired to the police force, the purge became self-perpetuating, for neither could serve comfortably with overtly conservative, racist, colleagues. Republican Samuel Mag-

---

52. G. Horton to Swayne, June 1, 1867; Dimon to Pope, August 13, 1867; and Pope to Dimon, August 7, 1867, box 3, Letters Sent, Records of the Third Military District, Office of Civil Affairs, 1867–1868, RG 393, pt.1. The reference here is to the Loyal, or Union, League.

53. Billy G. Hinson, "The Beginning of Radical Reconstruction in Mobile, Alabama, May–November 1867," *Gulf South Historical Review* 9 (fall 1993): 74; *MN,* July 4, 1867; memo of Mayor Horton, August 9, 1867, Mobile City Police Records.

54. Dimon to Pope, August 10, 1867, box 3, Records of the Third Military District, Office of Civil Affairs, 1867–1868, RG 393, pt.1; John O'Connell to Mayor Horton, August 10, 1867, Mobile City Police Records.

55. *MAR,* August 16, 1867.

56. Ovid Gregory to Dimon, August 28, 1867, Mobile City Police Records; *Mobile Tribune* quoted in *MN,* August 27, 1867; *MAR,* August 16, 1867.

ill, for example, presented the chief with a list of over a dozen disloyal officers, acting as something of a political commissar. There was also an unsigned document containing five more names of recently converted rebels, internal evidence suggesting espionage. "I am on the track of a few more," the mysterious informant concluded, adding that he would call on the recipient personally the following day. Dimon had little choice but to submit, though he resented it bitterly, recalling later that "4 officers and twenty eight of my most reliable men were dismissed in the month of July last without reason except they would not join the Loyal League." Horton apparently directed Dimon to assemble a force resembling the racial profile of the general population. Though this was never achieved, by the end of Horton's term in June 1868, some twenty of the sixty-seven privates on the force would be African American.[57]

Here was substantial change, delivered within weeks. Inevitably, though, the integration of the Mobile police force antagonized white opinion, with one paper threatening bloodshed for Horton's "wanton outrage on the feelings of his own race." A tense transition followed. Several whites were arrested for verbally abusing Horton and his police. In one instance an off-duty white sergeant found himself in a bar fight when patrons insulted the force.[58] The African American appointees encountered special hostility. They faced a mixed reception even within their own community, being, after all, agents of a distrusted formal legal system. Some freedpeople perceived being arrested by black officers as a gratuitous indignity. One drunken woman proclaimed that she "didn't give a snap for all the nigger policemen in Mobile."[59] With respect to the whites, the situation was far worse. One of the new officers, Roderick B. Thomas, had previously led the streetcar occupation, and perhaps this explained his difficulties on his beat. One clerk, a disabled Confederate veteran, taunted Thomas by "telling the citizens that I [Thomas] am his boy, and he is boss, and all such stuff."[60] Racial hostility similarly interfered with the performance of other

57. Samuel J. Magill to Dimon, September 27, 1867; anonymous to "Gen.," [1867]; Dimon to Lt. Col. Hudson, April 12, 1868; Dimon to Horton, August 21, 1867, Letterbook of Letters Sent; and memo, June 1, 1868, Mobile City Police Records.

58. MAR, August 11, 28, September 10, 18, 1867; petition, C. A. R. Dimon et al. to Mayor Horton, September 13, 1867, Mobile City Police Records.

59. MAR, November 6, December 5, 1867.

60. Roderick B. Thomas to Col. C. A. R. Dimon, October 27, 1867, Mobile City Police Records.

officers' duty. On one occasion whites under arrest by black officers called out to bystanders to free them, though unsuccessfully. Police Chief Dimon complained that there had twice been "danger of a serious outbreak occasioned by parties refusing to be arrested" by blacks, with one prisoner actually liberated.[61] The matter of arresting white females was especially sensitive. Major Lankford had a murky personal dispute with one woman on his beat, who called him a "b—— s—— of a b——." Lankford prevailed on his white colleagues to arrest her, which subjected him to violent abuse in the press. The possibility of such interracial arrests received much emphasis, though Forsyth's paper admitted that in practice black officers deported themselves cautiously in view of the prospect of "instant death."[62]

Facing a difficult task, the appointees sometimes compounded their own problems. The behavior of the new police occasionally raised issues of professionalism as they struggled with the divided loyalties inherent in the circumstances. Allen Alexander, for example, lost his position on the charge of leaking information to a burglary suspect, while another officer was reportedly fired for cowardice.[63] Certainly the conservative press pounced on any suggestion of partiality or inefficiency. The *Times* proclaimed the "notorious fact" that the blacks on the force were "totally unfit," despite the column's admission that the city had been unusually quiet of late. There clearly were missteps: one officer accidentally shot himself, and members of the night force were repeatedly brought before the mayor for falling asleep; after some hesitation, Mayor Horton eventually discharged several black officers for this reason. The *Nationalist* was embarrassed enough to urge new appointees never to sit down on the job; the paper also advised those who saw the night officers roaming about in the daytime to send them home to bed.[64] Mayor Horton eventually seems to have concluded that his experiment with black police had been a mistake, that African Americans were unsuited to this duty.[65] The firestorm of political abuse he received likely colored his appraisal, for in obvious respects they performed well. Mayor Horton's police prevented riot for over a year, a noteworthy

61. *MAR*, October 3, 1867; Dimon to Pope, August 18, 1867.
62. *MAR*, October 17, 19, 26, 1867.
63. C. A. R. Dimon to Mayor Horton, August 21, 1867, Mobile City Police Records; *MAR*, August 23, November 16, 1867.
64. *MT*, October 27, December 3, 1867; *MAR*, September 4, 1867; *MN*, September 12, 1867. See also *MN*, March 19, 1868.
65. Truman G. Avery Diary, March 15, 1868, William R. Perkins Library, Duke University.

accomplishment in Reconstruction Mobile. Moreover, for the freedmen, the changes looked benign: the police brutality that had been such an problem under Mayor Withers was now less in evidence. On the crucial vagrancy issue, city policy was transformed. From when Horton assumed office in May to the end of 1867, the mayor's docket revealed 1,765 arrests, but of these only eight were vagrants, six of them black.[66] The army's dissolution of the chain gang doubtless encouraged this change, but the decrease still represents a dramatic departure from the previous wholesale rousting of the black poor. There is, moreover, evidence that the Democratic claims of racial partiality toward blacks were exaggerated. Of the reported arrests, some 851 were blacks and 914 were white; this would be above the African American share of the population and a higher proportion than under conservative Mayor Withers. The figures might simply reflect better police protection in the suburbs, but if black suspects were arrested in increased ratio by the newly integrated force, racial favoritism obviously remained limited.

Mayor Horton's administration benefited African Americans in a variety of other ways. Late in 1867 the mayor opened soup kitchens for the destitute, drawing on the financial aid of the Freedmen's Bureau. The program operated through black-aid societies, with the city hiring L. S. Berry as agent and relying on other activists to certify need. Even reluctant city officials were prodded into increased social expenditures. Board member G. M. Parker, for example, wrote that "it is one of the blessings of freedom that the city has to support an average of 75 sick niggers. A new building is being erected for them and must be furnished, and the writer, one of the Hospital Committee, wishes to have it done as cheaply as possible."[67] Parker's hostility itself confirms the scope of direct change, while other civic initiatives benefited the freedpeople indirectly. For decades, Mobile's public markets had a legally enforced stranglehold on food sales. With the mayor's support, the city boards abolished the market "monopoly," as the *Nationalist* termed it, to substantial public acclaim. The new policy also allowed "men of small means" to enter the field, such as Allen Alexander himself, who opened a meat booth to the favorable notice of the *Times*. Competition worked to the freedpeople's benefit because they spent a dis-

66. "Transcript of the Different Violations of Law Taken from the Mayor's Docket from May 21st, 1867 to December 31st, Inclusive," folder 1, envelope 3, box 13, RMBACC.

67. J. Gillette to Asst. Comm., May 21, 1868, M809, RG 105, reel 18; G. M. Parker to Dean & Hale, March 26, 1868, Parker Papers.

proportionate share of their income on food, and the new system encouraged produce farming just beyond the suburbs, allowing producers direct access to consumers.[68]

Mayor Horton's more ambitious initiatives frequently stalled before the conservative-dominated city boards. Soon after assuming office, he proposed a city jobs program. During the war, great entrenchments had been built in the western periphery that bred mosquitoes and sickened residents as the city expanded in that direction. Recognizing the "great amount of destitution" in the city, he suggested that workers might be procured "at very low wages" for the task of draining or filling the trenches. This initiative went nowhere, as did his efforts on education. After the Reconstruction acts passed, Horton and Bromberg had been appointed by General Pope to the city school board in order to leaven the conservative incumbents. The schools had long been of interest to Horton, and he thought that the board would "probably adopt some general regulations, so as to embrace all classes of children." The attempt to establish public, if segregated, schools for blacks would engender controversy with the existing missionary school, the future status of which was unclear. Fiscal concerns also slowed progress, but at least Horton raised the issue of black public education.[69]

The mayor's efforts did not forestall further civil rights demands, rather the taste of success encouraged some of the more aggressive activists. Berry and Alexander along with other men and women boarded streetcars in a peaceful attempt to bring suit before the courts. The local courts, however, did nothing, which meant that the obvious recourse, a federal suit under the civil rights act, would be heard before the unsympathetic Judge Busteed. Berry, Alexander, and others concluded that the legal route was costly, slow, and uncertain, an accurate assessment as it turned out.[70] The mayor avoided acting on this instance of quasi-private racial discrimination, but he did instruct Chief Dimon that "the Police have no right to eject colored men from the street cars." Horton was more helpful on other issues. During

68. *MN,* August 22, 1867; *MT,* November 10, 1867; George H. Ewert, "Old Times Will Come Again: The Municipal Market System of Mobile, Alabama, 1888–1901" (Master's thesis, University of South Alabama, 1993), 36–45.

69. *MDR,* January 1, 1871; Horton to Boards of Aldermen and Common Council, August 1, 1867, folder 1, envelope 6, box 12, RMBACC; *MAR,* May 14, 1867; G. Horton to E. P. Smith, July 31, 1867, Alabama, AMA, reel 1.

70. *MAR,* June 29, July 2, 3, 9, 17, 1867; Allen Alexander et al. to Swayne, June 25, 1867, M809, RG 105, reel 10.

the summer, there was a popular mobilization on behalf of the Dog River case defendants. The Peters family provided inconsistent identifications of the suspects, one defendant in particular being innocent in the opinion of Chief Dimon.[71] A widespread petition campaign prompted support by Horton, Bromberg, and the *Nationalist* as well as the endorsement of General Swayne. The governor stayed the death sentence long enough to visit and review the evidence, witnessing another identification personally; he then allowed the execution to proceed. Still, with Mayor Horton's aid, the African American community had slowed hasty justice in the face of massive white pressure for an execution.[72]

The mayor's faction had one particularly effective voice in the black community, John Carraway, who combined egalitarian zeal with surprisingly temperate public advice. Carraway consistently showcased blacks' sobriety as well as their pervasive enthusiasm for education and the Protestant religion. He resented conservatives because they "invariably select the worst classes among us" to characterize his whole race, who were in reality "faithful, law abiding citizens." Carraway recommended that African Americans forget the past and "show nothing like a vindictive spirit" in order to win the cooperation of well-disposed whites. Carraway stressed the importance of responsible leadership. On numerous occasions he highlighted his own reasonableness by accusing white Radical leaders of whipping up racial resentments. W. W. D. Turner, he charged, sought street confrontations over the streetcar issues, whereas he had urged the freedpeople to trust to the ballot box. On the crucial civil rights issue, Carraway even disavowed the notion that African Americans sought "the greatest of all humbugs, social equality," because "we don't know where it begins or ends." All he wanted was fair treatment in public places, he assured his listeners. Carraway's various positions gained him a good deal of African American criticism, but he also won the enthusiastic endorsement of the *Nationalist,* whose editor explicitly defended him as the right sort of black leader.[73]

With the aid of spokesmen like Carraway, Mayor Horton's administration had solidified African American popular support by the time of its first

---

71. Horton to Dimon, June 15, 1867; and C. A. R. Dimon to Gov. Robert Patton, August 28, 1867, Mobile City Police Records.

72. S. S. Houston to Swayne, August 8, 1867; and Bromberg to Swayne, August 25, 1867, Swayne Papers, ADAH.

73. *MN,* August 22, September 12, 19, 1867, February 6, 1868.

electoral test in October. The Reconstruction acts called for elections, with black suffrage, to authorize a state constitutional convention and choose delegates to that body. In Mobile's Republican meetings, Mayor Horton's allies dominated proceedings. The official nominees included Horton, Griffin, Carraway, and Gregory, these being among the most prominent leaders in the mayor's following. Even an obscure moderate was nominated over the much more prominent Radical Yankee lawyers. For Harrington, this must have been particularly galling since he had recently confronted a conservative mob. Whatever Harrington's sense of personal grievance, he swallowed his resentment, but his ally W. W. D. Turner chose a truly desperate response. Turner announced the formation of a rival independent ticket, soliciting support from, of all places, Henry St. Paul's ultraconservative *Times*. W. W. D. Turner now called himself a Republican, though not a Radical, and he accused the mayor's faction of stirring up racial unrest. At this, nearly all the established black leadership turned on him and denounced the "scheming agitators," with Carraway leading the way. Even L. S. Berry, the most restive of the prominent black leaders, disavowed Turner as an opportunist. Griffin's *Nationalist* also lit into Harrington and Turner, repeating wild rumors of Harrington having shipped freedpeople into slavery in Cuba. On election day, since Democrats boycotted the election, Turner received a handful of votes.[74]

Turner experienced humiliation, while other Radical insurgents fared equally wretchedly, even the African Americans appealing to racial solidarity. Two militant spokesmen, John Stewart and the militia leader James B. Gibbs, tried to confront the moderate leadership; both men were apparently dark skinned, which is perhaps suggestive of the wider social tensions in play. On one occasion, Albert Griffin and John Carraway traveled across Mobile Bay to give a talk in Baldwin County, but Stewart and Gibbs gathered their followers to heckle them. A heated public exchange followed, and the resulting factional dispute was played out in the pages of the *Nationalist*. The editor denounced Gibbs for wanting to "turn the Republican party into a black man's party." In return, Gibbs accused Albert Griffin of stealing *Nationalist* funds, the finances of the paper being continually a sensitive issue. In the subsequent October elections, Gibbs ran for the constitutional convention from Baldwin County, which served as something of a resort for Mobile's out-of-favor politicians. In the *Nationalist*'s telling,

---

74. *MAR*, September 27–31, 1867; *MN*, August 22, September 19, 1867.

Gibbs supposedly contended that voters should promote racial balance regardless of formal qualifications. Griffin pointedly responded that "we do not want a rascal or a fool sent merely because he is black," again asserting the colorblind Republicanism that typified his rhetoric and buttressed his own position. On election day, the voters chose a scalawag over Gibbs. This essentially ended the African American activist's political career, and in early 1868 the isolated and impoverished Gibbs actually endorsed the Democrats. Political apostasy actually got him expelled from his church, a sure sign of popular repudiation.[75]

In this initial electoral venture, Mayor Horton demonstrated that his faction enjoyed the support of the black populace. If the more radical voices were eclipsed, the results were otherwise sobering for the mayor and his Unionist allies. In the face of massive media and social pressure, their carefully built white constituency shriveled. The first day's reported vote ratio was one hundred blacks to one white. The *Nationalist* estimated that only one in six white Republicans actually braved the boycott. Frederick Bromberg wailed: "We cannot rally a dozen [white] friends around us. The election test has proved to us that the oaths of the League . . . are straw in the fires through which loyalty is made to pass here." In Bromberg's case the metaphor was apt, for one of his father's homes was torched for the second time.[76] Despite temporary possession of power, Republicans could never win elections without white votes; nor, one suspects, was the prospect of white officeholders leading an all-black party that promising. For the wartime Unionists, holding office under the military had only made them more inviting targets of public hatred. The army inhibited actual violence, but this made social persecution even more intense. In the case of City Treasurer Bromberg and his family, the financial consequences can be traced graphically. In July 1866 the Dun Credit Agency rated the Brombergs as reliable with a toy store worth over fifty thousand dollars. The following February, however, the local agent noted that they had "lately come out strong for the 'Nigger' wh[ich] injures their trade & cr[edit]." By the time of the 1868 presidential contest, Bromberg had "destroyed his bus[iness]

---

75. *MN,* September 26, 1867; *MDR,* March 31, 1868; records 5627, 4362, M816, reel 2. The evidence on ancestry is not conclusive, but bank records have entries for J. B. Gibbs and John Stewart, with both having their complexion described as "black."

76. *MN,* September 26, 1867; F. Bromberg to Wager Swayne, October 27, 1867, box 5, Records of the Third Military District, Office of Civil Affairs, 1867–68, RG 393, pt.1; *MAR,* October 2, November 17, 1867.

utterly by taking violent radical principles into his head." Respectable citizens would do no business with him that they could do elsewhere, and the store had few customers except among blacks. These financial reverses perhaps encouraged Bromberg's penchant for plural officeholding. Prominent white Republicans undermined their prospects in most other forms of business, becoming more dependent on political patronage.[77]

Even more-modest Republican involvement could prove costly. For example, the wartime Union man Amos Towle, who headed Mobile College, was injudicious enough to join the white Union League. Down "like the vultures" pounced the "three rebel papers of Mobile," and a student boycott bankrupted the college, driving him into exile. Perhaps the most spectacular victim of this sort of harassment was Mayor Horton himself. Late in 1867 the Presbyterian congregation he had served for decades asked him to resign as elder, and his family withdrew in protest; not even during the war had the Union man brought so much hostility upon his kin.[78] More dramatic still was his prosecution in court: during the summer, a black *Times* news vendor named Archie Johnson had taken to belittling Republicans. As Horton testified: "those who employed him posted labels upon the back of his coat and on his hat abusing and ridiculing Union men. Then he would go about calling their names in a way to call attention to them."[79] Mayor Horton, thinking this nuisance a threat to public order, expelled Johnson from town repeatedly. W. W. D. Turner then charged Horton with violating the federal civil rights act, the case to be tried before none other than District Judge Richard Busteed. In a biased proceeding, Busteed excluded evidence that expulsion commonly had been used before, often with white defendants. Thus Horton was found guilty and briefly jailed, with Busteed blustering about a two-year sentence before decreeing a small fine. Only the judge's subsequent shooting by the U.S. district attorney "suspended his persecutions for the present," as Horton's wife, Eliza, observed.[80]

77. Credit ledgers, Mobile County, July 1866, February 1867, August 1867, November 1868, Alabama, vols. 17, 18, R. G. Dun and Company Collection, Baker Library, Harvard Business School.
78. James J. Gillette to A. O. Gillette, October 28, 1867, James Gillette Papers, LC; December 11, 18, 1867, Records of the Third Presbyterian Church of Mobile, Alabama, 1853–68, Sessional Records, Central Presbyterian Church, 1842–68, Mobile Public Library.
79. House, *Investigation of the Charges against Hon. Richard Busteed,* 263.
80. *Boston Evening Traveller,* February 24, 1868; Horton to Swayne, December 28, 1867; and Eliza Horton to Son, January 8, 1868, Gustavus Horton Papers, The Museum of Mobile.

For the whites in the dominant Republican faction, the results were sobering, and the immediate future looked hopeless, in Bromberg's estimation. Their black colleagues, however, were often more optimistic, for African Americans generally escaped the full public venom their colleagues encountered as renegades. If the white leagues had "proved miserable failures as election engines," this had the short-term advantage of making Horton all the more dependent on his African American popular constituency.[81] The social isolation of Unionists made them seem less susceptible to the blandishments of other whites, and the open persecution of Horton and Bromberg legitimized them as firm Republicans. Furthermore, the paucity of native white support also opened leadership opportunities, both to African Americans and to white newcomers who might be receptive to civil rights demands. Many freedpeople preferred northerners to the southern Republicans, especially those of Confederate antecedents. Bureau Agent James J. Gillette articulated the anomalous situation clearly. Mayor Horton's friends were "so few that there are not enough to fill the lucrative offices of the city." Almost "any intelligent northern man is received warmly as an accession to their ranks, and can be placed at once in an office by the colored vote." Gillette suggested that if a relation came down to Mobile, he could have a place worth several thousand, and somehow the bureau man soon found his way into Republican politics himself. The times were certainly "out of joint" when men refused to run for office "for fear of the darkey, and of being considered his friend."[82]

For African Americans, the times being "out of joint" had compensations, subordination being their standard lot. The recent progress must have seemed breathtaking, for in addition to African Americans on the police force, they also now were serving as grand jurors under General Pope's order.[83] The inspiring reality was that the freedpeople had flocked to the polls for the first time and sent the ex-slave Carraway and the Creole Gregory as delegates to Montgomery. At the November 1867 constitutional convention, the relatively urbane Mobile cohort gained considerable prominence. Gregory unsuccessfully tried to outlaw interracial sex, perhaps a reflection of his Creole background, while Carraway proposed a measure

---

81. F. G. Bromberg to Swayne, October 27, 1867, box 5, Records of the Third Military District, Office of Civil Affairs, 1867–68, RG 393, pt.1.

82. James J. Gillette to "Mother," January 7, [1868], Gillette Papers, LC.

83. *MT,* October 30, November 5, 1867.

protecting title to black church property.[84] One of the two promoted a common-carrier antidiscrimination bill, doubtless a response to the streetcar dispute. Overall, Gregory and Carraway cooperated well with Griffin and Horton, who were in some respects the more radical, having soured on conciliation. For example, Griffin now thought widespread disfranchisement of ex-Rebels essential.[85] The convention as a whole, however, rejected this advice, capitulating to northern Republican pressure for a moderate stance. Overall, the proposed constitution combined strong support for public education with cautious guarantees of civil rights, at least by modern standards, but the freedpeople of Mobile seemed supportive.[86]

In the months after the constitutional convention, the mayor's faction checked popular militancy and maintained its influence over the crucial black activists. In February 1868 Mobile's Republicans faced another election, this one to ratify the new constitution and select federal, state, and county officers. The Democrats determined on a statewide boycott, hoping to defeat the congressional requirement that half the registered vote be polled. In Mobile this actually helped Republican chances. The undoubted white majority locally was irrelevant, for if the constitution carried statewide, the boycott would place all offices in Republican hands. Despite the opportunity this presented for ambitious activists, black leaders proceeded cautiously. The African American leadership routinely promoted their educated white allies for higher office, even though blacks were well represented at party nominating conventions. As John Carraway pointed out, every federal- and state-level candidate in Alabama was white, and he recommended this "same wise course" of caution for Republicans throughout the South. Even for local offices, black leaders often pursued a similar policy. At the county Republican convention, for example, there was so little rivalry for nomination that nearly all the choices were made by acclamation.[87] When the delegates nominated a wealthy but unknown Creole, Joseph Fernandez, he declined the position, "being a colored man," with Bromberg's word choice suggesting that Fernandez's race contributed to his

---

84. *New York Herald,* November 11, 13, 1867; Kolchin, *First Freedom,* 171; *Moulton (Ala.) Union,* November 25, 1867.

85. *MT,* November 17, 1867; *MN,* October 24, 1867.

86. Kolchin, *First Freedom,* 167–71; Michael W. Fitzgerald, "Radical Republicans and the White Yeomanry during Alabama Reconstruction, 1865–1868," *Journal of Southern History* 54 (November 1988), 586–91.

87. *MN,* February 6, January 9, 1868.

action.⁸⁸ Given this tendency, the scarcity of white candidates allowed even the Radical George Harrington a nomination for state legislature, along with Carraway, Gregory, and James Shaw of the *Nationalist*. Mayor Horton ran for county probate judge, and though already city treasurer and on the school board, Frederick Bromberg received two more nominations, these for state senator and to the county commission. One candidate, the wartime Union man Caleb Price, was nominated for county commissioner even though he was "not looked upon as a Republican," surely striking testimony of the conciliatory tendencies of the black leaders. The *Nationalist* explained that it was the desire of the convention "that property-holders should feel assured that the finances of the county were in safe hands."⁸⁹

Carraway and the black leadership sought respectability, and their outright pragmatism was demonstrated in the only real internal controversy in the February election, the prized congressional nomination. At the Republican district convention, Mayor Horton nominated Frederick Bromberg, while Albert Griffin nominated F. W. Kellogg, the U.S. collector of internal revenue. After several ballots, Kellogg won, with the apparent support of Mobile's black delegates. This result was somewhat anomalous, for though Kellogg was a former Republican congressman from Michigan, he had "studiously avoided politics" in Mobile. According to Carraway, the capital needs of the ever destitute *Nationalist* determined the selection (an assertion the evidence supports). After the convention, Kellogg vowed to supply two thousand dollars for Griffin's *Nationalist* to appear as a daily, and he subsequently raised the money. Thus the financial exigencies at the newspaper resulted in a nominee who was not that well known, and as it turned out, retrograde on race issues. Kellogg privately commented that "the less said about the Negroes the better." Those who expected to put blacks in office had better join those "in favor of female suffrage and nominate Miss [Anna] Dickenson for Prest.," this being the very image of Radical excess. Griffin's counsel thus saddled Republicans with Kellogg, who was unceremoniously dumped at the next election, but the nomination did demonstrate the practical bent of the black leadership.⁹⁰

The menacing wider circumstances likely encouraged this profile.

88. Bromberg to Gov. William H. Smith, [1868,] Gov. William H. Smith Papers, ADAH.
89. *MN,* January 16, 9, 1868.
90. *MN,* January 9, 1868; *Montgomery Alabama Journal,* February 6, 1868; F. W. Kellogg to Medill, January 18, 1868; and F. W. Kellogg to Washburne, December 16, 1867, in E. B. Washburne Papers, LC.

Though the February election featured little direct violence, economic intimidation was rampant, orchestrated in the press. The Mobile bureau agent estimated one hundred freedmen lost their jobs after the election. The Democratic boycott of the polls made Republican voters conspicuous, and the harassment of white voters in particular reached new heights. The constitution received over five thousand votes in the county, a reported ninety-one of them white. The conservatives published the name of every white voter, allowing an unusually precise examination of this segment of Republican electorate. Thirty-three are listed as policemen, with another ten described as candidates and nine more as officeholders. Only a minority held no obvious stake in the outcome, and the total number of voters represented about 2 percent of the white electorate.[91] The newspaper also published a list of Creole voters in the country, over sixty of them. The *Register* concluded that they were "indifferent to the privilege of voting," but a rough estimate suggests that around half of the Afro-Creole adult male population likely cast ballots. The split vote indicates divided loyalties in the face of economic pressure against participation.[92]

Statewide, the Democratic boycott strategy succeeded, aided by President Johnson's timely removal of Generals Pope and Swayne. The Alabama constitution vote fell short of the majority participation prescribed by Congress. Black Republicans were bitterly disappointed with the apparent defeat, particularly those activists who now faced retaliation. Well before the election, freedmen approached the Freedmen's Bureau asking about emigration to Liberia, for they had become discouraged by the probable withdrawal of government protection. After the election about forty individuals applied to the American Colonization Society for aid. One leader simply explained, "we are nearly on starvation nothing to do under the heavens." These prospective émigrés included the vanquished ultramilitants James Gibbs and John Stewart and the popular firebrand Allen Alexander, which might have ideological significance as a reflection of these grassroots Radicals' inclination toward racial nationalism. Most of those expressing interest eventually abandoned the idea of emigration, but a small party did

---

91. Gillette to Asst. Comm., February 26, 1868, RG 105, reel 14; *MDR*, February 10, 1868.

92. *Roll of the Black Dupes and White Renegades Who Voted in Mobile City and County for the Menagerie Constitution for the State of Alabama* (Mobile, 1868), 6, 24. On Creole numbers, see the discussion in chapter 1.

depart for Africa in late April.⁹³ Some of the white Republicans were equally eager to leave Mobile. W. W. D. Turner, now again a Radical Republican, wrote a friend looking for work. Bewailing his wretched luck, Turner explained that he had built a reputation as a criminal lawyer, but his clients were so poor that he could not make anything. Besides, Republicans resented him because of his "many warm personal friends" who were "mostly rebels." He was so situated that he could not get the offices he wanted and would not take the offices offered. "What I now want is some money," he concluded his plea for employment elsewhere.⁹⁴

Most Republicans, especially prospective officeholders, took a different tack: Horton's followers asked Congress to admit Alabama under the apparently rejected constitution. They argued that the prescribed conditions had been unrealistic and undemocratic, since nonvoters counted against ratification. Albert Griffin urged readers to keep their spirits up, for Congress had not yet deserted them. Horton thought that if readmission failed, only drastic measures would suffice: "A more rigid Military rule, with the offices in the State filled by Loyal men . . . and . . . a little of Mr. Stevens' 'mild confiscation.'" Horton begged congressional leaders for swift action because "Loyal men here have suffered so much and so long, that their burdens are well nigh unendurable."⁹⁵ He had reason to fear, for that spring the Ku Klux Klan spread throughout northern and western Alabama, even putting in a momentary appearance in Mobile. Threats on Horton's life proliferated in the context of burgeoning violence. After several anonymous warnings, Horton went to the army's post commander, who comforted him with the observation that "if any one intends hurting you, he will not advertise it."⁹⁶ After the failed impeachment of President Johnson, Horton's son concluded, "Pa's life will be in danger as long as he lives in Mobile."⁹⁷ Later in the year, an incorrect press report of his death at Klan

93. James Gillette to William Coppinger, December 26, 1867; George Fears to William Coppinger, March 18, 1868; John A. Stuart to "Sir," February 14, 1868; and John A. Stewart to ACS, March 2, 1868, reel 101; and James Gillette to William Coppinger, April 25, 1868, American Colonization Society Papers, LC, reel 102.

94. Turner to H. C. Warmoth, April 6, 1868, Henry Clay Warmoth Papers, SHC, reel 2.

95. *MN,* February 20, 1868; G. Horton to Charles Sumner, March 21, February 13, 1868, in Sumner, *Papers,* reel 41.

96. *Athens (Ala.) Post,* April 8, 1868; Eliza Horton to George Horton, April 28, 1868, Horton Papers.

97. George Horton to F. S. Horton, May 22, 1868, Horton Papers.

hands allowed him to read the resulting condolences.[98] Even if Horton escaped violence, the social persecution of Republicans remained intense, and Horton's son tried to persuade his family to sell their possessions and leave: "what's the use of furniture in Mobile when nobody goes to the house, or condescends to associate with the folks?"[99]

After months of delay, Congress voted readmission of Alabama under the Republican constitution in late June 1868. This did not directly affect Mobile's municipal government save that civil rule logically superseded the military appointees and Mayor Horton would soon become county probate judge. One of the first duties of Gov. William Hugh Smith would be to choose his successor, even as the new, overwhelmingly Republican legislature pondered what to do with the state's largest city and its latent ex-Confederate majority. A ruinous transition followed, encouraged by the prospect of an immediate reshuffle of dozens of city jobs. To this time, the African American leadership had remained relatively united behind Horton and his scalawag-dominated following. The mayor had delivered significant change and painstakingly built a popular following for his administration. Though Radical critics challenged him, most activists sustained the mayor on grounds of necessity. Prominent leaders like Carraway sought respectability; they relied on the judgments of their white allies and often tried to restrain popular militancy. In the summer of 1868 this changed suddenly. Prodded by mass discontent, new grassroots activists challenged the established race spokesmen, demanding direct action and less deference to the sensitivities of Unionist allies. Two opposing factions coalesced, with distinctive social profiles and leadership styles, each having some claim to a wider constituency. The resulting polarization undergirded black politics from then on, recurring in various guises for the next decade and more.

Deteriorating prospects within Mobile's depressed economy provided the context for renewed popular unrest. In early 1868 African Americans flooded to the city, a tendency Horton's humane policies toward the poor encouraged. Whites abandoned Mobile by the thousands, but freedmen kept coming: some had been evicted for voting, some fled the Klan, and all had just experienced a wretched crop year. In January the Freedmen's Bureau estimated that five hundred people were in immediate need of food,

---

98. G. Horton to Eliza Horton, November 11, 1868; H. W. Robbins to Eliza Horton, November 17, 1868; and Eliza Horton to Frank Horton, December 15, 1868, Horton Papers.

99. George Horton to F. S. Horton, May 22, 1868.

helping establish soup houses to deal with the suffering. The agency reported increasing destitution, and employment sectors dominated by freedpeople became saturated.[100] The hard times meant insufficient work even for longtime residents, but the "large crowds of country vagrants" had little chance of earning a living. By May, the *Register* reported the wharves crowded with freedmen, but those unloading the boats were "incapable of doing it from *weakness.*" They were all "soup fed negroes" lacking "*stomachs* upon which to work." James Gillette of the bureau underscored the dimensions of this suffering.[101] In late June, on the eve of increasing political disorder, Gillette commented that the disastrous previous crop had "crowded the city with a wretched class." There were too many laborers by half in the city, while the surrounding country was denuded. Wages were so low on average that the employed could do "no more than live," while the rest sponged off them, keeping them poor. Gillette urged the jobless to leave, but the migrants preferred to be idle rather than work hard on the plantations and receive no pay. As sympathetic as Gillette was, he found the state of affairs frustrating; he contemplated forced removal, but in practice such a policy was too harsh to be acceptable. Though more conservative, Police Chief Dimon offered a similar diagnosis. The suburbs had been recently settled by a destitute "floating class from the county," primarily stealing for a living. Dimon's official reports revealed an increasing proportion of black offenders, now becoming a majority of all arrests. Most were charged with theft, and those arrested were generally common laborers, disproportionately under twenty years of age. Dimon saw the increasing misery as the direct cause of escalating crime.[102]

The newcomers' privations did not yield renewed labor agitation, perhaps because the summer was the slow season on the docks. Instead, their suffering infused Republican politics, turning factional disputes into a vehicle of popular discontent. Harrington's group of disaffected activists and office seekers, those most unhappy with Horton's faction, tapped this restive constituency to bolster its mass presence. The result was an explosive

100. Endorsement of James Gillette, on George Shorkley to Gillette, January 31, 1868, M809, RG 105, reel 15; Gillette to J. Hayden, February 11, 1868, entry 142, vol.108, Letters Sent, SAC Mobile, RG 105.
101. *MDR,* May 14, 1868.
102. Gillette to Asst. Comm., June 26, 1868, M809, RG 105, reel 18; Dimon to Mayor, July 10, 1868, folder 8, envelope 3, box 13, RMBACC; C. A. R. Dimon to Gillette, February 19, 1868, Mobile City Police Records.

situation on the streets, which statewide political developments compounded. The installation of the Republican government of Gov. William Hugh Smith produced immediate controversy. Despite Unconditional Unionist antecedents, Governor Smith moved immediately to distance himself from disfranchisement and other policies identified as Radical. He denounced carpetbaggers within the party, demonstrating little enthusiasm for civil rights. In his quest for native white support, he concentrated on economic development, especially railroads. Governor Smith's dogged pursuit of this strategy would produce a troublesome selection as Mobile's mayor, the key to subsequent internecine conflict. Here was perhaps the decisive moment in the city's Reconstruction political evolution: Governor Smith compromised Horton's moderate faction with the black populace and played into the hands of Harrington's militants. After this, controversy spread through the Republican ranks and engulfed the black community itself.

With Alabama formally reconstructed, the military-appointed government of Mobile became an anomaly. Democratic boycott of the recent elections had resulted in an overwhelmingly Republican legislature, and a bill passed quickly, giving Governor Smith the duty of reappointing the mayor and city boards, with similar legislation passing for other cities.[103] The Mobile legislation repealed the charter sections authorizing municipal elections, an unusual enactment to say the least. State senator Bromberg pledged a ballot soon, explaining that no election was possible "until provisions had been made for registration," and someone had to serve in the meantime. Thus the most pressing business at hand was the governor's choice of a new mayor. After consulting with the Brombergs, William Hurter, and other allies, Gustavus Horton recommended Dr. R. W. Coale for the position.[104] Coale was a colorless choice, a northern army doctor who was not well known, but he was considered Republican enough and respectable. An endorsement petition was circulated among the African American leadership, which reflected the distinctive priorities of the Horton faction. As Hurter explained, they could have gotten more signatures, "but we sought only the most influential colored people & all real estate holders,

---

103. State of Alabama, *Acts of the Sessions of July, September, and November 1868 of the General Assembly of Alabama* (Montgomery, 1869), 4–5; *Mobile Register,* September 28, 1868.

104. *Montgomery Mail,* October 4, 1868; Horton to F. G. Bromberg, July 23, 1868; and Horton to Smith, July 24, 1868, Smith Papers.

such men as Leavens, Wiggins, Bragg & Somerville." The petitions also contained such familiar endorsers as George Fears, Henry Austin, and Jacob Anderson from the old *Nationalist* board. For some of Horton's more cautious white allies, stability and bipartisanship became the overriding goal. Hurter hoped the governor would "make as few changes in the Boards as possible," for despite the Democratic majority, he proclaimed the existing members mostly "good."[105]

While this lobbying campaign was underway, a Radical candidate came forward. From Montgomery, many Republican legislators endorsed internal revenue official H. Ray Myers, perhaps in deference to his ally George F. Harrington, who would soon be elected Speaker of the Alabama House. Massive petitions began circulating in Mobile, with one endorsing Myers for mayor and Harrington for city court judge. That petition bore some familiar names, such as W. W. D. Turner, Allen Alexander, and Joshua Davis, though the bulk of the signatures were marked with an illiterate "X." Scores of black veterans' names were prominent among the reported two thousand total. This outpouring of support was curious; Myers until recently had been a supporter of President Johnson, as one might expect from a federal employee. Opponents saw him as the stereotypic carpetbagger: no one could tell "who he is or where he came from." Myers had however circulated "amongst the ignorant class of negroes," and his supporters claimed that four-fifths of the Republicans of Mobile endorsed him. One suspects that this popularity was not merely a matter of attending to a neglected constituency or of political ideology, though both dimensions existed. The mayoral transition would shake up the city jobholders, which promised employment opportunities to those outside the ranks of established black notables.[106]

Faced with this division of opinion, Governor Smith temporized, setting the stage for a contest of strength in Mobile. A mass meeting to endorse U. S. Grant for president would allow the militants to demonstrate their popular following. Harrington chaired the meeting, to be addressed by W. W. D. Turner, Ovid Gregory, Joshua Davis, and Major Lankford; L. S. Berry reportedly addressed the gathering too. All these speakers may not

---

105. James G. Steward et al. to Governor Smith, July 22, 1868; and William Hurter to Bromberg, July 23, 1868, Smith Papers.
106. A. W. McCormick to Smith, July 3, 1868, and Allen Alexander et al. to Smith, June 29, 1868, Smith Papers.

have known the full agenda, but H. Ray Myers gave a rousing pro-Radical speech, after which Allen Alexander offered resolutions endorsing him for mayor. The *Nationalist,* of course, denounced the rally as a fraud, but it conceded three to four hundred people were present, and it soon noted rumors that the freedpeople intended to integrate the streetcars by direct action.[107] A few days later, moderate Coale supporters staged a rally of their own to demonstrate their own popular appeal, but the results were less impressive. On the Fourth of July, a mass meeting gathered to select candidates for a state party convention, with Horton presiding. "Two or three hundred" Myers followers packed the meeting, some drunk if the *Nationalist* account can be credited. Albert Griffin proposed a list of delegates to the convention, which included such prominent figures as Carraway, Gregory, Berry, James Bragg, and the Reverends Leavens and E. D. Taylor. H. Ray Myers opposed the selections, proposing his own name among others, and the crowd backed him. The meeting broke up in disorder, with Horton abandoning the platform in the midst of a violent rainstorm. The Myers followers remained, in sodden triumph, to enjoy the scheduled picnic.[108]

Afterward, the Republican county committee overruled the meeting's Radical selections, but the implications of the controversy were nonetheless dramatic. According to H. Ray Myers, this episode was the origin of the rival Republican party structures that figured prominently in subsequent years.[109] Thereafter, the two factions were competitive on the streets, with the militants sometimes having the better of it. The *Nationalist* provided extensive, if hostile, social analysis of what had occurred. Myers had perhaps two hundred followers, "nearly all" of whom had "come in from the country within a year." Myers blamed other Republicans for their woes, intimating that if they will only follow him they would "all get lucrative employment and have 'biscuit to eat instead of cornbread.'" The image here is of destitute migrants swamping the established black political structure to gain access to city jobs. Economic grievances seem to have figured in the activists' motivations as well. The newspaper identified the black leaders of the Myers's following as Joshua Davis, Allen Alexander, and W. B. F. Bates, with Major W. Lankford mentioned elsewhere. Neither

107. Alexander et al. to Smith, June 29, 1868; *MN,* June 25, July 2, 1868.

108. *MN,* July 9, 1868. To my knowledge, the only existing copy of this crucial issue is at the Chicago Historical Society.

109. *MDR,* August 20, 1870.

Davis, a tailor, nor Lankford, the financially troubled barber, reported any property in 1870. Alexander, a former slave who arrived in Mobile during the war, was by one account a laborer; he probably had little property either as he had recently been planning emigration.[110] Bates did accumulate some property during the 1860s. However, he, Alexander, and Davis, were described as dark complexioned, which was then unusual among the African American political elite.[111] Relative to their followers, the Myers spokesmen were literate and perhaps even well off, but they were socially disadvantaged relative to their leadership rivals. These contrasts probably explain their popular appeal, for Bates and especially Alexander would be among Mobile's foremost black politicians by the 1870s.[112] Their influence would outlive that of the transient Myers and even Harrington and Turner themselves. Radical whites came and went, but the black leadership of the militant faction endured.

In Montgomery Governor Smith pondered a response to the factional disorder. One might have expected Smith to appoint the moderate faction's choice, but perhaps the strength of the popular mobilization against Coale dissuaded him. As a conservative scalawag seeking bridges to the opposition, the governor understood the undemocratic appearance of the Mobile legislation. Smith determined to ignore both controversial Republican candidates and select someone who could appeal more broadly across party lines. In a move that surprised even the appointee, he selected former council president Caleb Price, a rumored wartime Unionist whose political allegiances were nominal; the businessman Price had recently run on the county ticket on the understanding that he was not really a Republican. Price thus was well beyond the conservative fringe of Horton's moderate faction, and he was primarily known for his emphasis on fiscal restraint. The governor could not have chosen a mayor whose policies were more certain to antagonize the freedpeople. The response on the streets would be immediate and emphatic.

At this moment the streetcar issue came suddenly into focus. For over a year, Griffin, Carraway, and others had contended that peaceful means

---

110. *New York Times,* March 5, 1886; *MN,* July 28, 1869; U.S. Congress, House, *Affairs in Alabama,* 447; entries 1502, 1519, M816, reel 2.

111. City Tax Books, 1867–70, Mobile Municipal Archives; entries 289, 201, Population Schedules, Mobile City, Mobile County, Ala., Manuscript U.S. Census for 1860 (M653), RG 29, reel 17; entries 1502, 1527, 6859, M816, reel 2.

112. *MN,* July 9, 1868.

would desegregate the cars. As the legislature met, Carraway pressed for a common-carrier law, but by late July, he and his colleague Ovid Gregory concluded that the legislature would evade the issue.[113] The frustrated Carraway passed on this news, perhaps hoping that a demonstration would prod Republican lawmakers, but he likely got more than he bargained for. After a protest meeting and days of unrest over the new "Rebel mayor," on July 30, 1868, several hundred freedpeople stopped a Davis Avenue car, with many entering and demanding service. When the driver refused to continue, the crowd outside "shoved the car along for some distance" before giving up.[114] Even more massive demonstrations ensued the following day. Several hundred "transient negroes of bad character" boarded the streetcars, going from one line to another.[115] The new police chief, Morris D. Wickersham, reported disorder for the whole afternoon: "Vast throngs of white & black people gathered along the various lines of the city railways. From stores, warehouses and shops, the [whites] emerged fully armed to meet any emergency." Mayor Price had called on these citizens for aid, securing a thousand volunteer policemen in all, a show of force that eventually stopped the disturbances. That night the city hired one hundred fifty policemen for good measure, including about twenty blacks. Five "ring leaders" were arrested along with one Republican policeman who, bravely, tried to arrest another white for disorderly conduct. No one seems to have been hurt in the day's troubles, despite the *Register*'s threat of race war.[116]

After the troubles ended, observers generally agreed on who was responsible: H. Ray Myers. Chief Wickersham claimed, "Had Myers been arrested on the 4th of July as I advised, there would have been no more of the factions." But the police had no grounds on which to arrest him, much as Chief Wickersham wanted. The initiative rested with Myers's following, especially the more combative grassroots leaders. In the midst of the disturbances, "[Major] Lankford and another negro named Alexander harangued a crowd of negroes at the Court House." More strikingly, of the five blacks who were actually tried, all were obscure figures with no known

---

113. State of Alabama, *Journal of the House of Representatives during the Sessions Commencing in July, September, and November 1868,* 23, 53, 56.

114. *Mobile Evening News* quoted in *Montgomery Advertiser,* August 1, 1868.

115. *MDR,* August 1, 2, 1868; *New Orleans Picayune,* August 1, 2, 1868; *Mobile Tribune* quoted in *Selma Times and Messenger,* August 5, 1868.

116. M. D. Wickersham to Smith, August 1, 1868, Smith Papers; *Mobile Register,* August 3, 4, 1868.

political background. The likelihood is that the direct action drew on spontaneous militancy rather than being a tactic imposed by white prospective officeholders. The protest, moreover, was evidently effective; the Republican legislature subsequently passed legislation admitting blacks to Mobile's streetcars.[117]

Whatever the origin or motivation of the unrest, this was a crucial moment in the evolution of the Republican leadership. That spring, the *Nationalist* had called on "considerate men of color" to "restrain their more hasty brethren," and this the spokesmen of the moderate faction had often done. During the presidential election, for example, Carraway, Gregory, Bragg, and Joseph, among others, called on blacks to attend the polls without arms; there had been charges that black Democrats would be mobbed, and these leaders urged that they be left unmolested to demonstrate "obedience and reverence for law and order." As time went on, this sort of intervention became less common, and the most prominent African American leaders became less willing, or able, to check the more "turbulent spirits among the colored people." As for the white moderate leaders, they now concluded that they could not control black popular agitation and subsequently distanced themselves from civil rights demands. City Judge C. F. Moulton, for example, upheld the streetcar companies' practices, and his fellow established scalawags seemed particularly troubled by the behavior of their allies.[118] One alderman provided dramatic evidence of this sentiment just after the streetcar occupation. He boasted that Horton and Bromberg had come around to his view that "colored men should be advised in all matters pertaining [to] their interests" and generally should not hold office. In particular, "Mr. Horton acknowledges he committed a fatal blunder when he put the colored man on the police force."[119] There is some confirmation that Horton was indeed troubled by the confrontations. The social agony of the new migrants encouraged aggressive activism, which threatened to swamp the electoral viability of the Republican party and provoke chaos. The appeal of newcomers like Harrington, Myers, and G. L. Putnam, men he thought irresponsible, evidently undermined Gustavus Horton's confidence in the masses of the freedpeople.

117. Wickersham to Smith, August 1, 1868; *MDR,* August 3, 1868; *MN,* December 21, 1868.
118. *MN,* April 16, November 1, 1868; *MT* and *Mobile Tribune* quoted in *Selma Times and Messenger,* August 5, 1868.
119. William G. Johnson to Smith, August 8, 1868, Smith Papers.

Over the next several months, the Radicals gained popular influence because circumstances associated the moderates with Mayor Price's administration. Horton and Griffin were slow to break openly with the governor, and the legislature had left many city offices in their allies' hands through year's end. For several weeks, the most controversial issue was whether African Americans would serve in city government. The Mobile legislation called for the governor to appoint city boardmembers, and after initial reluctance, Horton, Bromberg, and their peers recommended several prosperous freedmen as aldermen. Governor Smith did appoint a handful, including two politically obscure Creoles. However, for bipartisan balance, he also added experienced boardmembers at Mayor Price's recommendation, including elite ex-Rebels G. A. Ketchum, George M. Parker, and G. Y. Overall.[120] These Democrats categorically refused to serve with black aldermen, and weeks of municipal deadlock ensued. Mayor Price now endorsed a whites-only appointment policy, for only such a policy could secure experienced business leadership. The city owed $1.5 million to bondholders, and should a taxpayer boycott or any mismanagement occur, Mobile would become bankrupt. Some of the more cautious Republicans agreed with Price that black representation could wait. "When the Colored men understand further the financial condition of the city," Judge John Elliot observed, "they will be perfectly willing to withdraw . . . and leave the old boards to manage things as they have done successfully for years."[121]

The freedpeople had followed this logic before, but no longer. They pressed for direct representation, and this time they carried their point. The Democratic appointees eventually realized that racist intransigence risked full Republican control of city government. Once the Democrats accepted their offices, though, the conservatives' "wealth and social position" allowed them to control the boards. According to James Shaw, the Republicans needed a preponderance of members or else "the Democrats could and would turn every Republican out of office" at the end of the year. Nor was the new mayor's conduct any comfort, for city government soon took on a Democratic cast. Price apparently replaced most of Horton's black police amid published complaints of special efforts to catch them napping. He

120. Memorandum of meeting, August 7, 1868, Smith Papers; *MDR*, August 24, 1868; *MN*, September 13, 1868.
121. Price to Smith, August 27, 1868; John Elliot to Smith, August 28, 1868; and M. B. Jonas to Smith, August 29, 1868, Smith Papers.

welcomed the Democratic vice-presidential candidate, Francis Blair, to the city, despite Blair's recent inflammatory statements promoting the overthrow of Reconstruction.[122] Price also issued a public warning against intimidation of the few black conservatives to the outrage of Republicans who pointed out that the real violence came from elsewhere. In September, in response to the ending of bureau subsidies, the mayor announced his intention to close the city soup kitchens. The municipal debt precluded such expenditures, and Price viewed soup kitchens as "an invitation to vagrancy and pauperism." And during the presidential election, in sort of a culminating insult, the allegedly Republican mayor of the city did not vote. By this point, even Price's Republican collaborators demanded that the legislature intervene. Ex-mayor Horton wanted to "place the City Government in loyal hands" until an election would be prudent—which was still not yet.[123]

The more dramatic response occurred within the African American leadership. After the factional struggles of the summer, even established black spokesmen became more assertive to keep in step with their restive mass constituency. Once they were deprived of city patronage, continued deference to Gustavus Horton and other moderate white leaders made less sense. Besides, white Radicals like Harrington seldom openly crossed their black constituents on civil rights issues, while Horton, Bromberg, and their allies did so frequently as a matter of political strategy. The black activists most associated with the moderates had to assert themselves or risk political isolation. At the same time, the whole language of colorblind equality and interracial leadership came in for reappraisal as racial assertiveness became more evident. In November L. S. Berry issued a public statement denouncing a proposed national black-labor convention publicized in the *Nationalist*. He did so on the classic Radical Republican grounds that "the sooner we, as a people forget our sable complexion, the sooner we cease to meet as a class in conventions, the better it will be for us as a race."[124] Berry, then in Montgomery, was immediately deluged with criticism from Allen

---

122. Price to Smith, September 16, 1868; and Shaw to Smith, September 12, 1868, Smith Papers; *Edwards' Mobile City Directory for 1869*, 3; *MN*, December 14, 1868; Caleb Price to Boards of Aldermen and Common Council, August 18, 1868, folder 3, envelope 2, box 13, RMBACC.

123. *MN*, September 6, 1868; Price to Lt. E. H. Weirman, September 17, 1868, entry 146, box 32, Letters Received by the Sub-Assistant Commissioner at Mobile, RG 105; G. Horton to Smith, December 10, 1868, Smith Papers.

124. *MN*, November 30, 1868.

Alexander and others warning him that his followers disagreed. Berry hastily retracted his letter, this time defending separate meetings as justified by common history and oppression. Berry offered black-nationalist rebuttals to his own equally plausible Radical egalitarian arguments of a few days before. The absent Berry clearly had misread the mood of racial militancy and the ideological flux then sweeping the community, and more militant spokesmen increasingly supplanted him.[125]

Perhaps the core issue among activists was feeling taken for granted, of being neglected in favor of tactical expediency and fiscal responsibility. The emerging free-school issue surely contributed to this sense. Under military rule, Horton, Bromberg, and Coale had been appointed to the county school board, which remained exempt from most state law and under conservative control. The board long considered funding black public schools, but "the School Commissioners had no money to rent or build separate schools, and nothing was done."[126] Even after the Reconstruction government took office, the board concluded that finances precluded free schools as provided for under state legislation everywhere else in Alabama.[127] The existing program subsidized education beyond the primary grades, and the boardmembers were reluctant to defund elite instruction in order to spread the benefits of basic education. Also, negotiations to take over the missionary-association schools broke down, apparently over how much autonomy the Yankee teachers should retain. As the descendent of the embattled Mobile Medical College school, the AMA's Emerson Institute enjoyed strong support, and several black politicians had attended or had children attending Emerson. In November, frustrated by these disputes, a Republican mass meeting demanded the abolition of the old school board altogether. Eventually, the state board of education created a rival "new" board under Superintendent George Putnam, the director of the Emerson Institute, and a protracted court battle ensued. Membership on the old board apparently co-opted Horton and Bromberg, for it was their one entree to respectable Mobile, their respite from pariah status. They stubbornly supported the old board in the face of vocal black opposition. Perhaps this was on principled grounds, for they likely believed the Emerson Institute a hotbed of irresponsible carpetbaggers that would benefit from different management.[128]

125. *Montgomery Alabama State Journal,* November 21, 28, 1868.
126. Gillette to Bromberg, March 17, 1874, Frederick G. Bromberg Papers, SHC.
127. Willis G. Clark, *History of Education in Alabama, 1702–1889* (Washington, 1889), 220–35, 279–81. Clark was a member of the "old board" with Horton and Bromberg.
128. *MDR,* May 15, 1870; *MN,* June 28, 1866; "Resolutions of Mobile County Republi-

If any of the moderates had maintained credibility with the freedpeople on civil rights, it was Albert Griffin, and his dramatic eclipse highlights the erosion of his faction. After the 1868 presidential election, Griffin and other Republicans secured legislation removing Mayor Price and vacating the city boards again.[129] This time the governor's appointments included John Carraway to the council and Lawrence S. Berry, Rev. E. D. Taylor, and several prosperous Creoles to the board of aldermen. In all, eleven African Americans were selected along with fourteen white Republicans and eight Democrats, so Republicans finally controlled the boards. The newly appointed members were to choose a new mayor and city officers in January 1869. Albert Griffin wanted to be mayor himself, but he lacked the votes, so he endorsed Alexander McKinstry, a recent scalawag convert and future lieutenant governor; Ulysses Grant's election had prompted a number of elite conversions to the Republicans statewide, and McKinstry was among the more prominent. Griffin reasoned that without a "large white accession" the party was doomed, and common whites would not enter "unless some of their leaders precede them." Griffin evidently came to some kind of terms with McKinstry, perhaps reminiscent of his earlier arrangement with Congressman Kellogg, for the *Nationalist* as always was in dire shape, owing the editor thousands in back salary. Whatever the specific terms, Griffin and McKinstry agreed that Horton's Unionist supporters were to receive the lion's share of the city offices.[130]

In response, a show of African American solidarity overrode all the prevailing factional divisions. In the joint ballot for mayor, all the blacks save one deserted Griffin and McKinstry. A united leadership rebelled and cast a protest vote for Mayor Price, who won reelection. In John Carraway's words, it was "only a choice between Democrats" anyway, so they might

---

can Union Club," November 5, 1868, Smith Papers; State of Alabama, *Official Report of the Superintendent of Public Instruction of the State of Alabama to the Governor for the Fiscal Year Ending 30th September 1869* (Montgomery, 1870), 35–6; Frances Annette Isbell, "A Social and Economic History of Mobile, 1865–1875" (master's thesis, University of Alabama, 1951), 111–5. The issue of racial integration, oddly enough, does not seem to have been raised by either faction.

129. *MN,* December 21, 1868, quoted in Works Project Administration, "Interesting Transcriptions from the *Mobile Nationalist,* 1868–1869" (Works Project Administration typescript, 1939), Mobile Municipal Archives; *Montgomery Alabama State Journal,* January 23, 1869.

130. Griffin to "Gen. Paine," January 30, [1869,] HR 40-A 21.1, no.13025, Records of the U.S. House of Representatives, RG 233, National Archives.

as well secure the best deal possible.[131] The blacks and a few white Radicals then divided the city offices with the Democrats. Here the personal interests of individual activists may have assumed predominant influence. The Democrats got most of the higher financial-oversight positions, but the deal made George F. Harrington city attorney and W. I. Squires of the Emerson Institute city engineer. African Americans fared reasonably well, securing their first substantial representation in city offices. James Bragg became street commissioner, and Allen Alexander became superintendent of the fire-alarm system, while others received lesser jobs. Griffin raged in the *Nationalist,* accusing Harrington and the African American boardmembers of having been bribed outright.[132] One Democratic newspaper, with mischievous intent, agreed that Griffin's charges of vote buying were accurate to the tune of five thousand dollars.[133]

Whatever the truth, there were other motives besides self-interest, and Griffin himself eventually conceded that not all the black aldermen had been bribed. His longtime ally John Carraway responded to the allegations of betrayal. Before the ballot, Carraway had tried to secure a mayoral candidate blacks could accept from the moderate faction, but Griffin insisted on the former Rebel McKinstry. No alternative existed to Griffin's dictation save the conservative Price. Carraway went on to defend his actions in terms of providing responsible city leadership. He wanted a mayor tolerable to "peaceable and law abiding citizens of both parties," and competent men were needed to run city departments, even if Democrats. Without Price's help, he added, few Republicans could have secured the property bonds to assume office anyway. Going on the offensive, Carraway then arraigned Griffin's record at the *Nationalist,* reciting a long—and accurate—litany of grievances: Griffin had demanded forty-five dollars per week in salary and "refused to take less"; he had borrowed money for the paper from the orphans' fund and never repaid it; he had promised repeatedly that the *Nationalist* would appear as a daily, saddling them with Congressmen Kellogg in the process, but the daily issues never appeared; the editor had even taken the *Nationalist* away from the original black trustees under duress. Carraway conceded he had long thought Griffin acted from pure

---

131. *MDR,* January 9, 10, 1869; *MN,* January 18, 1869, quoted in Works Project Administration, "Interesting Transcripts from the *Mobile Nationalist.*"

132. *MN,* January 9, 19, 1869. There was apparently considerable division in the black community at large over this strategy.

133. *Montgomery Mail,* January 21, 1869.

motives and had even tried to get him elected to the U.S. Senate the previous summer. Since that time, Griffin sought every imaginable "office in the gift of the people," culminating in his opportunistic support for McKinstry. The black boardmembers had not been bribed, Carraway concluded, they just did not trust Griffin any more.[134]

For years Griffin's control of the *Nationalist* had allowed him to define the ideological terrain of public debate, and he legitimized scalawag-dominated leadership and his own tactical moves with the goal of color-blind equality. Now the editor's antagonists had enough of his lectures, and after the vote for mayor the feud intensified. As alderman, L. S. Berry moved to strip the *Nationalist* of the city-printing contract, and while his colleagues balked, they insisted that the paper appear thrice weekly.[135] When Griffin left for Washington to seek a federal patronage post in Hawaii, his former allies moved against him. In April the black majority on the restructured *Nationalist* board—Berry, Carraway, and Jacob Anderson—removed Albert Griffin as editor.[136] Several issues of the *Nationalist* then appeared under their auspices, featuring denunciations of Griffin as a trickster who neglected the paper for private business, "mostly office seeking." It seems that Griffin's critics overplayed their hand, perhaps because their role in the hated Mayor Price's reelection looked dubious in hindsight. After some weeks, Griffin regained physical possession of the premises, with some of his black loyalists threatening Berry's life and even assaulting him, and Griffin actually asked his followers to desist in an editorial. The editor subsequently regained formal control of the paper at a meeting of the stockholders. Still, Griffin had suffered a ruinous loss of credibility within Republican ranks.[137]

Thus, by 1869, even established black leaders in the moderate faction, pressured by the ferment in the community, became less deferential to their former scalawag allies around Horton. One *Nationalist* column suggested that Berry, Carraway, and Gregory all supported Harrington for a federal patronage post that spring. By now, the rhetoric of colorblind equality and interracial leadership had worn thin, at least as employed by Albert Griffin in the *Nationalist*. Black politics had taken shape in the Union Leagues

134. *Montgomery Alabama State Journal*, February 6, 1869.
135. *MDR*, January 19, 1869.
136. Entry 2271, April 20, 1869, M816, reel 2; *MN*, May 3, 14, 1869, quoted in Works Project Administration, "Interesting Transcriptions from the *Mobile Nationalist*."
137. *Montgomery Mail*, January 12, 1869; *MDR*, July 4, 1869; *MN*, July 7, 9, 1869.

under the mentorship of Horton, Bromberg, Griffin, and other moderate whites seeking a biracial Unionist constituency. These spokesmen persuaded African American leaders to accept subordinate status, but factions consequently developed within the black community, dividing the leadership along class and caste lines and raising controversies over goals and tactics as well. To this time, black leaders had made only cautious demands of their Republican allies, but the struggle for grassroots support made this less possible. Horton and his scalawag followers could not satisfy even their closest African American allies because the former mayor could not offer enough to hold their loyalty or that of the black populace more broadly. Thus the black leadership pursued community interests ever more aggressively, with some activists going to the length of a tactical alliance with the conservative opposition. This reciprocal interaction would soon become the defining feature of Mobile's politics as the emerging Radical faction collaborated with powerful Democrats in search of office and influence.[138]

138. *MN,* January 9, 19, April 5, 1869.

4

The Fruits of Sagacity

Race, Business, and the Radical Ascendancy

During the early years of Reconstruction, relatively privileged men dominated Mobile's black political scene. Promoted by powerful white Republicans, these sober-minded, politically moderate individuals sought respectability in the wider community and discretion in their followers. By the late 1860s, a very different cohort of leaders challenged them for public favor, and these radicals were more willing to encourage popular militancy than their rivals. This contest would culminate in the assumption of the mayor's office by George F. Harrington, the carpetbagger leader of the Radical faction of the Republican party in 1870. Harrington's administration concluded the process of popular mobilization, offering both the fruits and perils of direct African American access to power. The Harrington interregnum delivered significant gains, but Radical Republican rule also was bedeviled by the sort of business-aid excesses so evident elsewhere in Gilded Age America. Modern historians of Reconstruction have not been much drawn to these economic topics, perhaps thinking them less significant than the wider struggle for racial justice, but these issues are crucial to understanding African American politics in Mobile.

In subsequent decades, when public discussion turned toward the era, Mayor Harrington's administration exemplified Reconstruction's evils. The traditional local account is that irresponsible Radical carpetbaggers and blacks destroyed the city's finances with extravagant business subsidies. The *Mobile Register* recalled that racially "mixed boards," having nothing personal at stake, "rioted and wallowed amongst the spoils of ill-gotten power." Editor Henry St. Paul similarly remembered the day when "an imbecile Governor turned over [Mobile's] manacled and pinioned people to the thieving crew of Harrington and his fellow plunderers."[1] Lurid rhetoric aside, this view colors even more recent discussions, despite the changes in Reconstruction historiography as a whole. One modern study observes that "several railroad projects launched during the Radical era" bankrupted Mobile, with most of these "sullied by corruption."[2] As a statement of bare fact, these descriptions have some validity. In 1870, under Radical Mayor Harrington, Republican-dominated boards passed aid legislation that contributed to later bankruptcy. All this is literally true yet misleading; Mobile's merchant elite played a major role as well, perhaps the decisive role in what transpired. The Republicans aligned with Harrington, and enacting the railroad legislation did exactly what the Mobile Board of Trade wanted over the opposition of other Republicans. African American political demands shaped the context for enactment, but the initiative came from the business community, and their evolving policies inspired subsequent political developments.

If Mobile's merchants and civic elite collaborated with Republicans on economic legislation, it was only out of perceived necessity. The Horton family's protracted social ostracism conveys some sense of elite sentiment toward Reconstruction's proponents. The community was awash in fiery rhetoric, encouraged by the Democratic press and the examples of local notables such as Adm. Raphael Semmes, Josiah Nott, and the novelist Augusta Evans. A British visitor recalled that Mobile was the first place he ever found Southerners talking about resuming the war.[3] Another Briton, chatting with a Mobilian, marveled at the most extreme position on racial matters he ever encountered.[4] Both the political leadership and the merchants vented similar hostility. For example, future Democratic mayor Gideon M. Parker found "niggers on top and nobody making money except the circus men."[5] Another conservative boardmember wrote that northern fiends were "instigating the negroes to deeds of violence rapine murder

1. *MDR,* August 8, 1877, February 3, 1875.
2. Doyle, *New Men, New Cities, New South,* 70, 78.
3. George Rose, *The Great Country; Or, Impressions of America* (London, 1868), 182.
4. David Macrae, *The Americans at Home* (1870; reprint, New York, 1952), 301.
5. G. M. Parker to C. Parker, December 26, 1867, G. M. Parker Papers, The Museum of Mobile.

thefts & house burnings."⁶ Private correspondence abounded with bitter references to Reconstruction and its local manifestations, generally expressed in terms of racist contempt. Mobile's civic elite thus had no enthusiasm for any aspect of Reconstruction, but they needed to respond to political realities. Black suffrage was the law and Republicans dominated the federal government, so worries closer to home preoccupied the local leadership. Cotton was the city's lifeblood, and the decline in Mobile's cotton trade was manifest to all. The city seemed doomed to a *New York Times* correspondent, and "the principal topic of discussion was the cause of this decline in her trade."⁷ As unprecedented as the political events were, business was business—and business was bad.⁸

William Ketchum, a prosperous cotton merchant, illustrates the balance of priorities in his letters to his long-absent wife, who was off exposing their daughters to culture in France. Outraged as he was by Reconstruction, Ketchum spent far more time bewailing the city's economic troubles. In November 1867 he observed: "my dear wife, the whole country is ruined, & the people broke. . . . I look upon the present as the darkest of my life, we Cotton men will have to hunt up some other business."⁹ A year later Mobile was suffering worse than elsewhere; cotton shipments had dropped, "and what else supports Mobile? *Nothing.*" The best merchants expected only a bare living, and gloom pervaded commercial circles to an extent he had never seen.¹⁰ Ketchum claimed that no one was making more than office expenses.¹¹ Some of his vehemence can be explained as attempts to rein in his family's spending, which well exceeded his income. Ketchum was and would remain a wealthy man, but his sense of relative deprivation was pervasive throughout the merchant class.¹² The commercial realities were so grim that desperate measures looked attractive to normally cautious businessmen.

Before Military Reconstruction began, elite opinion weighed economic-development initiatives to stave off the competition. Mayor J. M. Withers's opposition and political confusion prevented much concrete being done.

   6. William Ketchum to Wife, November 1, 1868, Creagh Family Papers, SHC.
   7. *NYT,* December 15, 1868.
   8. Ketchum to Wife, November 18, 1867.
   9. Ibid.
   10. William Ketchum to Wife, November 1, 1868, Creagh Family Papers.
   11. Ketchum to Wife, December 3, 1868, March 25, 1869, Creagh Family Papers.
   12. William Ketchum to Wife, May 31, 1869, Creagh Family Papers.

The inauguration of black suffrage only made this uncertainty worse, and subsidy measures remained on hold during 1867 and most of 1868. The reluctant businessmen on the city boards sought only fiscal caution from Mayor Gustavus Horton's administration. The primary goal of conservatives like Gideon M. Parker was to preserve the city's credit intact out of the ruin of war. Horton shared this priority and generally deferred to his merchant colleagues, passing on to his successor a bonded debt of well over one million dollars. However, with the appointment of Caleb Price as mayor, and the subsequent conservative influence on the city boards, civic elites pondered a more proactive role. Ulysses S. Grant's election as president in November 1868 suggested that Reconstruction would continue for some years, which made marking time less attractive. Furthermore, the Republican legislature enacted generous state subsidy measures for endorsement of railroad bonds to the extent of sixteen thousand dollars per mile for all roads built. Mobile's commercial rivals moved to take advantage of the legislation, and the city's business leadership saw little advantage to letting this subsidy expire. The political circumstances were not ideal, but further delay seemed unwise, and changes in the city's press intensified the demand for action. In January 1868 the *Advertiser and Register* merged with the *Times* to form the *Mobile Register*.[13] The purchaser was the Yankee entrepreneur and aspiring conservative politician William D'Alton Mann, an official in the U.S. Internal Revenue Service. The *Register* was "not thought to pay well," but it facilitated Mann's far-flung investments, especially in railroads.[14] For editor, Mann retained former mayor John Forsyth, who had already distinguished himself for his support of subsidy measures. The *Register* combined Democratic partisanship with relentless advocacy of every aid proposal imaginable. In control of the most influential newspaper in the state, Forsyth unstintingly promoted Mann's personal interests, becoming a virtual cheerleader for civic-subsidy measures. These press changes, combined with a newly active board of trade operating under the day-to-day direction of Forsyth's son Charles, set the stage for dramatic measures.

In the spring of 1869, the board of trade pushed economic initiatives with "unflagging zeal and industry," proposing several spending measures

13. *MT,* January 29, 1868.
14. Credit ledgers, June 1869, Alabama, vol. 18, R. G. Dun and Company Collection, Baker Library, Harvard Business School.

to the city government under Mayor Price.[15] The most important was the endorsement of $1.5 million in bonds for the Mobile and Alabama Grand Trunk Railroad to run toward the coalfields around modern Birmingham. The active managers were among "the oldest and best known" Mobile citizens, and a printed petition endorsing the measure was signed by over one hundred board of trade members, who reportedly represented two-thirds of the property in the city.[16] The signatories included three subsequent Democratic mayoral candidates, Martin Horst, G. M. Parker, and John Reid, along with W. D. Mann himself. Topping the list was Moses Waring, perhaps the premiere merchant in the city and worth over half a million dollars.[17] The railroad enterprise was "of vital importance" to Mobile, but "in the current depressed condition of our people," individual subscriptions would not suffice.[18] The petition lauded the utility of such municipal endorsements of railroad stock, and the *Register* termed it the short cut to the regeneration of the city.[19] Two additional proposals took shape that spring under similar auspices. The board of trade observed that harbor improvement was crucial to the commerce of the city.[20] It eventually recommended a city appropriation of one million dollars to deepen Mobile Bay, hoping that once the city commenced the task a federal appropriation would follow. While this was under discussion, a board of trade committee also looked into the status of the privately owned wharves, the subject of longstanding dispute. At the 1867 constitutional convention, Albert Griffin had inserted a provision restoring ownership of all wharves to the city, but litigation took the matter to the U.S. Supreme Court. The committee was appointed to explore a settlement with the wharf owners, and they approached the city government to participate.[21]

15. *MDR,* March 4, 1869.

16. Ibid., June 4, 1869; Frederick G. Bromberg, *The Reconstruction Period in Alabama,* Iberville Historical Society Papers, nos. 3, 4 (Mobile, 1911–14), 8.

17. Credit ledgers, May 2, 1866, Alabama, vol. 18, Dun and Company Collection.

18. M. Waring et al. to Mayor, Common Council, and Board of Aldermen, May 15, 1869, folder 2, envelope 6, box 13, RMBACC.

19. *MDR,* May 6, 1869.

20. Board of Aldermen, Minutes, March 11, April 1, 15, 1869, Mobile Municipal Archives, reel 5; Board of Common Council, Minutes, May 5, 1869, Mobile Municipal Archives, reel 21; W. J. Ledyard et al. to Mayor, March 30, 1869, folder 2, envelope 5, box 13, RMBACC.

21. *MDR,* March 31, 1869. On the background of the legal dispute over the waterfront, see Robert Saunders Jr., *John Archibald Campbell, Southern Moderate, 1811–1889* (Tuscaloosa and London, 1997), 39–56.

These three proposals, taken together, would have tripled the city's contingent debt. They were nonetheless popular with the business leadership, the Grand Trunk subsidy in particular. The *Register* termed it "*the great enterprise*" for the city's future.[22] One railroad proponent thought "nearly all the large property owners" were in favor, though it would be opposed by "some few small property owners."[23] On the whole the subsidy proposals were rationally conceived to respond to Mobile's economic problems. Unfortunately for the proponents, these initiatives prompted still others, which complicated the prospects for rapid enactment. The most significant of these was a proposal by the New Orleans, Mobile, and Chattanooga Railroad to locate its repair facility in the city in exchange for a direct gift of several hundred thousand dollars. Mann was a major contractor and spokesman for the line, and the *Register* promoted the grant enthusiastically.[24] Still, as one conservative alderman pointed out, the project lacked "the same strong endorsement by the tax-payers that the Grand Trunk Railroad ordinance had."[25]

All four economic-development proposals came before the board of aldermen at the meeting of May 20, 1869. Two aldermen, who had recently conferred with the board of trade, between themselves sponsored the four bills. Some preconcerted strategy appears likely in order to satisfy all the special interests by passing the bills simultaneously. The attempt failed, in part because Albert Griffin's *Mobile Nationalist* denounced the subsidy measures relentlessly. Though the *Nationalist* backed public-works spending in principle, it doubted the proposals under consideration. People were "pushing from one extravagant scheme of spending money into another," one letter editorialized, urging Republican officials to tread warily.[26] Griffin was particularly skeptical of the Grand Trunk Railroad, suspecting the managers' desire to use public money without risking their own capital. He feared the company could be milked for construction money and then bankrupted, leaving the city holding the bag. Griffin insisted that the proposals should not be approved without a popular referendum, and his intense scrutiny dampened the uncritical enthusiasm on the boards.[27]

22. *MDR,* May 6, 1869.
23. Ibid., May 28, 1869.
24. Ibid., June 22, 1869.
25. Ibid., June 26, 1869.
26. *MN,* May 24, July 12, 1869.
27. Ibid., May 24, July 2, 1869.

For several weeks the city government was "in a stew" over the proposals, and all four became mired in controversy.[28] The Grand Trunk Railroad, for its evident popularity among the businessmen, ran afoul of Griffin's moderate allies. The Mobile Common Council, led by Frederick Bromberg and Gustavus Horton, inserted a provision in the subsidy bill that the company had to raise $250,000 in cash before it received city endorsement for bonds. When it turned out that the company could not raise that sum, a bare council majority voted to waive the provision.[29] Bromberg and Horton then challenged the subsidy in court on the grounds that the bill had not received the legally required two-thirds vote of the entire number of council members. The shadowy status of the bonds rendered them unmarketable, and the railroad consequently lacked the capital to start construction. Similar problems beset the New Orleans and Mobile workshop grant. Aided by emphatic promotion in the *Register,* it passed quickly, over the objections of several Democratic boardmembers. Immediately thereafter, though, a meeting of wealthy opponents denounced the measure, with Moses Waring and scores of businessmen petitioning against it.[30] Waring and his colleagues challenged the legality of the grant in court on the strong grounds that an outright gift of city money to a private corporation was unsanctioned under state law. The railroad workshops were already under construction, but the legal challenge stopped payment of the promised subsidy.[31]

In pique, Forsyth and Mann turned on the other proposals. Their *Register* previously promoted all the contemplated subsidies, but now they assailed the wharf owners as public malefactors, specifically targeting wealthy Moses Waring for abuse. Perhaps the intention was to force Waring to abandon his lawsuit, but the legal dispute dragged on all summer. Passions grew heated, and one city official reportedly brained Frederick Bromberg with a heavy ledger.[32] Finally, aid supporters tried to "link the wharf-purchase question with the harbor question" so that the two ordinances might be "pulled through by the joint strength" of both.[33] A combined appropriation passed after John Carraway and his colleagues on the

28. *Montgomery Alabama Journal,* June 24, 1869.
29. Board of Common Council, Minutes, July 6, 1869, reel 21.
30. Board of Aldermen, Minutes, June 22, 1869, reel 5; *MN,* June 30, July 2, 1869.
31. *MDR,* June 24, 1869.
32. Ibid., June 9, 1869.
33. Ibid., October 8, 1869.

council drastically scaled it back.³⁴ Even this strategy miscarried, for Mayor Price vetoed the bill, eliminating the chance that any of the four aid measures would be implemented. City government now reached gridlock as the common council went for months in the fall without a quorum, Bromberg and other subsidy opponents absenting themselves. As the expiration of state railway-aid legislation approached, proponents of assistance grew increasingly desperate. Soon, however, an unanticipated but not unwelcome resolution presented itself: the African American community would resuscitate subsidy legislation by having Mobile reconstructed yet again. The freedmen would become crucial players in the fate of the board of trade proposals, though more by incident than by design.

What African Americans thought of these elite subsidy disputes is difficult to reconstruct. By this point, the black electorate was informed enough on matters of more pressing concern. At a rally in 1869, for example, Allen Alexander paused to assure an audience "you are all well acquainted with the principles of our party" before going on to lambaste the Democrats.³⁵ On the economic issues before Mobile, however, evidence is scarce on black opinion. These measures involved technical matters of high finance in fields from which African Americans had been excluded. The subsidy issue was not one of their urgent concerns; little evidence of popular sentiment exists in the form of petitions, public rallies, and the like. Still, African Americans were not wholly insulated from the dispute. The aid proposals were among the outstanding public issues facing the boardmembers; there were enough black members to sway the outcome, and all had to cast public votes. They generally offered critical support for subsidy measures, especially those most likely to benefit their constituents, while viewing the issue as subordinate to civil rights.

African Americans on the boards seldom proposed any of the subsidy measures, nor were most particularly active in the debates surrounding them, if the newspaper coverage is accurate. Still, there is some evidence of the thinking of the more prominent leaders. During the month that L. S. Berry and John Carraway helped control the *Nationalist,* the paper was mildly supportive of development initiatives, far more than the displaced Albert Griffin was.³⁶ The temporary expulsion of Griffin as editor coincided

34. *MN,* September 17, 1869.
35. Ibid., July 16, 1869.
36. Ibid., May 10, 12, 1869.

with the subsidy proposals' gestation, which might suggest the two bore more than an accidental relation to one another. There are other, more direct, indications of black leadership preferences. As alderman, Berry endorsed the Grand Trunk subsidy on the grounds that he was "decidedly in favor of internal improvements, and wanted to keep pace with the march of improvement." He was "surprised to see men of intelligence in favor of such a suicidal course" as trying to stop progress. The railroad, moreover, would "give employment to a large number of idle and hungry people" and thereby render everyone's cows, hens, and pigs more secure from theft.[37] Berry's observation perhaps expressed his identification with poorer constituents, who often lived near the outskirts of town. He promoted the subsidies in terms of the tangible benefit for his constituents, articulating a plausible economic rationale for African American support: railroad subsidies provided short-term jobs and might yield economic growth, while most freedpeople felt the resulting property taxes only indirectly. If the *Register* can be believed, the railroad work under way that summer drew many unemployed blacks from Mobile, improving the job prospects for everyone.[38] Completion took many months, and according to one railroad report, the construction of the line from New Orleans doubled the wages for railroad hands, making it impossible for other railroads to hire sufficient labor.[39] Laborers on the project even struck, forcing concessions, which suggested workers' awareness of their strong bargaining position.[40] More railroad construction could only help the labor market, while overwhelming support from the business community offered apparent assurance that the policies were safe. The unnoticed problem, however, is that this course left African American politicians dependent on the wisdom, expertise, and candor of commercial leaders.

In general, the aldermen passed the subsidy measures by overwhelming

37. *MDR,* May 28, 1869.
38. Ibid., August 22, 1869
39. *New Orleans Picayune,* October 30, 1870; Mobile and Ohio Railroad Company, "Proceedings of the Twenty-second Annual Meeting of the Stockholders of the Mobile and Ohio Railroad Company Held in Mobile, May 17, 1870" (Mobile, 1870), 15. In one small community along the line, railroad construction reportedly had an extraordinary benefit. At Bay St. Louis, the railroad "literally clothed the naked and fed the hungry. It has given employment at high wages, to every man who would work." *Handesboro Democrat* quoted in *New Orleans Picayune,* October 26, 1870.
40. *MDR,* February 9, 14, 16, 1869.

margins, which minimized any distinctive visibility for the African American members in debate. Only one of the aid votes had an apparent race-related dimension, the workshop grant for the New Orleans and Mobile Railroad. Democrats on the boards voiced business community skepticism toward the unpopular railroad, but strong black support provided the margin of passage. The proponents promised fifteen hundred jobs, well timed to get people through the slow summer season, while the *Register* claimed that half the city's laborers and mechanics were without work.[41] The Democratic paper actually invited the "the colored members of the Boards" to help the "hundreds of idlers of their own race."[42] The railroad, moreover, was already providing substantial employment opportunities for Mobile's blacks. Given the scarcity of industrial jobs, a concern with diversifying employment opportunities would make some sense. This proposal arguably offered more direct benefit to their constituents than any of the others. In this instance, moreover, the black aldermen rose above partisanship, supporting a measure identified with the violently Democratic W. D. Mann and his *Register*.[43] Still, if African American city officials favored aid measures, they were not enthusiastic about it, and they sometimes piggybacked other race demands at the proposals' expense. Alderman Wilber Strong offered an amendment to the Grand Trunk bill that there should be no distinction by race in treatment of passengers.[44] This was ruled out of order, but when a later vote came, only one black member voted for the subsidy. Of the three votes against the railroad, two were African Americans, including Alderman Strong, while several others apparently absented themselves, including Berry, who had earlier spoken for the proposal. If the fate of the antidiscrimination provision motivated this behavior, it would suggest that civil rights consistently overrode economic concerns in the freedpeople's priorities.[45]

After the reelection of Mayor Price, moreover, the civil rights issue became increasingly urgent. The factional divisions within the black leadership were overshadowed for the time being by Price's conduct. The *Register* boasted that the mayor's "severe manner" toward petty offenders drove them out of the city. There was another purge of the police force early in

41. Ibid., June 13, 1869.
42. Ibid., June 11, 1869.
43. Ibid., June 25, 26, 29, 30, 1869.
44. Ibid., June 4, 1869.
45. Ibid., June 4, 11, 1869.

1869, with several of the more prominent Republicans being replaced. Afterward, police conduct, always a concern, became more problematic. In one instance an officer ordered a man to move off the sidewalk and, when he protested, roughly arrested him. The affair wound up in court, where the officer was reprimanded and fined.[46] In another striking episode a policeman reportedly set dogs on black boys congregated at the wharves. When black alderman John Bryant interfered, the officer assaulted him, for which the policeman was fined in court. These judicial reprimands suggest brutal behavior by Price's police and that black officials closely attended criminal-justice issues. For example, Alderman Berry proposed to humanize the city's chain gang by unshackling the prisoners and providing pay for street work.[47]

The culminating grievance against Price's administration was yet another riot, this time with his police right in the middle of it. A congressional election occurred in early August 1869 between the Democratic nominee, W. D. Mann of the *Register,* and A. E. Buck, a Republican of the moderate faction. The First Congressional District being preponderantly black, Buck won, despite local Democratic majorities, some gunshots in the Seventh Ward, and the display of a cannon by white firemen near the polls. Afterward, Republicans planned a victory rally downtown, but a rumor spread that the blacks would burn Mann in effigy. Consequently, it was "circulated all that day that the meeting would be broken that night by a riot"— that is, by whites upset about the threatened insult. Republican leaders tried to call off the meeting, but according to the *Nationalist,* some freedmen insisted on defying the threats.[48] As the rally gathered on the evening of August 5, hundreds of whites organized themselves a block away under arms while scores more attended the Republican rally. At the meeting, there was some conservative heckling. When white fireman David Reed shouted "hurra for Mann," freedmen responded in kind, an exchange that ended in mutual curses. At that, someone (by some accounts Reed) fired once from near a group of police. The shooting became general, the whites took cover,

46. Ibid., August 22, 1869; *MN,* September 22, 1869, in Works Projects Administration, "Interesting Transcriptions from the *Mobile Nationalist*" (Works Project Administration typescript, 1939), Mobile Municipal Archives.

47. *MDR,* March 20, 23, February 19, 1869.

48. *Montgomery Alabama State Journal,* August 5, 1869; G. Horton Jr. to G. Horton, August 7, 1869, Gustavus Horton Papers, The Museum of Mobile; J. T. Foster to Smith, August 12, 1869, Gov. William H. Smith Papers, ADAH; *MN* quoted in *MDR,* August 8, 1869.

and, at police urging, black leaders Major Lankford and James Bragg hastened the freedmen away to the suburbs. Bragg was particularly helpful in calming the freedpeople, according to the police chief, but as the crowd departed, hundreds of organized whites arrived and more firing ensued.[49] The police chief claimed three of his men were shot from the retreating procession, and most of the whites injured were on his force, which reflected the widespread perception that they had taken the white rioters' side.[50]

The police headed off to patrol the suburbs, where groups of angry freedmen circulated on the streets. This left the downtown under the protection of armed white volunteers. A squad reportedly marched to Frederick Bromberg's residence, gave three cheers for Mann, then fired a volley over, or perhaps into, the house.[51] Gustavus Horton Jr. rejoiced that his father was out of town for the riot, noting that whites "shot a poor negro whenever they could find him alone." One squad reportedly followed Major Lankford, firing on him after his escort disbanded. Whites also searched for Albert Griffin all night, but he eluded them by hiding in a livery stable surrounded by black bodyguards. Two blacks and one white were reported dead in the disturbances, with many more seriously wounded, but the danger was not over. Horton's son wrote that "the only thing to be apprehended further is assassination. They have been after Griffin for three nights past, but they have not found him."[52] The *Register* chose this opportunity to even scores, the editor's venom perhaps exacerbated by Griffin's recent opposition to the various subsidy measures. The columns scarcely bothered to disguise its threats: "if these [carpetbagger] wretches are ambitious of dangling to lamp-posts, all they have got to do is turn loose their infuriated wild beasts once more." Forsyth's paper blamed Griffin directly for the riot, stating that unless he kept his followers in order, "his head and those of his fellow-conspirators will pay the forfeit." The

---

49. *Talladega Sun,* August 21, 1869; *Montgomery Mail,* August 7, 1869; *Mobile Tribune* quoted in *Montgomery Mail,* August 10, 1869; *Montgomery Alabama State Journal,* August 7, 11, 1869. As with all of Mobile's race riots, the partisanship of the press makes determination of the facts difficult.

50. *Mobile News* quoted in *New Orleans Picayune,* August 10, 1869; *MN,* August 5, 1869, in Works Project Administration, "Interesting Transcriptions from the *Mobile Nationalist*"; Police Chief Milne to Mayor Price, August 7, 1867, Smith Papers.

51. *MN* quoted in *National Anti-Slavery Standard,* August 28, 1869.

52. G. Horton Jr. to G. Horton, August 7, 1869; *Mobile Tribune* quoted in *Eufaula Bluff City (Ala.) Times,* August 12, 1869.

Register warned that the city would have no peace until Griffin left or he was "forced to stop scattering [his] firebrands in the community." After several days of this, Griffin called for a truce, apparently negotiating safe passage out of the city with the *Register*. He abandoned the *Nationalist* into the hands of his moderate allies and left for Kansas, never to return.[53]

After Griffin fled, Republicans found the sequel to the disturbances even more unsettling. Fifty Democrats met at the board of trade, constituting themselves as a "Committee of Public Safety" to help public authorities maintain order. The head of the group was Price Williams, who was also the head of the Democratic Central Committee. Even Mayor Price understood that sanctioning one party encouraged countermeasures, but the *Register* blustered that the mayor would have the vigilante aid whether he wanted it or not.[54] Republicans were outraged at the implication that they had been responsible for the riot, pointing out that none of the perpetrators of the riot had been arrested. Mobile's black population demanded martial law, and when Gov. William H. Smith refused, leaders urged the Republican legislature to vacate the city government yet again. A legislative election following the death of Ovid Gregory heightened the potential urgency of the situation. That November the disorganized Republicans were crushed, in part through the Committee of Public Safety's announced plans to patrol the Seventh Ward polls. Given the consequences of recent elections, the obligation of accepting the popular verdict seemed minimal and physically dangerous as well.[55]

The rising demand for another new city government meant more trouble for the moderate Republican faction, especially Gustavus Horton and Frederick Bromberg, who were long since on difficult terms with the freedpeople. The complicated struggle for control of the public schools added to their problems. For a year, Horton and Bromberg engaged in an effort, as members of the "old" school board, to bar County Superintendent George Putnam of the Emerson Institute from control of tax revenues. The bipartisan old school board saw Putnam as a carpetbagger opportunist of questionable probity. Having secured this one toehold into white respectability,

---

53. *MDR,* August 8, 1869; *MN,* August 25, 1869, in Works Project Administration, "Interesting Transcriptions from the *Mobile Nationalist.*"

54. *MDR* quoted in *MN,* October 1, 1869, in Works Project Administration, "Interesting Transcriptions for the *Mobile Nationalist.*"

55. W. G. Jones to Caleb Price, August 9, 1869, Smith Papers, ADAH; *Montgomery State Journal,* October 4, 1869; *MDR* quoted in *MN,* October 27, 1869.

one suspects that the long-suffering Horton and Bromberg were loath to give it up, though their general desire for fiscal austerity probably played some role too. But in opposing Putnam, these moderates placed themselves in opposition to free schools, Putnam's central demand.[56] In addition, the superintendent had secured state legislative authority to appoint a rival school board, which included prominent Catholic Democrats who resented Protestant direction of the schools.[57] Putnam's board also included L. S. Berry and Constantine Perez, and thus challenging the "new" board's authority made the moderates vulnerable on civil rights too. As Allen Alexander charged, Bromberg was "opposed to negroes holding positions on the Board of Education."[58]

Given these circumstances, Frederick Bromberg was not in a position to disregard demands that the legislature act. Still, he could hardly support another new municipal regime in his capacity of state senator. As a vociferous opponent of the pending subsidy measures, he doubtless feared a new city government would enact aid programs. During this period, Councilman Bromberg negotiated loans for the city to make up for unpaid taxes, a problem that was getting worse month by month.[59] Such financial worries aside, he was unwilling to do anything that might strengthen white Radical leaders like Harrington, Myers, and Putnam or their black allies. Furthermore, he had long pledged that civic elections were forthcoming, and he felt under some pressure to fulfill his promises. For all these reasons, Bromberg led the opposition against the Mobile municipal bill when it was proposed late in the year.

At this time, Bromberg still enjoyed good relations with several prosperous African American protégés, facilitated by his recent appointment as postmaster, which gave him several federal jobs to dispense. When Bromberg announced his opposition to the Mobile reorganization bill, his closest allies lost no time in expressing their dismay. A telegram arrived from James Bragg and the Creoles Philip Joseph, Charles Fernandez, and Constantine Perez, some of Mobile's wealthier activists. "Act with your party,"

---

56. *MN*, May 21, 1869, in Works Project Administration, "Interesting Transcriptions from the *Mobile Nationalist*."

57. Clark, *History of Education in Alabama*, 220–39. Willis G. Clark was a member of the "old" school board.

58. *MDR*, August 19, 1870; *Montgomery Mail*, October 3, 1869.

59. Ways and Means Committee, Minutes, August 22, December 13, 1869, Miscellaneous Books, Mobile Municipal Archives, reel 12.

these leaders implored, "letters from the people tomorrow." These men then published a statement to the legislature, signed as well by prosperous black leaders, including Durham Davis. Almost to a man, the prominent black activists associated with Bromberg and Horton's faction signed the petition, which disassociated themselves from their white allies as emphatically as possible. The statement insisted that a Republican government be installed in Mobile as the previous legislation had envisioned. Mayor Price's police force, "notoriously composed . . . of our most bitter enemies," had made honest elections impossible. The petition charged that Price discriminated against blacks in his capacity as judicial officer and that, in times of civic unrest, he had never called upon Republicans to help preserve order, only upon organized racist groups.[60]

In private, James Bragg further hectored the senator on behalf of the freedpeople, manifesting considerable frustration. Word of Bromberg's position spread like wildfire on the streets, he reported. Previous factional patterns were irrelevant because, for all Mobile's blacks, expelling the municipal administration was a matter of self-preservation. To Bragg, it made no sense to validate a vote so long as Democratic leaders and the press encouraged bloodshed: "The people here demand a change, and not by an election for you know we can not have a fair one." The undemocratic overtones of the legislation in the abstract made little impression on Bragg, given his experience as a target in the recent riot. Besides, politics within the black community were crystal clear since, in the face of Radical criticism, it was "hard for us to sustain men as Republicans and then have them to act with the Democrats in the Senate." Bragg's reading proved prescient, for as the decisive events of the following year unfolded, Bromberg's course undermined the popular appeal of the moderate faction. On this crucial issue, as Bragg observed, "every single Colored republican endorses that bill and it must go through."[61]

Bragg predicted that no black leader could be sustained under the circumstances, and his moderate allies' subsequent ordeal at the *Nationalist* bore him out. In May, Griffin's faction of stockholders had elected Bragg president of the *Nationalist* Board of Directors, electing as members Philip Joseph and others identified with the moderates. When Griffin fled in Au-

60. Bragg et al. to Bromberg, November 20, 1869, Frederick G. Bromberg Papers, SHC; *Montgomery Alabama State Journal,* November 27, 1869.
61. James Bragg to F. Bromberg, November 20, 1869, Bromberg Papers.

gust, he left as de facto editor Sara Stanley Woodward, a former missionary at the Emerson Institute; she was the light-skinned wife of Griffin's white business manager, C. A. Woodward.[62] A rival group of Radical trustees soon coalesced, led by longtime militants Allen Alexander and Major W. Lankford; they impeached Bragg as president and appointed new editors of their own. This factional bitterness culminated in several confused days of physical confrontation. In early December, during the Mobile reorganization bill controversy, Alexander and Lankford entered the *Nationalist* office and had editor Sara Woodward arrested for trespassing. Afterward, Philip Joseph broke the front door down with an ax, and Alexander threatened him at gunpoint, if the Democratic accounts can be believed. The contending parties wound up in court on various charges and placed under bond to keep the peace, but the matter was soon moot anyway. The bankrupt *Nationalist* ceased publication, with white moderates buying the press and issuing the successor *Mobile Republican* under their own control.[63]

In response to the grassroots outcry, the Republican legislature passed the Mobile reorganization bill in February 1870, obliging Governor Smith to appoint a new mayor and city boards and finally scheduling city elections for the following December. The circumstances suddenly broke the municipal logjam stalling the board of trade's economic-subsidy initiatives. For the freedpeople, the wishes of the business community were obviously not the issue. Representative John Carraway tried to abolish the board of trade at this very time and also secured a bill admitting blacks inside Mobile's streetcars, neither of which suggests interest in conciliating the merchant elite.[64] Still, the African American demand for a new government revived the prospects of the aid measures by displacing Mayor Price and the moderate Republicans who blocked them. The swift enactment of subsidy legislation came suddenly within reach, a fact that Mobile's commercial leadership soon recognized full well.

Gov. William H. Smith could not have relished the task of appointing Mobile's civic administration for the third time, considering his previous difficulties in that quarter. Having built some white following as a conservative Republican and facing reelection that fall, the governor sought to

---

62. On Sara Woodward's previous career, see Judith Weisenfeld, "'Who is Sufficient for These Things?' Sara G. Stanley and the American Missionary Association, 1864–1868," *Church History* 60 (December 1991): 493–507.
63. *MDR*, December 10, 11, 12, 14, 1869; *MN*, December 2 ,1869.
64. *MDR*, November 20, 1869.

avoid more controversy in Mobile. Though he naturally had to select a Republican as mayor, he also hoped to appoint a bipartisan, responsible body of boardmembers. He eagerly consulted with the city's business community and Democratic leadership as he had during the previous crises. Some of these contacts decried the endless postponement of elections, this being the fifth externally appointed government since the war ended. Still, realtor Price Williams, chair of the Democratic Central Committee, recommended the reappointment of nominally Republican Mayor Price as the best choice available. At the board of trade, however, very different counsel prevailed. A delegation was dispatched to Montgomery, led by wealthy merchant and wharf-owner Moses Waring. As one insider confirmed, "several gentlemen of wealth and influence" went to the capitol "at the request of our Board of Trade."[65] Their main recommendation Governor Smith found sufficiently arresting that he had his visitors commit it to paper: "we prefer the name of George F. Harrington to that of any other of his party that has been suggested as the Mayor of Mobile." Even in the face of this explicit endorsement, the governor hesitated. A dispatch from Mobile that the appointment would be "*satisfactory to our friends*" reportedly decided the case. As former mayor J. M. Withers concluded, Harrington would be "indebted to democratic, so called, influences for his appointment."[66]

Of all people, why endorse Harrington, the archetypal carpetbagger Radical? There is only one plausible answer: State Representative Harrington, now Speaker of the House, had distinguished himself as a proponent of railroad subsidies. He was an incorporator of two projected railroads, including one with Governor Smith himself.[67] He had been socializing fairly extensively with Mobile's leading Democrats as well, if the *Register*'s later account can be credited.[68] Moses Waring later explained the thinking of his delegation: "We had a conversation with Mr. Harrington. He gave strong assurances that he would use his position for the benefit of Mobile, its property owners and tax payers, and for their protection against oppressive

---

65. Price Williams to Smith, February 26, 1870; and Charles Walsh et al. to Smith, February 4, 1870, Smith Papers; *MDR,* February 13, 15, 1870; Robert H. Smith to William H. Smith, February 18, 1870, Smith Papers.

66. *Montgomery Alabama State Journal,* October 14, 1870; *MDR,* March 22, 1870; U.S Congress, House, *Affairs in Alabama,* 605.

67. "Corporation Papers, Railroads, 1868–1901," December 28, 1868, January 4, 1869, ADAH, microfilm reel M334.

68. *Nebraska City Chronicle* quoted in *MDR,* May 30, 1871.

action, if attempted by the Boards." After consultation with Harrington, Waring and his colleagues also recommended several appointments to the city boards. Afterward, W. D. Mann concluded that if Waring could pack the boards for his purposes, "there couldn't be any great harm in doing a little 'unpacking'" in the interest of the railroad workshop grant. Mann sent recommendations of his own to Governor Smith, who acted upon at least one of them.[69]

Not all conservatives were happy with the board of trade delegation or with the "*Register,* Mann and Harrington ring," as the *Tribune* described it. Some businessmen complained that Waring had placed his own personal interests ahead of the city's. "We are about to be taxed here to answer all sorts of personal schemes," one critic told the governor, specifying the wharf purchase and the workshop grant. The correspondent described Harrington as the worst mayor possible, and he begged Governor Smith to reconsider in favor of one of the moderate Republicans. Others expressed a more generalized dismay at the odd alliances. One unreconstructed ex-Confederate complained that "many of our people," either from interest or inclination, were working "hand in glove" with the hated Yankee rulers.[70] Whatever local support Mayor Harrington would enjoy, his accession to power did not proceed easily, for it was bitterly contested by the outgoing mayor and was only resolved by Caleb Price's arrest.[71] Later, editor Forsyth chose to "congratulate our fellow citizens on the appointment of the new mayor" on the grounds that Harrington was the "honestest rogue of the

69. *MDR,* March 26, June 11, 1870.

70. Ibid., June 11, 1870; Robert H. Smith to W. H. Smith, February 18, 1870; C. H. Maston to "Doctor," May 28, 1870, W. L. Minor Collection, Alderman Library, University of Virginia.

71. The circumstances of Mayor Harrington's accession to office are extraordinarily complicated. Just as Harrington was swearing in the new boardmembers, arresting news came from Montgomery. Someone had physically tampered with the Mobile bill to exempt certain officers, including W. I. Squires, who was probably the party responsible for the forgery. Harrington, as Speaker of the House, had been told of the alterations, but he allowed the bill to proceed anyway. After the discovery of the changes, Caleb Price refused to relinquish the mayor's office. Harrington telegraphed the governor for troops, but Smith preferred to await the decision of the courts. Several confused days followed. The *Register* urged caution, assuring whites this was not their fight, and there was some talk that Major Lankford's followers might install Harrington, but nothing of the sort materialized. After his eventual arrest, Price turned over the office in the face of a judicial order. *MDR,* February 19, 24, 1870; Harrington et al. to Smith, February 16, 1870, Smith Papers.

whole bunch."⁷² Backhanded praise, perhaps, but the *Register* refrained thereafter from abusing or threatening Mayor Harrington as it had Griffin or Horton.

Under these curious auspices Harrington finally assumed power. Over the next ten months, his administration afforded Mobile's African Americans the most direct influence they would ever enjoy. They represented a large minority on the board of aldermen, though Carraway remained the only black on the eight-member council. Several African American moderates accepted Governor Smith's offer of appointment as aldermen, apparently thinking the opportunity too good to decline. Besides, Frederick Bromberg and his scalawag colleagues had deserted them so that further loyalty in that direction perhaps seemed misplaced. Mayor Harrington apparently welcomed these black leaders, and several of the members of the opposing faction were selected as city officers, though the boards froze out the white moderates. James Bragg retained his position as street commissioner, a position worth fifteen hundred dollars a year, Constantine Perez became inspector of weights and measures, and two other Creoles received appointments. In fact, a number of the administrative positions went to blacks previously identified with the moderate faction. To a striking extent, it seems the literacy, standing, and skills of these established leaders held them in good stead as individuals. However, even under Harrington, the African American appointments gravitated to the more modest positions, where little or no official bond was required to assume office, while white Radicals mostly gained the higher-paying city offices.⁷³

Once in office, Mayor Harrington primarily interested himself in economic development, but he countenanced expanded social spending and civil rights measures too. Moreover, with the resignations of Horton and Bromberg, the major proponents of fiscal restraint departed. On municipal matters, at least, the factionalism within the black community became less evident once the new administration assumed control. Black politicians took advantage of their opportunity, though the circumstances only allowed modest practical benefits for their constituents. The problem was that social expenditures the freedpeople sought were temporary, but the subsidy measures under consideration were permanent. This reality dictated that business interests would receive the lasting benefits if the proposals came to fruition.

72. *MN,* February 12, 15, 1870.
73. *MDR,* April 1, 1870.

Immediately upon Harrington's taking power, the city government reaffirmed the legality of the Grand Trunk grant, which was validated by the legislature for good measure. The endorsement included a provision to pay interest on the bonds for three years, a direct liability for the city of up to $360,000. This railroad subsidy was the linchpin of the board of trade recommendations, and the mayor did everything possible to ensure the success of the road, which soon began construction. The remaining three proposals remained in limbo for some time, however. The harbor appropriation proved unnecessary as the Mobile County government, which remained under the control of Gustavus Horton, Frederick Bromberg, and Caleb Price, undertook some reluctant expenditures under legislative prodding; Congressman A. E. Buck secured a federal appropriation as well.[74] The wharf purchase and the New Orleans and Mobile workshop grant remained under consideration, but it seems the acrimony between W. D. Mann and Moses Waring forestalled implementation of either project.

While several major aid proposals remained embroiled in controversy, the freedpeople pressed their demands during this rare moment when their preferences influenced policy. Harrington's police chief, W. W. D. Turner, claimed he received two thousand job applications. Turner proposed a substantial increase in the force in part so that "many worthy men" could "get something to do, thereby making a living for themselves and [their] families." The police budget increased dramatically under Harrington, so perhaps Chief Turner got his wish, and blacks clearly did well in terms of employment. African Americans held 37 percent of police jobs in 1870, an all-time high and approaching their proportion in Mobile's population.[75] While most of these officers were designated as mulattoes in the census, a sizable minority were described as black. Harrington's policies thus eroded the caste preference that had been so divisive when Mayor Horton first sought to integrate the force. Moreover, most of the officers were both propertyless and without activist backgrounds, suggesting that the benefits

---

74. State of Alabama, *Acts of the General Assembly of Alabama, 1869–1870* (Montgomery, 1870), 28–9; *MDR,* June 1, 1870; Board of Common Council, Minutes, June 21, 1870, reel 21; Board of Revenue Commissioners, Minutes, May 23, 1870, February 23, 1871, Mobile County Commission, Mobile Government Plaza.

75. *MDR,* June 11, 1870; W. W. D. Turner to Harrington, March 10, 1870, folder 2, envelope 5, box 14, RMBACC. On the census figures in a national context, see Rousey, *Policing the Southern City,* 137.

from the police jobs spread beyond the established ranks of black notables.[76]

The changing civil administration and the city's encouragement of job growth likely strengthened the freedpeople at the workplace too. In October 1870 the "draymen, press gangs, and other workingmen" went on strike in support of a $2.50 daily wage. The short stoppage was peaceable and the employers quickly capitulated.[77] There were other gains in the private sector. After years of legislation and litigation over excluding blacks, the streetcar companies finally made concessions. In compliance with state and local law, all the companies save one admitted black patrons to the inside of all cars.[78] Councilman Carraway proposed an ordinance to compel admission on the remaining line, but the issue of segregation inside the cars remained unresolved. In April, reportedly in celebration of the Fifteenth Amendment's ratification, several black women entered the white compartment on the Conception Street line. Lacking police assistance, company superintendent P. J. Pillans ordered his employees to remove one rider, who promptly had him arrested for assault. The affair wound up before Mayor Harrington, who fined Pillans $50 and suggested the matter would be resolved in a higher court. Carraway was present at Pillans's trial, following the outcome closely, which suggested the importance he and his constituents placed on the issue. Through the early 1870s, the streetcar companies sought a practical solution. In one case blacks were separated by a grille from white patrons, but the situation on the other lines is unclear.[79] In the end the freedpeople apparently gained their point on this intensely contested symbolic issue. By the next decade, Mobile's streetcars

---

76. An examination of the manuscript census reveals fifteen mulatto and twelve black officers. While mixed-ancestry individuals thus were disproportionately represented, the diversity of those employed seems noteworthy. While a few known activists, such as Wilborne Boyd and Samuel Wilson, were on the force, the bulk seem to have been politically obscure. Eighteen of twenty-seven officers reported no property at all. Population Schedules, Mobile City, Mobile County, Ala., Manuscript U.S. Census for 1870 (M593), RG 29.

77. *Mobile Republican,* October 20, 1870; *MDR,* October 18, 19, 21, 1870. For a subsequent strike by steamboat hands, see *MDR,* December 3, 1870.

78. *MN,* July 5, 1869, Works Projects Administration, "Transcriptions from the *Mobile Nationalist*"; *MDR,* April 29, 1870; State of Alabama, *Acts of Alabama, 1869–1870,* 28–9.

79. *MDR,* April 29, 1870; Maria Waterbury, *Seven Years among the Freedmen* (Chicago, 1890), 115.

were effectively integrated, both de jure and to some extent de facto, and would remain so through the turn of the century.[80]

Given the attainment of substantial governmental influence, the more experienced African American politicians naturally provided leadership for their less seasoned comrades. Their conduct suggests a fiscal dimension to the other factional contrasts. Alderman Lawrence Berry distinguished himself as an advocate for aggressive measures to benefit black constituents, especially the poorer ones. He proposed having the city physician attend ill destitute persons upon the certification of city officers. He also secured an inquiry into the sufficiency of police pay and endorsed reform of the chain gang as well.[81] Berry backed Putnam's free public schools as well as the expansive economic-subsidy measures explicitly as a vehicle for benefiting his needy constituents. His colleague John Carraway provided a counterweight on the common council. As a state legislator and a newly minted attorney, Carraway had expertise upon which to draw as a local lawmaker. He was Berry's longtime rival, since the days they had struggled over the *Nationalist,* in state as well as local politics. Carraway even denounced Berry before the legislature, blaming him as sergeant at arms for the fraudulent alteration of the Mobile municipal bill. Carraway was more identified with the Horton faction, which inclined him toward relative fiscal caution and varied positions on the individual subsidy proposals under consideration. Though aggressive on civil rights, especially the streetcar issue, he was less identified with the sort of spending bills Berry promoted relentlessly.[82]

The African American popular constituency also pressed directly for more civic services. Mobile, like most cities, had concentrated its infrastruc-

---

80. August Meier and Elliott Rudwick, "The Boycott Movement against Jim Crow Streetcars in the South, 1900–1906," *Journal of American History* 55 (March 1969): 758–60, 762–4; David Ernest Alsobrook, "Alabama's Port City: Mobile during the Progressive Era, 1896–1917" (Ph.D. diss., Auburn University, 1983), 135–51. In 1902, after repeated stalled efforts, the Mobile city government moved to segregate the streetcar system by law. A massive African American boycott ensued, lasting over the next several months. Though eventually defeated, the implication of the resistance is evident. The changes brought by the Reconstruction challenge to subordination presumably were substantial enough in practice to elicit this response.

81. "Ordinance to Provide Medical Treatment for Destitute and Indigent Persons," September 8, 1870, folder 3, envelope 4, box 14; and resolution, August 11, 1870, folder 2, envelope 4, box 14, RMBACC; *MDR,* February 19, 1869.

82. Foner, *Freedom's Lawmakers,* 41; *Montgomery Advertiser,* January 11, 1870.

ture spending downtown to facilitate commerce and satisfy the wealthier neighborhoods. Now, though, demands for spending came from elsewhere. One Republican club petitioned for street lamps for the northwestern portion of the city. There were "fewer lights in the streets therein in proportion to the population and supporters of the Union than any other portion of the city." Crime being a problem in the suburbs, these requests made sense and met with official favor. City Engineer W. I. Squires reported in August on the "large number of lamps recently erected." His report revealed that they went disproportionately into the long neglected interior areas like Davis Avenue, the principal thoroughfare through the African American neighborhood. The majority-black Seventh Ward in particular received much of the new construction.[83]

These initiatives inevitably cost money, especially in conjunction with the railroad subsidies. A later fiscal report claimed that municipal spending under Harrington went from $23,000 per month to $41,000. These numbers are difficult to substantiate because of a subsequent change in the method of reporting figures, but spending clearly went up, increasing by over one-third for the police alone. By the summer of 1870, moreover, taxes were coming in unusually slowly. The city government encountered an unanticipated cash-flow crisis, necessitating a short-term loan of $60,000.[84] African Americans on the boards, along with their white Republican colleagues, were shaken into greater scrutiny of city finances. They soon acquired some surprising credentials as budget cutters, reining in their colleagues' spending habits and examining the mayor's actions more carefully. John Carraway, for example, served on a subcommittee to investigate the Grand Trunk bonds. The councilmen concluded that they had been removed from the possession of the city unlawfully. It seems that the full $1.5 million in bonds were delivered to the company rather than just the initial installment of $300,000 as called for under the aid law. Carraway and his colleagues concluded that "informality was practiced by the officials of the city," and they forced the return of the excess bonds. Carraway and his colleagues censured the company's actions, successfully insisting that the grant's original provisions be adhered to. Drawing on his experience as

---

83. Franklin D. Turner et al. to Mayor, June 28, 1870, folder 2, envelope 5, box 14; and W. I. Squires to Common Council, August 16, 1870, folder 2, envelope 5, box 14, RMBACC.

84. U.S. Congress, House, *Affairs in Alabama*, 607–16; Ways and Means Committee, Minutes, March 23, May 8, June 24, 1870, Miscellaneous Books, Mobile Municipal Archives, reel 12; ordinance, June 16, 1870, folder 3, envelope 4, box 14, RMBACC.

state representative, Carraway personally accused the company of lying to the legislature to evade the requirement for $250,000 in cash. On another occasion, Carraway proposed investigating conflict of interest on the common council and whether City Engineer Squires could be removed for cause.[85]

Well might Carraway have been concerned for Mobile's interest and for his own reputation. By the summer, rumors of bribery in city government were becoming common. It is difficult to evaluate the merit of the accusations or to assess the precise involvement of African American leaders. Still, while black boardmembers were unified on most issues of constituent concern, on peripheral matters they might pursue individual gain without much political damage. Perhaps the most revealing study of this complex interaction can be seen in the Nicholson Pavement proposal. In the summer of 1870, W. D. Mann proposed paving the downtown with treated wood, which was then in brief vogue in Memphis and other cities. The cost was half a million dollars, and Mann was president of the only local company capable of undertaking such a job. Mann and Forsyth's *Register* relentlessly promoted the measure: the city debt after all was "not heavy," and it was "no argument against this improvement that the city and county have done their duty in reference to other improvements—Harbor, Grand Trunk, etc., etc." The owners of the company were prominent Democrats, such as Forsyth, G. M. Parker, and G. A. Ketchum, but the paving measure proved controversial as Moses Waring mobilized the board of trade in opposition. Among the freedpeople, Berry endorsed the proposal, while Carraway seemed less supportive, insisting that the contract must be let to the lowest bidder. After considerable debate, the city boards agreed on a public referendum, which meant that the African American electorate would have a major role in the outcome. Both sides rushed to secure the endorsement of popular figures in public rallies.[86]

85. "Report of the Special Committee," June 14, 1870, folder 2, envelope 6, box 17, RMBACC; "Report of Special Committee on Missing Bonds of Mobile and Alabama Grand Trunk Railroad Company," May 24, 1870, in Works Projects Administration, "Interesting Transcriptions and Cataloging Notes from the Aldermen Minutes of the City of Mobile" (Works Projects Administration transcript, 1938), Mobile Municipal Archives; Board of Common Council, Minutes, April 19, 1870, reel 21.

86. *MDR,* June 1, 1870; "Report of Select Committee," May 31, 1870, folder 4, envelope 5, box 14, RMBACC. On the Memphis pavement issue, which helped bankrupt that city during Reconstruction, see Lynette Boney Wrenn, *Crisis and Commission Government in Memphis: Elite Rule in a Gilded Age City* (Knoxville, 1998), 17.

The African American leadership openly divided on the Nicholson Pavement measure. Some of the established leaders in the Horton faction, such as Philip Joseph, opposed it, whereas several of the more militant spokesmen like Berry were conspicuous among the proponents. W. B. F. Bates, for example, voiced the common arguments for aid. Naysayers had claimed that railroad grants would ruin the town, but they had not—yet—and neither would pavements. Bates promised that the proposal would give the members of the audience jobs and "a chance to lay up something toward buying a home, instead of lying round idle all summer" during the slack work season. Allen Alexander agreed that the city needed more money in circulation, alleging that the black opponents of the measure had been bought off. He charged that his old ally Major Lankford had offered to carry the Seventh Ward for the proposal for five hundred dollars. When Lankford did not receive the cash, he "went to the other [antipavement] side where he probably did get it or more, as they had $7,000 to distribute." Whatever the truth of this charge, the divided counsel of these leaders seemed to make little difference. Voters rejected the scheme, and even wholesale ballot stuffing, cheerfully admitted by the *Register,* could not turn the tide. The Seventh Ward voted it down by a gigantic margin, which would suggest that even poorer African Americans were not uncritical proponents of public expenditure. "The negroes defeated the pavement," noted the paper, "and they did it in defiance of their accustomed leaders."[87]

Accepting money for public advocacy of measures was legal and common in that era, but the sense that officials were for sale colored the public discourse. For example, in July 1870 Councilman William Miller pushed for an investigation of reports that city officers were selling positions on the police force. There was some plausibility to this claim, given the mercenary motives of some public officials. Police Chief W. W. D. Turner privately wrote, "I am not seeking office for the honor of the thing, for I have arrived at a time of life when those things have little temptation for me."[88] The *Register* later alleged that no necessary measures for business interests could be had "without cash down." In one case aldermen touched on such rumors with reference to themselves. During the pavement campaign, Alderman J. R. Eastburn, upon being appointed to a subcommittee, asked if

---

87. *MDR,* June 11, July 1, June 3, 14, 1870.
88. "Report of Special Committee on Missing Bonds," May 24, 1870; Turner to Warmoth, January 23, 1871, Henry Clay Warmoth Papers, SHC, reel 2.

it would pay since "he understood that was the rule here." One of his colleagues joked that he should be allowed five hundred dollars from "the corruption fund" for his services. It is difficult to evaluate the precise meaning of such talk, but the boardmembers often were men of modest means assuming unpaid duty, and the necessity of gaining a livelihood impinged on public duties.[89]

The most ethically suspect action of the city government occurred late in Harrington's term with the enactment of the long-delayed wharf purchase. It seems that after the pavement measure was defeated, Waring and Mann finally arrived at an accommodation; the wharves would be purchased by the city for $360,000, with Mann receiving $13,000 from the wharf owners' share.[90] Mann later denied this, but the evidence is overwhelming that Harrington gave him the bonds. Democratic officials alleged in emphatic terms that bribes had been paid to secure the approval of the boards. A memo in the city records claims that aldermen had sold their votes for "what was put in their individual pockets." Upon assuming office, Harrington's successor similarly observed that the "manner in which this pretended wharf purchase was consummated is but too painfully apparent to the citizens of Mobile." One strong piece of evidence suggests something of the sort occurred. After the wharf vote, moderate Republican councilman C. F. Moulton resigned his seat, citing the "public disgrace some of the members are bringing upon the body." He wrote his colleague James Gillette that "to your knowledge, & mine, a quorum was twice defeated, while members stood at the door of the Council Chamber, refusing to enter until they [were] bribed to enter. It is enough for me."[91] The testimony here, in a private letter to a fellow eyewitness, seems persuasive, though the wording might suggest a distinction between being bribed for votes and being paid to attend a meeting. Moulton does not directly allege that the wharf bill passed by actual bribes for votes, which might suggest a concern for appearances if nothing more. Some years later, however, several former

89. *MDR*, December 1, August 10, 1870.
90. E. M. Underhill to Boards of Aldermen and Common Council, December 6, 1871, folder 2, envelope 6, box 15, RMBACC.
91. Memo, "Jennings 1869 & 1870 vote on Wharf and Grand Trunk," folder 2, envelope 4, box 14; and M. Horst to Boards of Aldermen and Common Council, January 2, 1871, folder 2, envelope 7, box 16, RMBACC; C. F. Moulton to James Gillette, October 8, 1870, James Gillette Papers, LC.

boardmembers accused Republican wharf-owner M. D. Wickersham of having bribed them.[92]

In the midst of these frenzied efforts to finalize the subsidy measures, the repeatedly postponed municipal elections occurred as scheduled in December 1870. There had been some talk that the Republican legislature might delay the elections yet again at the last minute. The November statewide canvass ended that possibility, for the election of Democrat Robert B. Lindsey as governor and a Democratic House of Representatives transformed the wider political context. In the subsequent city elections, liquor merchant Martin Horst defeated George F. Harrington for mayor by a substantial margin, 4,759 to 3,113. The entire Democratic ticket won, ending the era of direct black political influence in Mobile. Still, irreversible decisions had been made during Harrington's administration, and not everyone on the Democratic side was displeased with what had been achieved. One conservative later conceded that, except for the wharf purchase, the various subsidies were "generally approved" by the citizens. As a board of trade report observed, "All of the projects now completed and in progress being realized, Mobile may congratulate herself that her whole duty in that line is done, and may rest from her labors, and await the ripening of the fruits of her capital and sagacity."[93]

Mayor Harrington's defeat finished his public career, but it had a revealing sequel. The ex-mayor took his repudiation to heart, especially the lack of gratitude of those who had helped place him in office. Harrington penned an essay on the fate of Yankee visitors in the South for a Nebraska newspaper. The typical newcomer, he wrote, was "taken to the 'Board of Trade,' where he listens to elaborate discussions of great schemes and projects for the improvement of the city and State and country." These commercial boards, he concluded, were delusively welcoming. They were really "among the most dangerous of political and sectional organizations," bitterly hostile to all things northern. The widely decried carpetbaggers and ignorant black officeholders Harrington blamed on conservative intransigence. The ex-mayor apparently felt he had been deceived by the blandishments of his late collaborators, and indeed his own financial benefit from

---

92. *MDR,* January 22, 1878. By the late 1870s, Morris Wickersham was so unpopular in the black community that former boardmembers implicated themselves in the hope of costing him his position as U.S. postmaster.

93. *MDR,* December 8, 10, 1876; Mobile Board of Trade, "Annual Report of the Mobile Board of Trade for the Year Ending November 30, 1870" ([Mobile,] n.d.), 18.

public service proved short lived. He died a few years later, his destitute widow reduced to begging his former political associates for help.[94]

As for the African Americans who served in municipal government during this period, a fair evaluation of their performance during this Radical interregnum is difficult. The disruption of the racist monopoly of state power opened a window of political opportunity that they utilized effectively for short-term gains. Taking advantage of Harrington's receptivity to their demands, black boardmembers expanded social spending and opened up city-government jobs to African Americans. On the aid issue, some, especially those identified with the moderates, such as John Carraway, demonstrated some fiscal caution. L. S. Berry, however, articulated the dominant tendency: collaboration with those in the business community who favored aid, for blacks would benefit from any successful program of economic development. Special-interest money apparently flowed, tainting public discourse, but it probably only facilitated measures that made sense for an impoverished constituency. The subsidies were far riskier than the African American boardmembers realized, but as subsequent events revealed, the Radical faction had plenty of Democratic assistance in wreaking the city's finances.

Beginning in January 1871, Democratic Mayor Horst moved quickly to reverse the policies of his predecessors, firing the whole police force outright. One local woman found that "the politics of the country are better" because "you see no negro policemen now, all white folks." The press professed satisfaction with the mayor's policies, despite the rapid dismissal of several of Horst's new officers for drinking on the job. The *Register* also praised the new officials for again cracking down on unemployed freedpeople: "We are glad to see that our energetic Mayor manifests a purpose to deal rigorously with these idlers, and rid the city of their presence." On fiscal matters, his all-white, all-Democratic boards complained bitterly of the incompetence of their predecessors. Horst discovered there was no provision to pay the city debt, which was due the very day he took office. To pay interest on the bonds, he had to leave the police and other employees unpaid for months.[95] There were more mundane problems to be dealt with

94. *Nebraska City Chronicle* quoted in *MDR,* May 30, 1871; Mrs. Harrington to Gillette, August 2, 1877, Gillette Papers.

95. Maria Barnwall to "Augusta," April 26, 1871, quoted in Henry Allen Lowe Jr., *The Journals of Henry Allen Lowe Jr., 1869–1877* (N.p., 1992), 32; *MDR,* April 25, 15, 7, July 2, 1871.

too. The tax collector found the records of his predecessor thoroughly confused. The minutes of the board of alderman actually had been removed from city hall. According to an investigating committee, City Clerk Lou Mayer had been appropriated $514 for the task of indexing the 1870 minutes and had not yet finished; the committee concluded he had tampered with the text to provide legal cover for his behavior. (The volume is still missing.)[96]

Over the coming months, it became clear that Mobile was in financial trouble. The property-tax rate had increased fourfold since before the war. The city treasurer reported that unpaid taxes went up from $125,000 in July 1871 to $215,000 eighteen months later. Mobile's economic woes meant that taxpayers were staggering under the added burden, which suggested that cutbacks were essential. The problem for Horst was that the spending lobby remained powerful within his own Democratic party. In January 1871 the board of trade immediately recommended "a well ordered system to improve the sanitary condition of the city," even if this might cause "increased expenditure."[97] A casual visitor observed that same month that the dredging of Mobile's harbor and the extension of railroads were the "chief topics of interest among the merchants," who were eager to keep pace with rival ports. Even as it became evident that cutbacks were urgent, the board of trade stubbornly resisted retrenchment, and the wharf dispute illustrates the wider problem. Upon assuming office, the Democratic boards repealed the workshop grant, and they tried to void the wharf purchase but were stopped by the courts. Officials then looked for a way to pay the $28,800 annual interest on the bonds and decided to charge rent for use of the wharves. The board of trade publicly denounced the policy, as did the *Register*. Stung, the Democratic boardmembers recalled the recent history of the issue: "under urgent pressure from the Board of Trade and the mercantile community," the city had loaned its credit "so largely to railway enterprises" that it would require taxation to the limit allowed by law.[98]

96. John McGrath to Mayor Horst, March 14, 1871, folder 3, envelope 7, box 16; and "Report of Special Committee Relative to the Removal of a Record Book from the Clerk's Office," January 17, 1871, folder 2, envelope 6, box 15, RMBACC.

97. Board of Aldermen, Minutes, September 5, 1871, reel 5; "Report of City Treasurer on Redemptions of Property Purchased at Tax Sales to July 1st, 1873," folder 2, envelope 5, box 19; and Board of Control of Board of Trade, Resolutions, January 28, 1871, folder 2, envelope 7, box 16, RMBACC.

98. Robert Somers, *The Southern States since the War, 1870–1871,* ed. Malcolm McMil-

The fate of William D. Mann's most ambitious project demonstrates the wider trend of events. Mann now was the prime mover in yet another enterprise, the Mobile and Northwestern Railroad from the gulf to the Mississippi delta. The proposed railroad was thinly capitalized relative to the Grand Trunk line; Mann by this time had sold the *Register,* being overextended financially. The timing of the proposal was moreover unfortunate, given statewide developments. Late in 1870, incoming Democratic governor Robert B. Lindsey discovered massive irregularities in his predecessor's endorsement of railroad bonds, with hundreds of thousands in unauthorized issues. When in January 1871 the Alabama and Chattanooga Railroad suspended interest payments, Governor Lindsey was unwilling to honor the state's obligation to pay until the legality of the bonds was resolved. Lindsey was indeed in a quandary, but his upright course had catastrophic economic consequences. When Alabama defaulted on its state-endorsed bonds, it compromised the funding for all projects then underway, dooming many of them to bankruptcy. Mobile's civic leadership blithely ignored these developments, and one visitor marveled at the continuing support for Mann's railroad, for "the promoters must be aware that the resource of State bonds is for the present played out in Alabama."[99] The visitor was downright skeptical that it could be built: the markets were already saturated with Mobile securities, and the Grand Trunk bonds were being sold at a heavy discount. Despite the troubling omens, the board of trade "unanimously" recommended the grant of one million dollars to Mann's project, with the emphatic endorsement of the *Register.* The Democratic boards endorsed the measure, the aldermen by a vote of twenty-two to one, with a later provision that the subsidy be paid at a premium in gold. If Harrington's Radical administration had irresponsibly overextended the city finances, his Democratic successors' additional outlays were even more reckless.[100]

Mann headed off to bribe the Mississippi legislature for more subsidies, and the unfortunate sequel was perhaps predictable. Both the Mobile and Northwestern and the Grand Trunk encountered trouble unloading the city-endorsed bonds on investors. The Grand Trunk built fifty-nine miles of

---

lan (University, Ala., 1965), 182; "Ordinance of January 3, 1871," Ordinance Books, Mobile Municipal Archives, reel 5; *MDR,* September 19, 1871.

99. Mobile and Northwestern Railroad, *The Mobile and Northwestern Railroad Project* (New York, 1871), 7, 21; *MDR,* March 13, 1871; Somers, *Southern States since the War,* 183.

100. *MDR,* July 2, January 8, June 15, 1871.

track before running out of money, and in December 1871 the *Register* noted the company's unpaid and destitute black laborers in the city. Mann's railroad made even less progress, grading only a few hundred yards at either end of the line. Both railroads suspended construction well before the crash of 1873 hit, essentially finishing them off. Both collapsed before they could qualify for the full city subsidy, but they doomed Mobile to eventual bankruptcy nonetheless. Nor did the new administration restore the city government to probity: the incoming city attorney soon resigned after being implicated in an arson-for-profit scheme involving members of the fire department. Major bribery scandals shook the city in the early 1870s under Democratic rule.[101]

In all, Mobile's fiscal ruin was a bipartisan, interracial community project. African American leaders bore significant responsibility, and some sought mercenary goals, but the prime movers were elsewhere—among them the Democratic business leaders that helped put Harrington in power and Mann and Forsyth's *Register*. The mingled responsibility eventually became so obvious that even the white electorate rebelled. In an ironic way, moreover, the railroad program held the promise of political survival for the Republicans who formally enacted it, for it was such a disaster that Democratic successors could not cope with the consequences. For the next decade, the city's woes, combined with the details of how these events transpired, fueled "independent" political movements against the elite business leadership. The dire circumstances allowed an anomalous resurgence of black and Republican local political influence even as Reconstruction wound down nationally. Republican control of the U.S. government, moreover, allowed African American activists to redirect their energies toward influence over the federal bureaucracy, and they increasingly turned their attention toward this remaining venue in the years ahead.

101. Ibid., December 21, 1871; John Willis, *Forgotten Time: The Yazoo-Mississippi Delta after the Civil War* (Charlottesville and London, 2000), 94–6; "Testimony Taken by Dumping Ground Investigating Committee," August 7, 1872, folder 2, envelope 6, box 17, RMBACC.

Mobile scenes suggestive of the casual character of labor on the docks. The ship is the *Hard Cash*, and the photographs probably date to the late nineteenth century.
Courtesy Michael McEachern Collection, University of South Alabama Archives, Mobile

Creole Fire Station, built ca. 1869. This imposing building, bearing the name "Creole," suggests the pride members took in their longstanding organization. *From* Souvenir History of the Mobile Fire and Police Departments *(Mobile, 1902), courtesy University of South Alabama Archives, Mobile*

Albert Griffin, editor of the *Mobile Nationalist,* moderate
Republican leader and eventual political exile.
Courtesy Riley County Historical Society, Manhattan, Kansas

This front-page racist caricature from *Frank Leslie's Illustrated Newspaper* (November 4, 1865), depicting voodoo in Mobile, illustrates the cultural distance many whites felt from Mobile's emancipated slaves.

Harper's Weekly rendering of the explosion of the United States Receiving Magazine at Mobile on May 25, 1865.

The aftermath of the ammunition explosion, north of downtown Mobile. *Courtesy Massachusetts Commandery Military Order of the Loyal Legion and the U.S. Army Military History Institute, Carlisle Barracks, Carlisle, Pennsylvania*

5

The Mainspring of It All
The Racial Politics of Federal Employment

From the beginning of Reconstruction, Mobile's black leadership divided along lines of wealth, education, and caste, and once established, these alignments persisted, along with wider continuities of popular support. Thus the collapse of Republican rule in Mobile did not end African American internal struggles, rather it intensified them and gave them broader significance. Defeat propelled local conflicts into state and national politics as existing rivalries were absorbed in the larger controversy surrounding the reelection of Pres. U. S. Grant. Popular factionalism peaked in the early 1870s, and to a striking extent, this mobilization turned on the allocation of federal employment. In the heyday of the spoils system, Mobile's Republican internal struggles revolved around patronage. For activists, the issue of government jobs fused an urgent practical concern with matters of wider significance.

If federal employment became a pressing matter, it made sense in the context of bitter electoral defeat. Democratic state and local victories marked a political milestone for activists dependent on politics for a living, often in dramatic personal terms. For instance, Lawrence S. Berry's life unraveled quickly once the Democrats won. Money woes had long beset him, and for years Berry threatened to leave depressed Mobile, believing jobs would be more readily available elsewhere. He tried several professions in his quest for a livelihood. In mid-1868 he opened a school, and he also went into a short-lived grocery partnership with his fellow activists Durham Davis and Constantine Perez. Berry also had been sergeant at arms of the Alabama House of Representatives, but the November 1870 election results eliminated such Republican state patronage posts. He spent the early weeks of 1871 unemployed and apparently withdrew money from a joint bank account without the knowledge of his former partners. An unmarried man with no property, Berry reportedly found solace for his troubles in the bottle. One Saturday morning he was found in an outhouse behind a tenement on Conception Street with "his throat cut from ear to ear." The *Mobile Daily Register* hailed his apparent suicide, suggesting other Republicans might follow his example.[1]

The freedman Berry, of course, had been the longtime voice of the more restive elements in the political community from his first days at the *Mobile Nationalist*. His main rival, John Carraway, fared little better after the Democratic sweep despite all his cultivation of respectability. In the late 1860s Carraway was the most distinguished black politician in Mobile, having served in the constitutional convention, the legislature, and as a city councilman. Despite his prominence, when Carraway died in April 1871, he had no real property to his name. He had just opened a business with several hundred dollars in merchandize, but it was little enough to support the wife and baby he left behind.[2] The circumstances of his passing must have been particularly galling, for he had just been implicated in a major Reconstruction scandal, the Alabama and Chattanooga Railroad's wholesale corruption of the legislature.[3] One of his black colleagues claimed that Carraway had taken a bribe of five hundred dollars for his vote. Carraway resolutely protested his innocence to the point of a literal deathbed denial of wrongdoing. The denial may have been true, for his accuser, future congressman Jeremiah Haralson, admitted to taking bribes and perhaps was not a reliable source. Even if guilty, Representative Carraway at least manifested some concern for his reputation, for he spent his last hours penning defenses of his official probity.[4]

1. *MN,* June 18, 1868; *Durham Davis, C. Perez, L. S. Berry, Copartners, v. Freedmen's Savings and Trust Company,* spring term 1871, Records of the Circuit Court, Mobile County, University of South Alabama Archives, Mobile; City Tax Lists, 1867–70, Mobile Municipal Archives; *MDR,* January 19, February 19, March 29, 1871.

2. Foner, *Freedom's Lawmakers,* 41; City Tax Lists, 1867–70, Mobile Municipal Archives; Population Schedules, Mobile County, Ala., Manuscript U.S. Census for 1870 (M593), RG 29, reel 31.

3. *MDR,* April 16, 1871.

4. *Montgomery Alabama State Journal,* March 3, 1871; State of Alabama, *Report of Com-*

The unquiet demise of these two leaders emphasizes the wider significance of how political activists supported themselves while they attended to public business. Modern historians of Reconstruction seldom attend much to this practical issue, but it absorbed much of the energy of African American politicians. Activists cut off most employment opportunities when they became prominent as Republicans, rendering themselves dependent on political patronage. One African American jail inmate described his profession to a census taker as "Politician," which suggests the volatility of this line of work.[5] With the reverses the Republican party experienced in late 1870, most municipal and state jobs abruptly closed to blacks. For the moment, little possibility of a comeback seemed likely. In Mobile, however, there was one alternate source of political employment remaining safely in party hands. The scores of federal positions in the customhouse became increasingly important to the material welfare and status of Republican activists. But who would get these jobs? Patronage positions became the focus of intense controversy in the coming years, as local factional rivalries were redeployed on a wider state and federal canvass. Harrington's Radical faction and Bromberg's moderate following dovetailed into national patterns of factional alignment by the early 1870s, largely fueled by this very concern. As the issue of employment for black activists became heated, moreover, it took on wider implications, becoming a civil rights issue for the community more broadly.

Mobile's apple of discord, as it were, was the Treasury Department post of collector for the port, the most important federal job in Alabama. The collector received perhaps a million dollars in collections annually. Paying a generous salary of approximately $5,000 in fees, the position allowed valuable business contacts among the merchants. In the 1870s the collector also dispensed some fifty or more jobs in addition to lesser temporary posts.[6] These allowed the collector, in combination with the postmaster and internal revenue officials, to influence state and local Republican conventions. Such organizational meetings normally were the preserve of those

---

mittee to Investigate Alleged Frauds in Issuance of Railroad Bonds and Bonds of the State for the Use of Railroads (Montgomery, 1871), 29.

5. See William Walker (no. 440), Population Schedules, Mobile City, Mobile County, Ala., Manuscript U.S. Census for 1880 (T9), RG 29, reel 25.

6. Willard Warner to Mrs. Lyman Warner, November 18, 1871, Willard Warner Papers, Tennessee State Library and Archives, reel 1; "Statement of Numbers of Persons Employed," June 30, 1876, box 4, AP-246, RG 56.

with professional interest in the proceedings. The expectation was that subordinate officials would follow their superior's lead or risk their positions. The collector of the port thus occupied an intensely political position, subject as it was to congressional confirmation. The position had important ramifications for local party politics too, as was reflected in Collector William Miller's appointment to the city council. It also held intense interest for the black community of Mobile as a visible symbol of an administration's commitment to them.

With U. S. Grant's inauguration as president in the spring of 1869, Alabama's congressional delegation united on a choice for collector, William Miller. Miller was the one truly wealthy Republican in the city, owning a ten-thousand-acre plantation, and was also a cotton merchant with longtime business interests in Mobile. He was a strong Union man, the prewar employer of Gustavus Horton, in fact. Miller had little political experience but had demonstrated considerable audacity in Greene County, having utilized his social position to assume office as probate judge under Military Reconstruction. The local Freedmen's Bureau agent marveled at his "iron will" in the face of being "hooted" in the streets. His son-in-law, Alexander Boyd, would soon be murdered in a spectacular Klan raid. Miller's Republican credentials were thus strong. In addition, his means made it possible for him to bankroll the local party press, the *Mobile Republican,* giving him some independence of his political sponsors. Still, his social standing and priorities placed him in tension with the African Americans who composed the bulk of the party in Mobile and elsewhere.[7]

Given the prevailing expectations of the spoils system, Republicans anticipated dramatic local changes from the party's national triumph. As Congressman F. W. Kellogg observed, the new collector might "very properly wish to fill the offices under him with his friends."[8] Given the circumstances, the advent of Republican rule raised novel racial issues. Up to this time, African Americans held only menial federal positions in Mobile, conservatives having held most of them under Pres. Andrew Johnson. With the new administration, Republicans widely anticipated both conditions would change. For the *Nationalist,* it was "scarcely necessary to remind" the new officeholders where Republican votes came from, adding that blacks were

7. R. A. Wilson to Beecher, January 9, 1869, M809, RG 105, reel 18; *Talladega Sun,* April 19, 1870; *MDR,* December 1, 1870.
8. F. W. Kellogg to Grant, March 29, 1869, box 5, AP-247, RG 56.

not even asking for jobs they could not fill well. The *Montgomery Alabama State Journal* came to precisely the same conclusion, warning the officeholders that the freedpeople would not be trifled with. Incoming postmaster Frederick G. Bromberg, for one, got the message. Democrats soon complained of the indignity of receiving their mail from black employees, Philip Joseph and Rev. Wilber Strong prominent among them.[9]

Collector Miller saw things differently. All his initial customs appointments were white, as were those in the internal revenue office. The *Register* gleefully observed that blacks were "left out in the cold," though criticism did induce Miller to make some appointments thereafter.[10] More strikingly, the collector retained several conservative or apolitical white employees. As he admitted, "I have failed to find Republicanism the only qualification necessary." Of the Republicans Miller did appoint, several were members of the legislature, using federal work to supplement their salaries. Even the lieutenant governor secured a position, and Miller's policy effectively muted criticism in Montgomery. However, in Washington, Miller's bipartisan appointments raised immediate criticism from Republican leaders to the Grant administration. Sen. Willard Warner repeatedly descended on the customhouse for personal inspections, making little effort to hide his displeasure.[11]

Miller defended his bipartisan appointment policy in various ways. As a businessman, he prized efficiency, and experienced officials facilitated a smooth transition. Whatever the criticism, Miller could not "run the Custom House so as to make it a success without competent men."[12] Being absent from Mobile a good deal on personal business, he wanted subordinates who were proved trustworthy, given the rampant postwar corruption scandals among his predecessors. He privately informed superiors that personally honest Republicans were scarce, an issue of some urgency during Mayor George Harrington's municipal rule. Furthermore, higher U.S. officials dealt extensively with the merchant community, who could hardly be

---

9. *MN,* April 23, 1869; *Montgomery Alabama State Journal,* April 8, 1869; *MDR,* May 21, 1871.

10. Newspaper clipping in Charles McCord to "Respected Sir," June 6, 1869, box 1, AP-246, RG 56.

11. Miller to Boutwell, March 5, 1870, November 13, 1869, box 1, AP-246, RG 56; J. H. Parker to Miller, June 21, 23, November 2, 3, 1869, Letters Sent, Customhouse, Mobile, Ala., letterpress book, 1869–71, RG 36.

12. Miller to Boutwell, February 14, 1871, box 1, AP-246, RG 56.

expected to cooperate with blacks in such roles. Then there were the political benefits: federal officials were deluged with twelve hundred applications for jobs, reportedly mostly from Democrats, which offered some opportunity to reach out to a formally hostile constituency.[13]

The customhouse afforded Republican politicians an independent power base. An enhanced white following might insulate the party from black political demands, stabilizing Republican rule under socially respectable leadership. This fit well with the longtime political strategy of the moderates. From his exile in Kansas, Albert Griffin defended the necessity of this policy, arguing that white converts could be had in Mobile if the freedmen and their demands could be controlled. It was crucial that federal officials should be men to whom the freedmen could look for "sound advice and proper guidance."[14] Griffin offered a disillusioned account of dealing with his former allies: while blacks were true Republicans, they were "generally ignorant and often vicious." Only responsible, moderate leadership backed by federal patronage could keep them in line. The strategic motivations aside, there was an additional agenda, less openly expressed but pressing nonetheless. Federal officials had to live in Mobile, in a community where the opposition had demonstrated every capacity to hound Republicans out of town. The *Register,* in particular, turned public ridicule on and off like a spigot. Under the circumstances, Republican officials tended to make concessions to stave off abuse, as the *Nationalist* observed. Among federal officeholders, this trend was particularly strong since they had something tangible to offer in exchange for elite toleration. Mobile's businessmen often saw the logic of coexisting with federal bureaucrats as long as they facilitated commerce and did not make themselves too obnoxious as Republican partisans. Collector Miller prided himself that the "wealth and intelligence" of Mobile had more confidence in him than in "any Republican in the State." His estimate was accurate: future mayor Gideon M. Parker praised the collector for allowing businessmen all the latitude he could as an official, given that others were angling after his job.[15]

The key to (white) social respectability for federal officials was in distancing themselves from blacks and their demands. One Union veteran and

---

13. *MN,* May 12, 1869, in Works Project Administration, "Interesting Transcriptions from the *Mobile Nationalist.*"

14. *Manhattan (Kans.) Nationalist,* June 30, 1871.

15. *MN,* September 13, 1868; Miller to Boutwell, February 21, [1873], box 5, AP-246, RG 56; Parker to anonymous, [April] 1870, G. M. Parker Letterbooks, The Museum of Mobile.

longtime officeholder suggested the price of violating this rule. Despite years of residence in the city, his obituary described him as having no friends at all among whites, being "a man of peculiar manners and of few associates except colored people." Few government employees faced this prospect with much resolution. In human terms the social pressure toward prevailing racial mores proved strong, especially among established scalawags like Miller. Customhouse officials mostly shied away from a platform presence at Republican rallies, preferring to limit their political participation to financial contributions. Miller himself conceded that he gave few speeches. This low profile may well have been office policy, at least selectively. According to a removal petition, the collector told jobseekers that he did not "want any man in his employ who takes any active part either in local, State, or National politics." In one instance Miller indeed complained of a subordinate's excessive talk about politics.[16]

None of this escaped Republican notice. The *Nationalist* reported an overheard conversation between a government employee and a white conservative; the jobholder avowed his white supremacist views, assuring his listener that he was in Republican politics for the money. Allegations of such opportunism were rife, and Collector Miller's pursuit of social and political acceptability antagonized many activists, white and black, who saw suspect men occupying federal positions. Given the expectations generated by the spoils system, Republicans viewed themselves as morally entitled to the jobs. Officials had "uniformly filled a majority of the subordinate Federal positions with Democrats," this at a time when competent Republicans were "almost starving in the streets of Mobile for want of employment."[17] After the Democrats regained office locally, these complaints became urgent, often expressed with considerable emotion. Miller's notion that Republicans did not have the talent to do these jobs struck many activists as false, even insulting. One petition observed that Miller embarrassed and humiliated Republicans by keeping Democrats on his staff. Activists resented the standoffishness of officeholders whose prime qualification was "their acceptability to Democrats." One petition signed by W. B. F. Bates and a biracial group of Republicans delineated the social

---

16. *MDR,* January 19, 1886; petition, June 13, 1870, box 5, AP-247; and Miller to Boutwell, March 5, 1870, May 17, 1871, box 1, AP-246, RG 56.

17. *MN,* September 8, 1869; John Elliott et al. to President Grant, [1871,] box 250, AP-247, RG 56.

implications, noting that prosperous customhouse officials had "nothing in common with the great mass of Republicans." By ignoring the freedmen, these federal employees forfeited whatever wholesome influence over them they might have exercised. Instead of restraining the freedpeople, as Griffin might have argued, such leadership sowed racial resentment, encouraging the idea among the freedmen that "no white man is to be trusted." Through their quest for white acceptance, federal officials abdicated their responsibility to the party.[18]

These complaints resonated with the Republican constituency at large. By June 1870, in the midst of the Harrington interregnum, substantial pressure built to remove Collector Miller. Harrington and W. W. D. Turner complained of Miller's "sectional prejudice" against northern men, alleging that he fired a subordinate for his actions as alderman. Removal petitions bearing thousands of names were sent to Washington, signed by the more radical black activists like W. B. F. Bates, Major Lankford, and Allen Alexander.[19] On the city council William Miller was a fiscal conservative, generally aligned with Horton and Bromberg on spending issues. As the *Register* observed, Miller was guilty of "belonging to the weakest wing of the Republican split," a factional division that was already institutionalized in the form of rival party organizations. A counterpetition materialized from black and white Republicans associated with the moderate faction, signed by John Carraway and Philip Joseph along with his numerous Creole relations. Several of these activists were already connected with Bromberg's post office or other federal employment.[20]

Collector Miller offered a straightforward explanation for the criticism to his superiors in Washington. His unpopularity resulted from his being "*too honest,*" and honesty was below par in Mobile. Malcontents were circulating a "monster" removal petition among "the most ignorant of our . . . very ignorant people." Few men of standing had signed the petitions, and the attacks on him were a combined effort of the "Outs."[21] Miller here

---

18. Petition, June 13, 1870; Elliott et al. to Grant, [1871].

19. Petition of Mobile Republicans to G. P. Boutwell, [May 1870,] box 250, AP-247, RG 56; petition, June 13, 1870; resolutions signed by James L. Patterson et al., [mid-1870,] box 5, AP-247, RG 56.

20. *MDR,* January 1, 1871; petition, "Let Us Have Peace," [1870,] box 7, AP-247, RG 56.

21. Miller to Boutwell, June 28, 1870, May 4, 1871, February 21, [1873,] box 5, AP-247, RG 56.

oversimplified broader motivations, though self-interest certainly was involved. Freedmen generally understood the necessity for supporting white officeholders, but they insisted on public displays of solidarity as the price of their support. Furthermore, federal employment policy legitimately became a civil rights issue, of interest beyond the ranks of activists. Republicans who supported black officeholding, such as H. Ray Myers, immediately gained an enthusiastic constituency. In frustrating such expectations, and in cultivating social acceptability to white Democrats, Collector Miller necessarily alienated Republican activists and their African American mass base.

For the moment, the Grant administration retained Miller and the other U.S. officials. In this, Republican grievances in Mobile may well have been less significant than the wider political circumstances, especially what was happening in Congress. A bitter rivalry between Alabama's two Republican senators overshadowed local sentiment, for neither wished to risk a potentially hostile successor. However, Mobile's activists soon projected their existing concerns and factional alignments into this wider dispute. Mobile would become the storm center of one of the more dramatic internecine struggles of southern politics, to the advantage of black activists in search of personal and collective advancement.

When Alabama was readmitted in 1868, the all-Republican legislature elected two Yankee generals, Willard Warner and George E. Spencer, to the U.S. Senate. Despite the apparent similarities in background, these stereotypic carpetbaggers had very different approaches to politics. Warner was a decade older than Spencer and already a politician in his native Ohio, where he was actually serving in the legislature at the time of his election to the Senate. A lawyer, Warner had antislavery antecedents as a supporter of Salmon P. Chase, though he was initially skeptical of black suffrage, and was well connected politically to the powerful Sherman clan. Having purchased a plantation in Alabama, he considered himself a substantial property owner, and he sought to accommodate the views of the opposition as far as possible through economic development and a generous pardon policy for ex-Confederates, though he was supportive of civil rights as well. General Spencer had a different profile (and he has suffered from the reputation as the personification of the Yankee freebooter). Having led the First Alabama (Union) Cavalry during the Civil War, he came to the state looking for "any job that would pay," in his own words. Episodes of peculation marked his career, but his very pariah status among whites reinforced a certain political consistency in support of black demands. He wanted no part of amnesty for former Rebels, given the continuing persecution of his constituents in the countryside.[22]

Clear distinctions of style and substance separated Alabama's two Republican senators, generating considerable ill feeling. To Warner, Spencer represented "the thugs of the party," and Spencer disliked Warner with equal intensity. For all the political differences between them, personal rivalry over influence and patronage seems to have propelled the feud. President Grant was not generous with Alabama in provision of ranking federal appointments, but of the positions given the state, the president deferred to Senator Warner. In Spencer's estimate, Warner monopolized "five-sixths of the Federal patronage."[23] In Mobile, Collector Miller's subordinates complained of Warner as a nuisance relative to Spencer, who had "shown a higher tone of character" in making more cautious patronage demands.[24] Still, the grassroots agitation against Miller in Mobile pushed him toward Warner, who was considered the more moderate of the two senators and the one with more influence in Grant's administration.

By 1870, Spencer decided to challenge the renomination of his colleague.[25] In response, Senator Warner made common cause with the more conservative Gov. William H. Smith, ensuring Warner's renomination.[26] Warner also pursued the divisive policy of running separate tickets against Republican legislative candidates not committed to his reelection. This happened in Mobile, and at Collector Miller's apparent direction, a factional Republican convention nominated five federal employees, among them James Bragg and Philip Joseph.[27] Perhaps the intent was to force a compromise ticket, but the strategy backfired, both locally and at the state level. In November the Mobile "bolting" candidates received a mere two hundred votes, which was dwarfed by the nearly five thousand received by the regu-

---

22. Spencer to Dodge, May 1, 1865, Grenville Dodge Papers, State Historical Society of Iowa. An overview of the careers of Warner and Spencer appears in Richard Nelson Current, *Those Terrible Carpetbaggers: A Reinterpretation* (New York, 1988), 30–7, 68–73, 153–71.

23. Willard Warner to Reid, July 19, 1871, Whitelaw Reid Papers, LC, reel 189; George Spencer to U. S. Grant, July 6, 1871, box 7, AP-247, RG 56. On the controversy, see the documents in Grant, *Papers*, 22:18–26.

24. John H. Parker to Judge Miller, November 5, 1869, Letters Sent, Customhouse, Mobile, Ala., letterpress book, 1869–71, RG 36.

25. G. Spencer to W. E. Chandler, October 8, 1870, vol. 18, W. E. Chandler Papers, LC.

26. I. D. Sibley to Boutwell, June 25, 1871, box 7, AP-247, RG 56.

27. *Mobile Herald*, September 28, 1871.

lar Republicans. Against the split opposition, the Democrats carried all five seats by a narrow margin. This defeat cost the Republicans the U.S. Senate seat; the Democratic candidate won by a single legislator's vote, reportedly with the collusion of Senator Spencer. Republican disunity helped doom Governor Smith's reelection bid as well.

Warner's spoiler strategy rendered Collector Miller vulnerable by demonstrating he had *"no influence* with the Republican masses" in Mobile and could sway "no one, save his appointees." Miller and his colleagues arguably bore responsibility for disaster, which hurt them with rank-and-file voters. As one Republican observed, those who ran the "bolting" ticket "cut themselves off from all hope of office except through Warner's agency."[28] They reinforced their isolation in the spring of 1871, when County School Superintendent George Putnam ran for reelection. Putnam had organized the "new" school board, and his free-school agitation facilitated inroads into the Catholic Democratic vote by promising funding for parochial schools. In the March elections he ran unusually strong in the immigrant neighborhoods, carrying the two-thirds-white Sixth Ward.[29] Putnam "would have won had it not been for the course of the bolters." There is some evidence that Warner's followers indeed voted the Democratic ticket, and the moderate-dominated *Mobile Republican* denounced Putnam. Miller's and Bromberg's names appeared prominently in this context, which eroded their already suspect reputation for party loyalty.[30]

By early 1871, with the Democratic statewide victory, two lines of criticism of Miller and his allies in the customhouse converged. Republican activists resented their appointment policies, while Republican voters blamed their factional intransigence for the recent political reverses. Spencer now pressed his claims for administration patronage more strongly as the remaining Republican senator from Alabama, contending that the federal officials in Mobile had undermined party unity. In early 1871 Grant began removing members of the bolting ticket.[31] After a meeting with Spencer, the

---

28. B. S. Turner to Grant, April 3, 1871, box 5; and George Turner to Boutwell, June 23, 1871, box 7, AP-247, RG 56.

29. *MDR,* March 5, 1871. These comments reflect the author's tabulation of the ethnicity of the adult male population as reported in Population Schedules, Mobile County, Ala., Manuscript U.S. Census for 1870 (M593), RG 29.

30. C. T. Stearns to Boutwell, June 24, 1871, box 7, AP-247, RG 56; *MDR,* March 4, 1871.

31. Spencer to Boutwell, January 9, 1871, box 250, AP-247, RG 56.

president replaced Postmaster Bromberg with the recently defeated George Putnam, a Spencer protégé, and a similar transition occurred in the Internal Revenue Office. Miller's collectorship, however, was the obvious prize: "a change *must be made there* or we will have no party in Alabama," Spencer wrote.[32] These demands were strengthened by the recent election of the African American congressman Benjamin F. Turner, who proclaimed Miller's removal "one of the issues on which I was elected." In Mobile another massive petition drive developed against the federal officials.[33] Most of these pleas promoted another candidate for the position, the newcomer Timothy Pearson of Massachusetts. Pearson was a confidant of Congressman Turner, and he apparently made expansive promises to his African American supporters.[34]

With the agitation against the collector and Grant's other removals, ex-senator Warner took advantage of the situation and abandoned his ally Miller. Warner opportunistically asserted his own claim to the position, telling the president that ten years hard work left him "penniless and for the time stranded."[35] An interracial delegation of his supporters arrived in Washington to press his claims. Beyond the financial advantages to Warner, the position would allow him to challenge Spencer's own reelection in 1872. Wholly alarmed at the prospect, Senator Spencer reversed course and sought accommodation with Miller.[36] After securing what he thought was Grant's firm agreement to retain the collector, Spencer left for Alabama, but Grant then appointed Warner as collector in late June 1871, pending Senate confirmation.[37] If the president's intent was to satisfy both factions, he failed, for the position gave Warner the means and motive to renew the battle. The outraged Spencer accused the president of breaking his solemn word. Grant had made a repugnant choice, wholly destructive of party unity, in aiding a "dishonest, disreputable and vicious" man. Spencer announced his intention of defeating the appointment when Congress recon-

---

32. Spencer to B. F. Butler, April 1, 1871, box 5, AP-247, RG 56.

33. B. S. Turner to President Grant, April 3, 1871, box 5; and John Elliott et al. to President Grant, [1871,] box 250, AP-247, RG 56.

34. T. Pearson to B. Butler, May 19, 1871, box 60, Benjamin F. Butler Papers, LC.

35. Willard Warner to Grant, April 23, 1871, Letters of Application and Recommendation during the Administration of Ulysses S. Grant (M698), RG 59, reel 65.

36. John Sherman to Warner, May 20, 1871, John Sherman Papers, LC; Miller to Boutwell, June 6, 1871, box 1, AP-246, RG 56.

37. O. E. Babcock to Spencer, May 25, 1871, U. S. Grant Papers, LC, reel 3.

vened in December. He had little choice, Warner being too direct a threat to ignore, but this set the stage for a major confrontation on the streets of Mobile.[38]

The Warner-Spencer feud was primarily just that, a personal dispute over issues of tangential concern to the freedpeople. But the leadership split presented genuine opportunities, for the factional struggle empowered black activists to pursue various agendas. A bidding war broke out for the loyalty of African Americans in the strategic port city. This may not have helped the Republican party's electoral prospects, but it certainly emboldened black activists to pursue their claims for position. It also gave the grassroots an opportunity for direct influence on government policy. In the electoral sphere, Republicans necessarily targeted their appeal toward potential defections from the white majority; for example, after 1871, black nominees were rare in municipal politics. But in patronage matters this pragmatic calculus applied less strongly, for the Democratic electorate at large was not that concerned about which Republicans received jobs. Indeed, for tactical reasons the Democrats often encouraged blacks in their demands for a fair share of the patronage. African Americans could seek office in this venue with few negative consequences.

To defeat Senator Spencer, Collector Warner needed to demonstrate popularity with black constituents, which had been a problem for the local moderate faction in the past. Having just supplanted the disliked Miller, Warner engendered some grassroots enthusiasm, and Mobile would showcase his popular appeal if he handled the patronage issue correctly. Upon his arrival in the city, he was welcomed by a group of "prominent colored Republicans" and a Creole brass band. After much shaking of hands, Warner addressed the crowd. He implausibly denied responsibility for the earlier bolting ticket fiasco, calling on Frederick Bromberg to testify to his innocence. He then came to the crux of the matter, his personnel policy: "In the first place, I want honest men; next, competent men; next, sound Republicans." Interrupted by applause, he added that listeners would "not be able to point to a man in the custom house of doubtful politics," to which someone in the crowd responded "Good" amid cheers. He concluded by endorsing the reelection of President Grant, which was greeted

---

38. Spencer to Grant, June 30, box 7, AP-247; and Spencer to Grant, July 6, 1871, box 1, AP-246, RG 56.

with more applause. Despite his local scalawag connections, Willard Warner finally had an issue that was legitimately popular with the freedpeople of Mobile.[39]

The new collector wasted no time fulfilling his pledge to fire Democrats. He also transformed the complexion—literally—of federal service in Mobile. By early 1872, a list of those working on detached duty reveals eighteen blacks and eleven whites. This represented a dramatic, and enduring, change in the composition of the federal workforce, and Warner understood the public effect. He recommended hiring one janitor for his *"fine appearance,"* along with other attributes, and Stewart Bell came "recommended for political reasons." While African Americans mostly received subordinate positions, some received conspicuous posts. Philip Joseph, for example, was recommended for clerk in the auditor's office, a job worth fifteen hundred dollars per year. Warner explained the motivation for hiring Joseph quite explicitly: "the colored people pretty generally asked the appointment of one of their number to some place in the Customs building as a matter of principle." Warner claimed that he had hired members of both factions, but his own followers received most of the positions, and the others were expected to shift loyalties.[40]

Once ensconced in the customhouse, Warner fell heir to the African American alliances of the Bromberg-Horton moderate faction in city politics, recapitulating earlier patterns of popular support. Even so, the collector obviously could satisfy no more than a fraction of those seeking jobs. To protect the government service and to secure maximum political influence, Warner consciously turned to a select segment of the African American community. Joseph, for example, was Warner's premiere black spokesman. The collector described him as "a creole of unusual intelligence and force: of strictly pure private character."[41] Born into a slaveholding family of independent means, Joseph was not altogether typical, but other prominent appointees shared similar backgrounds. Inspector James A. Summerville, for example, was light skinned and a free man before the war; in 1870 he a was cotton sampler worth sixty-five hundred dollars. James Bragg was a grocer worth five thousand dollars, a competent man of "abil-

39. *Montgomery State Journal,* July 21, 1871.
40. Warner to Boutwell, August 4, 29, 1871, box 1, AP-246, RG 56.
41. Warner to Boutwell, August 4, 1871.

ity and influence." Walter Brazil had been a prewar free black who had some college education.[42] Warner opened midlevel federal jobs to well-credentialed, property-holding, established African American males. Strong practical reasons existed for this policy in terms of education and acceptability to a business clientele. The practice also meshed well with the existing composition of black support for the moderates. Still, the limitations of this version of preferential hiring exacerbated caste and class divisions within the African American community.

Warner's policies solidified the support of a powerful bloc of his African American constituency. If one examines publicly identified leaders supporting Warner's confirmation, a familiar pattern is clearly in evidence. Prosperous men predominated as Warner spokesmen, not surprising in view of the number enjoying lucrative employment at his hands. Along with Joseph, Bragg, and Summerville were men like Constantine Perez, a Creole cigar manufacturer who spoke four languages and worth seventy-five hundred dollars, and C. D. Nicholas, another Creole who lived with an apparent sibling worth ten thousand dollars. Of fifteen Warner faction activists in 1871, at least six were Creole, and most were prewar free blacks. All were identified as mulatto save one. Nine reported property, mostly substantial amounts, and the bulk were quite literate.[43] These men were not Warner's toadies; on civil rights issues, leaders like Joseph and Bragg were aggressively egalitarian, the Creoles as much as anyone. Warner's version of colorblind equality suited them well, for they were among the better-educated and more prosperous Republicans of either race. If the walls of caste came down in public service, and in the community more generally, such individuals could be expected to prosper.

The distinctiveness of Warner's following is most evident in comparison

---

42. Ibid.; Miller to Boutwell, February 14, 1871, box 1, AP-246, RG 56. The wealth and occupation data are taken from Population Schedules, Mobile City, Ala., Manuscript U.S. Census for 1870 (M593), RG 29.

43. C. Perez to Secretary of Treasury, July 20, 1881, box 250, AP-247, RG 56. The wealth figures are tabulated from Population Schedules, Mobile City, Ala., Manuscript U.S. Census for 1870 (M593), RG 29; and the prewar status from *Directory for the City of Mobile* (Mobile, 1859); *Farrow and Dennett's Mobile City Directory* (Mobile, 1867); *Henry Farrow and Company's Directory of the City of Mobile* (Mobile, 1870); and City Tax Rolls, 1860–70, Mobile Municipal Archives. The following African American activists were identified with the Warner faction in the 1871 dispute: Louis Avendorph, W. J. Boyd, James Bragg, Durham Davis, George Fears, Joseph Gomez, Henry Vincent, Eli Hopewell, Philip Joseph, Major Lankford, Willis Moore, C. D. Nicholas, Constantine Perez, Wilber Strong, and John Truyer.

with their opponents, African Americans who led anti-Warner rallies or whose names headed removal petitions. Spencer's supporters were dramatically poorer and darker skinned than their counterparts. Though familiar names like Allen Alexander or W. B. F. Bates appear, most were relatively obscure men. Of eleven activists with known backgrounds, perhaps two were free before emancipation and none were Creole. Most of these men were described as black or dark mulatto, and two or possibly three had property within their households. Several were young newcomers to politics. Henry J. Europe—the father of jazz great James Europe—was in his early twenties, a former slave who was probably freed during emancipation. Spencer Terrell, soon to be a prominent figure, was a steamboat hand about twenty years old, though he lived with relations with means. Though literate, such men often lacked the educational attainments of their rivals.[44] They were, however, more representative of the African American population, a fact that became increasingly relevant as time went on. The Spencer-Warner rivalry thus affected Mobile's blacks in twofold fashion: it opened professional positions to privileged African American leaders, while it emboldened less-established activists to challenge them for community leadership and jobs. The clash of egalitarian visions made Mobile the "scene of war" as different groups of activists sought grassroots sanction.[45]

In June, as Miller's removal loomed, both sides roused their popular followings. Warner's appointment generated a flurry of activity, and agitation continued until Congress reconvened in December. The factions hastened to demonstrate majority support, but how? Warner's followers solidified their control of the *Mobile Republican,* while Spencer funded another paper, the *Mobile Herald,* both claiming to represent party opinion. Rival Republican central councils sent resolutions to Washington, each denouncing the other as illegitimate in the national press. Warring party bodies would characterize Mobile's Republicans for decades thereafter. Mass peti-

---

44. Reid Badger, *A Life in Ragtime: A Biography of James Reese Europe* (New York and Oxford, 1995), 10–3. The social variables for this group were tabulated from Population Schedules, Mobile County, Ala., Manuscript U.S. Census for 1870 (M593), RG 29. It should be mentioned, though, that because Spencer's supporters were poorer and less visible in the records, the identifications for several of them are less certain. Nevertheless, the following African American activists were identified with the Spencer faction in the 1871 dispute: Allen Alexander, W. B. F. Bates, Columbus Canty, Isadore McCloudis, Joshua Davis, Samuel Digg, H. J. Europe, Albert Gallatin, Harrison Ray, Abe Royal, and Spencer Terrell.

45. A. W. Dillard to C. Hays, August 27, 1871, box 7, AP-247, RG 56.

tions were circulated, each being challenged by the other group as forged; widespread illiteracy facilitated such charges. From Washington, Grant's exasperated attorney general wrote that "the feud in Alabama is a shameful thing, but how can we tell who is to blame?" Both sides, he concluded, had "a popular following." The issue came down to proof that could not be easily manufactured. Control of the streets became the test of factional strength, and that contest became increasingly physical.[46]

At first, Warner's followers enjoyed the advantage, the recent employment reshuffle generating substantial enthusiasm. Here was a tangible civil rights victory, near at hand, welcomed by the black community. The new customhouse employees furnished a nucleus for street-corner rallies, which lauded Warner and demanded the removal of Spencer supporters from all remaining federal jobs. Warner also enjoyed the endorsement of the most prominent established African American leaders. The composition of Warner's faction seems to have held true for his popular following as well. The *Mobile Herald* taunted one crowd as "*Custom House flunkies*" and "*Creowls.*"[47] This account also mentioned the presence of cotton samplers, one of the skilled trades most open to antebellum Creoles. Warner's rallies clearly mobilized a substantial social constituency, but he left little to chance. In one instance Philip Joseph and other government employees reportedly solicited signatures demanding martial law against the Klan; they then allegedly tore off the headings and glued the signatures to other petitions.[48]

On the streets the conflict became quite bitter, with violence a recurrent threat if the *Register*'s reporting can be believed. In July Joseph was expelled from a meeting, whereupon "pistols, knives, clubs, etc." were drawn. Several participants were arrested. Two months later, Joseph found himself in court for fighting the Spencer activist A. B. Royal.[49] It became routine to disrupt opposition Republican faction rallies. On one occasion

---

46. A. T. Akerman to John D. Cunningham, November 30, 1871, Letterbooks, Amos K. Ackerman Papers, Alderman Library, University of Virginia.

47. *Mobile Herald,* October 2, 1871.

48. George Turner to Spencer, December 5, 1871, box 4; and C. Mayer to Spencer, December 5, 1871, box 7, AP-247, RG 56.

49. *Mobile Republican,* August 12, 1871; *MDR,* July 1, August 27, 28, 29, 1871. Here, as elsewhere, the necessity of relying on hostile Democratic sources presents a problem. But the more straightforward statements of fact would seem worthy of some credence, especially where substantiated by court appearances and other evidence.

Warner followers descended on a Spencer meeting with threats and guns drawn, according to the *Register*. In another instance the Radical *Herald* actually commended Spencer followers both for crashing a meeting and forbearing to beat the opposition. These were not mass outbreaks along the line of Mobile's perennial race riots, and there was little actual bloodshed. Those arrested for disorderly conduct were familiar names, the black spokesmen for the two factions. The dispute, it would seem, was of more passionate concern to the activists than the grassroots following, though the attendance at the rallies suggests some popular interest. At first, neither group enjoyed a decisive advantage with the black population at large. As William Miller observed, it was initially "difficult to say which was the stronger."[50]

All that fall Warner assured uneasy Treasury superiors that things were going well. He claimed he had "succeeded in uniting the people," gaining the support of every ward in the city except one. There was some basis to his claim: in October the *Register* reported that a Warner rally outdrew a rival Spencer gathering 250 to 150.[51] Warner skillfully utilized the November county elections to build his popular appeal. The Spencer faction selected a ticket comprising white Radicals in the hope that divisions among Democrats might allow victory. Warner's group responded with a very different ticket, dominated by Joseph, Constantine Perez, C. D. Nicholas, and other African Americans; the candidate for sheriff was Durham Davis, one of the Mobile's wealthier black merchants, worth $4,250.[52] Warner's followers thus put forward one of the few Republican tickets of the era with a strong black presence. The *Register* commented that neither faction had any hope of winning, but each wanted to show they were endorsed by the "'loil' masses" and thereby "secure the Federal patronage." Congressman B. S. Turner denounced Warner's maneuver, urging his constituents against the "delusive cry" of "Colored men vote for your color." It was to no avail. Spencer's followers withdrew their ticket just before election day to avoid a humiliating third-place finish.[53]

50. *MDR*, September 27, 1871; *Mobile Herald*, October 2, 1871; William Miller to Boutwell, July 27, 1872, box 4, AP-246, RG 56.

51. Warner to Boutwell, September 6, 1871, box 1, AP-246, RG 56; *MDR*, October 11, 1871.

52. Population Schedules, Mobile County, Ala., Manuscript U.S. Census for 1870 (M593), RG 29, reel 31.

53. *MDR*, October 11, 1871; *Greensboro (Ala.) Beacon*, November 18, 1871; *Mobile Herald*, November 6, 1871.

Warner's momentary success notwithstanding, as Congress gathered in December 1871, his detractors became quite vocal. In part this was simply numbers: there were always more activists without jobs than with them, and as William Miller explained, no appointment ever pleased more than one man in three.[54] A black activist exhorted Spencer to use all his "enfluence to defeat Gen. Willard Warner," revealingly adding that it was in Spencer's interest "as well as ours." Spencer Terrell noted he was a stranger to the senator, but he too asked him to press the fight against Warner.[55] The senator hardly needed the urging, but these scores of earnest pleas suggest independent motivation. Most of these petitions renewed the campaign for Timothy Pearson as Warner's replacement, apparently on the basis of promises of future favor. Abe Royal praised Pearson as wholly identified with the black community. One activist said he would practice what he preached, another that he would give the black man a chance.[56] W. B. F. Bates, among others, pressed Spencer to stand by Pearson because "we as colored men . . . have always stood by you." Pearson himself boasted that he was stronger in Mobile than the senator. Spencer would abandon Pearson without hesitation, but his local followers clearly acted on their perceived interests rather than passively following their leaders' dictates.[57]

Perhaps the avalanche of petitions resulted from the novel circumstances, for Pearson had called on his African American backers to make their preferences known in Washington. While patronage obviously dominated discussion of the customhouse, Warner's critics raised wider concerns. One group of mostly illiterates praised Pearson as "the poor man's friend regardless of color." Isadore McCloudis urged Warner's replacement by someone who would "unite us as a Colord people."[58] Members of Warner's faction had led insurgent local efforts, most obviously the bolting ticket, splitting the Republican vote on two recent occasions. In both cases they received much the smaller portion of the vote, which opened them to

54. Miller to Boutwell, July 8, 1871, box 4, AP-246, RG 56.
55. George W. Caldwell to G. E. Spencer, December 4, 1871; and Spencer Terrell to Senator Spencer, December 5, 1871, box 5, AP-247, RG 56.
56. Isodore McCloudis to B. F. Butler, December 11, 1871; and A. B. Royal to B. F. Butler, December 4, 1871, box 5, AP-247, RG 56.
57. W. B. F. Bates et al. to Spencer, December 8, 1871, box 5; and Pearson to Boutwell, [1871,] box 4, AP-247, RG 56.
58. Petition, [September 18, 1871]; and I. McCloudis to B. Butler, December 4, 1871, box 5, AP-247, RG 56.

the charge of disruptive behavior in the face of the racist enemy. For the black electorate, with its overriding loyalty to the Republican cause rather than individual leaders, the charge proved effective.

For all the local controversy, General Warner's fate was largely determined elsewhere. Continuing ferment had punctured Warner's promises to restore harmony in Mobile. Ex-collector Miller's scalawag comrades resented Warner's abandonment of him, and some neutral Republicans suggested the appointment could only perpetuate the feuding. By August, Spencer predicted victory: "Grant is already scared and will soon do what we want."[59] The senator vowed to "carry the war into Africa," aware that across Alabama Warner's egalitarian hiring practices made less impression than locally among Mobile's blacks. When Congress reconvened, Spencer stalled Senate confirmation, which rendered the nomination increasingly vulnerable to the approaching presidential campaign of 1872. Grant faced an impending Liberal Republican revolt from within the party. Spencer threatened to join the liberal opposition, and local elections elsewhere in the state suggested he enjoyed majority support among Alabama's Republicans. As Collector Warner complained, Congress had dithered until reelection fears made "a coward" of Grant.[60] Warner threatened to resign, but he never got the chance. The president concluded to pull the nomination, asking Warner's former senate colleagues to convey him the news. The public story was that a technical problem developed with his appointment, that his predecessor had never formally resigned, leaving administration officials criminally liable for violating the Tenure of Office Act. Grant withdrew Warner's name in late January, which restored the office to William Miller.[61]

Back in Mobile, Spencer's *Herald* headlined the "DEFEAT OF THE ARCH DISORGANIZER," and it was indeed a dire blow to Warner. His wrath knew no bounds. He cut off contact with the president, icily rebuking him years later for having "wounded and humiliated" him.[62] The Liberal Republican

59. Spencer to G. Putnam, August 12, 1871, quoted in State of Alabama, *Report of the Joint Committee of the General Assembly of Alabama in Regard to the Alleged Election of Geo. E. Spencer as U.S. Senator, together with Memorial and Evidence* (Montgomery, 1875), 16–7.
60. *MDR,* December 19, 1871; Warner to Sherman, February 29, 1872, Sherman Papers.
61. U. S. Grant to Roscoe Conkling, January 17, 1872, in Grant, *Papers,* 22:350–1; *New York Herald* quoted in *New York Tribune,* February 13, 1872.
62. *Mobile Herald,* January 23, 1872; Willard Warner to U. S. Grant, November 6, 1880, Warner Papers, reel 2.

revolt, however, gave Warner an apparent opportunity for revenge. In pique, he, Bromberg, Horton, and most of their white followers denounced Grant, eventually endorsing the Liberal Republican/Democratic presidential candidate, Horace Greeley. It was a dramatic move by the most established Republican leaders in Mobile, the culmination of years of party strife. In addition, Bromberg ran as the Liberal Republican nominee against Congressman Turner, with the Democrats obligingly nominating him too. The *Mobile Herald* concluded that everything had gone smoothly in the Republican party so long as the scalawags had kept the freedmen "at a respectful distance and under submissive rule, something in the manner of a slave master." When the freedpeople resented such treatment, these half-hearted leaders took flight. Good riddance to such Republicans, taunted the paper.[63]

For the mass of black voters, Warner's apostasy clarified everything. As Collector Miller observed, even Warner's African American supporters might not swallow Greeley, and Spencer's followers now gained a decisive popular majority. While customhouse jobs were important to activists, they were not as decisive with the voters, but President Grant's reelection was another matter. African American votes could hardly be swayed from the hero of Vicksburg, and Warner's black spokesmen could never sell a coalition with Democrats. Buoyed by public approval, Spencer's activists organized a Republican militia, the National Guard, in preparation for the fall campaign. Initially formed in Montgomery, this marching club was used "exclusively by one set of Republicans against the other," especially in Alabama's hotly contested cities. The National Guard claimed nearly three thousand members in Mobile, which represented two-thirds of the Republican electorate, according to Miller.[64] Guardsmen reportedly pledged only to vote for those in regular attendance, while "leading, intelligent and influential Colored men" were barred, according to several black activists. The implication here and elsewhere is that the National Guard functioned as sort of a rowdy political arm of the black poor. Even the hostile *Republican* admitted that the organization effectively lured unwary freedmen into the factional dispute in the guise of a pseudosanctioned militia.[65]

63. *Mobile Herald,* May 7, 1872.
64. J. A. Minnis to A. Akerman, November 18, 1871, Letters Received by the Department of Justice from the State of Alabama (M1356), General Records of the Justice Department, RG 60, National Archives, reel 3; William Miller to Boutwell, July 27, 1872, box 4, AP-246, RG 56.
65. *MDR,* August 20, 1872; *Mobile Republican,* August 17, 1872.

Perhaps they were not that unwary. The military trappings of the National Guard intersected with wider political concerns. Grant endorsed federal action to crush terrorists, which became a major issue in his reelection campaign after several enforcement acts passed Congress. As the *Herald* proclaimed, no one else could "so successfully secure the enforcement of the laws and the suppression of the Ku Klux." Spencer backed Grant's policy emphatically, but Warner had been more hesitant, and his moderate faction had been aligned with Gov. William H. Smith, widely regarded as weak on Klan suppression. Though the Klan was not much of a presence around Mobile, the city's freedmen cared about terrorism, especially with so many being migrants from the countryside. A recent trial of accused terrorists in Mobile highlighted the issue. Federal District Attorney J. P. Southworth prosecuted the Eutaw rioters, who fired upon a rally at which then-senator Warner himself spoke. The jury acquitted the accused, all reportedly Klansman, in the face of strong evidence of guilt. W. W. D. Turner complained that as long as Southworth was in office, there would be "no conviction of the Ku Klux." Southworth wailed that if a district attorney could not convict Klansmen, "his *semi* party friends immediately ask his removal, no matter why he failed." Southworth was a Warner ally, and the high-profile acquittals emphasized Warner's vulnerability on the issue.[66]

By mid-1872, Spencer's supporters had achieved the weight of numbers in Mobile, which they put to muscular use. In April a teacher in the Emerson Institute observed that politicians were "acting on the aggressive plan of warfare," with turbulent times expected. The following month a Republican district convention ended in the expulsion of several of the moderate faction, reportedly at the hands of the National Guards. The *Herald* reported that "some of the anti-Grant men got their heads hurt," taking evident pleasure in that outcome.[67] Twenty or so Republicans were arrested, including Allen Alexander, who reportedly hit someone with a table leg. After another disturbance on the Fourth of July, the *Register* concluded that all the black celebrations generated rows and that the authorities could hardly maintain order. Collector Miller was emphatic that white federal of-

---

66. *Mobile Herald,* March 14, 1872; W. W. D. Turner to Spencer, January 27, 1872, George E. Spencer Letter, William R. Perkins Library, Duke University; W. B. Woods to Department of Justice, February 7, 1872, reel 6; and J. P. Southworth to G. Williams, January 22, 1873, M1356, RG 60, reel 6.

67. Maria Waterbury to Cravath, April 1, 1872, Alabama, AMA, reel 2; *MDR,* May 7, 1872, September 29, 1876; *Mobile Herald,* May 7, 1872.

ficeholders had no hand in the disturbance. He could scarcely guess which faction behaved worse, though he was perhaps not an unbiased observer. Still, Miller's conclusion seems difficult to dispute: "the desire for Federal offices has been the main-spring of it all."[68]

After Grant's renomination, Warner, Bromberg, and their moderate allies backing Greeley reconsidered their strategy. The blacks were "blindly for Grant but they *can* be broken," Warner thought, and with sufficient "work and money," he could carry them for Greeley. Warner was mistaken, and perhaps his African American allies enlightened him on that point. Warner's faction eventually conceded that their black followers could not oppose the Republican presidential nominee and maintain any credibility. The Liberal Republicans might, however, prevail in an important local race with the help of their black allies. Bromberg and his colleagues decided to run Philip Joseph as a factional Republican against Congressman B. S. Turner, claiming Joseph to be the legitimate party nominee. They could thus split the vote against the Liberal Republican/Democratic candidate, Frederick Bromberg himself. Joseph's willingness to perform in this role was encouraged by a reported five-thousand-dollar subsidy from Democratic leaders, though he certainly had ample political motive to wish to defeat Turner, Spencer's leading black ally.[69]

Joseph's candidacy reinforced his faction's appeal to his fellow Creoles, and prosperous light-skinned spokesmen were especially predominant among his supporters. The Mobile delegates to his factional convention, for example, included Joseph, Louis Avendorph, Joseph Gomez, and W. E. Cruzan, all Creoles. Joseph's campaign, however, secured little enthusiasm among the freedpeople more broadly, these auspices perhaps not being universally welcomed. More importantly, Joseph's collaboration with the Democrats was widely rumored. His supporters had difficulty operating in Mobile's public spaces, given the intimidation practiced by their Republican opposition. Warner was to address one Seventh Ward meeting, but hecklers insisted that H. Ray Myers speak instead, breaking up the gathering. At another Joseph rally, National Guardsmen attended in force with a band. So long as the speakers praised Grant and the state Republican

---

68. *MDR,* May 10, 11, July 6, 1872; Miller to Boutwell, July 27, 1872, box 4, AP-246, RG 56.

69. Warner to Reid, July 15, 1872, Reid Papers, reel 189; *MDR,* July 12, 20, 1877. Some years later, the paper's editors claimed personal knowledge of the payment.

ticket, they listened in silence, but whenever Philip Joseph's name was mentioned, an "infernal din" drowned out the speaker. No violence occurred, but after the speeches ended, the guardsmen tore down the speaker's stand for emphasis.[70]

These obstructions notwithstanding, the election worked out much as Joseph's sponsors hoped. Against a divided opposition, Bromberg won and became the sole Liberal Republican congressman from the entire South. Joseph placed last, but his third-plus share of the district's Republican vote was enough to ensure Congressman Turner's defeat by a substantial margin.[71] However, Joseph did much less well in Mobile, which suggests the state of black opinion in that politicized and savvy enclave. Turner trounced him in the city by seven to one, despite it being Joseph's home town.[72] He ran best in the wealthier downtown wards, receiving a sizable minority of the Republican vote, but in the outskirts Republicans repudiated Joseph by staggering margins. Since both factions supported the Republican national and state tickets, the outcome provides a fair measure of their relative strength within the Republican electorate. Philip Joseph's vote correlated positively with the number of mulatto adult males by precinct, as opposed to those described in the census as black.[73] The evidence thus suggests that the obvious social contrasts in the leadership reflected a wider pattern, that they paralleled a division in their popular following as well. The resulting polarization also suggests why Spencer's faction prevailed.

Grant's triumphant reelection in 1872, combined with the Republican statewide sweep under incoming governor David P. Lewis, confirmed Senator Spencer's leadership. Warner's expulsion from the collector's office, with the defection of his faction, ironically left Spencer the inevitable leader of his party for Alabama. Even the remaining moderates in the party con-

70. *Mobile Republican,* August 24, 1872, August 12, 1871; *MDR,* August 28, 1872.

71. Bromberg received approximately 44 percent; Congressman Turner, 37 percent; and Joseph, 20 percent. Michael J. Dubin, *United States Congressional Elections, 1788–1997: The Official Results* (Jefferson, N.C., 1998), 223.

72. *MDR,* November 13, 1872.

73. The calculation was as follows: A hand tabulation of mulatto and black adult males was done by precinct from Population Schedules, Mobile County, Ala., Manuscript U.S. Census for 1870 (M593), RG 29. The percentage by ward of mulatto out of the total nonwhite population was compared with the percentage voting for Joseph out of the total Republican vote. The result was a moderately strong +.54 correlation, which suggests a significant tendency for mulatto voters to support Joseph and black voters to support Turner. The pattern is thus fairly consistent with the wider argument.

ceded his preeminence for the time being. Spencer would be reelected to the Senate in a bitterly controversial contest featuring rival legislatures and wholesale bribery. This episode, and Spencer's leadership in general, may not have done party chances much good, for the revelation of how he was reelected left him damaged goods before the national public. The *New York Times* editorialized against Spencer's "simply amazing" frauds, which demonstrated the "utter rottenness of politics in Alabama."[74]

Spencer's followers in Mobile, however, found the results more attractive. For the next decade and more, activists once identified with Spencer's following directed black politics in Mobile, and the pattern of informal exclusion of darker-skinned and ex-slave activists dissipated. Factional controversy continued, of course; in 1880, for example, a delegate to the Republican state convention complained that Mobile delegates were "always fighting among themselves," adding that they "almost always had double delegations." Still, after Grant's reelection, everyone recognized who spoke for the black masses. Men like Allen Alexander, W. B. F. Bates, and Spencer Terrell dominated party counsels thereafter, though they gradually ceased to act as a unified group. Joseph and his colleagues continued to fight them for years, generally on the losing end regardless of educational and class attainments. Thus, whatever the wider implications, from the point of view of local activists, Grant's reelection was the watershed, empowering a broader range of African American leaders and politicizing their popular following as well.[75]

These trends were reflected at the customhouse, the inevitable focus of attention among Republican activists. As the *Register* complained, one daily saw "idle and worthless negroes standing or sitting about the Customhouse" talking politics in a "loud and frequently excited manner." In the building itself, William Miller resumed his duties as collector in early 1872, but he did not have an easy time of it. His federal superiors initially suggested he keep some of Warner's appointees in place as a gesture toward unity. They proved insubordinate, especially Philip Joseph, whom Miller tried repeatedly to dismiss. Miller eventually ordered him to "get out of here d—— you," informing him that it was "not in the power of the Ad-

---

74. State of Alabama, *Alleged Election of Geo. E. Spencer; NYT,* May 13, 1875. See also *New York Tribune* quoted in *Mobile Tribune,* May 18, 1875, on the bipartisan nationwide criticism.

75. G. Cotton to Sherman, May 25, 1880, Sherman Papers.

ministration to put you back here." This confrontation, which Joseph characterized as rude and potentially violent, doubtless encouraged his subsequent bid for Congress against Miller's factional allies.[76]

Having switched camps, Miller did not find his newfound pro-Spencer political connections all that comfortable either. He reportedly had trouble controlling his allies in the National Guard, who became a combative grassroots force in their own right.[77] Furthermore, Miller found Spencer's oversight problematic. Just before the presidential election, he complained that Spencer padded his payroll with activists doing campaign work. Miller's Treasury superiors overruled him, insisting that Miller make the hires. The collector clearly bridled at the political interference, but still his vigilance allowed his operation to escape the financial troubles evident in some other departments, especially in the post office. There Spencer requested his ally, Postmaster George Putnam, to divert federal money toward the Republican campaign. When Putnam, despite allegations of previous financial misdeeds, refused, Spencer had him dismissed. Ironically, Putnam reemerged as a Liberal Republican as did the equally disappointed Timothy Pearson, who had not received the coveted position as collector. After Putnam's removal from the post office, Spencer approached his successor, J. J. Moulton, for a ten-thousand-dollar loan. Postmaster Moulton complied, but he was left exposed to charges when Spencer could not or would not replenish the diverted funds. Moulton would be indicted for his actions, though Spencer escaped punishment before the Senate.[78]

From the point of view of the freedpeople, these unedifying developments had compensating features. For one thing, according to the *Register,* the genial J. J. Moulton commonly provided bail money when activists were arrested, as happened a good deal during the contentious presidential campaign.[79] At the customhouse, Miller had once resisted black patronage demands, but now he was subject to Spencer's influence. The senator dictated several appointments over Miller's objections, and on one occasion, he intervened to have one black employee receive a wage increase. By February 1873, when Miller left office, the customhouse had twenty white em-

---

76. *MDR,* August 13, 1872; Philip Joseph to H. S. Vanderbilt, June 29, 1872, box 4, AP-246, RG 56.

77. *MDR,* October 30, 1872.

78. Miller to Boutwell, August 17, 1872, box 4, AP-246, RG 56; *MDR,* May 7, 1872, January 6, March 22, 1876; *Chicago Times* quoted in *MDR,* May 21, 1876.

79. *MDR,* August 11, 1872.

ployees and fifteen black ones. Whites occupied the higher offices in greater numbers than under Warner, but still the contrast with previous administrations was dramatic. Furthermore, the expectation was that African Americans were to receive a substantial portion of the offices, and anyone who departed received substantial local resentment. As Spencer Terrell complained in 1880, "not since the Hon. Willard Warner was collector of the port had there been a Colored inspector." In point of fact, Terrell exaggerated, but the underlying assumption is evident. Warner's affirmative-action precedent proved powerful so long as Republicans controlled the presidency. From then on, activists seeking removals generally pressed their demands effectively in the name of the black masses.[80]

Thus, even after Redemption in Alabama, African American political influence remained potent within the federal bureaucracy. As Constantine Perez observed, President Grant "always told us [blacks] that should we have an occasion to wish for anything we should apply in person and we will be heard." White Republicans frequently blamed black patronage influence for the party's woes. One conservative scalawag in the interior was particularly emphatic in his denunciations, slipping easily into racist language. A. W. Dillard concluded that it was simple to use blacks to put incompetent men into office, and that recommendations and petitions from them were "easily to be had"—though presumably not at random. In 1875 Dillard recalled that "Last fall, we had Phillip Joseph & co. clamoring for the removal of District Attorney Geo. M. Duskin, because he would not become their tool & do their bidding." This influence, he thought, was one of the worst consequences of universal suffrage because African Americans wanted to run the Republican party. Dillard's hostility notwithstanding, he had a point; Joseph pressed the issue of black representation in government jobs in his *Mobile Watchman*.[81]

Equity in patronage was a civil rights demand subject to verification and within the control of local federal officials. Officeholders could disregard the pressure of local Republicans, but only at the risk of antagonizing the majority of party constituents, as Morris D. Wickersham discovered during his long tenure as Postmaster J. J. Moulton's successor. Formerly somewhat

---

80. Miller to Boutwell, January 7, 1873; and "Officers and Employees, Mobile Customs House," February 5, 1873, box 4, AP-246, RG 56; Spencer Terrell to John Sherman, March 22, 1880, box 7, AP-247, RG 56.

81. C. Perez to Hayes, March 31, 1877, box 4; and A. W. Dillard to R. A. Mosely, June 12, 1875, box 250, AP-247, RG 56; *Mobile Watchman,* August 30, 1873, April 26, 1874.

sympathetic to black concerns, upon assuming his duties at the post office, Wickersham changed his tune, eventually endorsing the Hayes administration's civil service policies insulating federal offices from politics. The postmaster's close ties to Democrats also raised hackles. Throughout the 1870s, he engaged in a running feud over the number of conservatives among his subordinates. At one Republican rally, a disturbance broke out: there was "a determination on the part of the crowd that Col. Wickersham should not be allowed to speak."[82] Amid hisses and vociferous objections, Wickersham abandoned the attempt. Afterward, black leaders called on the postmaster to demand that he hire good Republicans. Even officials associated with Spencer's Radical faction received the same sort of scrutiny, often in personal terms. A gathering of militants simultaneously denounced the moderate Postmaster Wickersham and Collector of the Port Calvin Goodloe, a Spencer protégé.[83] In 1875, African Americans denounced Goodloe as "a well-known *sporting man*" whose time was "much occupied with such amusements." At one black Republican gathering, W. B. F. Bates accused him of failing to appoint black subordinates because ship captains did not like them. James Bragg, however, defended the collector on the grounds that he knew personally of three black men working in the customs office. Obviously, African Americans weighed the performance of even Radical factional allies in such tangible terms before their popular following.[84]

Over the subsequent decade and more, the two factions' leaders rotated in and out of the various federal offices as the Spencer-era rivalries perpetuated themselves.[85] In time, Pres. Rutherford B. Hayes's conciliatory southern policy would assist the moderate faction, but both groups employed significant numbers of local black activists. Indeed, Philip Joseph was briefly appointed internal revenue director under Pres. Chester A. Arthur, though the president soon suspended the appointment under pressure. Competent African American employees often held their jobs regardless of

---

82. *MDR,* August 5, 1876, May 5, 1877, June 15, 17, 1880. After Garfield's nomination, Wickersham tried again, spending twenty minutes on stage, receiving catcalls of "Democrat" and "Traitor," before giving up. Even Lou Mayer could not get the crowd to desist. *Mobile Gazette,* June 17, 1880.

83. *MDR,* September 3, 1880, April 4, 1876.

84. W. G. Strong et al. to B. H. Bristow, October 18, 1875, box 4, AP-247, RG 56; *MDR,* September 14, 1875, April 18, 1876.

85. Wiggins, *Scalawag in Alabama Politics,* 108–27.

who was in favor in Washington. Walter Brazil, for example, survived a change of regime at the customhouse, winning press notice in the process.[86] Despite Collector Miller's misgivings as to ability, the African American federal employees seemingly performed well. Except for Moulton's troubles at the post office, there were no major scandals in Mobile for the next decade or more, certainly nothing to rival the cascade of scandals under Andrew Johnson.

African American public officials won a certain pragmatic toleration from the merchants and the Democratic elite once Redemption made the Republicans less threatening. Prominent Democratic businessmen repeatedly recommended Constantine Perez for office on the grounds that he was competent and helpful, a longtime property holder and taxpayer.[87] Mobile's Democratic congressman endorsed a pay increase for A. B. Royal, once a combative Spencer militant.[88] Probate Judge Price Williams Jr. and other Democrats similarly endorsed a black inspector on the grounds that he was a "good orderly citizen" who belonged to "the best class of our colored population."[89] Black officeholders received little abuse in the press so long as they kept a modest profile. When the former Spencer activist Spencer Terrell died in 1884, he received an appreciative obituary in the *Register* contending that he was a sensible, conservative sort of Republican. That same year the *Register* praised black post-office employees for being polite and engaging in politics no more than necessary. In partisan terms this made some sense; black officeholders were politically less threatening than white Democratic renegades, who became increasingly common in the late nineteenth century.[90]

In their pragmatic drive for government jobs, Mobile's black leaders hardly covered themselves with glory, and modern historians of the era have not been particularly attentive to such patronage issues. In comparison to egalitarian issues of greater moment, the pursuit of individual self-interest in this venue looks uninspiring. Still, in the midst of the larger collapse of Reconstruction and the egalitarian hopes it generated, the outcome

86. *MDR,* September 27, 1882, June 30, 1883; *Huntsville (Ala.) Gazette,* July 10, 1880.
87. A. Baurman et al. to J. W. Burke, August 11, 1880, box 250, AP-247, RG 56.
88. Endorsement of J. T. Jones on A. B. Royal et al. to C. C. Folger, December 13, 1883, box 250, AP-247, RG 56.
89. Price Williams Jr. et al. to Secretary of Treasury, April 5, 1883, box 250, AP-247, RG 56.
90. *MDR,* February 24, 12, 1884.

of Mobile's patronage struggles may well have looked like victory, both for themselves and their cause. Wholesale cynicism, one suspects, came less easily for members of a recently enslaved race than for their white allies; African American demands for federal office inevitably raised issues of racial justice, certainly for the individuals involved, and apparently for their followers too. The changes in the federal bureaucracy were among the few civil rights gains to outlive Reconstruction in Mobile, changes that were peacefully and effectively implemented. For a generation, activists undermined caste and class exclusion in government service. Given the circumstances, perhaps they achieved all they could for racial equality, leaving the rest to better men in better times.

6

Let Us Serve the Rich

Black Politics in an Era of Diminishing Prospects

In the literature on the aftermath of emancipation, the bracing political battles of Radical Reconstruction possess a compelling appeal for historians. The era's forthright struggle for justice contrasts starkly with the depressing national retreat from equality that characterized the final decades of the nineteenth century. In practice, though, the Reconstruction regimes' grip on power was so tenuous that they made only limited gains for their core constituents, at least in areas where African Americans did not numerically predominate. The short-term gains of the Republican ascendancy, both material and symbolic, must also be weighed against the wholesale embitterment of the white population. In Mobile's case, the strategy of maintaining office without elections had obvious drawbacks, for sooner or later, the conservative white majority was bound to return to power. So long as the Reconstruction governments clung to office, African Americans remained a central focus of resentment to be expressed in ferocious rhetoric and recurrent riots. Redemption's significance was thus double edged in Mobile. The return of the Democrats to power certainly meant a return to white supremacy as a public priority, but it was only as the stark racial polarities of Reconstruction eroded that black suffrage could create a relatively normal voting bloc, one whose preferences conservatives increasingly had to take seriously.

This evolution had much to do with the changing behavior of black activists. While Republicans were in power, African American leadership rivalries fueled popular mobilization and progressively more-radical civil rights demands. After repeated electoral defeats, though, the process reversed itself. African American leaders no longer had the luxury of disregarding the nuances of conservative opinion, and they became progressively more adept at locating fissures within the monolith of white hostility. Furthermore, once the Radical faction obtained supremacy, insurgents ceased rousing followers for direct-action campaigns just as the pressure of poor migrants coming in from the countryside lessened. By abandoning the more advanced civil rights demands, black activists focused on those tangible goals that seemed most salvageable. The practical necessities of the situation now pushed activists toward pragmatism or even opportunism in seeking the favor of various groups of conservative whites. Activists' very reputation for self-seeking and mercenary behavior made black suffrage a less frightening reality once Reconstruction ended. In local politics, activists flexibly sought to reconfigure the electoral equation in the face of a certain white majority.

As with the struggle for jobs and influence within the federal bureaucracy, the local political scene thus offered African American leaders some compensation for the collapse of Reconstruction nationally. In Mobile the loss of Republican control permitted black activists surprising leeway for the next decade and more in a setting marked by increasing political civility. Democrats presided over protracted fiscal disaster, with repeated crises and eventual city bankruptcy. Fiscal stringency starved social spending, which, combined with other economic troubles, encouraged restiveness in the white population. The circumstances exacerbated divisions among conservative whites, both over rivalries for office and abuse of the democratic process. Thus, despite the obvious liabilities of the Republican record and a continuing minority status in a racially hostile electorate, African Americans maintained some political relevance. The very finality of Republican defeat at the municipal level undermined Republican partisanship; chastened party leaders sought tactical alliances with dissident Democrats. Black activists secured some concessions, perhaps all that were possible, though the benefit for the African American population as a whole is less clear.

Municipal fiscal collapse provided the context for resurgent black political influence. Triumphant Democrats enacted generous railroad subsidies as well as free wharves and other policies demanded by the board of trade. But construction of the railroad projects soon stalled, leaving the city liable for quantities of endorsed bonds.¹ In late 1871 the city borrowed $100,000 from local banks, "owing to the unexpected difficulties in negotiating the unsold bonds of the city."² The Democratic state government's default placed all local bond issues under a cloud. The city found itself at a financial impasse in late 1872 as the next semiannual interest payment loomed and tax payments trickled in. To add to the general frustration, several major municipal scandals broke, and Mayor G. M. Parker faced "wholesale and indiscriminate charges of fraud and corruption" against his administration.³

"Mobile is in a sad state, going down, down, down."⁴ Such was a religious leader's appraisal at the end of Parker's term, and the municipal disarray emboldened attacks on the leadership. Criticism focused on Mayor Parker, John Forsyth's *Mobile Daily Register,* and the longtime head of the Democratic Central Council, Price Williams Sr.⁵ The Democratic establishment's leading opponent was former mayor J. M. Withers, who had long opposed subsidy measures and targeted the board of trade for abuse. Withers now edited the *Mobile Tribune,* and after years of vocal dissent, he challenged Mayor Parker's renomination late in 1872. Although beaten in the ward meetings, Withers claimed that he "was fraudulently 'counted out' and the nomination given to *the favorite of the Central Council.*" It was probably true since for years afterward observers recalled it as the most corrupt nomination proceeding in memory.⁶ In response Withers and some

---

1. "Testimony Taken by Dumping Ground Investigating Committee," August 7, 1872, folder 2, envelope 7, box 17, RMBACC, Mobile Municipal Archives; *MDR,* April 6, 1871, August 1, 1872; Board of Aldermen, Minutes, June 18, 1872, Mobile Municipal Archives, reel 5.

2. Board of Aldermen, Minutes, December 12, 1871, June 11, 1872, reel 5; Parker to Walsh, Crawford, and Co., October 22, 1872, G. M. Parker Papers, The Museum of Mobile.

3. G. M. Parker to Walsh, Crawford, and Co., October 22, 1872; *MDR,* November 22, 1872.

4. Richard H. Wilmer to Bishop Quintard, January 2, 1873, Charles Todd Quintard Diaries, Louisiana State University Libraries.

5. *Mobile Tribune,* August 11, 1872, quoted in Works Projects Administration, "Interesting Transcriptions from the *Mobile Tribune*" (Works Projects Administration typescript, 1939), at Mobile Municipal Archives; *MDR,* November 26, 1874, March 2, 1886; *NYT,* October 21, 1874; Alma Esther Berkstresser, "Mobile, Alabama, in the 1880s" (Master's thesis, University of Alabama, 1951), 42.

6. *MDR,* June 13, November 10, 30, 1872, November 22, 1874, April 13, 18, 1877.

of the city's creditors sought tactical cooperation with the Republican leadership.[7]

The timing was opportune. Republicans had been so embroiled in the Warner-Spencer customhouse dispute that they barely contested the previous municipal election, and the apparent hopelessness of their partisan chances made them receptive to broader alliances. Withers was apparently reluctant to run himself against the Democratic mayor, so he agreed to support Republican judge Cleveland F. Moulton on a nonpartisan "Citizens ticket."[8] The established scalawag Moulton had been associated with the moderate faction. During the Harrington administration, he was conspicuous for his personal probity, Moulton having resigned his position as councilman over the wharf purchase. As for Withers, he was to be nominated as city treasurer, and his supporters were to divide the remaining nominations with white Republicans, leaving the more popular Democratic choices unopposed.[9] Withers and his followers proclaimed loyalty to the national Democratic party and orthodoxy on racial matters, so the Citizens ticket was clearly a marriage of convenience.

Faced with Democratic disarray, the African American leadership mustered a unified response, one of the few times that decade. It would seem that there was implicit agreement that direct black representation on the Citizens ticket was counterproductive as was formal party endorsement. Instead, Republican leaders endorsed an all-white bipartisan electoral ticket that was made public just hours before the election. There is no evidence of dissension among black or white Republicans at the time. Perhaps chastened by their previous experience, African American leaders concluded that rather than insist on unpaid positions on the city boards, they would look for compensating advantages elsewhere, especially jobs in the federal bureaucracy. Also, some of the white nominees were strong Spencer allies in the customhouse, such as L. H. Mayer, who were expected to protect black interests in city government. This striking display of racial realpolitik allowed Moulton, Withers, and the Citizens ticket to take full advantage of white disaffection with the Democratic leaders.[10]

    7. Ibid., November 25, 1873. The evidence is circumstantial, but the following year the press reported an effort by Waring to have the Democrats endorse the reelection of Mayor Moulton.
    8. C. Clay to "Wife," December 4, 1872, Clement C. Clay Papers, William R. Perkins Library, Duke University.
    9. *MDR,* May 19, 1876, November 22, 1874.
    10. J. C. Lawrence to [unknown], April 14, 1873, box 36, AP-258, RG 56.

Moulton ran upon the platform of "economy, retrenchment, and general municipal reform" and won a landslide victory. One Republican happily observed, "we beat the Democrats by nearly five thousand majority," but the margin was embarrassingly huge.[11] Moulton got almost ten thousand votes, more than the total vote normally cast. The Democrats commonly alleged repeat voting by African Americans, claims generally minimized by modern historians, but in this instance the evidence looks strong. It seems that the wholesale defections from the Democrats disrupted that party's traditional stakeout of the ballot box. As the *Register* observed, on election day "the renegade whites worked actively and energetically, seeming to have a particular spite against the party with which they had formerly acted." Still, most Democrats implicitly conceded that the Citizens ticket had won by a substantial margin of the legitimate ballots. Cleveland Moulton came to power with a degree of Democratic acquiescence that his unelected Republican predecessors had lacked.[12]

Upon assuming office, Moulton sought a drastic one-quarter reduction in city expenditures.[13] He urged efforts to collect back taxes and demanded cutbacks in official salaries. He even proposed aggressive measures to prevent newcomers from using the city hospital as well as residents who were not truly destitute. The mayor warned that his administration might commence with "the humiliation of a temporary inability to meet the bonded debt of the city." Unfortunately for him, this came to pass; outgoing Mayor Parker had not provided for the next interest payment, which fell due at the first of the year. Moulton tried to secure a temporary loan from businessmen, but public criticism deterred them from cooperating with the mayor. Even Forsyth's *Register* blanched at this destructive show of Democratic partisanship. As a result, the city defaulted on its interest payments, and the market value of Mobile's securities instantly evaporated.[14]

Mayor Moulton's efforts to salvage the city's finances soon generated dissent among Republicans. After the Citizens ticket won, the white Republicans on the boards demanded the lion's share of city patronage. Several

---

11. *Mobile Tribune,* December 3, 1872, quoted in Works Projects Administration, "Interesting Transcriptions from the *Mobile Tribune*"; W. Irving Squire to Cravath, December 21, 1872, Alabama, AMA, reel 3. It should be added that the Democratic totals look suspiciously high themselves.

12. *MDR,* December 3, 4, 1872.

13. Ibid., August 19, 1873, January 3, 1872.

14. Ibid., January 1, 10, 1873; U.S. Congress, House, *Affairs in Alabama,* 616.

boardmembers were elected to city posts, which raised the issue of conflict of interest, given an existing ordinance prohibiting such appointments. A motion to enforce the ban, reportedly at Mayor Moulton's suggestion, infuriated some of his Republican allies, especially Alderman James Lomery. After substantial controversy, the mayor got his way, and several Republicans resigned from the unpaid boards. Thereafter, as the *Register* noted, the board of aldermen became a rather "conservative body." After this demonstration of the mayor's bipartisanship, Moulton and Withers finally received some Democratic cooperation on enacting cutbacks. The mayor achieved a substantial reduction in the city budget, from $300,000 in 1872 to $240,000 the following year, the lowest figure since the war.[15]

What Moulton's African American constituents made of his priorities is unclear, but some of his cost-saving initiatives ought to have raised issues. The city maintained its severe vagrancy legislation, sentencing "all idlers, paupers, disorderly and vicious persons" to up to one month on the chain gang.[16] Moulton's administration boasted of working prisoners on the streets cheaply, calculating it cost but sixteen cents a day in added costs. He also worked female prisoners on the streets, which even his Democratic predecessor had not done.[17] More broadly, Moulton's fiscal priorities would seem inconsistent with the wishes of the Republican electorate, given the previous history of black support for social spending and economic development measures. Still, the city's financial context had changed, lowering expectations. Perhaps Mayor George Harrington's legacy was a certain wariness of expenditures and an enhanced appreciation of personal honesty in officeholders. Support for retrenchment policies made sense in one other respect. Under the Democrats, African Americans were not receiving anything like their share of jobs or public services anyway, so city cutbacks were not likely to affect them that directly.[18]

Moulton was able to deliver gains in criminal justice. According to the county solicitor, Judge Moulton had long insisted on black jurors, contending they were strikingly impartial. Also, police statistics reveal a substantial decrease in the number of arrests under Moulton, vagrancy proceedings being especially rare.[19] As mayor, he directly controlled police hires and

15. *MDR,* January 22, March 1, 1873, December 5, 1872, November 28, 1876.
16. Ordinance of March 15, 1873, RMBACC, reel 6.
17. *MDR,* July 12, November 30, 1873; *Mobile Watchman,* September 6, 1873.
18. *MDR,* September 26, October 1, 1873.
19. U.S. Congress, House, *Affairs in Alabama,* 561; Isbell, "Social and Economic History of Mobile," 85; *MDR,* July 21, 1874.

presided over a notably smooth reintegration of the police force. Before the election, the Democrats had warned of the risk of incompetent black officers, but perhaps mollified by Moulton's bipartisan approach, the *Register* found "no complaints of the few negroes on the police, who, so far, have behaved very well." Even after falling out with the mayor, the paper continued to praise them. These officers were usually posted in "the most disorderly beats, where the worst portion of our black population congregate," yet they made their arrests effectively without undue violence. This growing public acceptance occurred despite what must have been substantial numbers of black policemen. At one point they held a parade and even formed a militia company, but not even their drilling under arms initially occasioned press criticism.[20]

These successes notwithstanding, Moulton's basic goal, fiscal solvency, proved impossible. Wall Street crashed in September 1873, and most regional banks suspended specie payments, which virtually stopped the sale of cotton "except at ruinous prices."[21] Of course, the dramatic onset of the depression, which would last for the next five years, killed off whatever hopes remained for the various railroad projects and undermined any prospect of the city paying the bondholders. By 1874, one conservative reported that the city was insolvent and that the crisis was likely beyond solution.[22] The depression undermined Moulton's bipartisan political balancing act. If this did not pose him sufficient difficulty, discontented Republicans challenged his reelection as well. Alderman Lomery vehemently opposed Moulton's evenhanded patronage policies, and he declared his candidacy for mayor.[23]

As was often the case, feuding within the white Republican leadership reawakened dormant divisions within the African American community. Lomery reached out to the most disaffected elements within the black leadership, especially Philip Joseph and his following. It appears some of the tensions of the previous conflict between the Spencer and Warner factions

20. *MDR,* January 7, 1873, January 28, March 1, 1874; *Mobile Watchman,* September 18, 1873.

21. *MDR,* October 5, 1873; Mobile Board of Trade, *Annual Report of the Mobile Board of Trade for the Year Ending December 5, 1873* (Mobile, 1874), 39; E. P. Lord to Cravath, October 7, 1873, Alabama, AMA, reel 3.

22. William G. Jones to Henry Watson, July 30, 1874, Henry Watson Papers, William R. Perkins Library, Duke University.

23. *MDR,* November 27, May 2, 1873.

played themselves out again in this local contest. One Republican meeting was contentious, according to the *Register,* because "the blacks and the creoles . . . do not seem to work together very harmoniously, politically or socially." Once again, divisions within the white Republican leadership offered opportunities to individual African American activists, though at a cost in group unity. In October a meeting led by the Creoles Constantine Perez and J. Truyer tried to nominate Lomery for mayor. Moulton supporters heckled them, with one white Republican accusing the Lomery supporters of "selling we Republicans out for money and a drink of whiskey."[24] An uproar ensued, with several politicians cursing one another on the stage according to a witness. Subsequently, there were several street fights reported between adherents of the two Republican factions.[25] The *Register* described Moulton's supporters as "the very scum and dregs" gathered out of "the slums of the black population," suggesting a class distinction in the two factions. If this was indeed the case, the outcome was perhaps to be expected. At the December 1873 election, Moulton's ticket outdistanced Lomery's by a vote of approximately 2,900 to 800, a substantial majority that nonetheless manifested significant black disunity.[26]

In this three-way race, though, Moulton's main opponent was the Democratic candidate, John Reid. Despite the divisions within Republican ranks, the mayor retained some standing among white voters for his rigorous fiscal policies. His supporters emblazoned retrenchment slogans on their banners and carried them about the streets. On election day the outcome was close in a ballot that was not marked by wholesale fraud, at least not on the Republican side. It seems that after the polls closed, Mayor Moulton and the Democratic sheriff entered the Fifth Ward and discovered Democratic election observers stuffing the ballot box. The *Register* nonetheless proclaimed Reid and his ticket victorious by a margin of nineteen votes. Forsyth's paper concluded that even if there was fraud at the Fifth Ward, there were likely even "greater frauds in the remaining SEVEN WARDS" in favor of the Republicans. Unpersuaded by this logic, Mayor Moulton would not concede defeat, and his police barricaded themselves in City Hall as months of litigation followed.[27]

24. Ibid., June 4, October 18, 24, 25, 1873.
25. Ibid., October 17, November 14, 15, 16, 20, 21 November 1873.
26. Ibid., November 16, 29, December 2, 10, 1873.
27. Ibid., November 30, December 4, 1873, January 29, January 3, 1874.

In terms of the city's needs, the disputed outcome could not have been worse. As a northern correspondent observed, the governmental confusion undermined Mobile's faltering credit and business prospects. When it became clear that Republican judges would not uphold Reid's claim of victory, Democrats became increasingly confrontational. "By Heaven!" John Forsyth intoned, "The RIGHT has licked the dust long enough at the feet of lawless power." He promoted a mass meeting, at which members of the crowd called for a physical seizure of City Hall. Alarmed, one railroad president addressed the crowd, "You counsel bloodshed and violence; we must have no violence or mob law; you who counsel violence are attempting to lead us all into wrong." It required the intervention of prospective mayor Reid himself to forestall an attempted putsch, and a lawless mood remained evident thereafter. In May 1874, for example, the first full-scale lynching in years occurred. A white wastrel was caught in the act of sexually molesting a four year old, whereupon a crowd of thousands gathered, took him from the sheriff, and hanged him just off Broad Street—that is, well within the city limits and in the middle of the day. Thus was "MOBILE VINDICATED," as the *Register* headline proclaimed, manifesting a certain enthusiasm for mob activity.[28]

To this point, Mayor Moulton had governed with some Democratic acquiescence, but his bipartisan legitimacy could not survive such a hotly disputed election. Maintaining office under the circumstances was perhaps a mistake, for the relative civility that had characterized the city for several years unraveled, and the freedpeople as always would suffer for it. Mobile became ungovernable in 1874, the year of the Redeemers' final triumph in Alabama. Few of the boardmembers elected with Moulton were now willing to serve, so the mayor called upon the previous incumbents to hold office extralegally. City officials could do little more than draw their salaries, and they had run out of plausible ideas for dealing with the fiscal crisis as the budget skyrocketed. Insurrectionary Democratic rhetoric gradually gave way to the simple but effective strategy of a taxpayer strike. The city defaulted repeatedly on its interest payments, and even City Treasurer Withers began talking of partially repudiating the debt. All the while public services deteriorated. Moulton had long since abolished the board of health in a city prone to recurrent epidemics. As the *Register* observed, "the streets

28. *NYT*, October 21, 1874; *MDR*, February 2, 7, May 12, 1874.

and gutters of the city are in deplorable condition," and other city departments suffered similarly.[29]

From the perspective of the African American populace, these events were bitterly ironic: blacks were being wretchedly repaid for their pragmatic, responsible approach to governance. They had disavowed demands for elective office and had subordinated their demands in a coalition administration under a fiscally conservative mayor. Now that mayor's disputed reelection exposed them to torrents of abuse, popular racism being the Democratic target of choice as partisan passions heated up. During Reconstruction's final throes in Alabama, blacks remained the racial bogeymen regardless of how cautiously they comported themselves locally. Moderation under Moulton served African Americans no better than Radicalism under Harrington and perhaps worse, given the growing physical threat. Furthermore, the economy continued to worsen, adding to the general frustration with Republican promises. One black Democrat charged that the Radical leaders had fooled blacks, making them believe they were going "to give them all [an] office a Piece." The freedmen were bitterly disappointed, given hard times in which only half "could get any thing to do."[30]

In this atmosphere of growing crisis, a mood of grassroots racial assertiveness and social radicalism became more evident. As the November 1874 statewide elections neared, the police reported increased martial drilling by African Americans. Despite total exclusion by the white unions, moreover, there were rumors of clandestine black labor organizing, efforts doubtless encouraged by declining wages. The *Register* reported that agitation was conducted through a shadowy "Society," which the paper distinguished from the more benign benevolent and religious groups. Supposedly, this entity enforced a minimum wage for chopping wood, threatening those who undercut the scale for this unskilled work with whipping. One group reportedly mandated that "Confederate Captains and Colonels" were to be called "Mister," while the Union Band of Sisters tried to enforce a standard wage for cooking and ironing. Radical rhetoric also circulated freely in these meetings, and these little excitements served to "bring the faithful together and keep up the payment of monthly dues during the off months of politics."[31]

29. Edward King, *The Great South,* ed. W. Magruder Drake and Robert R. Jones (1875; reprint, Baton Rouge, 1972), 341; *MDR,* December 13, August 22, March 4, 28, April 26, November 13, 24, 1874.

30. *NYT,* October 21, 1874; *MDR,* September 6, 1874.

31. U.S. Congress, House, *Affairs in Alabama,* 569; *MDR,* March 17, 18, 19, 24, 1874.

Widespread popular frustration fueled a tempestuous year of internecine political conflict. African Americans now insisted on direct representation on the party legislative ticket. More controversial was the demand for federal civil rights legislation outlawing segregation in public places along with state legislation to the same end. For once, Republican factionalism coincided with a clear public issue, one of egalitarian principle verses political necessity. Most Republican officeholders dreaded discussion of the subject, especially the mayor. At one gathering it was "understood that Moulton and his policemen had stocked it with delegates . . . in favor of keeping the Civil Rights question out of the canvass."[32] Given the racial dynamics, white Republican officeholders naturally turned to their black allies—often their employees—as spokesmen. Former militants holding patronage jobs, such as Spencer Terrell, voiced pragmatic arguments. Robert Europe, for example, opposed formal resolutions in favor of the civil rights bill. It was necessary, he thought, to be "prudent, until the Republican party in Alabama can get the power in their hands." Perhaps the most dramatic transformation of this sort was that of Allen Alexander, long a fiery Radical inclined toward physical confrontation. He previously sued streetcar lines over exclusionary policies and even led mass occupations. His wife, Charlotte, recently went to federal court over segregated steamboat accommodations; according to an eyewitness, Alexander himself was almost pitched overboard in a confrontation over the issue.[33] Thus Alexander had not abandoned his combative style, but he was now Moulton's most prominent black spokesman with strong ties to the white Republican leadership seeking bipartisan support. "Custom House Alexander," as the *Register* termed him, was also seeking to retain his federal job, from which Lomery's former supporters demanded his ouster. The beleaguered black Radical suddenly saw the logic of caution on civil rights, becoming the leading public opponent of the proposed measure. At one meeting he commented, "We have adopted too many resolutions already, and they did no good." At another convention he arraigned a colleague for "having forced the race issue and put that weapon in the hands of the Democrats."[34]

For a discussion of labor agitation among domestics in Atlanta and elsewhere, see Tera W. Hunter, *To 'Joy My Freedom: Southern Black Women's Lives and Labors after the Civil War* (Cambridge, Mass., 1997), 44–97.

32. *MDR,* May 27, 29, August 5, 1874.

33. Ibid., August 26, 1874, August 6, 7, 1873; U.S. Congress, House, *Affairs in Alabama,* 378.

34. *MDR,* August 5, 26, 1874.

As entrenched black jobholders resisted the civil rights pressure, other activists pressed the demand. Prominent among them were the displaced black spokesmen of the former Warner-Bromberg following. James Bragg, for example, reported on the civil rights bill's prospects from Washington, urging Mobile Republicans to stand firm. His old associate Philip Joseph assumed leadership of the bill's proponents. For years, Joseph led the moderate minority grouping among black Republicans, but the alliance with the scalawag leadership had disintegrated after Horace Greeley's disastrous presidential campaign and the loss of administration patronage. However, circumstances provided Joseph a popular issue with which to flail his longtime rivals. Now editing a newspaper, he soon acquired a reputation as a ferocious racial militant. "What is the matter with Joseph?" the *Register* wondered, recalling that he "used to be rather a mild-mannered colored man."[35] His conversion may not have been opportunistic, though; he and his fellow Afro-Creoles had been among the most emphatic opponents of racial exclusion, and Joseph himself had been arrested in a street railway confrontation. Whatever the motive, his *Mobile Watchman* editorialized that the civil rights bill "has been allowed to slumber too long in Congress, and has been dodged too often." At a series of Republican conventions throughout the state, Joseph fought attempts by Alexander and his comrades to bury the issue. "Why dodge the question of [the] race issue and the equality of all men?" he asked from the floor of one gathering, threatening to walk out. Joseph vowed to force white Republicans on record.[36]

All through the summer of 1874, the civil rights issue roiled black Mobile. The *Tribune* suggested that "Royal Street, especially the Custom House corner," was "given up to the politicians," mostly discussing the civil rights bill. Activists debated on the steps of the post office and elsewhere, with several altercations reported in the press. Republican dignitaries descended on Mobile to plead for discretion, but they met a cool response at public meetings and were sometimes heckled.[37] Overall, it seems there was real grassroots enthusiasm for the measure, given the pervasiveness of discrimination in daily life. In congressional testimony one Mobile man termed his treatment in white bars and on streetcars as an af-

---

35. *Mobile Watchman,* August 30, 1873; *MDR,* May 26, 27, October 6, 1874.

36. *Greensboro (Ala.) Beacon,* January 8, 1870; *Mobile Watchman* quoted in *MDR,* July 21, 1874; *MDR,* August 5, 1874; *Selma Times* quoted in *MDR,* August 5, 1874.

37. *MDR,* June 4, 19, August 4, 28, 1874; *Mobile Tribune,* October 23, 1874.

front to his liberty. With the passage of the Civil Rights Act the following year, there would be repeated enforcement tests by private citizens, who persisted even in the face of threats of violence.[38]

Given the black representation at party gatherings—almost a four-to-one majority in one county convention—one might suppose the Republican party machinery would inevitably back the bill. However, the civil rights measure's opponents prevailed locally by a variety of means. The *Watchman* claimed that a "crowd of desperadoes, with brass knuckles, slung shot, bowie knives, etc.," took control of a Seventh Ward election of Republican delegates.[39] Such conduct was unusual, for patronage employees, black and white, normally controlled formal party gatherings with less trouble. Conventions were dominated by those with a professional stake in the outcome, those whose political participation was subsidized directly or indirectly.[40] The *Register* claimed undemocratic procedures prevailed at Republican conventions, especially when Allen Alexander chaired. At one, whenever "the [Postmaster] Wickersham party, the anti–Civil Righters" decided to carry a point, Alexander would vacate the chair, "get on the floor, make a motion, then take the chair again, put the motion to the house, and ... declare it *unanimously* carried." Philip Joseph eventually led an interracial bolt of civil rights militants, but the effort proved unnecessary. At the state Republican convention, the pro–Civil Rights forces swept all before them, brushing aside the objections of the Mobile delegates. The party also nominated for Congress a black proponent of the bill, Jeremiah Haralson of Selma, over Allen Alexander himself, one of his leading rivals.[41]

After the decisive outcome, the Republican factions in Mobile sullenly regrouped for the fall campaign. At contentious meetings, they managed to agree upon a single ticket, with both Joseph and Alexander nominated for

38. U.S. Congress, House, *Affairs in Alabama,* 341; MDR, February 7, March 4, 5, 13, 22, July 10, 1875.

39. MDR, August 2, 1874; *Mobile Watchman* quoted in MDR, August 16, 1874. A *Register* account, apparently of the same gathering, also alleged wholesale fraud. MDR, August 2, 1874.

40. The depiction here of nineteenth-century party politics is certainly not unique to Reconstruction or the southern Republicans. See the excellent discussion in Glenn C. Altschuler and Stuart M. Blumin, "Limits of Political Engagement in Antebellum America: A New Look at the Golden Age of Participatory Democracy," *Journal of American History* 84 (December 1997): 855–85.

41. MDR, October 9, June 4, August 6, 1874.

the legislature. The contest was shaping up in menacing terms. As Alabama Democrats geared up for the climactic "White Line" campaign of 1874 that would finally finish Reconstruction, Moulton's disputed reelection added a local grievance. Democrats vowed that this election they would not lose by fraud (or otherwise, it seems). One lawyer observed that it was customary in Mobile to go armed at election time, and many observers predicted trouble. Some weeks before the election, the Democratic leadership approached Mayor Moulton with the report that black militia companies were drilling outside town. The Democrat Central Council told the mayor to disarm them or else they would do it. The mayor complied, but as the balloting approached, Moulton and other Republicans telegraphed repeatedly for military aid. "Only the presence of U.S. soldiers on election day can prevent riot & violence by bodies of men organized for that purpose," Moulton concluded.[42]

The crisis atmosphere within the black community encouraged increasingly harsh pressure on dissidents. Democrats were distributing cash, jobs, and alcohol to their few black allies, who were widely viewed as sellouts. Mayor Moulton himself conceded that the feeling against them was quite bitter.[43] At elections black Democrats often complained of intimidation, but in 1874 the evidence seems unusually strong. In one instance a mob broke into a Democratic club meeting, demolishing the furniture. The crowd reportedly beat a black Democrat, York Tunstall, firing on him as he fled. The mob assailed the home of another leader, and several Republicans were arrested for their participation. The Democrats claimed these were preconcerted political riots, but they were probably spontaneous outbursts.[44] Outside town, one group of "boisterous and frantic black women" reportedly forced a man to vote Republican. They "kept saying that the white people wanted to put their children back into slavery, and that they would die first." Various sources note the involvement of women in similar episodes, suggesting something beyond normal political tactics.

42. *MDR,* October 11, 1874; *Mobile Tribune,* November 6, 1874; U.S. Congress, House, *Affairs in Alabama,* 569; Moulton to Attorney General, October 30, November 2, 1874, Letters Received by the Department of Justice from the State of Alabama (M1356), General Records of the Department of Justice, RG 60, National Archives, reel 6.

43. U.S. Congress, House, *Affairs in Alabama,* 455.

44. *MDR,* October 30, 1874; U.S. Congress, House, *Contested Election, Bromberg vs. Haralson, Alabama,* 44th Cong., 1st sess., H. Doc. 47, 42–6, 49–51.

While this intimidation paled by comparison to that of the Democratic opposition, it was pervasive, reflecting genuine fears.⁴⁵

By late fall, the threat of racial violence was palpable, manifest in combative Democratic rhetoric. "The mongrels must be defeated so overwhelmingly that they will never again attempt to make a contest," one Democrat proclaimed. The summer's civil rights agitation only sharpened the racist backlash. One group of black Republicans, hoping to stave off opposition, marched around the city with banners proclaiming "No Social Equality" and "No Mixed Schools."⁴⁶ The Democrats derided these gestures, promoting forceful measures. The *Mobile Tribune,* now under conservative ownership, urged young whites out to the polls, "To prevent negro repeating, it is necessary to have a strong and vigilant force at every voting precinct in the city." The Democratic county sheriff appointed scores of conservative activists as mounted deputies, and other horsemen operated under party authority. Guns from the armory suddenly appeared in the hands of whites.⁴⁷ Faced with this menacing predicament, and perhaps having concluded that resistance was futile, Mayor Moulton tried to co-opt the opposition. He appointed white special deputies, some of whom were soon seen distributing Democratic tickets. More fatefully, the mayor commissioned a white volunteer militia, under the command of the Democrats' campaign treasurer, to keep order at the polls. The militia stationed a cannon at one of the fire companies, convenient in the event of emergency. On election morning whites strung up an effigy of Ben Butler downtown, suggesting that once again bloodshed would bring national attention to Mobile.⁴⁸

Throughout the day, there were rumors of organized groups of black repeat voters, reports that had basis, as several second-tier Republican activists later confessed.⁴⁹ The bands of whites watching the polls made scores

45. U.S. Congress, House, *Contested Election,* 79; U.S. Congress, House, *Affairs in Alabama,* 460.
46. MDR, September 12, 1874; October 31, 1874; *Mobile Tribune,* October 22, 1874.
47. *Mobile Tribune,* October 22, 25, 1874; U.S. Congress, House, *Affairs in Alabama,* 347.
48. MDR, November 7, 1874; *Mobile Tribune,* November 4, 5, 1874.
49. Charles Nordhoff, *The Cotton States in the Spring and Summer of 1875* (New York, n. d.), 86–7; U.S. Congress, House, *Contested Election,* 13–24, 24–31, 31–8, 46–9, 52–7, 67–70, 73–5. The testimony from former Republican activists of the drilling of hundreds of African American repeaters is very strong. Allen Alexander, however, does not appear in this context. U.S. Congress, House, *Affairs in Alabama,* 11.

of arrests, and Democratic deputies killed one alleged repeater in the course of capture.[50] A riot nearly broke out then, but the real confrontation came later that afternoon. When Democratic challenges jammed the Seventh Ward poll, Allen Alexander led several hundred freedmen to the Fourth Ward, a legal proceeding since voters were entitled to cast ballots at any box. Democratic deputies blocked the way, and Alexander strode out to meet them. The sheriff ordered Alexander's arrest, on uncertain grounds, and Alexander shouted for his followers to continue to the polls. As the Democratic deputies shoved him into a carriage, members of the crowd interfered. Someone, probably a deputy, fired a shot, and a melee followed. Two blacks, William Kinney and Cyrus Roberts, were reported killed, with several others shot as well. The well-armed whites scattered the crowd, suffering no reported injuries.[51]

As Alexander himself observed, this made the fourth riot in Mobile, and each time Republican leaders had "advised the negroes to go unarmed." Discretion had not helped, and even after the firing stopped, Alexander remained in peril, surrounded by infuriated whites. A policeman heard cries of "Shoot him; kill him; the damn son of a bitch." Another white witness saw a dozen pistols drawn, all pointed at Alexander.[52] He was "jerked out of his vehicle . . . begging for his life," according to the *Tribune,* and but for the intervention of several prominent Democrats, he "would have been roughly handled."[53] The more restrained white conservatives stalled long enough for U.S. soldiers to arrive, and thus bolstered, the sheriff and his deputies conveyed the prisoner to jail. Alexander concluded that he was safer in custody than outside and refrained from posting bond. That night there was apparently some discussion of killing him in jail, but he lived to tell the tale.[54]

Even before the riot, the mayor had determined to arrest Alexander, without real charges, to keep the peace. After the trouble, the mayor "begged" the freedmen to go home, telling them to "leave the election alone."[55] Facing an impossible plight, Moulton turned control of the situa-

50. U.S. Congress, House, *Affairs in Alabama,* 346.
51. *MDR,* November 4, 1874; *Mobile Tribune,* November 4, 5, 1874; U.S. Congress, Senate, *Elections of 1874, 1875, 1876,* 44th Cong., 2d sess., S. Rept. 704, 37–8.
52. U.S. Congress, House, *Affairs in Alabama,* 349, 346, 455.
53. *Mobile Tribune,* November 4, 1874; U.S. Congress, House, *Affairs in Alabama,* 346.
54. *MDR,* November 5, 1874; U.S. Congress, House, *Affairs in Alabama,* 346, 453.
55. U.S. Congress, House, *Affairs in Alabama,* 453, 451.

tion over to his Democratic militia chief, thinking his force more restrained than the sheriff's deputies. The militiamen removed the occasion for disorder—black voting—by training their cannon on the Seventh Ward poll. The black men "left in droves," and the Democratic press confirmed the riot frightened many from voting. The mayor's actions prevented further bloodletting, but some Republicans felt betrayed. One black leader accused Moulton of deserting his party. Ex-mayor Gustavus Horton also criticized his use of the Democratic militia, having surmounted worse trouble himself.[56]

After the election ended, the freedmen congregated on the corner of Royal and Government waiting for news. Jeremiah Haralson had defeated Congressman Frederick Bromberg, but otherwise the results were grim amid widespread reports of violence and intimidation. Democrats under George S. Houston had swept the governorship in a landslide, along with the legislature and most of the Congressional seats, thus bringing a decisive end to Alabama's Reconstruction era. After the outcome became clear, a correspondent reported that "the darkies do not seem to understand the situation at all, and are constantly talking in groups on the street corners about 'the 'lection done gone 'gin us.'" Conditions remained tense throughout the city. In mayor's court several days later, a man was on trial for carrying concealed weapons. One lawyer asked a witness, "Do you suppose there are five men here right now that are not armed?"[57]

Under the circumstances, the Democratic statewide triumph made the mayoral elections of December 1874 a foregone conclusion. The new Redeemer legislature paused long enough to rewrite Mobile's election laws, tightening voter registration and changing city elections to once every three years. With apparent justification, Republicans claimed a systematic attempt to deter black registration. After the election the *Register* commented on the "wonderful reduction of the Republican majority in the Seventh Ward," implausibly crediting it to black defections. The registration-law changes made little difference in the final outcome, though; mayoral candidate J. M. Withers was crushed by a two-to-one margin by John Hurtel, with the Democrats sweeping every office. Soon ex-mayor Moulton left

56. U.S. Congress, House, *Contested Election*, 22, 86, 23; U.S. Congress, House, *Affairs in Alabama*, 375.

57. *Greenville (Ala.) Advocate,* November 19, 1874; *Mobile Tribune,* November 5, 6, 1874.

town for St. Louis, and Withers lapsed into years of public silence, their independent movement thoroughly discredited. The end of Reconstruction in Alabama was thus a watershed in local politics too. For a century thereafter, known Republicans seldom held elective office. Blacks thenceforth would represent something over a third of the electorate, which deprived them of any real prospect of direct power in a racially polarized city. Even the Republican press concluded it was "folly for Republicans to nominate candidates for office" in Mobile, given that they could not win and would never be permitted to assume office anyway. Whatever African American political influence remained would unfold in this apparently unpromising context.[58]

Despite the unfavorable wider developments, the local situation after Redemption remained surprisingly fluid in practice. The end of Reconstruction statewide closed off the prospects for direct Republican exercise of power, but it opened avenues of indirect influence.[59] The Democratic registration laws, whatever their unfairness, minimized black "repeating" as a public issue in the city. African Americans who managed to register would cast ballots with little trouble thereafter, though getting their votes counted in tight races remained problematic. Once the Redemption turmoil ended, Mobile's black minority again attended the polls in increasing numbers. In 1875, for example, local voters nearly rejected the Democratic proposal for a new constitutional convention. The Alexander affray was the last significant partisan violence for a decade, despite a series of closely contested elections. White opinion leaders also became more sensitive to their civic reputation, open lawlessness being a problem with U.S. marshals near at hand. As Reconstruction receded, the prospect of black rule became less plausible.[60] Republicans refrained from endorsing party nominees in local races, and serious black candidacies effectively ceased. The African American minority seemed less threatening, which allowed black leaders more

58. U.S. Congress, House, *Affairs in Alabama,* 454, 461; *MDR,* December 23, 24, 1874; January 29, 1874; *Mobile Tribune,* December 11, 1874; *Montgomery Journal* quoted in *NYT,* June 18, 1877.

59. On the long history of the dilution of the influence of the African American vote, see Peyton McCrary, "History in the Courts: The Significance of *The City of Mobile v. Bolden,*" in *Minority Vote Dilution,* ed. Chandler Davidson (Washington, D.C., 1984), 47–63. Mobile's Reconstruction precedents were featured in a major U.S. Supreme Court decision in 1980 concerning "at large" voting arrangements under the Voting Rights Act.

60. *MDR,* August 8, 1875.

maneuvering room in a context of lowered expectations. Paradoxically, it was the very finality of the defeat of larger Radical egalitarian goals that made some gains possible. Unlike some other cities with competitive post-Reconstruction politics, in Mobile the modest black success minimized the resulting racist backlash.[61]

Of course, the passions of the election campaign and recent riot persisted for some time. In the spring of 1875, the federal Civil Rights Act integrating public facilities prompted apparently spontaneous enforcement tests. One fellow mistakenly anticipated passage of the bill and had "several chairs broken over his head" in a coffeehouse, to the delight of the *Register*. In March African Americans repeatedly tried to gain service at barrooms, theater houses, and other public facilities.[62] The Democratic papers debated the appropriate response: the *Tribune* suggested that whites simply wait out the blacks, who would weary of intruding, while the *Register* preferred intimidation or subterfuge.[63] After several weeks the challenges passed as the resulting cases worked their way through the courts. Whites seemed a bit relieved by the lack of mass confrontation. One correspondent observed that Mobile had only modest trouble, blacks were proudly riding the apparently integrated streetcars but were otherwise "shy." It had been feared they "would make trouble by forcing the civil rights [act] on us, but thus far they have been very quiet."[64] By the fall, the papers were congratulating Mobile's residents that the disturbances had passed. African Americans apparently reconciled themselves to a measure

---

61. The goal of black politics everywhere after Redemption remained unchanged: racial equality, which represented the underlying issue regardless of whatever pragmatic compromises were made. In some areas, such as Virginia under William Mahone's Readjuster movement and later on in North Carolina under the Populists, African Americans employed their ballots so effectively as to win major concessions on patronage and other issues. In both cases, though, this success eventually galvanized racial bloodbaths in urban centers reminiscent of the overthrow of Reconstruction. In Mobile the civil rights gains remained so modest and the divisions among conservative whites so intractable that black voters were able to remain politically relevant for years without creating violent racial polarization. On the situation in contemporary Virginia under the Readjustors, see Jane Dailey, *Before Jim Crow: The Politics of Race in Postemancipation Virginia* (Chapel Hill and London, 2000).

62. *MDR*, February 7, March 3, 13, 16, 1875. See also the issue of May 29, 1875, for a report of a streetcar altercation.

63. *Mobile Tribune*, March 10, 1875; *MDR*, February 4, March 7, 1875.

64. *Greenville (Ala.) Advocate*, April 1, 1875.

of de facto segregation, or even exclusion, in settings dominated by elite whites.⁶⁵

A gradual accommodation to political circumstances became evident in other areas. The American Missionary Association's Emerson Institute, for example, once exemplified carpetbagger activism, its faculty taking a leading role in the early years of Reconstruction. As the 1870s wore on, Superintendent E. P. Lord resisted association with controversial political figures, believing the partisanship of his predecessors damaged his school's reputation. He had some cause for concern: the former AMA teacher and Radical politician W. Irving Squires would be arrested in St. Louis while trying to counterfeit Mobile securities.⁶⁶ The institute began courting public opinion and in 1874 sent commencement invitations out to residents in the vicinity. Some thirty whites attended the exercises, among them businessmen and Democratic politicians. "They all congratulated us and pronounced it wonderful, splendid, etc.," the superintendent enthused.⁶⁷ As part of this changed profile, the missionaries emphasized religious work and personal moral uplift, which won some support from Mobile's white ministers. The Emerson Institute briefly printed a small newspaper, which even won modest praise in the *Register* for its moderate political views. Though the institute would again go up in flames, reportedly torched by whites who thought the paper was not moderate enough, this time the teachers at least won some local white sympathy for rebuilding.⁶⁸

Growing toleration, such as it was, had some social basis. The African American influx had exacerbated Mobile's racial turmoil during the early years of Reconstruction. White fears of an invasion of rural freedpeople encouraged harsh policies and police severity. As the postwar agricultural

---

65. *MDR*, October 29, 1875; *Mobile Tribune*, May 22, 1876. Howard Rabinowitz argues that desegregation was not the most pressing issue for urban blacks in general. In Mobile the support for civil rights legislation on the streetcars and elsewhere was emphatic during Reconstruction. Still, after Redemption, the issue was seldom raised in the political sphere, suggesting other priorities took precedence given the circumstances. See Rabinowitz, *Race Relations in the Urban South*, 182–97.

66. E. Lord to E. Cravath, June 19, October 23, 1874, Alabama, AMA, reel 4; *NYT*, May 14, 1875; *St. Louis Republican* quoted in *MDR*, May 16, 1875.

67. E. P. Lord to E. Cravath, October 12, 1874, June 13, 1874; and Kate Lord to Miss Emerson, December 31, 1875, Alabama, AMA, reel 4.

68. *MDR*, February 18, 1876; Abbie Holton to M. E. Strieby, April 18, 1876; and E. P. Lord to Strieby, April 21, 1876, Alabama, AMA, reel 5.

crisis sorted itself out during the 1870s, these circumstances changed. The board of trade reported at mid-decade that the "vagabond negroes" were diminishing in numbers, and Mobile's black population in 1880 declined from the previous reported census figure.[69] One political result was that the bloc of impoverished newcomers who had fueled earlier Republican mass factionalism became less evident, and activist struggles became more focused on individuals and jobs. The 1873 depression, however, brought a different concern. Each winter the newspapers were alive with the tramp menace, the fear that Mobile was overrun with white vagrants from the northern and western states. In one instance a white man in rags, reportedly starving, was picked up by police.[70] Confronted by such social agony, humane sympathy often lost out to fears of the roving poor. "The only way to get rid of them," the *Register* observed, "is to have every one arrested and made to work on the streets."[71] On occasion, the paper recommended whipping vagrants or even that individuals shoot thieves. The threat of lawlessness among growing numbers of white vagrants, combined with increasing class tensions during the depression, diluted the obsession with African American behavior. For whites, blacks were still identified with crime and disorder, but the relationship became more obviously problematic.[72]

As John Hurtel and the Democrats assumed power, these changes in racial climate made little immediate difference in municipal policy. In the race-drenched recent canvass, the Democrats had promised to expel blacks from city jobs, and they did so from all but the most menial positions.[73] One jobseeker explicitly applied to the "honorable boddies" for a position under the "white mans pollicy."[74] The *Register,* voice of the Democratic

---

69. Mobile Board of Trade, *Annual Report of the Mobile Board of Trade for the Year Ending November 30, 1875* (Mobile, 1876), 73; U.S. Bureau of the Census, *Compendium of the Tenth Census* (Washington, D.C., 1883), 380–1. In 1870 there were national complaints of underenumeration of black residents, which if true in Mobile would have made the decline over the subsequent the decade correspondingly larger. *Mobile Tribune,* January 24, 1875; *MDR,* June 10, 1875.

70. *Mobile Tribune,* January 24, 1875; *MDR,* June 10, October 12, 1875.

71. *MDR,* December 31, 1875. The *Mobile Tribune* made similar statements. *Tribune,* October 5, 1875.

72. *MDR,* April 14, 1875, March 20, 1876.

73. One *Register* letter suggests that black children were paid to trap stray dogs, but even here it is not clear the procedure was authorized. *MDR,* June 10, 1875.

74. Richard Files to Mayor, January 1, 1875, folder 2, envelope 7, box 17, RMBACC.

leadership, urged city officials not to trifle with their whites-only employment promises: "The appointment of negroes upon the police or to city offices would be made simply because they are negroes, and not because they are competent."[75] There was no point to irritating poorer whites to please blacks since blacks always voted Republican anyway. The appointment of a mixed constabulary would persuade the rank and file that "our protestations of last year arose simply from policy and not from principle." This overt discrimination goaded the African American community to oppose the Democrats, even if accommodation might have otherwise seemed expedient.

At least the new administration fulfilled its mandate with respect to racial matters. On the crucial debt issue, the Democrats found the problem as intractable as their predecessors. Mayor Hurtel cautiously observed that it would be wisest "not so much to do but rather to undo much of what has been done." The city's debt now exceeded three million dollars, with a backlog of half a million in unpaid taxes, and the recent taxpayer boycott only exacerbated the problem.[76] The city seized some fifteen hundred delinquent properties, but public resistance prevented actual tax sales. In 1875, following the state's example of partial repudiation, Mobile admitted bankruptcy and negotiated to scale back the city's debt. Most of the bondholders settled for fifty-one cents on the dollar, though some of the dissatisfied ones sued in federal court and seized city properties piecemeal. That embarrassment aside, the city had worse problems: given the continuing depression, even the renegotiated terms proved too difficult. As one critic observed, a fatal error was committed, "*an overestimate of the ability of the people to pay.*" Yet another crisis was soon at hand.[77]

After years of tight budgets, public services in the city deteriorated. A city report found the downtown streets impassable after rains, no small problem in a cotton port. A group of mostly black residents complained that the nearest water of any sort was three blocks away.[78] Water lines stopped before the outskirts, which left whole neighborhoods uninsurable for fire; in one fearful instance, firemen watched helplessly as twenty-five

75. *MDR,* May 8, 1875.
76. Ibid., January 3, February 6, December 5, 1875.
77. *Mobile Tribune,* December 4, 1875; *MDR,* October 6, 1875, November 19, 1876.
78. Report of the Joint Committee on Streets, October 14, 1875, folder 2, envelope 5, box 21; and Alonzo Lennan et al. to the Mayor, August 8, 1877, folder 3, envelope 2, box 23, RMBACC. See also *MDR,* February 6, 1875, January 17, 1879.

homes perished.[79] Law enforcement was another problem, for policemen were seldom seen in the suburbs at night.[80] Even the board of health, reinstituted under Democratic rule, denounced the boardmembers' financial nitpicking, and a founder of the board, the prominent physician Jerome Cochran, became a leading critic.[81] As the crisis worsened, City Auditor Henry St. Paul commenced an aggressive campaign to write off Reconstruction-era debts. Why should the city starve itself for a "greedy band of creditors" whose debts originated in Radical "fraud, corruption or imbecility."[82] The still-belligerent St. Paul's rhetoric generated considerable criticism, but both the Democratic papers became increasingly sympathetic to this logic.[83]

City officials temporized on the debt issue, and their increased tenure in office shielded them from public frustration. Widespread discontent soon found other political expression, however, as a contested congressional nomination prompted years of popular insurgency. After his defeat in 1874, ex-congressman Frederick Bromberg remained popular among Mobile Democrats despite his Reconstruction background as a moderate Republican. He had, after all, opposed the railroad subsidy program and the other catastrophic economic initiatives. As the son of an immigrant, Bromberg also appealed to the city's ethnically diverse white working class. In Congress he had effectively bartered his Liberal Republican status to secure choice committee assignments, gaining the first substantial federal funding for clearing Mobile Bay. Many business leaders thought the city still needed Bromberg's services, fearing that a less effective representative might leave "the best port of the Gulf hermetically sealed." In 1876 Bromberg sought to regain his First District seat, now gerrymandered Democratic. His Mobile supporters swept the Democratic precinct meetings, but at the district convention a dispute over the unit rule led to a walkout by Bromberg's supporters. After initial hesitation, the *Register* and the local Democratic hierarchy lined in behind James T. Jones, the official nominee, while

79. *MDR,* February 5, 1875, October 12, 15, 1876.
80. *Mobile Tribune,* January 12, 1876; *MDR,* November 26, 1876; Board of Common Council, Minutes, November 16, 1876, Mobile Municipal Archives, reel 22.
81. *MDR,* March 25, 1875, November 25, 1877; Isbell, "Social and Economic History of Mobile," 99. On Cochran's career as an Alabama medical leader, see Allen Johnson Going, *Bourbon Democracy in Alabama, 1874–1890* (1951; reprint, University, Ala., 1992), 198–9.
82. *MDR,* February 3, 1875, April 2, 1876.
83. *Mobile Tribune,* April 1, 1876; *MDR,* February 2, 1875.

Bromberg's Mobile followers and the *Mobile Tribune* found themselves in full-scale revolt.[84]

These circumstances distinctly favored the Republicans. As one federal official observed, the factional ill will diverted Democratic hostility "to some extent from the colored voters."[85] To win, the insurgent Bromberg needed Republican support, no mean feat in the midst of a hotly contested presidential campaign between Republican Rutherford B. Hayes and Democrat Samuel Tilden.[86] The African American electorate thus faced the opportunity of returning Mobile's most prominent Republican turncoat to Congress, this time in rebellion against the Democrats. The irony of the situation notwithstanding, an appropriate response was not immediately apparent, and it generated substantial debate over strategic issues that would remain contentious in the coming years. For moderate Republicans, such as Gustavus Horton, there was no chance of success in Alabama "except in the disintegration of the Democratic party."[87] There was also a tactical consideration: supporting Bromberg would make it more likely that black ballots would be polled and counted, benefiting the rest of the Republican ticket. Sen. George Spencer's local operative, L. H. Mayer of the Internal Revenue Office, sardonically suggested their campaign banners should read Hayes and Bromberg on one side and Tilden and Bromberg on the other.[88]

Shaken by defeat and the violence of Redemption, Mobile's black leadership seized on the counsel of expediency with enthusiasm. Allen Alexander chaired the district convention that endorsed Bromberg, and he denounced the notion of running a Republican for the seat, especially an African American. The Bromberg campaign, he thought, would break down the color line and inaugurate an era of good feeling, and he felt certain most Mobile blacks agreed. Spencer Terrell likewise hoped that the division would allow blacks to bar the most reactionary Democrats from power, those who still rejected the Reconstruction amendments.[89] Henry J. Europe offered the most upbeat portrayal, depicting the Democratic dis-

84. *MDR,* October 3, May 21, August 21, 1876.
85. U.S. Congress, Senate, *Elections of 1874, 1875, 1876,* 32.
86. *MDR,* September 17, 1876.
87. Ibid., April 18, 1877.
88. Ibid., September 17, October 28, 15, 1876.
89. *Mobile Tribune,* October 11, 18, 1876.

unity as providential, literally God's doing. If Bromberg won, his white supporters could never "go back to Price Williams and affiliate with his [Democratic] ring. They will seek our votes in future political contests, and Price Williams and his adherents will also seek our votes, and then they will wish there were a few more niggers! [Laughter]." Europe welcomed the prospect that African Americans could permanently exercise the balance of power. Under the old condition of things, blacks' rights were never secure, but the alliance with Bromberg offered more safety than thousands of occupying federal soldiers. Another black leader agreed, observing that "we don't want any of Grant's troops, because if you kill niggers now you kill them for voting for a Democrat," a prospect he thought unlikely.[90]

A few other Republican activists opposed such ploys, citing Bromberg's previous betrayal. As congressman, he had played a conspicuous role in the revelations that brought down the Freedmen's Bank and had long called for the removal of federal troops from the South.[91] Some Republican activists preferred to run an actual Republican candidate against the two feuding Democrats. The white politician W. W. D. Turner, Mayor Harrington's old law partner, announced himself as the real party candidate in the race. Turner's motivation for his spoiler campaign was unclear, but many charged afterward that he sold the party out for Democratic money. Turner denied it, and firm proof is lacking; such allegations became endemic after Redemption, with the blurring of partisan lines locally. The ethics of the situation were murky anyway: if a given election was simply a choice of Democrats, why should Republican political professionals not cash in? (In Turner's case, after a decade of trying to make a living in politics, he got married in Florida and dropped from sight following the 1876 election.)[92]

If Turner indeed accepted Democratic money, the local black electorate likely had some inkling, for he fared badly in the raucous street canvass that characterized Republican politics. At a Turner rally, Allen Alexander led hecklers who were "so disorderly and insulting" that the candidate could scarcely make himself heard. Alexander mounted the stand to respond, but another black activist shoved him off, resulting in a general scuf-

90. Ibid., October 29, 19, 1876.
91. *MDR,* May 21, 1874, January 22, 1875, August 27, October 15, 1876; Carl R. Osthaus, *Freedmen, Philanthropy, and Fraud: A History of the Freedmen's Savings Bank* (Urbana, 1976), 187, 194–5.
92. *MDR,* October 15, 18, 1876, December 13, 1877; *Mobile Tribune,* November 12, 1876; *Pensacola Herald* quoted in *MDR,* June 5, 1877.

fle followed by arrests. Democratic Mayor Hurtel, who was in attendance, declared "it was the evident intention of Alexander and his crowd to break up the meeting."[93] He may well have been right, and the mayor's presence at the Turner rally demonstrated why it was deemed necessary. The Democrats always promoted the weaker opposition factions, with subsidies flowing freely toward the most disruptive Republicans, even the most radical. To read the *Register*, one would assume that Turner represented the bulk of Republican voters rather than a mere handful. Given the press manipulation, activists necessarily confronted each other directly at meetings, verbally or otherwise, and in the street. The *Register* complained that blacks were "regularly employed" in such pursuits and that they felt they had "a perfect right to go to a meeting and disturb its proceedings by their noise and confusion."[94] Basic civil liberties suffered, but circumstances allowed Republicans limited options if they hoped to forge some sort of consensus.

Divided as they were by faction and individual interest, Mobile's Republican activists were seldom unified, but by election day, black voters generally were. Dissident candidates were always plentiful, and increasing literacy logically ought to have facilitated ticket splitting, but seldom after Redemption did Mobile's blacks allow themselves the luxury of a significantly divided vote. In this instance Bromberg rolled up a gigantic local majority over the regular Democratic candidate, carrying the city by a three-to-one margin and winning the predominantly immigrant wards heavily.[95] As for Turner, he received only about a hundred or so votes in the city. The rumors of Democratic vote buying notwithstanding, the well-informed black electorate of Mobile shunned his candidacy. In the congressional district as a whole, however, Turner did better, draining off enough votes in the interior to give the Democrats a majority, or at least allow them to claim one. As predicted, Bromberg's white following remained restive, becoming the nucleus of a continuing movement against the entrenched Democratic leadership. In the summer of 1877, Mobile's voters prepared to elect a sheriff and other county officers. Widespread pressure existed for a

93. *MDR,* October 15, 1876.
94. Ibid., July 27, 1877.
95. Ibid., November 13, 1876. Bromberg ran furthest ahead of the Republican ticket in the heavily immigrant Third, Fifth, and Sixth Wards. In the Fifth, for example, Bromberg bested Jones 490 to 100 in a ward where Rutherford B. Hayes, the Republican presidential candidate, received only 254 votes.

more open nomination process, but a proposal for a primary was voted down, and the choice of candidates again proved controversial. The "Straightout" Democrats blamed much of this discontent on the impatience of younger men, for in the midst of "business depression and financial distress," government work was "regarded as a panacea for all pecuniary ills."[96]

Whatever the cause, an opposition People's Democratic party solidified and nominated James A. Shelton, a longtime Democrat of Irish extraction, for sheriff. One spokesman, George G. Duffee, proclaimed that Shelton had waged "the fight of a poor man against the ring." Class and ethnic consciousness were thus implicit in an insurgent appeal, and Mobile's white labor movement, modest though it was, proved receptive.[97] Against the backdrop of the great railroad strike in the summer of 1877, the independent votes clearly existed to defeat the Democratic candidate, Peter Burke, but only if the black Republican constituency cooperated. Again having the prospect of real influence, African American activists debated a response. The obvious option, presenting Republican party candidates, again received little consideration. U.S. Marshal George Turner observed that black voters in Mobile were "perhaps more timid than they are in any other southern city of like size."[98] Given the recent riot, Turner thought that any election disturbance caused panic and that blacks would scarcely leave their homes afterward. The marshal exaggerated, but black activists quite possibly concluded a serious bid for power too dangerous, even, or perhaps especially, if it showed prospects for success. As one party meeting observed, Republicans had concluded it was "proper and wise" not to run candidates locally. That decision left the two feuding Democratic factions, and activ-

96. *NYT,* November 30, 1876; *MDR,* April 20, July 3, 1877; *Mobile Tribune,* February 4, November 2, 3, 1876.

97. *MDR,* December 11, 1877. One of the People's Democratic Convention officers was Gregor McGregor, longtime leader of the Baymen's Benevolent Association, Mobile's most powerful union. His skilled cotton screwmen, two hundred strong, were exclusively white, heavily immigrant, and previously Democratic. The *Register* observed that the baymen carried "a considerable influence in elections." *MDR,* August 4, 1876, June 6, 12, 15, 1877, May 12, 1878.

98. U.S. Congress, Senate, *Elections of 1874, 1875, 1876,* 32. The U.S. marshal was W. W. D. Turner's brother in a white Republican leadership that was notably nepotistic. Spencer's allies Charles and Louis Mayer were two brothers who held high federal positions throughout the 1870s, and of course J. J. and Cleveland Moulton were brothers as well. The same pattern is much less evident among the African American leadership.

ists quarreled so openly over what to do that a group of Methodist ministers stepped in to broker a solution. A published statement observed that blacks were "very much divided" over the partisan situation, adding that for the moment they should "cease political strife." The ministers promised in good time to enlighten the black community as to how it should vote. In response, one group of activists denounced the ministers for their audacity, warning them that they should avoid temporal matters thereafter.[99]

On this issue the black leadership split, with most activists backing the People's Democrats, but others, such as Allen Alexander, supporting the Straightout Democrats. The resulting debates were tumultuous. At one meeting, if the *Register* can be believed, "there were three lively fights, and at one time the prospect was that of a lively row." The police were reportedly called in to maintain order, but the meeting broke up in confusion. For weeks thereafter, controversy continued. In the Sixth Ward three rival Republican organizations claimed official status, and similarly irregular clubs proliferated throughout the city. Strikingly, however, on election day the leadership disunity again made little difference. Mobile County voters buried the Democratic candidate by two thousand votes in orderly balloting. By all accounts, the People's insurgents received almost all the black vote, perhaps two hundred backing the Straightouts.[100] The African American electorate resisted voting for a Straightout Democrat, whatever leadership advice they received. One black activist concluded that Republicans were generally sold out by their leaders, and "last summer they were sold, that is they got the money, but they [Republicans] voted as they pleased."[101] George Duffee concurred that Democrats thought they had bought the black vote but received a rude surprise on election day. This might explain the injudicious fury with which the *Register* turned on its black collaborators. It blamed defeat on the disgust whites felt for the resort to black spokesmen, specifying Alexander among others.[102] This disrespect humiliated and infuriated those leaders who had backed the Democrats, just in time for the fall city campaigns.

Republican voters again demonstrated they could help humble the regular Democratic candidate, even under the adverse circumstances of Re-

99. *MDR,* July 1, May 13, 1877.
100. Ibid., June 19, July 13, August 12, 22, 1877.
101. Ibid., December 11, 1877.
102. Ibid., August 8, November 20, 1877.

demption. This occasioned some gratification, and the effective exercise of the franchise perhaps merited it, but the intervention did not necessarily advance a racial-justice agenda much. Before election day, People's Democratic leaders had dropped "Democratic" from their name, and they privately assured Republican leaders that if successful, civil rights concessions would be forthcoming. The streets were "full of the rumors of these pledges," which featured African Americans as deputies and on juries. Once installed in office, however, Sheriff Shelton found it inadvisable or impossible to comply with such expectations. Democrats maintained most of the county offices, and Shelton soon reconciled his feud with the Straightouts. Shelton's black supporters found themselves frustrated. At one Republican meeting, a black speaker wanted to know if the People's party had "given even the place of porter or watchman at the Courthouse to the colored allies who had won the victory. A deep disgruntled 'nary time' came from the audience." In future, things would be different; having proven their influence, Republicans pressed for public pledges from officials who could be held accountable.[103]

With perhaps a hundred policemen and seventy-five positions on the street force at stake, city jobs remained an inviting goal, especially with a municipal election coming that December.[104] One petition headed by Rev. E. D. Taylor but mostly signed by political unknowns combined conciliatory gestures with forthright requests. The signers admitted that blacks had been "led into wrongs by unprincipled and unscrupulous men," presumably the much reviled carpetbaggers. This policy alienated them from their true friends, southern whites. The black population, having come to their senses, now prayed that as a gesture of forgiveness the Democratic officials would "give them a recognition in the giving out of the public spoils."[105] The city boards discreetly delayed responding to the petition until after the county election, then dismissed it. Afterward, the *Register* marveled at the insolence of the request, petitions from black constituents being quite rare after Redemption.[106] The conciliatory language actually cloaked bold demands, suggesting the priority the black community accorded the patronage. This issue functioned as a talisman for more abstract issues of racial

---

103. Ibid., July 22 1877, May 23, 1878, November 20, 1877.
104. Ibid., August 4, 1877.
105. E. D. Taylor et al. to Mayor, May 30, 1877, folder 1, envelope 1, box 24, RMBACC; *MDR,* August 12, 1877.
106. *MDR,* August 12, 1877.

respect, uniting the self-interest of the activists with the egalitarian aspirations of the wider black community.

As the municipal election finally drew near, the fiscal crisis worsened, playing into the hands of the insurgents. The city managed to meet its renegotiated debt payments, but at immense cost. By the fall, the police and street force were two months behind on their pay, while city contractors were often four months behind in payment. The city ceased honoring its warrants—"IOUs"—in payment of taxes, thus rendering them temporarily valueless to the city employees who received them. Public services suffered badly. One Republican mass meeting referred to the "foul and filthy" streets, the "neglected public pumps," and the "want of gaslights in many parts of the city."[107] Furthermore, the seizures of city property in federal court accelerated, threatening a parade of auctions. Worse still, the court began to levy taxes directly in support of its judgments. Like everyone else, African Americans were weary of retrenchment and growing restive. One Republican faction apparently placarded the streets "with a communistic appeal to strike down and stop the wheels of municipal government, to repudiate public debts."[108]

These dire circumstances facilitated the appeal of insurgent whites to the African American electorate. In the tumultuous year 1877, the People's candidates sought black support through the rhetoric of class resentment. Mayoral candidate George G. Duffee had personal motivations as well as political ones. After starting out as an office boy, he rose to become a cotton merchant. He was regarded as "honest and popular" but lost heavily in speculation and suffered "a complete extermination of his bus[iness]."[109] Downwardly mobile and needing office badly, Duffee fell easily into denunciations of the wealthy: "They charge me, fellow citizens, with being a Communist—class against class." He contested the charge but added it was "these bank men and rich that talk about running class against class." He concluded one speech with the observation, "I eat a cold dinner every day, for I am a poor man." He called on blacks to teach their children that men of modest means might aspire to office. Though Duffee articulated few clear ideas of how to deal with the fiscal crisis, his denunciations of bankers

---

107. Ibid., September 23, 28, 1877.
108. Ibid., April 13, 1878, December 15, 1877.
109. Entries for Geo. G. Duffee, credit ledger, Mobile County, January 17, March 17, 1877, Alabama, vol. 18, R. G. Dun and Company Collection, Baker Library, Harvard Business School.

and bondholders apparently resonated well with black listeners as well as white.[110]

Duffee and his People's allies also addressed black concerns specifically, if not with conspicuous enlightenment. In private Dr. Jerome Cochran urged caution, reportedly stating that "the colored men were ignorant yet, and must let the white people act for them, and trust to the white people's good intentions." When pressed, however, he made public concessions, as when one black man interrupted a People's meeting to ask what they would offer blacks. Cochran responded that he recognized "all the rights of the colored people, the right to vote, and the right to be recognized in the employment of the city."[111] He then welcomed any black man who cared to speak to the platform. As for Duffee himself, he vowed: "I am your friend, I mean it. I don't want the black men to lose their vote and they must enjoy it." Duffee argued that black suffrage meant more southern congressmen, and the mostly white crowd cheered. On another occasion Duffee offered the somewhat disquieting assurance that he would govern the whole people, like the Redeemer governor Wade Hampton of South Carolina. He would see that blacks received their rights, equal and undivided. Duffee privately promised that blacks would serve on his police force but refused to sign a pledge to that effect.[112]

The threat of a Republican alternative encouraged Duffee's overt solicitation of black support. He heard downtown rumors that Democrats intended "to try that job they tried in August, throwing their money everywhere. They want to try that [W. W. D.] Turner job again"—a reference to the spoiler candidacy that defeated Bromberg in 1876.[113] That is to say, when pressed, Straightout Democrats with means could generally induce some disaffected Republican activists to offer a party ticket to drain off black votes. As Duffee feared, a separate Republican slate appeared, heavily publicized in the Democratic press, under the Radical scalawag Paul Ravesies. It received support by some federal officeholders who resented the Hayes administration's patronage policy, which sought Democratic collaboration at the expense of loyal Republicans. L. H. Mayer, Senator Spencer's closest local ally, lambasted Duffee's vague promises on

110. *MDR,* December 6, 11, 1877.
111. Ibid., November 20, December 8, 15, 1877.
112. Ibid., December 6, 7, 15, 1877.
113. C. C. Pontiac et al. to Hayes, December 31, 1877, box 4, AP-247, RG 56; *MDR,* December 6, 1877.

behalf of the People's party: "what do they propose to give you? Nothing—not a single thing."[114] Six blacks submitted petitions to Sheriff Shelton for positions as porter or watchman, and they had been ignored. Black federal employee Henry J. Europe argued that true Republicans should force the People's party to "give a decided yes or no to the colored people" rather than rely on nebulous assurances of future favor.[115] Aided by the *Register,* Ravesies's followers could articulate a Radical Republican viewpoint publicly so long as they provided covert aid to the Democratic candidate thereby. For some activists and officeholders, black and white, it was an opportunity that might yield both political and personal benefit.

Ravesies's supporters complained that federal officials misapplied party "money & supplies" to Duffee's independent campaign. The situation facilitated the flow of money from Democrats to cooperative Republicans. The universal currency of such reports makes establishing the facts difficult, but cash subsidies apparently were much in evidence in this bitterly contested election.[116] Ravesies publicly denied receiving a fifteen-hundred-dollar bribe, so prevalent were rumors of Democratic money. One black activist went to the People's party leaders for money to canvass; when they refused, he defected to Ravesies, publicly using the rebuff to illustrate that Duffee was a cheapskate.[117] Duffee himself testified to the pervasiveness of corruption with an unorthodox bit of platform advice. He warned his listeners that Democrats would spend money like water to beat him but that the People's party could hardly follow suit. He concluded: "I tell you, colored men, if they offer you money take it—take it, and then vote as you think best. Let them know the rich man cannot have everything his own way." Black activist Spencer Terrell added that Democrats were buying up registration papers, thus preventing blacks from voting. He urged them not to part with their right to vote: "don't sacrifice your certificates and yourselves, too."[118]

On election day, Duffee defeated the Democratic candidate for mayor by a thirty-seven-vote margin, though the Democrats carried the majority of the unpaid positions on the city boards. The Ravesies ticket received

114. *MDR,* November 20, 1877.
115. Ibid., December 13, November 20, 1877.
116. Pontiac et al. to Hayes, December 31, 1877; *MDR,* December 11, 1877.
117. *MDR,* December 13, 1877.
118. *MDR,* December 8, 11, 1877; Charles Nordhoff, *The Cotton States in the Spring and Summer of 1875* (reprint; New York, n.d.), 20, 85.

slightly over two hundred votes, a tiny proportion of the Republican total but enough to turn several races toward the Democrats. The election was the fairest since the war, the *Register* conceded; the paper actually discouraged challenges by the defeated Democratic candidates on the ground that they would tend to keep divisive issues alive. Duffee now entered upon a three-year term as mayor with the public intensely aware of the promises made to his black allies. The Democratic opposition had no intention of making his task easy, reminding the new mayor that he was "at the mercy of the boards." If Duffee had the right to appoint the police under the charter, the *Register* observed, the city boards could reduce the size of the force to one man, then appoint another constabulary to preserve public order.[119]

Unlike Sheriff Shelton, Mayor Duffee tried to fulfill his pledges to his African American constituents. He appointed seven black policemen, reportedly assuring his caucus they would be stationed in the suburbs and "kept out of sight as much as possible." He also appointed black detectives, apparently on the same principle of invisibility. The *Register* proclaimed the appointments a "declaration of war" and called upon the Democratic legislature to intervene.[120] The Democratic city boards tried to interfere, but it seems Mayor Duffee carried his point.[121] Even so, much of the African American community still felt he had not followed through on his pledges. One black leader, S. S. Davis, observed that Duffee "had not done one-half that he promised to do when he was seeking the office," adding that some of the new policemen, apparently whites, harassed blacks on the streets needlessly. On one occasion a black crowd tried to liberate a drunken man who was resisting arrest from Duffee's police.[122] The police chief also found himself embroiled in a public controversy with black ministers, one growing out of his interfering with church festivals for not paying city license fees. The ministers complained of the "great injustice" perpetrated against "our class of citizens" by the current administration.[123]

Mayor Duffee's mixed record inspired intense internal debate among African Americans, which was reflected in the legislative races the following summer. Supporters and opponents of the People's alliance offered legislative tickets that, for once, divided the Republican vote, assuring an easy

119. *MDR,* January 8, 1878, December 23, 1877.
120. Ibid., December 28, 1877, January 4, 1878.
121. G. G. Duffee to Boards, May 18, 1878, folder 2, envelope 3, box 24, RMBACC.
122. *MDR,* August 1, December 27, 1878.
123. Ibid., August 27, 28, 1878.

Democratic victory. The African American criticism seems to have honestly perplexed Duffee. Encountering a case of resisting arrest, he mused that "the colored people were hard to please. If he didn't make officers of some of them, they would find fault; and when he did, they would not be arrested by them." It was not black discontent, however, but the financial issue that proved Mayor Duffee's undoing. Though he came to office on a wave of popular frustration, he had not sketched out a clear position on what to do about the debt. Several of the more outspoken proponents of repudiation did poorly at the election, among them Henry St. Paul, who ran far behind his Democratic ticket.[124] Duffee's class rhetoric did not grant him a clear mandate for a specific course of action, and he shied away from drastic measures. That summer, the city failed to meet its renegotiated interest payments. This caused "disappointment and indignation" among bondholders, and the resulting federal lawsuits and tax judgments threatened citizens with "the destruction by confiscation" of citizens' property.[125] By August, the city was four months late on its payrolls too.[126] The crisis festered and the mayor's popularity ebbed away.

For the Democrats, Duffee's election provided a wholesome jolt. At a subsequent election, a Democratic legislator remained "considerably anxious" that the few disaffected Democrats would be "joined by the solid phalanx of Republicans and Niggerdom" and thereby win.[127] The continuing dissident threat prompted internal reforms. After years of controversy, the leadership finally agreed to party primary elections, and Mobile became the first large city in Alabama to nominate by direct primary vote.[128] On the crucial debt issue, the Democrats moved vigorously since repudiation now could be blamed on Duffee's maladministration. Swift action was essential after Mobile defaulted to avert the flood of litigation underway. The young lawyer Hannis Taylor examined the precedents, especially the recent bankruptcy of Memphis, and he concluded that federal law precluded collection of debts against defunct municipalities.[129] If the legislature repealed

124. Ibid., August 11, March 12, December 23, 1878.
125. Board of Aldermen, Minutes, December 24, 1878, Mobile Municipal Archives, reel 6; *NYT,* January 20, October 7, 1879.
126. Board of Aldermen, Minutes, August 6, 1878, reel 6.
127. S. C. Muldon to Schroeder, October 22, 1878, S. C. Muldon Letterbooks, The Museum of Mobile.
128. Allen Woodrow Jones, "A History of the Direct Primary in Alabama, 1840–1903" (Ph.D. diss., University of Alabama, 1964), 112–3; *MDR,* June 27, 1878.
129. Wrenn, *Crisis and Commission Government in Memphis,* 15–40; Tennant S. McWil-

Mobile's charter, the successor government might deal with creditors from a position of strength, forcing more-realistic terms. The Democrats were well placed to secure swift enactment of the proposal from a sympathetic legislature. The possible repeal also had the partisan advantage of bringing Duffee's three-year term to a premature end and trimmed the boundaries of the proposed "Port of Mobile" to exclude the northern and southern suburbs, eliminating several hundred mostly black voters.[130] Taylor presented his plan publicly in late 1878, winning the endorsement of a powerful committee of business leaders. The *Register* backed it too, simply confessing that "the burden is far in excess of our ability to pay. . . . we might as well admit this plain fact in all of our calculations."[131] A year before such talk was communistic, but now that it had become Democratic orthodoxy, the boards endorsed it.[132]

The swift emergence of the Taylor proposal placed Mayor Duffee in an impossible position: he could either obstruct a solution to the city's fiscal woes or watch his elective office disappear. In early 1879 Duffee led public opposition to the proposal, arguing "that the city could arrange with its creditors without the resort to giving up the charter. He considered this repudiation, and he was opposed to repudiation."[133] The mayor stressed the undemocratic overtones of the legislation, noting that all local offices were to be filled by appointment from the governor. Duffee did win some following among African American voters, who were aware of the racial gerrymander incorporated in the proposal. Even here, however, the *Register* discerned some tendency for blacks who "own their homes and who have acquired property" to "break away from the leadership of the politicians."[134] Whatever blacks thought, the legislature paid minimal heed to the criticism of the opposition. After restoring local elections and making a few other concessions, the legislature quickly passed the charter repeal just before adjourning. The City of Mobile ceased to exist in March 1879, to the outrage of creditors across the nation.[135]

---

liams, *Hannis Taylor: The New Southerner as American* (University, Ala., 1978), 11–3; *MDR*, February 15, 1882.
    130. Berkstresser, "Mobile, Alabama, in the 1880s," 219.
    131. *MDR*, January 14, 1879.
    132. Berkstresser, "Mobile, Alabama, in the 1880s," 6.
    133. *MDR*, January 13, 1879.
    134. Ibid., January 26, 1879.
    135. Berkstresser, "Mobile, Alabama, in the 1880s," 3–7; *NYT*, October 8, 1879.

In elections soon thereafter, the Democrats won full control of the new Port of Mobile, with Mayor Duffee running weakly on his ticket.[136] The People's movement disintegrated, yielding smaller and more labor-identified groupings and leaving African Americans badly divided. Given the favorable circumstances, Democrats finally anticipated the stable control Redemption had promised. The legislature had certainly done its part to assure permanent Democratic supremacy. One merchant, for example, praised the "at-large" voting procedures for the new eight-member governing body, the board of police. If representation was by wards, "some objectionable man" might win, but citywide voting made that impossible.[137] With the national economy finally beginning to come out of the depression and given the enhanced white majority in the reconfigured Port of Mobile, one might have assumed African American political influence would come to an end. The Democrats won easily for the near future, but the local economy remained troubled, and the Port of Mobile legislation was so fiscally restrictive that the white population remained dissatisfied. Thus African American political leaders retained some real political leverage well into the 1880s.[138]

In the years after Redemption, black politics evolved in a pragmatic direction. No basic challenge to the social order would be tolerated anyway, so incremental gains loomed increasingly larger. Some black leaders expressed positive relief that the violent struggles of the Reconstruction era were past. One petition, signed by C. C. Pontiac and others, praised President Hayes's conciliatory southern policies for "a season of repose with a feeling of security such as we have never known."[139] Increasingly, debates revolved around municipal and federal patronage rather than more abstract issues of racial justice, though these wider issues always lurked in the background. Perhaps the most concrete way to observe the implications of this is to examine the course of individual leaders. While activists' calculations of personal benefit were always significant during Reconstruction, jobs and money became more obvious motivations afterward. In the cases of Allen Alexander and Philip Joseph, the city's two most prominent black leaders, one can trace the influence of personal interest upon leadership. Both men

---

136. Berkstresser, "Mobile, Alabama, in the 1880s," 12; *MDR,* March 12, 1879.
137. *MDR,* July 26, 1879.
138. Doyle, *New Men, New Cities, New South,* 71.
139. Pontiac et al. to Hayes, December 31, 1877.

struggled with maintaining credibility while surviving as Gilded Age political professionals.

After entering politics early during Reconstruction as a combative young militant, Alexander remained "under the public gaze" for nearly two decades, longer than "any other negro" in the vicinity.[140] His sometime ally Cleveland F. Moulton described the former slave as a smart man whom nature had favored.[141] After losing a bid at the legislature in 1869, Alexander served for some years as a justice of the peace in Baldwin County. Indicted for official misconduct, apparently on flimsy grounds, he fled to Mobile.[142] As Moulton observed, Alexander was arrested a good many times, but nothing substantial was ever proven.[143] Alexander reemerged as a spokesman for the Republicans, securing a position as inspector in the customhouse. In early 1874, factional opponents sought his removal from the position, and "the nature of the accusations against me was such as to prevent me, almost entirely, from obtaining any employment."[144] Without the help of friends, he observed, his "large and dependent family" would have suffered. Moulton and his allies lobbied for almost five months before Treasury officials restored Alexander to the position, which paid a modest $3.50 a day. Alexander's rescue may have encouraged his aggressive opposition to the civil rights bill on behalf of his white allies. After the 1874 riot, which nearly cost him his life, the controversial Alexander again lost his patronage position.[145]

Between insecure jobs and Democratic gunmen, Alexander had ample reason to ponder the personal cost of his political career. Such calculations likely shaped the evolution of his politics. Immediately after Redemption, he led the militant opposition to Postmaster Morris D. Wickersham, head of the local party structure. African Americans widely distrusted Wickersham for his politics and his tendency to hire white Democrats as subordinates. Alexander chaired a party gathering that accused Wickersham of leaking information to Democrats and of telling them that "whenever he

140. *MDR,* March 5, 1886.
141. U. S. Congress, House, *Affairs in Alabama,* 454.
142. Judge John Elliot to R. M. Reynolds, January 30, 1874; and Statement of Charles E. Mayer et al., April 22, 1874, box 4, AP-246, RG 56; *MDR,* November 19, 1870.
143. U.S. Congress, House, *Affairs in Alabama,* 454.
144. Allen Alexander to Secretary of Treasury, July 31, 1874, box 4, AP-246, RG 56.
145. U.S. Congress, House, *Affairs in Alabama,* 349.

wanted the aid of niggers he could easily buy it."¹⁴⁶ Alexander proclaimed the postmaster worse than the opposition, but soon thereafter, he accepted a position as clerk in Wickersham's post office, a job that he held into the early 1880s. The Radical "Customhouse Alexander" promptly morphed into "Post Office Alexander" and became Wickersham's longtime spokesman. The postmaster could barely speak before black audiences without being heckled, but he retained some influence so long as Alexander articulated his positions, if only in deference to Alexander's demonstrated capacity to physically confront detractors.

If not entirely mercenary, Alexander's newfound position certainly entailed different political alliances. In 1877, as the People's Democratic campaign of James Shelton gathered steam, Wickersham proclaimed his official neutrality on the grounds that the Hayes administration preferred nonpartisan behavior. In private, though, he tried to "control a few negroes for the Straight-Outs, the candidate for Sheriff on that ticket being one of his bondsmen."¹⁴⁷ That is to say, the Democratic candidate, Peter Burke, had signed the postmaster's property bond, Republicans notoriously having difficulty meeting such requirements for holding office. Thus Alexander, following Wickersham's lead, endorsed the Democratic nominee and, as party official, muscled supportive resolutions from Republican meetings. He consequently encountered a firestorm of criticism, finding himself "all alone by himself in the Radical party just now" as the *Register* pointed out.¹⁴⁸ One Republican leader openly accused him of pocketing a five-thousand-dollar bribe, and others made similar charges. Alexander took the criticism with ill grace. After being denounced at one meeting, he responded that he could "buy every 'nigger' in the Seventh Ward," this perhaps an oblique boast of Democratic largesse. The massive black vote for Shelton was a personal humiliation compounded by the Democrats blaming Alexander's prominence for causing the low white turnout.¹⁴⁹

The Democrats assumed that venal black leaders controlled their followers like puppet masters, but as Alexander discovered, this was not true. No individual leader could exact unquestioning obedience from the African American community, if only because all the talk of Democratic payoffs

146. *MDR,* September 15, 14, 1875.
147. Ibid., August 5, 1877, January 22, 1878.
148. Ibid., June 3, 1877.
149. Ibid., October 1, June 2, 3, August 8, 1877.

encouraged independent judgment. After this damaging episode, it took some time for Alexander to recover. That autumn a suggestion at a Republican meeting that he be asked to speak was rejected without comment, perhaps in response to his role in the election. By the time of the Duffee campaign, though, Alexander again assisted the Democrats by supporting Ravesies, the spoiler Republican candidate. He also defended his earlier behavior with vigor. "Of the two Democratic parties," he observed, "the straight-outs are much the best, for they are aristocrats, they are the rich; the others want our votes because they are poor." The People's Democrats would not even promise positions as porter or watchman before the election, and Alexander discerned no chance for concessions once they won.[150]

"If we are to be servants let us serve the rich; it is preferable to serving the poor."[151] This credo of Alexander's may have been opportunistic, but it made a certain amount of sense in the context of Redemption. Perhaps the statement manifested Alexander's actual belief, but it certainly expressed his practice. Repeatedly during the late 1870s, Alexander opposed fusion with insurgent Democratic factions, preferring hopeless Republican tickets. This implicit aid to the Straightout Democrats manifested the cold-eyed pragmatism that typified his leadership. In 1880, for example, he was the only local delegate to the Republican National Convention not to support U. S. Grant's bid for a third term. He conceded that Grant was popular with Mobile's blacks, but southern Republicans could not deliver a single electoral vote, and Alexander thought political reality prevailed. Despite having been formally instructed to vote for Grant, Alexander had "laid aside all favorites" and was "for the man that the Northern States believe they can elect."[152] That fall, Wickersham and Alexander backed a factional Republican bid for Congress, that of the black politician Frank Threatt. In Mobile County the effort racked up 140 votes to 3,240 for the regular Republican, James Gillette. Threatt's candidacy assured the defeat of Gillette, the nationally recognized party candidate. Gillette was identified with Spencer's old following and long considered hostile to the postmaster, and Wickersham and Alexander certainly knew how to punish their enemies within the Republican party.[153]

150. Ibid., December 9, November 20, 1877.
151. Ibid., November 20, 1877.
152. Ibid., June 3, 1880.
153. Handbills signed by Spencer Terrell, February 11, 16, 1881, James Gillette Papers, LC; *NYT,* November 11, 1880.

In one respect, however, Alexander's political style changed but little. Having faced Klansmen and Democratic deputies, he still stood his ground in a confrontation. The *New York Times* observed that Alexander "ruled conventions by his turbulence, and he was known as a fighting man."[154] Not surprisingly, Alexander spent more time in court than any other activist, perhaps more than all the rest combined.[155] He was charged with everything from assault to inciting riot, generally—though not always—growing out of political altercations and more often than not involving Republican rivals. A most revealing instance occurred in 1882, after Wickersham and he finally lost their federal positions. As a party official Alexander became involved in a personal dispute with Collector of Customs Joseph W. Burke, whom the now jobless Alexander reportedly resented for not hiring him.[156] The two men had a political disagreement, during the course of which Alexander publicly accused Burke of directing his subordinates not to contribute money to the party. The collector admitted that he had done so, stating that Alexander could not be trusted with party funds. The enraged Alexander then struck him over the head with an umbrella. Burke did not respond, concluding it injudicious in a meeting primarily composed of African Americans, and the episode subjected the collector to months of ribbing in the Democratic press. Alexander's behavior overtly grew out of the financial dispute and was compounded by his short fuse. Still, one suspects it was freighted with wider issues of respect, of his treatment by the most powerful white patronage official in the state.

Perhaps Alexander's bare-knuckles personal style enhanced his popular appeal. If so, it eventually cost him dearly. After losing his federal clerkship

154. *NYT*, March 5, 1886.
155. Alexander's full police record would be difficult to reconstruct, but the highlights as recorded in the *Register* include: a fine for disorderly conduct (September 24, 1869); public drunkenness (October 5, 1869, and November 3, 1869); charges growing out of the *Mobile Nationalist* confrontation (December 10–14, 1869); hitting someone with a table leg at a political meeting (May 10, 11, 1872); fourteen indictments growing out of his service as an official in Baldwin County as well as locally (February 1, 1874); an arrest at a political riot (October 15, 1876); a conviction for inciting riot, in which he was reportedly sentenced to three months (January 17, 1877); involvement in a barroom fight, during the course of which he discharged a pistol into the ceiling (July 13, 1877); a charge of assault with a pistol and during the course of his trial assaulting an officer in the courtroom (May 30–31, 1878); and a charge of disorderly conduct (May 20, 1882). While one would be ill advised to accept such accusations at face value, wholesale fabrication of the entire list seems unlikely.
156. *MDR*, October 4, 1882.

at the post office, Alexander pulled together enough money to open a "low bar" that catered to a gambling clientele. On Christmas night, 1885, Alexander was playing craps in the back poolroom. A dubious customer entered, "Crab Alf" Hamilton, who had been recently acquitted on charges of arson. Alexander thought it best to withdraw his money from the table, which Hamilton resented as an insult. He pulled a knife and lit into the group, striking Alexander and another man. Eventually, someone clubbed him with a metal bar while Alexander stabbed him in the chest. The press accounts suggest obvious provocation, but Democratic city officials still charged Alexander with murder, some witnesses claiming he had inflicted the fatal injury after Hamilton was subdued. Two months in custody followed, with Alexander unable to raise the several thousand dollars for bail. While awaiting trial, Alexander contracted pneumonia in the drafty jail and died. He had only made it to his midthirties, with his *Register* obituary announcing the "Death of a Bad Citizen."[157]

Alexander's rival Philip Joseph perhaps lived a less colorful life, but he pursued an similarly inconstant political trajectory. As a young man Joseph had emerged early during Reconstruction as the city's most prominent Creole politician. Of privileged background, the "always scrupulously dressed" Joseph was thought "well educated and of fine address." In the early 1870s he worked under Frederick Bromberg in the post office and ex-senator Willard Warner in the customhouse, becoming the leading black spokesman for their moderate Republican faction. After Warner's defeat in the customhouse fight with Sen. George Spencer, Joseph edited a Republican newspaper and became an aggressive proponent of black officeholding and civil rights legislation. With the success of Redemption in Alabama, Joseph left Mobile, encouraged by a ten-thousand-dollar libel judgment against his paper.[158] He relocated to Louisiana, receiving a job in the post office and a position under the Republican state government as well.[159] The

---

157. Ibid., November 16, December 27, 30, 1885, March 5, 1886; *New Orleans Picayune*, December 27, 1885, March 5, 1886; *NYT,* March 5, 1886.

158. MDR, February 21, 1907, July 19, 1877, March 10, 1875. Joseph's paper featured a gossip column that publicized interracial liaisons, and he was sued repeatedly over the issue. *Mobile Watchman,* August 30, 1873, January 31, April 26, 1874.

159. MDR, June 17, 1877; U.S. Congress, Senate, *Report and Testimony of the Select Committee of the United States Senate to Investigate the Causes of the Removal of the Negroes from the Southern States to the Northern States,* 46th Cong., 2d sess., 1880, S. Rept. 693, 2:393, 412.

collapse of Reconstruction there prompted another move, a return to Mobile in time for Shelton's campaign for sheriff, though he reportedly dabbled in Louisiana politics for some years to follow.[160]

Upon his return to Mobile, Joseph went from civil rights zealot to spokesman for the insurgent People's Democrats. In one speech he argued that failure to hire blacks as porters in Sheriff Shelton's courthouse did not matter. The position was "not worth much," and "as for himself he wanted a better office," a comment that perhaps reflected his own privileged background relative to most other black activists.[161] As the People's party declined under Mayor Duffee's rule, the independent movement took on an increasing identification with organized labor. Joseph concluded that the Greenback party's "laboring men" were "courting the colored vote."[162] He thought this a wonderful opportunity, noting that the Greenback congressional candidate was "as near a Republican [as] a fellow can get to be and not be one."[163] His efforts to force endorsements split the local Republican party, but national party officials approved of his actions, and it appears he secured employment as a federal election supervisor.[164] He actually served as a county official for the third party, predicting that the Greenbackers would show such strength at the next election as to astound the major parties. It did not happen in Mobile, but the third party did pick up a number of congressional seats, including a win in North Alabama. Afterward, Joseph established a nominally Republican newspaper, the *Mobile Gazette,* by one account on a press furnished by his Greenbacker associates.[165]

Most Mobile Republicans resisted Joseph's strategy. If they rejected Wickersham and Alexander's promotion of the Straightout Democrats as the lesser evil, they also doubted the wholesale embrace of class-based Democratic insurgents. For the federal jobholders, the patronage implication was that dissident Democrats would be rewarded at the expense of loyal Republicans, black and white. Lou H. Mayer and other Spencer followers mostly criticized fusion arrangements, preferring to maintain an in-

160. Pamphlet, "Daring Impudence," in Spencer Terrell to John Sherman, March 22, 1880, box 7, AP-247, RG 56.
161. *MDR,* December 13, 1877.
162. Joseph to Gillette, October 7, 11, 1878, Gillette Papers.
163. Joseph to Gillette, October 11, 1878.
164. *MDR,* July 21, 1878; Joseph to Gillette, October 7, 14, 19, 1878, Gillette Papers.
165. *MDR,* October 11, November 10, 1878, April 7, 1880, June 25, 1881. The truth of the allegation was in dispute.

dependent Republican organization. Their arguments often made sense to African Americans, for a few federal jobs went a long way for black activists. Besides, as one government worker observed, the customhouse irregularly employed "about one hundred vagrant negro-spotters, who go around and inform on unsuspecting individuals."[166] Why forfeit whatever jobs and influence they had in search of a few Democratic dissidents, generally as racist as the Straightouts themselves?

Joseph's strategy of alliance with Greenbackers had other drawbacks besides the obvious one that blacks cared little about deflation—though given the city's debt problem, perhaps they should have. The real problem was the alliance with white labor radicals. One Republican gathering observed that Joseph's paper was "controlled by an element that has always been jealous of the negro as regards labor."[167] Since the formal union movement excluded Mobile's blacks, the criticism of collaboration with a labor-based party had obvious credibility. The white Baymen's Association had long since solidified a near monopoly of loading cotton onto ships, and other laborers tried to follow suit.[168] In early 1878, for example, anonymous stevedores petitioned the city government, complaining that black stevedores were taking contracts to load lumber. The specifics are unclear, but it appears there was some violation of local law or protocol: "The Negro is represented as working by the day, but such is not the case."[169] Subsequent press reports suggest the white workers won their grievance, to the distress of the board of trade, and it appears a timbermen's association eventually solidified racial control over this work too.[170] Mobile's leading businessmen, by contrast to the white unions, commonly professed appreciation or an actual preference for black laborers.[171]

Given these realities, the *Register* found it puzzling for "the unskilled-labor black" to profess unity with "the skilled-labor white," and the paper

166. Ibid., August 14, 1878.
167. Ibid., April 14, 1880.
168. Ibid., June 4, 1876.
169. Petition of "Many Stevedores" to Mayor, January 10, 1878, folder 2, envelope 3, box 24, RMBACC.
170. *MDR,* May 12, July 18, December 22, 1878, November 2, 1885, February 25, March 23, April 23 1886.
171. U.S. Congress, Senate Committee on Education and Labor, *Report of the Committee of the Senate upon the Relations between Labor and Capital and Testimony Taken by the Committee,* 48th Cong., 2d sess., S. Rept. 1262, 4:67, 103, 110.

was not alone in doubting that the two groups had common interests.[172] Still, circumstances increasingly aided Joseph's strategy of political alliance with the labor movement. In 1878 the Knights of Labor arrived in Mobile's vicinity, starting the first significant interracial labor mobilization in the city's history.[173] While the more established unions apparently held aloof, the Knights generated substantial popular notice.[174] By early 1880, the white organization was "making a strong effort to organize the colored element," they being about the first labor activists to do so. In Mobile the "Colored Creoles" were organized separately, and at one time the Knights claimed a membership that would have embraced much of the Creole male population.[175] The Knights anticipated challenging the Democrats in the August 1880 county elections but fell victim to internal dissension over "too much *politics*."[176] Even so, the labor agitation may have borne fruit in subsequent strikes among black draymen, railway workers, and boatmen. The walkouts continued for nearly two weeks and seem to have had an enduring effect. In 1883 business leader A. C. Danner observed that the blacks had "a great many associations of their own" and even "some labor unions." "The stevedores have organized," he concluded.[177]

Even if the labor insurgency fizzled politically, Joseph's strategy secured him favorable notice in Washington. From the nation's capital, local officeholders' job fears were not a crucial concern. Republican leaders wanted to win elections, and the encouragement of independent Democrats made sense, even to politicians previously supportive of black rights. Joseph personally sought the sanction of Washington officials, reportedly with some success. He claimed that President Hayes endorsed "supporting

172. MDR, May 19, 1880.

173. Jonathan Garlock, comp., *Guide to the Local Assemblies of the Knights of Labor* (Westport, Conn., 1982), 7–8; MDR, October 18, 1879. There is some evidence in Knights of Labor records of activities in the vicinity in 1878, but the first substantial public effect seems to have been in the fall of 1879.

174. *Journal of United Labor,* July 18, October 15, December 15, 1880, May 15, December 15, 1881; Melton McLauren, *The Knights of Labor in the South* (Westport, Conn., 1978), 43.

175. T. L. Eastburn to Powderly, January 19, February 2, 1880, Terence V. Powderly Papers, Catholic University, Washington, D.C., reel 2.

176. T. L. Eastburn to Powderly, February 2, 1880; and F. M. Simms to Powderly, June 21, 1880, Powderly Papers, reel 2.

177. MDR, September 27–October 8, 1881; U.S. Congress, Senate, *Report of the Committee of the Senate upon the Relations between Labor and Capital,* 4:103.

the independent movement" in Mobile and condemned "meddling Custom House officials."[178] The well-publicized victory of the antidebt Readjuster movement in Virginia made this strategy look promising, and in the early 1880s Presidents James Garfield and especially Chester A. Arthur pursued it.[179] In Alabama Joseph was the most prominent black spokesman for this approach, and Arthur considered him for several federal posts. In September 1882 President Arthur appointed Joseph as collector of internal revenue, reportedly as "encouragement to the negroes."[180] Ferocious local opposition apparently induced the president to suspend and then withdraw the appointment, but Joseph certainly came closer to a major federal position than any other African American leader in Mobile.[181]

After this disappointment, Joseph's subsequent life was a sad one: He went to jail for shooting a woman and became a habitual user of morphine and other drugs. Joseph overcame that addiction, but his inherited wealth gradually dissipated. He died in poverty in 1907. If neither Allen Alexander nor Philip Joseph found wealth or conspicuous moral stature through their political careers, at least they made a living in politics. They probably differed from their peers more from their visibility and the scope of their ambitions than in substance. Alexander was prominent enough to be bought, and both men had unusually lengthy careers, long enough for inconsistencies to mount. For run-of-the-mill activists, the pattern seems similar on a more modest scale: political issues were filtered through individual and factional interest in a wider Gilded Age political culture that legitimized individual gain as the lifeblood of politics. The vigorous courtship of Mobile's black politicians before the 1880 presidential campaign nicely illuminates the behavior of more-typical activists.[182]

Even after Redemption, the presidential nominating process made southern Republicans significant in national politics every four years. As

178. *Mobile Watchman* quoted in *Huntsville (Ala.) Gazette*, April 10, 1880.
179. Vincent P. De Santis, *Republicans Face the Southern Question: The New Departure Years, 1877–1897* (1959; reprint, New York, 1969), 133–81; Stanley P. Hirshson, *Farewell to the Bloody Shirt: Northern Republicans and the Southern Negro, 1877–1893* (Chicago, 1961), 78–122; Bess Beatty, *A Revolution Gone Backward: The Black Response to National Politics, 1876–1896* (New York, 1987), 46–7. On the Readjuster insurgents, see Dailey, *Before Jim Crow*.
180. *MDR*, September 27, 1882.
181. *NYT*, September 24, 26, 27, 1882.
182. *MDR*, February 21, 1907.

the Republican national convention of 1880 approached, Secretary of the Treasury John Sherman used Hayes administration patronage to enhance his prospects, working with a particularly heavy hand in the South.[183] His Alabama supporters, most notably ex-senator Warner, labored toward gaining a supportive delegation, but they were obstructed by ex-president Grant's continuing popularity among the black population. Several of Spencer's protégés in Mobile also backed Grant, often maintaining their federal jobs with impunity under the Tenure of Office Act. With black support they were in a position to control Republican meetings. Internal Revenue Collector Lou Mayer, for example, spent money freely in "packing primary meetings in Mobile" and "generally [defeated] Postmaster Wickersham in Conventions."[184] Another correspondent agreed that Mayer would spend whatever was necessary to carry the convention for Grant.[185] Clearly, the white officeholders in Spencer's old following cultivated their African American colleagues. A Grant supporter offered James Gillette striking advice about one black leader: "I think it would be a good idea for you to write to [Frank Threatt]—he will appreciate it. You know how they [blacks] like to be consulted & c."[186]

To overcome Grant's advantages, Warner proposed to spread some money around himself.[187] Alexander and Joseph backed other candidates, so the more visible black leaders were already spoken for. Instead, Sherman's supporters contacted Spencer Terrell, C. C. Pontiac, and other less prominent black activists. Several offered to go "to other counties where they are well known and elect unpledged but undoubted Sherman delegates."[188] It might cost fifty dollars apiece, but Sherman's lieutenants assured him it was worth it. As the state Republican convention approached, the demands for additional revenue increased. Sherman's supporters had pulled together a contesting delegation from Mobile that would attempt to gain seats on the floor. "Nearly all of these delegates are colored men and have not a dollar in the world," one Sherman manager wrote, adding that

183. *NYT,* December 1, 1882
184. Memo, "Alabama," in W. Warner to John Sherman, January 2, 1880, John Sherman Papers, LC.
185. Memo from M. C. Osborne in W. Warner to Sherman, January 2, 1880.
186. J. W. Dereen to Gillette, April 29, 1880, Gillette Papers.
187. W. Warner to John Sherman, May 14, 1880, Sherman Papers.
188. B. J. Spaulding to Sherman National Committee, April 27, 1880, Sherman Papers.

they could not attend unless expenses were paid.[189] Press accounts suggest that any delegate who pledged support was indeed offered liberal aid.[190] Despite the enthusiasm generated by Grant's visit to Mobile that spring, most of Sherman's contacts assured him that prospects were good, but they were mistaken.[191] Grant's forces swept the Selma convention, brushing aside Warner and his men in a tempestuous meeting.[192]

Afterward, Sherman's dispirited Alabama lieutenants took stock and concluded they had been had. One complained to the *New York Tribune* that the black delegates were for Grant, but they would not have been except for money and false friends.[193] One Mobile supporter, George Cottin, exploded in a litany of black betrayal. Spencer Terrell was a traitor, while other blacks were tampered with or sold out. One of Sherman's presumed black supporters made a "long harangue" about Republican disunity in Mobile, thus completely undercutting the Sherman faction's delegate challenge. Cottin concluded that Grant's men had outbid and out–wined and dined their opposition. There were "very few colored men who can be trusted, they don't know what gratitude is, the more you do for them the more they will expect from you."[194] Cottin felt that blacks ought to be "more grateful toward those who helped to set them free." This was perhaps the most novel argument ever employed against the presidential aspirations of Gen. U. S. Grant.

Willard Warner had an equally unflattering view of the outcome, concluding that nothing could overcome the "ignorant" devotion of Spencer's black supporters for Grant. Blacks preferred Grant and no one else. Warner recalled that in Grant's 1872 race, blacks "did not know Greeley or Sumner" either, for no antislavery record could match the general's appeal.[195] Warner at least implicitly conceded that there were real political issues involved, but another correspondent offered a more subtle reading. R. M. Moore wrote from Mobile that "it was a mistake for Gen. Warner to at-

189. G. L. Tichnor to John Sherman, May 11, 1880, Sherman Papers.
190. *NYT,* May 15, 1880.
191. W. Warner to John Sherman, May 5, 14, 1880, Sherman Papers.
192. *New York Tribune,* May 22, 29, 1880; *Washington Post,* May 22, 1880; *NYT,* May 21–23, 1880. Several accounts suggest mild surprise at how little difference Sherman's money had made.
193. *New York Tribune,* May 29, 1880.
194. George Cottin to "Colonel," May 25, 1880, Sherman Papers.
195. W. Warner to John Sherman, May 14, 23, 1880, Sherman Papers.

tempt to manage a convention composed, as that was, by a majority of colored delegates, as he had alienated many of them by his course in '72."[196] That is to say, blacks long remembered Warner's defection to Horace Greeley after he lost the Mobile collectorship, and they never forgave him. In either account the basis of the outcome is conceded to be substantial, a response of African American activists to popular pressure or their own convictions. Mobile's black activists were clearly self-interested, even opportunistic, but they also tried to maintain some credibility with their followers and, perhaps, with their own consciences. For these poor men, political fidelity consisted in not staying bought.

They were hardly alone. Before one crucial election, a white Democrat approached Peter Murphy, a carpenter who headed a First Ward Republican association. The Democrats offered him fifty dollars to distribute their tickets to his followers, and after some hesitation, he took the money. At a subsequent meeting Murphy carried in the tickets, "showed the crowd the $50, advised them to let the tickets alone, and they did so." The crowd apparently saw the humor in the situation, and no one reproached him—or asked to share the money for that matter.[197] So long as he served their interests and kept faith with them, he could pocket the Democrats' cash with their blessing. The point applies more broadly. After Redemption, compromise and political opportunism of one form or another was inevitable. Politics was a sordid, self-interested business, but so long as their leaders kept faith, people understood. If not, no one trusted them blindly anyway.

196. R. M. Moore to John Sherman, May 24, 1880, Sherman Papers.
197. U.S. Congress, House, *Affairs in Alabama,* 376.

Epilogue
Black Mobile Enters the New South

By any modern standard, African Americans confronted bleak realities after Reconstruction failed. As they approached the 1880s, blacks experienced discrimination and social segregation in a thousand forms. One minister, Wiley Bryant, observed that their rights were ignored in southern courts under conservative rule. Bryant called on President Hayes and the northern public to fund emigration since blacks were too poor to leave on their own. His letter concluded, "our rights and privellages are so small that we are no more than a target."[1] In retrospect, such observations seem apt, given the subsequent capitulation of southern society to extreme racism. By the early twentieth century, Mobile would share fully in the lynchings, legal segregation, and disfranchisement that swept the region.[2] In the context of the eighties, though, this prospect seemed remote, and in some respects the omens looked reasonably promising. The passing of Reconstruction racial conflict combined with rising black educational levels suggested a gradual amelioration of race relations. Community leaders used their suffrage to broker modest political gains from the system. Black lead-

---

1. Henry Edwards and Wiley Bryant to President Hayes, June 3, 1879, Rutherford B. Hayes Papers, Rutherford B. Hayes Library, Fremont, Ohio. Internal references suggest this letter came from Mobile or its vicinity, but the evidence is not conclusive.

2. For the grim record of Mobile in the early twentieth century, see Alsobrook, "Alabama's Port City," 152–235.

ers saw cause for hope in the years after Redemption, illusory as such expectations proved.

Optimists could point to the continuing racial representation in federal jobs, always a topic of importance for Republican activists. When Philip Joseph commenced his lobbying in Washington for a major appointment, he argued that white Democrats retained many jobs in the government service. Rival black activists countered that even under the existing white Republican leadership, African Americans enjoyed substantial benefits. One newspaper account claimed that seven of sixteen employees under Postmaster M. D. Wickersham were black, including most of the mail carriers. Similarly, in J. W. Burke's customhouse, "at least one half of his force is colored." Whites monopolized the ranking jobs, but blacks held four of the ten middling positions as inspectors, Collector Burke having doubled the number. The article pointed out that prominent political figures like Allen Alexander, Charles D. Nicholas, and Henry Europe held federal positions. "In fact," he concluded, "all the colored officeholders here are representative men." Constantine Perez, a Joseph ally, disputed the specific numbers, claiming that many of the blacks employed were night watchmen. The exact reality in this instance remains murky, but the general point seems incontestable. By Perez's own count, African Americans had secured substantial representation in federal jobs under the Republicans—around their proportion in the general population. Black adherents of the various factions generally argued their case in these terms, providing a person-by-person ethnic reckoning. This pattern underscores the centrality of racial equity in patronage to the political culture, while the substantial count demonstrates that federal officers paid heed. The "goodly number" of black customhouse employees, in one visitor's upbeat appraisal, made an impression on activists, dependent as they were on government jobs. As one black correspondent commented from the scene, those "persistent and active in politics, who have done much 'stumping' feel that they are entitled to something, and would not . . . refuse an office. The truth is that most of them hanker after it." Given a natural tendency for political activists to conflate their concerns with those of the race, continuing success in this venue seemed important, perhaps more significant than circumstances actually warranted.[3]

3. Newspaper clipping in C. Perez to Secretary of the Treasury, July 20, 1880, box 250, AP-247, RG 56; *Huntsville Gazette,* June 25, 1881, September 3, 1883, July 30, 1881.

Republican control of federal jobs had another consequence of broader relevance. The presence of U.S. law-enforcement officials provided a useful check on Mobile's race relations. Federal election laws remained on the books after Reconstruction, and even in the rural hinterland, U.S. marshals repeatedly arrested people for civil rights violations. In the late 1870s, Mobile's district attorney Charles E. Mayer was among the most aggressive federal officials in the South, bringing scores of election cases to court.[4] Democrats complained of the "constant annoyance of our people" by indictments "wherever a pretext can be found." The papers claimed that Republican boss L. H. Mayer himself cleared selections for federal court jurors.[5] If conviction proved difficult, the threat of trial intimidated racist behavior, especially during federal elections, in which Congress might seat Republican challengers if fraud was sufficiently overt. In some instances federal intervention could save black lives. Choctaw County whites in 1882 lynched Republican activist Jack Turner after his arrest on the basis of forged evidence of insurrection. Immediately afterward, county officials sought his brother, Moses Turner, in connection with the presumed plot. In Mobile, federal officials seized the fugitive man themselves on bogus charges that were "simply a pretext to prevent him from arrest by the state authorities." U.S. officials soon ushered Moses Turner out of Alabama, thereby ensuring that he would escape his brother's fate.[6] In addition, white Republican leaders denounced the lynching one after another, even the most conciliatory like M. D. Wickersham and Collector Burke. Their intervention facilitated national attention, to the outrage of their white Democratic contacts and the delight of Mobile's black activists.[7]

The benign federal presence aside, African American leaders also hoped that Mobile's environing white community might become less hostile. Re-

4. *NYT,* August 26, 1882. On the very real threat of federal intervention, see Xi Wang, *The Trials of Democracy: Black Suffrage and the Northern Republicans, 1860–1910* (Athens, Ga., 1997). On Mayer's zeal, see Robert M. Goldman, *"A Free Ballot and a Fair Count": The Department of Justice and the Enforcement of Voting Rights in the South, 1877–1893* (1990; reprint, New York, 2001), 55–61.

5. [*Mobile Register(?),*] "Attention Citizens! Of the First Congressional District of Alabama" (N.p., [1882]), 4; *MDR,* April 16, 1879.

6. *MDR,* September 20, 1882. For a modern examination of this episode and the role of U.S. officials in it, see William Warren Rogers and Robert David Ward, *August Reckoning: Jack Turner and Racism in Post–Civil War Alabama* (Baton Rouge, 1973), 89–93, 169, 173.

7. *MDR,* September 6, 8, 1882; "Attention Citizens!" 2–3; *New York Tribune,* August 23, 1882; *NYT,* August 26, 1882.

construction was receding in popular memory, the more hated carpetbaggers were generally gone, and Republicans had long refrained from endorsing a party ticket in local elections.⁸ The independent Democrats' occasional victories had not prompted a renewal of Reconstruction racial disorder, and substantial black participation in elections became routine. As Henry Europe observed, "Negro votes have ceased to be obnoxious to the white people of this community since the two branches of the Democratic party had begun such a lively bidding for them." The choice of a cautious strategy was not entirely unconstrained, for a serious partisan effort generally induced strong countermeasures. In August 1880 Republican L. H. Mayer, the pro-Spencer official, had his own name placed at the last minute on the independent ticket as candidate for probate judge, perhaps as a ploy to increase black turnout. This violation of post-Redemption political etiquette met a heavy-handed conservative response. Mayer received not a single vote in one Seventh Ward ballot box, though the rest of his ticket fared well, an outcome indicating blatant fraud. If the stakes were high enough, the Democrats manipulated voting returns, but this was a last resort rather than the preferred option.⁹

Elite embarrassment over electoral irregularities provided Republican leaders some leverage. Collector of Customs J. W. Burke informed his superiors that a strong federal law-enforcement presence was necessary, but thus bolstered, talks with the opposition could yield results. Burke acknowledged his approach was controversial with local Republicans, but however distasteful it was, the proper plan was "to seek out 'the Captains of the Fraud' and make a treaty with sufficient numbers of this party" to have the returns accurately made. "We got a fair count in this (Mobile Co.) last Congressional election [November 1880] and it was brought about by negotiations." He added that the continuing feuds in the Democratic ranks made it likely that similar deals could be made again. Burke concluded that rather than independent insurgents, it was precisely the established Bour-

---

8. George E. Spencer's remaining supporters antagonized Secretary of the Treasury John Sherman in the 1880 campaign by supporting Grant. Once it became clear that Grant had not received the nomination, Sherman immediately removed the most prominent of them from their federal positions in violation of administration policy requiring cause for removals. Most seem to have followed Lou Mayer's example and left the state. *NYT,* July 6, August 1, 1880, September 26, 1882.

9. *MDR,* May 19, August 10, 1880.

bon Democrats who were in the best position to implement such arrangements.[10]

As time went on, the city's commercial leadership recognized that Mobile's reputation for political extremism and electoral fraud might not be helpful. They watched the dramatic growth of rival Birmingham as well as the textile mill campaigns under way elsewhere in the South. Racist as it was, the emerging New South model promoted a certain businesslike decorum in racial matters.[11] The city already absorbed fearful national publicity for its repeated bond defaults, and urban disorder would only exacerbate the bad press.[12] Moreover, in every national election the "bloody shirt" rallied northern voters to the Republicans, and civic leaders were conscious of the political import of their actions. Mobile's newspapers obsessively monitored northern commentary on southern social relations.[13] As visible as events in the city were, its leaders wanted to appear as reasonable as possible on racial matters since "public tolerance" was "watching these Southern States." For example, when the brief "Exoduster" enthusiasm for migration to Kansas reached Mobile, the response of white city leaders was not good riddance but polite assurances of concern toward their black fellow citizens. A *Register* editorial actually concluded that, overall, Mobile was unusually fortunate because "our colored population is orderly and well behaved." Only the more partisan Republican politicians were described as the exception.[14]

One legal development symbolized these wider changes in attitude. Ever since Redemption, the exclusion of African Americans from the jury box had been a political issue. In 1880, black leaders circulated a handbill denouncing the practice, calling attention to federal legislation and court decisions on the issue. Judge O. J. Semmes, the son of Confederate admiral Raphael Semmes, chose to address the topic from the Mobile bench. He found racial exclusion unwarranted and urged that city officials desist from the practice. The judge called on the local bar association for support, and

10. J. W. Burke to Chandler, June 8, 1882, W. E. Chandler Papers, LC.
11. Paul M. Gaston, *The New South Creed: A Study in Southern Mythmaking* (New York, 1970), 125–50.
12. *NYT*, January 20, October 7, 1879, August 27, 1881. See also Ernst von Hesse Wartegg, *Travels on the Lower Mississippi, 1879–1880,* ed. and trans. Frederic Trautmann (Columbia, Mo., and London, 1990), 237–8.
13. *MDR,* January 30, August 19, September 3, 1885.
14. Ibid., March 12, 1885, May 24, 1879, March 27, 1880, February 19, 1884.

the lawyers unanimously endorsed his position. Even the *Register* concurred, observing that large numbers of "our colored citizens" were "possessed of an average common school education, and have accumulated property." They would make fine jurors, and besides, the community needed their cooperation in repressing crime. While still upholding segregation, the paper concluded that the day was past when partisanship and "blind race prejudice" should prevail.[15] This enlightened response to an African American protest is significant, and in subsequent years, blacks composed a significant minority of local jurors.

The *Mobile Register* was the longtime voice of the Democratic establishment, and its positive role in the court dispute reflects the wider evolution of its editorial policy. During Reconstruction, the *Register* had epitomized Democratic racial extremism. With the death of editor John Forsyth in 1877, his successors adopted a more responsible tone, though always within the context of white supremacy and partisan regularity. For example, when ex-president U. S. Grant visited Mobile in the spring of 1880 and received an uproarious welcome from the African American community, the paper managed a civil response to his campaign stop. In another instance the paper denied press reports that blacks opposed prohibition, strikingly contending that temperance advocates were about as numerous in one race as in the other.[16] The *Register* also promoted education in somewhat enlightened terms, favoring federal aid and black teachers while denying that schooling would unfit blacks for work. "Do we not today see a great improvement in the race," the paper asked, "compared with what they were ten years ago?"[17] Of course, tactical calculations often underlay polite affirmations of respect, which tended to proliferate during national elections. Still, when the *Register* assured northerners "the negroes are protected in their rights not only by public opinion, but by the state laws," they placed themselves under some pressure to ensure compliance.[18]

Given the paper's rhetorical posture, the *Register* reacted to the increasing wave of Southern lynchings with some gravity. The paper denounced one extralegal murder, emphasizing that "When we say crime we mean

15. Ibid., March 9, 1880; *Harper's Weekly,* March 27, 1880, 194.
16. William Warren Rogers Jr., "The Past Is Gone: Ulysses S. Grant Visits Mobile," *Gulf South Historical Review* 5 (fall 1989): 6–19; *MDR,* April 10, 14, 1880.
17. *MDR,* February 26, 1886.
18. Ibid., April 6, 1880.

it."[19] Under Democratic rule no excuse existed for mob activity. "The rowdy must go," the paper observed, with the choice of wording perhaps mitigating the benign intent. The only solution for extralegal violence was to "enforce the law without regard to race, color, partisan influence, or any other consideration."[20] The editors suggested that the militia confront mobs, confident that determined resistance would prevent such outbreaks: "Those engaged in any lynching affair also should be brought to justice, and made to feel the vengeance of outraged law."[21] Admittedly, the *Register*'s opposition to extralegal violence was not entirely consistent. In the notorious Jack Turner episode, the paper made excuses for an obvious lynching, arguing against the evidence that the murder of the Republican leader was not politically motivated; in the midst of a congressional election, the editors feared giving Congress an excuse to seat a Republican challenger.[22] Even so, the overall positive evolution of the newspaper's viewpoint is striking, given its earlier near-promotion of riot and the Ku Klux Klan. From Reconstruction through the end of the nineteenth century, vigilante episodes remained uncommon locally. If lynching was "absolutely unknown" in Mobile County, as Frederick Bromberg stated, the powerful newspaper's editorial influence probably deserves some credit.[23]

The enlightened tendency of elite opinion remained modest, with public discourse defending segregation in particular as a necessary principle. The conservative resolve on this issue was bolstered by the 1883 U.S. Supreme Court decision overturning federal civil rights legislation. One controversial episode in mid-decade sharply illustrates the limits of white toleration. On a train headed from the North, an African American minister, J. T. M. Lindsey, and his wife were ordered out of the first-class compartment by the conductor. A nearby white passenger, Thomas J. Morrow, was drawn into the dispute, and he expressed the—now questionable—opinion that

19. Ibid., April 18, 1882.
20. Ibid., September 3, 1883.
21. Ibid., September 17, 1880. See also March 19–23, 1886.
22. *NYT,* August 28, 1882. For the *Register*'s tortured and partisan editorial course in this episode, see Rogers and Ward, *August Reckoning,* 106, 112, 125, 153–5. Even on less politically charged cases, the paper occasionally allowed stories of lynching elsewhere to pass unremarked if the circumstances were inflammatory enough. One such account covertly suggests approval on the grounds the mob was interracial. See *MDR,* December 29, 1885.
23. See Bromberg to Charles W. Eliot, December 27, 1901, in Alsobrook, "Alabama's Port City," 152.

the couple had a legal right to the seats. The conductor then gathered an angry group of white passengers who expelled all three from the car, apparently stabbing the minister in the process. Upon arrival in Mobile, the conductor encountered Morrow and assaulted him in the street. The conductor's subsequent arrest prompted days of press discussion, with the *Register* sympathizing with the assailants. "Is it any wonder," the paper asked, "that white people should object to the colored people using the cars especially provided for white people?" Still, there was no criticism for the city officials who arrested and fined the conductor for his conduct.[24]

Clearly, segregation and black subordination were priorities, but elite sentiment sought some racial accommodation within this context. The continuing importance of the black vote encouraged restraint. Fresh divisions within the white majority empowered the African American electorate, for the recent legislative settlement actually settled nothing. In establishing the Port of Mobile in 1879, the Democratic legislature placed the city in a fiscal straightjacket, limiting municipal spending to $100,000 annually; the hope was to mollify northern creditors by permanently devoting the extra revenue to paying off a portion of the defaulted debt. This figure represented less than half of the previous budget, around a third by some estimates, with unauthorized excess spending reportedly rendering port officials criminally liable.[25] The bond crisis was solved by a second partial repudiation, but the spending limitations meant that the city ran out of money toward the end of each calendar year. As one modern historian has written, the Mobile legislation "guaranteed a weak city government unable to provide public services that would be desperately needed and more affordable in the years ahead."[26] Once whites overcame their initial relief at the solution of the city's longstanding debt woes, it gradually dawned that local government still did not work.

The *Register* openly wondered what other community was "conducted upon a basis of expense as small as that now fixed for this city?" The resulting fiscal stringency yielded obviously counterproductive results. The police force was down to forty members, an "utterly inadequate" number in the opinion of a grand jury.[27] According to the published 1880 census, the en-

24. *MDR,* May 23, 24, 26, 28, 1885.
25. Ibid., March 16, 1879, November 10, 1882; "Private Circular," July 9, 1880, John A Soto Scrapbook, William R. Perkins Library, Duke University.
26. Doyle, *New Men, New Cities, New South,* 71.
27. *MDR,* January 11, 1881, February 19, 1882, November 7, 1886.

tire police force went off duty from six to seven o'clock every morning, apparently on the assumption that felons slept late.[28] Firemen complained that their hoses had worn out, being frequently damaged in use by streetcars passing over them. Despite public complaints by fire department officials, nothing could be done to rectify the problem, that is until the insurance companies threatened rate hikes. In February 1881 one city official complained that "the Port is now without money to pay her next pay roll." These familiar problems refused to go away, and the continued stagnancy of the cotton trade for the next decade promised little relief.[29]

The permanent crisis sapped white loyalty for the Straightout Democrats, at least in local races, where Republicans still did not formally contest elections. As one Democrat concluded, "men will not obey conventions unless there is a party fight in sight." Few whites abjured the Democrats in national and state politics, but they felt differently about nominally nonpartisan local races. Given the white majority and cautious deportment of the black minority, conservative voters felt they could split tickets without inviting racial upheaval. The *Register* observed that locally the independents comprised debt repudiationists and those passed over by the Democrats for some office. The white opposition was "the disappointed, the unappreciated, the enemies of law and order, the anti-tax-payer, the agitator and the communist." One "Workingman" observed that the claims of party loyalty rested lightly upon the laboring classes, but, in truth, frustration with the city administration increasingly spread across the social spectrum.[30]

For several years after the creation of the Port of Mobile in 1879, the Democratic architects of the debt settlement had swept the polls. Declining taxes certainly had an initial appeal.[31] By early 1882, however, a substantial opposition again coalesced in local elections under the "Citizens" label. As usual, black leaders pressed their demands upon the independent Democrats. In a First Ward meeting, several urged support for the insurgents. One observed that the Democratic administration had been "pretty hard

28. George E. Waring Jr., comp., *The Southern and the Western States,* bk. 2 of *Report on the Social Statistics of Cities,* vol. 19 of U.S. Bureau of the Census, *Tenth Census of the United States,* 22 vols. (Washington, 1887), 197.
29. *MDR,* March 22, 1882, February 11, 1881; Berkstresser, "Mobile, Alabama, in the 1880s," 140.
30. *MDR,* February 7, August 10, 1882, March 8, 1883, August 31, 1882.
31. Ibid., June 4, 1879.

on the black man" and recommended that blacks support the Citizens ticket and "get their share of the spoils." Another leader similarly argued that since blacks were employed in white stores and houses, "it was time that they should have employment upon the police and street force." After the Democrats won, some black community notables approached the victors. One postelection petition, signed by W. B. F. Bates and fraternal association leaders, asked the triumphant Democratic officials to change employment policies. Having been "a potent vote in the last election," Bates and his comrades thought that in deference to their numbers, the city should hire some of the community's able black citizens. Such recognition was "just before the divine and Human laws." Presumably, the basis of the request was that the petitioners somehow facilitated Democratic victory, but if so, authorities dismissed the plea without comment.[32]

As the decade wore on, continuing urban disarray allowed African American leaders increasing success in pressing their issues. Democratic rule did nothing to solve the circumstances of the city government as infrastructure decay became increasingly obvious. The *Register* itself conceded that of late "the question has been repeatedly asked, 'How long is this thing to last?'" The paper acknowledged that excessive economy had become galling to most of the public.[33] If these difficulties were not enough, municipal officials also irritated lower-class white voters on an unrelated and somewhat unlikely issue. Steven Hahn's classic *Roots of Southern Populism* drew historians' attention to the issue of the open range for livestock as a class-tinged political issue. Hahn and his critics generally depict this topic as a backwoods concern, but surprisingly, in urban Mobile it was a divisive issue too.[34] Into the 1880s, pigs and goats roved the streets with apparent legal sanction. Cows chased women down Royal Street, right "in the heart of the chief city of the State of Alabama."[35] Beyond the practical problems this presented, it also damaged Mobile's image as a progressive, businesslike New South city. Thus, in 1883 officials moved to deal with the issue with a pound ordinance, banning the ranging of livestock in the streets.

32. *Mobile Chronicle,* March 2, 1882; *MDR,* March 7, April 4, 1882.
33. *MDR,* April 20, 1883.
34. Steven Hahn, *The Roots of Southern Populism: Yeoman Farmers and the Transformation of the Georgia Upcountry, 1850–1890* (Oxford, 1983); Shawn Everett Kantor and J. Morgan Kousser, "Common Sense or Commonwealth? The Fence Law and Institutional Change in the Postbellum South," *Journal of Southern History* 59 (May 1993), 201–42.
35. *MDR,* May 24, 1883.

A firestorm of controversy resulted. One of the measure's sponsors promptly abandoned it, having received "strong intimation that the ordinance will be unpopular with his constituents." Petitions and handbills circulated, with several mass meetings protesting the ordinance. One meeting denounced "the outrage on poor people caused by the passage of the pound ordinance." Another claimed that nine-tenths of the population of the outlying precincts opposed the bill.[36] Still another vowed physical resistance to the new law, adjourning with three cheers for liberty and free men.[37] The opposition was most vocal among the poorer whites of the outlying districts, whereas the African American population did not figure that prominently in the dispute. Perhaps the bulk of the black population were too poor to maintain livestock themselves, but whatever the reason, Mobile officials could scarcely ignore the opposition among Democratic voters. The administration eventually made concessions, exempting the portion of the city west of Broad Street and other areas away from the downtown business district. Even so, the compromise solution was unsatisfactory in practice, cows not respecting legislative boundaries. The issue kept "bobbing up" for years.[38]

Divisive as the livestock debate was, it was tangential to the fiscal realities faced by the municipal government. Another issue struck at the core of Democratic rule, raised by well-connected conservative businessmen. In recent years housing for the wealthy had expanded along the major thoroughfares and streetcar lines radiating out of the city. Mobile now had "its fashionable West End."[39] Even today, the palatial homes along Government Street testify to the social ostentation of the wealthier residents in a time of economic stringency.[40] A growing segment of the elite thus shared the public-service woes of the outlying areas. One leading citizen complained of "our not having any police in that part of the city." Inland of Broad Street, the most pressing issue was standing water and the incapacity of the twenty-man street force to provide adequate relief.[41] As the U.S. cen-

36. Ibid., June 16, 1883.
37. Ibid., May 24, June 14, 16, 1883.
38. Ibid., June 19, October 19, 1883; Berkstresser, "Mobile, Alabama, in the 1880s," 80.
39. Quoted in Elizabeth Barrett Gould, *From Fort to Port: An Architectural History of Mobile, Alabama, 1711–1918* (Tuscaloosa and London, 1988), 191.
40. For Mobile's architectural achievements during this era, see Gould, *From Fort to Port,* 163–225.
41. *MDR,* June 1, August 1, 1883.

sus reported, the city lacked a drainage system: "A large amount of work is done annually, but, as it is not permanent, there is no real improvement." Indeed, the work done on the smaller streets often diverted water toward the large thoroughfares, causing disastrous flooding after heavy rains.[42]

City officials faced withering criticism from constituents used to having their wishes taken seriously. At one heated meeting at the board of trade, Recorder Owen claimed that "all possible has been done." He pointed out that the legislature had tied the police board's hands and city officials did the best they could with $100,000 annually. The legislature would be out of session for some time, he observed, so no immediate change was in prospect. The audience was not mollified, emphasizing the urgency and possible danger of the situation. Harry Pillans Jr., a former city official, observed that in his neighborhood, "We have gaslight, but nothing else: no police, no scavenger cart, no water—nothing but light." The ability to see his flooded Government Street surroundings at night apparently gave him little comfort. The water was a foot deep on his property, and Pillans accused city officials of tolerating inefficient street laborers for partisan purposes.[43]

A. C. Danner, a banker and wealthy businessman, sharpened the political indictment. He blamed the Democratic leadership for exacerbating a difficult problem through their personnel policies. The street force simply did not work; they were expensive and inefficient primarily because of political exigencies. The city engineer told Danner that he could not hire enough laborers because there were "not enough Irish in town." That is to say, the Democratic machine's policy of steering city jobs to poorer white residents meant necessary work did not get done. Some of Mobile's street laborers had been on the force for forty years, hardly a sign of youthful vigor. As the employer of large numbers of African American laborers himself, Danner pointed out that efficient workers could be had for a dollar a day, substantially less than the city was currently paying. Danner concluded that, politically popular or not, it was only fair to do something for black residents: "Since we go to negroes and say 'We want your votes,' and since we say this is a white man's government—and it is, and I hold that it must be—I am willing to say also that 'such places as you are fitted for we shall give you. We want your votes, and we will give you work.' We must give it to the best workmen, regardless of color." This enlightened, practical ver-

42. Waring, *Southern and the Western States,* 19(2):195–7.
43. *MDR,* June 1, 1883.

sion of white supremacy was greeted with applause by the crowd. After the protest, city officials suddenly found the money to repair the drains, and the laborers reportedly worked with unaccustomed vigor. Still, temporary exertions only provided a short-term fix for an impossible situation.[44]

One Irish resident pointed out that his "overflowed and abandoned" neighborhood just east of Broad Street had worse problems than those of his "silk stocking" betters. In truth, the problems with inadequate services cut across class lines. As frustration with Mobile's Democratic leadership festered, the next major election would be the county and legislative canvass, scheduled for August 1884. The Democratic primary election of that year yielded the typical complaints of fraud, prompting another wholesale revolt. This time, however, the leadership for the Citizens Democratic ticket came from a powerful segment of the white population. One hundred businessmen gathered to nominate independent candidates, with considerable fanfare, calling for state regulation of primary elections. The published manifesto proclaimed that "the interests of the tax payer, rich and poor, white and black, are one and inseparable." The Straightout Democrats conceded that "men of great wealth and respectability" led the opposition, and indeed, they tried to class-bait their adversaries as the spoiled rich. The upshot was that, once again, African American voters would determine the outcome of another insurgent Democratic bid, this one with unusual elite sanction.[45]

Faced with this now familiar scenario, the black leadership once again divided. The *Register* observed that there appeared to be several Republican executive committees left over from previous feuds. At one meeting someone suggested trying to "harmonize with other Republican bodies in this city," but members voted the motion down because the other groups were bogus. At another crucial meeting, Democratic plants allegedly tried to cause trouble, and according to the Citizens' newspaper, the *Mobile Item,* the Republican proceedings were "of the usual turbulent character."[46] Negotiations with the Citizens resulted favorably, and the insurgents agreed to place a white Republican businessman, O. L. Crampton, on their ticket for the school board. This proved sufficient for most of the Republicans, though Allen Alexander eventually led another bolt of "his half a

44. Ibid., July 13, June 1, 1883.
45. Ibid., June 2, July 6, June 11, 29, 1884.
46. Ibid., April 3, June 14, 15, 1884; *Mobile Item,* June 7, 1884.

dozen personal friends."[47] His followers nominated a rival Republican ticket in the apparent interest of the Democrats, but Alexander's habitual divisive behavior was hardly unique. As the election approached, Joe McWilliams, claiming the status of treasurer of the Republican Executive Committee, publicly denounced his predecessor for misuse of party funds. The specifics are vague, but McWilliams wrote that "if the 'Citizens' candidates expect to get elected through such manipulators," they would lose. The flow of partisan money to activists only exacerbated such issues, and a crowd of fifty to one hundred blacks reportedly gathered around the Citizens' headquarters every day. After the election, the *Register* alleged that "men have been lying around idle for weeks making their living by politics," absorbing all the liquor they could get. "The skirts of neither party are clean in this matter," the paper concluded.[48]

Personal motivations notwithstanding, serious issues were under consideration. Just after the Citizens' convention, Republican leaders circulated a handbill calling for fairer education funding in order to equalize school terms in rural Mobile County with those of the city. The handbill also disavowed the intention of nominating a Republican slate, calling instead for representation on the Citizens' ticket for unpaid offices. The *Register* described the subsequent nomination of the Republican Crampton as "the signet seal of a dark and hidden alliance," but the Citizens sought black votes openly. In defending Crampton's nomination for school board, the Citizens found "nothing inconsistent with fairness that a person recognized by the colored population as their friend" should be consulted.[49] This language of racial inclusion typified the movement's statements. The *Mobile Item,* for example, allowed black sympathizers space in its columns. One letter, signed H. V. Cavanah, argued that many blacks were taxpayers and deserved the right to vote without molestation. He pointed out that the Straightout Democrats had "plainly said that they did not care for the negro vote, they could do without them, and if in need, they could *buy* them." He urged voters to disprove the slur. Another *Item* column reprinted resolutions that the best interest of the black schools demanded black teachers.[50]

47. *Mobile Item,* June 28, 1884.
48. *MDR,* June 15, July 1, 18, August 6, 1884.
49. Ibid., June 8, 20, July 8, 1884.
50. *Mobile Item,* June 28, 1884.

A violent episode occurring in the midst of the campaign encapsulates the wider change in Mobile's racial climate. On July 4, Democrats held a campaign barbecue outside town for the benefit of both blacks and working-class white supporters. It seems some racial insults were exchanged at the picnic, which featured a fair amount of drinking. Afterward, a wagonload of white Democrats headed back toward the city and were followed on foot by a group of blacks, who exchanged taunts with the passengers. A white policeman, Ulysses Cleveland, rode up and "told the boys they had better get down and drive the negroes away," in Cleveland's words. Several white passengers demurred, fearing a fight, but a few made the attempt. When they were resisted, Officer Cleveland discharged his gun twice without effect, reportedly into the air. At that, Frank Winney, a black and a reported ex-convict, fired into the wagon, killing one white and injuring eight others. Here was the first significant election violence in a decade, with an African American assailant shooting white Democrats; the victims, moreover, were largely innocent of any wrongdoing, being those who sought to avoid trouble. The Democratic Central Committee blamed this "deliberate assault at the hands of hidden assassins" on the Citizens, urging that, in the presence of common danger, "those who now propose to be loyal to their race must stand resolutely together."[51]

A few years previously, such an inflammatory racial incident would likely have unified white opinion behind the Democrats. People elsewhere were lynched for less. In Mobile, though, a decade after Reconstruction, things proceeded differently. The *Register,* party organ though it was, contradicted the claims of the Democratic Central Committee, perhaps in the interest of restraining further violence. Aggressive reporting demonstrated that Officer Cleveland's provocative behavior contributed to the bloodshed, which all hands condemned. A Citizens' response gleefully seized on the *Register*'s account, then rose to a rousing denunciation of Democratic race baiting: "Fellow-citizens! let us, on the fourth of August, show to the world, that the race issue in Alabama is a thing of the past, dead beyond resurrection; that we of Mobile belong, in fact, to the new progressive South, determined to have, at home, peace and good will amongst all classes of citizens, and abroad, respect and confidence." Despite the apparent provocation for racist resentment, such appeals for interracial amity had surprising effectiveness in the New South context.[52]

51. *MDR,* July 6, 1884.
52. Ibid., July 6, 8, 1884.

Faced with indications of electoral defeat, the *Register* forlornly asked if the men of 1884 had forgotten their fathers' struggles of 1868.[53] The answer was apparently affirmative, because the Citizens' ticket crushed the Democrats by a vote of approximately 5,400 to 1,500. Several independents were elected to the legislature. Even the Republican businessman Crampton won a school-board seat, running just a few hundred votes behind his ticket, which suggested that most white independents lived up to their end of the bargain. The poll was peaceful, save for a polling-place dispute involving Allen Alexander, whose factional Republican ticket received about thirty votes. Despite the squabbling between their leaders, the unity among the black electorate must have been overwhelming, with the Seventh Ward rolling up a six-to-one margin. On election night the Citizens' headquarters was crowded with an interracial throng of celebrants. According to the *Register,* jubilant blacks shouted "We's got 'em dis time!" and "Done beat de Democrats!"[54] After the result, one conservative mused on the unsettling implications. With partisan lines becoming blurred in local elections, blacks were becoming increasingly clever about utilizing their votes. They were "peculiarly susceptable to the influence of the almighty dollar" because the "main idea of the colored voter has been that politics is simply a struggle for office."[55] The author confessed that the Democrats had not provided much of an example, but what he thought the excessive pragmatism of the black electorate had other origins. Dramatic racial change had been taken off the political agenda by the Redeemers. African Americans knew it, and rather than risk violent repression, they settled for a more circumspect challenge through dissident white intermediaries. In an ironic way, the perception that black activists and voters were motivated by mercenary goals had perverse utility: it muffled the racial challenge implicit in universal suffrage. It reassured anxious white elites that continued black voting did not mean ruin and thus helped nudge all parties from racial confrontation toward negotiation. Venal politicians after all could be reasoned with.

With the realistic possibilities so constrained, blacks relished effective deployment of their suffrage for limited victories all the more, as one tantalizing contemporary account suggests. In the spring of 1885, the northern

53. Ibid., July 20, 1884.
54. Ibid., August 5, 12, 1884.
55. Ibid., January 30, 1885.

writer Charles Dudley Warner attended the cotton states' exposition in New Orleans. He chatted with a quadroon widow from Mobile who was in charge of the display of African American handicrafts. Despite her "confirmed social prejudice against black people," the light-skinned woman nonetheless manifested much zeal for her race, and she cited the previous summer's election in Mobile as an example of the progress occurring throughout the South.[56] By her account, the woman realized that the "reformers" wanted and needed the black vote: "I went, therefore, to some of the chief men, who knew me and had confidence in me, for I had had business relations with many of them [she kept a fashionable boarding house], and told them that I wanted the Opera-house for the colored people to give an entertainment and exhibition in."[57] This, she conceded, was an extraordinary request, for nobody but white people had ever been admitted. After hesitation, the white leaders agreed. A large charity exhibition was held, with numbers of leading whites invited. "It really was a beautiful affair," she enthused, "lovely tableaux, with gorgeous dresses, recitations, etc., and everybody was astonished that the colored people had so much taste and talent, and had got on so far in education." Her white contacts asked for a repeat performance, but she thought it better to leave them wanting more, with the promise that the next exhibition would be even more impressive. The woman continued with the observation that the August election turned out all right, and "now the colored people in Mobile can have anything they want." She concluded her tale, "There is the best feeling in Mobile," and people would get on beautifully if the "politicians would let us alone."[58]

The woman's account clearly offers a flawed picture of what was happening. One suspects she embellished her own importance and that access to the Opera House surely was more an issue for the Creole elite than the general black electorate. Jobs, respect, and immediate favors were more rel-

---

56. Charles Dudley Warner, *Studies in the South and West with Some Comments on Canada* (New York, 1889), 13–5. The woman in question was probably Mrs. Carrie Bryant, who reportedly supervised the African American handicrafts exhibit from Alabama. *New Orleans Picayune,* December 26, 1885. If this was indeed the woman, her zeal for her race had some substance, for she soon opened an asylum supporting "a number of helpless old people and children." *Mobile Blade,* October 27, 1888.

57. Warner, *Studies in the South and West,* 13–5. The material in brackets is in the original text, added by the author Warner.

58. Warner, *Studies in the South and West,* 15.

evant for the activists and the average voter than charity balls. The aforementioned northern reporter suspected as much, for he noted that after the election, "the negroes were put in minor official positions, the duties of which they were capable of discharging." By early 1885, even Democratic municipal authorities had finally hired a few black policemen. The Mobile woman's account is nonetheless revealing, conveying a sense of the centrality of African American agency to the political process. The climate was such that this woman, at her own initiative, felt empowered to approach white community leaders with a concrete request—and negotiate what she wanted in the name of the race. Bracing possibilities were in the air when an African American woman could even assert such influence.[59]

A concluding episode at middecade brings this issue into focus, typifying the odd mixture of accommodation and racial assertion possible under the circumstances of the New South. A tactical alliance with the Democrats prompted the first mass mobilization in years around a limited objective, one that garnered substantial elite sanction. In the port elections held during the spring of 1885, George G. Duffee attempted a political comeback at the head of an independent ticket. The former mayor apparently remained unpopular with his earlier black supporters, and the "colored element mostly voted the straightout Democratic ticket." This was the first time blacks had voluntarily voted for the regular Democrats in large numbers, and whites heralded the dawn of an era of racial concord. Though regretting defeat, the independent *Item* observed that "the color line is broken in Mobile," conceding that this aspect of the outcome was positive. One might depict this episode as the culminating abandonment of the egalitarian hopes of Reconstruction, a betrayal of Mobile blacks' Republican loyalties, but the reality is more complex. Having contributed to Democratic victory, African Americans soon sought a major concession. They called on the white Democratic leadership to hire qualified blacks as teachers, which school-board policy had promised for over a decade. The practice was common in black schools elsewhere, and the topic had been raised in recent elections, but now circumstances made it an urgent demand.[60]

That spring two former residents, L. W. Cummings and F. A. Stewart, returned to Mobile after having graduated from Fisk University. Both sought teaching jobs, pointing out that they were substantially better quali-

59. Ibid.; *MDR,* January 30, 1885.
60. *Mobile Item,* March 7, June 28, 1885; *MDR,* September 16, 1885.

fied than the whites then employed in the Davis Avenue School in the Seventh Ward. The school board offered them subordinate positions, but the two instead turned to the public, feeling they were being wronged. Months of agitation followed. Petitions circulated contending that black teachers would do a better job and that those who pursued higher education deserved encouragement. Thirteen hundred African American signatures appeared, with "some of the common people" signing the petition "quicker than the ministers." The transparent fairness of the demand within the context of segregation also won some elite support. Twenty leading whites signed supportive petitions, including the recently reelected Democratic head of the port government, R. B. Owen, and Probate Judge Price Williams Jr. The *Register* endorsed the proposal, at least at first, terming it a movement that deserved to succeed. However, the school board refused to displace the existing employees, though they did find some positions for less confrontational black activists. This set the stage for an open discussion of Mobile's post-Reconstruction racial settlement in the public press. As one published letter complained, "no young colored man can serve as an apprentice in any foundry, printing office or counting house in the city of Mobile. How can he, under the circumstances, become a true man?"[61]

The two graduates were "urged by friends"—perhaps white—to " 'go slow,' and to rely upon their power at the polls to get what they wanted." Rather than await a vacancy, they instead chose direct action. A mass meeting gathered in one of the black churches to ask for "colored people for colored schools, and demand that the colored people have their rights." L. W. Cummings accused the Republican school-board member, O. L. Crampton, of half-hearted support, adding that black ministers too had been reluctant to make strong demands and were circulating less explicit petitions. His comrade F. W. Stewart urged a boycott: "we will compel them to give us colored teachers." He called on those who backed the boycott to stand, and four-fifths of the audience did so. The *Register* deplored the meeting, denouncing the militant sentiments and coercive tone toward other blacks, but when the school opened, the boycott proved effective. Student attendance was "quite small," perhaps 25 out of 250. School officials implausibly claimed that the boycott was not responsible for the attendance problem, but they expressed their determination to wait out the opposition regardless. Nearly a month later, over half still were not attend-

61. *MDR,* September 7, 9, 13, 22, 1885.

ing, but it appears the boycott gradually faded, especially once L. W. Cummings took another teaching job in the Alabama interior.[62]

The boycott did not succeed. The school board held firm, doubtless concluding that these particular college graduates were not the sort of employees they wanted. Elite white sympathizers fell away in the face of aggressive black demands. Still, community discontent had forced the hiring of "several colored teachers of colored schools" and public acknowledgment of their grievances, with violence being strikingly absent.[63] The point has broader implications. By middecade, African Americans had achieved a modest headway through informal influence and the political process. Powerful civic leaders bid openly for black votes and even defended their legitimacy, Democrats as well as independents. A generation had passed since emancipation, a decade since Reconstruction, and African American leaders had come to terms with the pragmatic possibilities their situation afforded, both in terms of individual self-interest and collective betterment of the race. As C. Vann Woodward argued decades ago, they might reasonably have concluded that the New South settlement permitted real progress within certain limits.[64]

It was a false dawn; the moment of relative racial civility would pass. The Democrats regained control of the White House in 1885, eliminating the hard-won black enclave in federal jobs. The Democrats also regrouped locally, making substantive and procedural concessions to dissident white sentiment.[65] The legislature sanctioned the reestablishment of the City of Mobile in 1887, loosening the financial straightjacket in the new charter. Mobile's economy and fiscal prospects finally began to improve.[66] The divisions within the white populace became less pressing in Mobile, narrowing African American opportunities to broker concessions. Soon after, another firestorm of racial hatred passed through the region, sweeping away the incremental gains of decades. Disfranchisement, legal apartheid, and even mob violence would come to Mobile after the turn of the century; Mobile County nearly led Alabama in lynchings in the decades after 1900.[67] The

62. Ibid., September 22, 23, October 2, 4, 29, 1885.
63. Ibid., September 19, 1885.
64. C. Vann Woodward, *The Strange Career of Jim Crow*, 3d rev. ed. (New York, 1974).
65. *MDR,* January 21, February 22, 1885.
66. Alsobrook, "Alabama's Port City," 1–3; Doyle, *New Men, New Cities, New South,* 78–86, 330.
67. Glen Feldman, "Lynching in Alabama, 1889–1921," *Alabama Review* 48 (April 1995), 126.

struggle for basic civil equality would all have to be done over again at immense cost. Still, African American voters and their leaders could not read the future nor could they have stopped the avalanche if they had known. For a time, African Americans used the available means about as wisely as possible and for as long as the circumstances would allow.

What, then, can one conclude about the first generation of African American politics in Mobile? In the wider historical literature, the polemical needs of the second Reconstruction obscured certain aspects of African American political behavior in the first. Perhaps identification with the goals of Congressional Reconstruction inhibited discussion of how crucially patronage and livelihood impinged on political leadership. Scholars have implicitly celebrated grassroots black activists by de-emphasizing the pursuit of individual self-interest. In Mobile, and likely elsewhere, this approach yields a sanitized version of events, given the practical needs of activists trying to make a living in politics. As the preceding account demonstrates, black leaders divided between themselves at nearly every opportunity. Mobile's concentration of government jobs and intense popular upheaval encouraged endemic factionalism. Early during Reconstruction, these leadership divisions occurred along fissures of social division within the community, but as time went on, a pattern of individual self-seeking became increasingly evident. By the 1870s, factionalism largely followed lines of actual or prospective federal employment as interracial clusters of activists struggled for patronage and mass support. The scramble for government jobs and political preference threatened to turn African American politics into the vehicle of activists' personal priorities.

By and large this did not happen, which was perhaps the hidden accomplishment of black politics during the era. Historians often focus on the actions of individual activists, but the collective intelligence of a skeptical black populace seems more crucial. The electorate overruled their squabbling leadership, insisting on a certain practical consistency. Loyal to the national Republican party as the vehicle of their highest aspirations, at the local level black voters did whatever it took to advance concrete interests—and generally vexing the Democrats wherever possible. Republican voters imposed unity upon the self-interested activists, disregarding their most prominent leaders when necessary. Allen Alexander, for example, was a physically brave and articulate spokesman, the most flamboyant politician of his day. Despite this, he seldom could deliver the black vote unless he could provide a persuasive rationale—something based on more than his personal interests. In Gilded Age politics, a certain self-serving style among activists was common, but no one in Mobile could secure the loyalty of the masses on trust alone. Black voters insisted that their values and concrete interests be served.

The modern preoccupation with racial equality as the crucial issue of the era also has distracted scholars from the aftermath of Reconstruction—a time when utopian aspirations were in retreat and black politicians settled for less inspiring goals. In Mobile the period of Republican control offered mixed practical results for African Americans, with civil rights gains undercut by racial conflict and municipal financial ruin. The aftermath of Republican rule proved surprisingly fluid, however. Fiscal debates rivaled race as the overriding public preoccupation of the 1870s and beyond. Conservative whites divided over the financial crisis, with class and labor issues becoming prominent. Under these circumstances, blacks skillfully manipulated their suffrage to yield occasional electoral victories, though carefully enough to avoid galvanizing a racist backlash. They thus avoided the sort of urban bloodletting that marked the end of Readjuster power in Virginia or the Populists' overthrow in North Carolina. African Americans were able to maintain political relevance safely in Mobile, no mean feat given the wider context of federal abandonment of racial justice. Their efforts pushed civic leaders toward a rhetoric of fairness, of toleration of basic black rights, and a rejection of extralegal violence. The relative civility of the post-Redemption decade in Mobile underscores the full tragedy to come as the region, and the nation, embraced a violent white tribalism as destiny.

Bibliography

PRIMARY SOURCES

Manuscripts

Alabama Department of Archives and History, Montgomery
Corporation Papers. Railroads, 1868–1901.
Houston, Gov. George S. Papers.
Lewis, Gov. David P. Papers.
Lindsey, Gov. Robert B. Papers.
Parsons, [Provisional] Gov. Lewis E. Papers.
Patton, Gov. Robert M. Papers.
Semmes, Raphael. Papers.
Smith, Gov. William H. Papers.
Swayne, Wager. Papers.

Alderman Library, University of Virginia, Charlottesville
Ackerman, Amos K. Papers.
Minor, W. L. Collection.
Wilson, Augusta Evans. Papers.

Amistad Research Center, Dillard University, New Orleans
American Missionary Association Archives.

Baker Library, Harvard Business School, Cambridge, Mass.
R. G. Dun and Company Collection.

Bowdoin College Library, Brunswick, Maine
Howard, O. O. Papers.

Catholic University, Washington, D.C.
Powderly, Terence V. Papers.

Historical Society of Wisconsin, Madison
Wittenberger, Frank. Diary (translation).

Illinois State Historical Society, Springfield
Burke, Lemuel. Diary.

Indiana Historical Society, Indianapolis
Schlagle, John W. Diary.

Louisiana State University Libraries, Baton Rouge
Quintard, Charles Todd. Diaries.

Manuscript Division, Library of Congress, Washington, D.C.
American Colonization Society Papers.
American Home Missionary Society Papers.
Butler, Benjamin F. Papers.
Chandler, W. E. Papers.
Chase, Salmon P. Papers.
Garfield, James A. Papers.
Gillette, James. Papers.
Grant, Ulysses S. Papers.
Johnson, Andrew. Papers.
Reid, Whitelaw. Papers.
Sherman, John. Papers.
Squier, Ephraim G. Papers.
Washburne, E. B. Papers.

Manuscript Division, New York Public Library, New York City
Executive Committee of the Mobile Committee of Safety. Minutes, 1862–63.

Minnesota Historical Society, St. Paul
Andrews, C. C. Papers.

Mississippi State University, Starkeville
Nannie Herndon Rice Family Papers.

Mobile County Commission, Mobile Government Plaza, Mobile, Ala.
Board of Revenue Commissioners. Minutes, 1865–76.

Mobile County Courthouse, Mobile, Ala.
Records of the Probate Court of Mobile County.
    Petitions to Become Slaves, 1860–62.
    Record Book of Runaway Slaves, 1857–65.

BIBLIOGRAPHY   271

Mobile County School Board Offices, Barton Academy, Mobile, Ala.
Board of School Commissioners. Minutes, 1865–79.

Mobile Municipal Archives, Mobile, Ala.
Board of Aldermen. Minutes, 1865–79.
Board of Common Council. Minutes, 1865–79.
City Tax Lists, 1867–70.
Guard House Docket, 1862–63.
Ordinance Books, 1865–75.
Records of the Mayor, Board of Aldermen, and Common Council. RG 3, 1865–79.
Ways and Means Committee. Minutes, 1869–73.

Mobile Public Library, Mobile, Ala.
Records of the Third Presbyterian Church of Mobile, 1853–68. Sessional Records, Central Presbyterian Church, 1842–68.

The Museum of Mobile, Mobile, Ala.
Creole Fire Company Papers.
Horton, Gustavus. Papers.
Muldon, S. C. Letterbooks.
Parker, G. M. Papers.
Records of the Creole Social Club.
Schroeder, H. A. Papers.

National Archives and Records Service, Washington, D.C.
Appointment Papers, Customs, and General Records of the Department of the Treasury. RG 56.
Case Files for Mobile County. Approved Claims Records of the Southern Claims Commission. RG 217, National Archives and Record Service Microfilm M2062.
General Records of the Department of State, RG 59. National Archives and Record Service Microfilm M698.
Letters of Application and Recommendation during the Administration of Ulysses S. Grant, National Archives and Record Service Microfilm M968.
Letters Received by the Department of Justice from the State of Alabama. General Records of the Department of Justice, RG 60. National Archives and Record Service Microfilm M1356.
Letters Received, Department of the Gulf. Records of the U.S. Army Continental Commands. RG 393.
Letters Sent, Customhouse, Mobile, Ala. Records of the U.S. Custom Service. RG 36.
Records of the Bureau of Refugees, Freedmen, and Abandoned Lands. RG 105.
Records of the Headquarters of the Army. RG 108.

Registers and Signatures of Depositors in the Freedmen's Savings and Trust Company. Records of the Office of the Comptroller of the Currency. RG 101. National Archives and Record Service Microfilm M816.
Records of the Bureau of the Census. RG 29. Population Schedules, Mobile County, manuscript U.S. Census for 1860, 1870, and 1880. National Archives and Record Service Microfilm M653, M593, and T9.
Records of the U.S. House of Representatives. RG 233.

Rutherford B. Hayes Library, Fremont, Ohio.
Hayes, Rutherford B. Papers.

Schomburg Center for Research in Black Culture, New York Public Library, New York City
Carpenter, John. Papers.

Southern Historical Collection, Davis Library, University of North Carolina, Chapel Hill
Bromberg, Frederick G. Papers.
Bullock and Hamilton Family Papers.
Creagh Family Papers.
Mordecai Family Papers.
Platt, Eldridge B. Papers.
Reynolds, Henry Lee. Papers.
Warmoth, Henry Clay. Papers.

State Historical Society of Iowa, Des Moines
Dodge, Grenville. Papers.

State Historical Society of Missouri, Columbia
France, Charles B. Papers.

Tennessee State Library and Archives, Nashville
Warner, Willard. Papers.

University of South Alabama Archives, Mobile
Records of the Circuit Court, Mobile County.
Croom, Velma and Stevens J. Correspondence.

W. S. Hoole Special Collections, University of Alabama, Tuscaloosa
Mobile City Police Records.
Yuille, Gaven. Papers.

William R. Perkins Library, Duke University, Durham, N.C.
Avery, Truman G. Diary.
Clay, Clement C. Papers.
Soto, John A. Scrapbook.

Spencer, George E. Letter.
Watson, Henry. Papers.

Newspapers and Periodicals

The American Missionary, 1865–68
Athens (Ala.) Post, [1868]
Aurora (Ill.) Beacon News, [1915]
Anglo-African, [1865]
Boston Evening Traveller, [1868]
De Bow's Review, After the War Series, 1865–68
Christian Advocate and Journal, 1865
Christian Recorder, 1865–68
Eufaula Bluff City (Ala.) Times, [1869]
Greensboro (Ala.) Beacon, [1871]
Greenville (Ala.) Advocate, [1875]
Grove Hill (Ala.) Democrat, [1867–68]
Harper's Weekly, 1865–86
Huntsville (Ala.) Gazette, 1880–84
The Independent, 1865
Journal of United Labor, 1880–81
The Liberator, 1865–69
Manhattan (Kans.) Nationalist, 1871–72
Mobile Advertiser and Register, 1861–66
Mobile Army Argus and Crisis, 1864–65
Mobile Blade, [1888]
Mobile Chronicle, [1882]
Mobile Evening News, [1862, 1864]
Mobile Herald, 1871–72
Mobile Item, 1884–85
Mobile Morning News, 1865
Mobile Nationalist, 1865–69
Mobile News, 1865, 1877–78
Mobile Register, 1868–86
Mobile Republican, [1871–72]
Mobile Times, 1865–67
Mobile Tribune, 1874–76
Mobile Watchman, [1873–74]
Montgomery Advertiser, [1865–70]
Montgomery Alabama State Journal, [1868–75]
Montgomery Mail, 1868–69

Montgomery State Sentinel, 1867–68
Moulton (Ala.) Union, [1867]
The Nation, 1865–80
National Anti-Slavery Standard, 1865–69
New Orleans Black Republican, 1865
New Orleans Picayune, 1865–67, 1886
New Orleans Tribune, 1865–68
New York Herald, [1865–67]
New York Times, 1865–86
New York Tribune, 1865–68, 1880
New York World, [1865–69]
Selma Times and Messenger, [1867–69]
Talladega Sun, [1870]
Washington Post, [1880]
Zion's Herald, 1865

Government Documents

Congressional Globe. 46 vols. Washington, D.C., 1834–73.
State of Alabama. *Acts of the General Assembly of Alabama, 1869–1870.* Montgomery, 1870.
———. *Acts of the Sessions of July, September, and November 1868 of the General Assembly of Alabama.* Montgomery, 1869.
———. *Official Journal of the Constitutional Convention of the State of Alabama Held in the City of Montgomery, Commencing on Tuesday, November 5th, A.D. 1867.* Montgomery, 1868.
———. *Official Report of the Superintendent of Public Instruction of the State of Alabama to the Governor for the Fiscal Year Ending 30th September 1869.* Montgomery, 1870.
———. *Report of Committee to Investigate Alleged Frauds in Issuance of Railroad Bonds and Bonds of the State for Use of Railroads.* Montgomery, 1871.
———. *Report of the Joint Committee of the General Assembly of Alabama in Regard to the Alleged Election of Geo. E. Spencer as U.S. Senator, together with Memorial and Evidence.* Montgomery, 1875.
U.S. Bureau of the Census. *Compendium of the Ninth Census.* Washington, D.C., 1872.
———. *Compendium of the Tenth Census.* Washington, D.C., 1883.
———. *Eighth Census.* Washington, D.C., 1864.
———. *Ninth Census.* Washington, D.C., 1872.
———. *Preliminary Report on the Eighth Census.* Washington, D.C., 1860.
U.S. Congress. House. *Affairs in Alabama.* 43d Cong., 2d sess., H. Rept. 262.

———. *Contested Election, Bromberg vs. Haralson, Alabama.* 44th Cong., 1st sess., H. Doc. 47.

———. *Report of the Select Committee on the Freedmen's Savings and Trust Company.* 44th Cong., 1st sess., H. Rept. 502, vol. 3.

———. *Testimony Taken before the Judiciary Committee, House of Representatives, in the Investigation of the Charges against Hon. Richard Busteed.* Washington, 1869.

———. *Testimony Taken by the Joint Select Committee to Inquire into the Condition of Affairs in the Late Insurrectionary States.* 42d Cong., 2d sess., H. Rept. 22.

U.S. Congress. Senate. *Elections of 1874, 1875, 1876.* 44th Cong., 2d sess., S. Rept. 704.

———. *Message of the President of the United States, Communicating, in Compliance with a Resolution of the Senate of the 12th Instant, Information in Relation to the States of the Union Lately in Rebellion, Accompanied by a Report of Carl Schurz on the States of South Carolina, Georgia, Alabama, Mississippi, and Louisiana; Also a Report of General Grant, on the Same Subject.* 39th Cong., 1st sess., S. Exec. Doc. 2.

———. *Report and Testimony of the Select Committee of the United States Senate to Investigate the Causes of the Removal of the Negroes from the Southern States to the Northern States.* 46th Cong., 2d sess., 1880, S. Rept. 693.

———. Committee on Education and Labor. *Report of the Committee of the Senate upon the Relations between Labor and Capital and Testimony Taken by the Committee.* 48th Cong., 2d sess., S. Rept. 1262, 5 vols.

U.S. War Department. *War of the Rebellion: A Compilation of the Official Records of the Union and Confederate Armies.* 128 vols. Washington, D.C., 1880–1901.

Works Projects Administration. "Interesting Transcriptions and Cataloguing Notes from the Aldermen Minutes of the City of Mobile." Works Projects Administration typescript, 1939.

———. "Interesting Transcriptions from the *Mobile Nationalist,* 1868–1869." Works Projects Administration transcript, 1939.

———. "Interesting Transcriptions from the *Mobile Tribune.*" Works Projects Administration transcript, 1939.

Books, Articles, and Other Published Sources

Anders, Leslie. "Men from Home: Missouri Volunteers in the Pacification of Mobile, Alabama, 1865–1866." *Missouri Historical Review* 69 (April 1975): 250–9.

Andrews, Christopher C. *History of the Campaign of Mobile: Including the Cooperative Operations of Gen. Wilson's Cavalry in Alabama.* New York, 1867.

———. *Recollections: 1829–1922.* Cleveland, 1928.
Andrews, Sidney. *The South since the War as Shown by Fourteen Weeks of Travel and Observation in Georgia and the Carolinas.* 1866. Reprint, Boston, 1971.
Belous, Russell E., ed. "The Diary of Ann Quigley." *Gulf South Historical Review* 4 (spring 1989): 89–99.
Bergeron, Paul H., ed. *The Papers of Andrew Johnson.* Knoxville, 1967–.
Berlin, Ira; Joseph P. Reidy; and Leslie S. Rowland, eds. *The Black Military Experience.* Series 2 of *Freedom: A Documentary History of Emancipation, 1861–1867.* Cambridge and New York, 1982.
———. *Freedom's Soldiers: The Black Military Experience in the Civil War.* Cambridge and New York, 1998.
Biddle, Ellen McGowan. *Reminiscences of a Soldier's Wife.* Philadelphia, 1907.
Brewer, Willis. *Alabama: Her History, Resources, War Record, and Public Men, from 1540 to 1872.* 1872. Reprint, Tuscaloosa, 1964.
Bromberg, Frederick G. *The Reconstruction Period in Alabama.* Iberville Historical Society Papers, nos. 3, 4. Mobile, 1911–14.
Clark, Willis G. *History of Education in Alabama, 1702–1889.* Washington, D.C., 1889.
Chase, Salmon P. *Salmon P. Chase Papers.* Vol. 1, *Journal, 1829–1872,* edited by John Niven et al. Kent, Ohio, and London, 1993.
Craighead, Erwin. *Mobile: Fact and Tradition.* Mobile, 1930.
Cumming, Kate. *Gleanings from Southland: Sketches of Life.* Birmingham, 1895.
———. *Kate: The Journal of a Confederate Nurse.* Edited by Richard Barksdale Harwell. 1959. Reprint, Baton Rouge, 1987.
Dennett, John Richard. *The South as It Is, 1865–1866.* 1866. Reprint, New York, 1965.
Elder, Donald E., ed. *A Damned Iowa Greyhound: The Civil War Letters of William Henry Harrison Clayton.* Iowa City, 1994.
Evans, Augusta Jane. *Macaria.* [1864.] Reprint, Baton Rouge, 1992.
Fleming, Walter Lynwood, ed. *Documentary History of Reconstruction: Political, Military, Social, Religious, Educational and Industrial: 1865 to 1906.* 2 vols. 1906–7. Reprint, Gloucester, Mass., 1960.
Fondé, Charles H. *An Account of the Great Explosion of the United States Ordnance Stores which Occurred in Mobile on the 25th Day of May 1865.* Mobile, 1865.
Grant, Ulysses S. *The Papers of Ulysses S. Grant.* Edited by John Y. Simon. 24 vols. Carbondale and Edwardsville, Ill., 1967–.
Hatch, Carl E., ed. *Dearest Susie: A Civil War Infantryman's Letters to His Sweetheart.* New York, 1971.
Holt, Thad, ed. *Miss Waring's Journal: Being the Diary of Miss Mary Waring of Mobile during the Final Days of the War between the States.* Chicago, 1964.

Houzeau, Jean-Charles. *My Passage at the* New Orleans Tribune: *A Memoir of the Civil War Era.* Edited by David C. Rankin. Translated by Gerald F. Renault. Baton Rouge and London, 1984.

King, Edward. *The Great South.* Edited by W. Magruder Drake and Robert R. Jones. 1875. Reprint, Baton Rouge, 1972.

Lowe, Henry Allen, Jr. *The Journals of Henry Allen Lowe Jr., 1869–1877.* N.p., 1992.

Macrae, David. *The Americans at Home.* 1870. Reprint, New York, 1952.

McKinstry, Alexander, comp. *The Code of Ordinances of the City of Mobile, Alabama.* Mobile, 1859.

McMillan, Malcolm C., ed. *The Alabama Confederate Reader.* Tuscaloosa, 1992.

Mobile and Northwestern Railroad. *The Mobile and Northwestern Railroad Project.* New York, 1871.

Mobile and Ohio Railroad Company. "Proceedings of the Twenty-second Annual Meeting of the Stockholders of the Mobile and Ohio Railroad Company Held in Mobile, May 17, 1870." Mobile, 1870.

Mobile Board of Trade. "Annual Report of the Mobile Board of Trade for the Year Ending December 5, 1873." Mobile, 1874.

Mobile Board of Trade. "Annual Report of the Mobile Board of Trade for the Year Ending November 30, 1875." Mobile, 1876.

Mobile Board of Trade. "Twelfth Annual Report of the Mobile Board of Trade for the Year Ending November 1, 1880." Mobile, 1881.

Nordhoff, Charles. *The Cotton States in the Spring and Summer of 1875.* Reprint. New York, n.d.

Palmer, Beverly Wilson, ed. *The Papers of Charles Sumner.* London, 1987. Alexandria, Va., 1988. Microfilm.

Powers, Stephen. *Afoot and Alone: A Walk from Sea to Sea by the Southern Route.* Hartford, 1871.

Rachleff, Marshall, ed. "Economic Self Interest Versus Racial Control: Mobile's Protest against the Jailing of Black Seamen." *Civil War History* 25 (March 1979): 84–8.

[Raviesies, Paul.] *The Mobile Oyster and Its Destiny and Other Attractions.* Mobile, 1884.

Reid, Whitelaw. *After the War: A Tour of the Southern States, 1865–1866.* Edited by C. Vann Woodward. New York, 1965.

Roll of the Black Dupes and White Renegades Who Voted in Mobile City and County for the Menagerie Constitution for the State of Alabama. Mobile, 1868.

Rose, George. *The Great Country; Or, Impressions of America.* London, 1868.

Silber, Irwin, comp. and ed. *Songs of the Civil War.* New York 1960.

Smith, C. Carter, Jr., and Sidney Adair Smith, eds. *Mobile, 1861–1865: Notes and a Bibliography.* Chicago, 1964.

Somers, Robert. *The Southern States since the War, 1870–1871.* Edited by Malcolm McMillan. University, Ala., 1965.

Stockwell, Elisha, Jr. *Private Elisha Stockwell Jr. Sees the Civil War.* Edited by Byron R. Abernathy. Norman, Okla., 1958.

Warner, Charles Dudley. *Studies in the South and West with Some Comments on Canada.* New York, 1889.

Wartegg, Ernst von Hesse. *Travels on the Lower Mississippi, 1879–1880.* Edited and translated by Frederic Trautmann. Columbia, Mo., and London, 1990.

Waterbury, Maria. *Seven Years among the Freedmen.* Chicago, 1890.

Williams, Hiram Smith. *This War So Horrible: The Civil War Diary of Hiram Smith Williams.* Edited by Lewis N. Wynne and Robert A. Taylor. Tuscaloosa, 1993.

Williams, James M.. *From That Terrible Field: The Civil War Letters of James M Williams, Twenty-first Alabama Infantry Volunteers.* Edited by John Kent Folmar. University, Ala., 1981.

———. "Post–Civil War Mobile: The Letters of James M. Williams, May–September, 1865." Edited by John Kent Folmar. *Alabama Historical Quarterly* 32 (fall/winter 1961): 186–98.

Woodruff, Matthew. *A Union Soldier in the Land of the Vanquished: The Diary of Sergeant Matthew Woodruff, June–December 1865.* Edited by F. N. Boney. University, Ala., 1969.

Woodson, Carter G. *The Mind of the Negro as Reflected in Letters Written during the Crisis.* 1926. Reprint, New York, 1969.

Secondary Sources

Books

Altschuler, Glenn C., and Stuart M. Blumin. *Rude Republic: Americans and their Politics in the Nineteenth Century.* Princeton and Oxford, 2000.

Amos, Harriet E. *Cotton City: Urban Development in Antebellum Mobile.* University, Ala., 1985.

Arneson, Eric. *Waterfront Workers of New Orleans: Race, Class, and Politics, 1863–1923.* Oxford, 1991.

Bailey, Richard. *Neither Carpetbaggers nor Scalawags: Black Officeholders during the Reconstruction of Alabama, 1867–1878.* Montgomery, 1991.

Barney, William L. *The Secessionist Impulse: Alabama and Mississippi in 1860.* Princeton, 1974.

Beatty, Bess. *A Revolution Gone Backward: The Black Response to National Politics, 1876–1896.* New York, 1987.

Bell, Caryn Cossé. *Revolution, Romanticism, and the Afro-Creole Protest Tradition in Louisiana, 1718–1868.* Baton Rouge and London, 1997.

Bergeron, Arthur W., Jr. *Confederate Mobile.* Jackson, Miss., 1991.

Berlin, Ira. *Many Thousands Gone: The First Two Centuries of Slavery in North America.* Cambridge, Massachusetts, and London, 1997.

———. *Slaves without Masters: The Free Negro in the Antebellum South.* New York, 1974.

Blassingame, John W. *Black New Orleans.* Chicago and London, 1973.

Bond, Horace Mann. *Negro Education in Alabama: A Study in Cotton and Steel.* Library of Alabama Classics. 1939. Reprint, Tuscaloosa, 1994.

Brown, D. Alexander. *The Galvanized Yankees.* Urbana, 1963.

Cimbala, Paul, and Randall Miller, eds. *The Freedmen's Bureau and Reconstruction: Reconsiderations.* New York, 1999.

Current, Richard Nelson. *Those Terrible Carpetbaggers: A Reinterpretation.* New York, 1988.

Curtin, Mary Ellen. *Black Prisoners and Their World, Alabama, 1865–1900.* Charlottesville and London, 2000.

Dailey, Jane. *Before Jim Crow: The Politics of Race in Postemancipation Virginia.* Chapel Hill and London, 2000.

Delaney, Caldwell. *A Mobile Sextet: Papers Read before the Alabama Historical Association, 1952–1971.* Mobile, 1971.

Denman, Clarence P. *The Secession Movement in Alabama.* 1933. Reprint, Freeport, N.Y., 1971.

De Santis, Vincent P. *Republicans Face the Southern Question: The New Departure Years, 1877–1897.* 1959. Reprint, New York, 1969

Dorman, Lewy. *Party Politics in Alabama: From 1850 through 1860.* 1935. Reprint, Tuscaloosa and London, 1995.

Doyle, Don H. *New Men, New Cities, New South: Atlanta, Nashville, Charleston, Mobile.* Chapel Hill, 1990.

Dubin, Michael J. *United States Congressional Elections, 1788–1997: The Official Results.* Jefferson, N.C., 1998.

Du Bois, W. E. B. *Black Reconstruction in America: An Essay toward a History of the Part which Black Folk Played in the Attempt to Reconstruct Democracy in America, 1860–1880.* 1935. Reprint, New York, 1972.

Dulaney, Marvin. *Black Police in America.* Bloomington and Indianapolis, 1996.

Fairman, Charles. *Reconstruction and Reunion, 1864–1888.* Vol. 6 of *History of the Supreme Court of the United States.* New York, 1971.

Fidler, William Perry. *Augusta Evans Wilson, 1835–1909.* University, Ala., 1951.

Fitzgerald, Michael W. *The Union League Movement in the Deep South: Politics and Agricultural Change during Reconstruction.* Baton Rouge, 1989.

Fleming, Walter Lynwood. *Civil War and Reconstruction in Alabama.* New York, 1905.

Foner, Eric. *Freedom's Lawmakers: A Directory of Black Officeholders during Reconstruction.* Rev. ed. Baton Rouge and London, 1996.
———. *Nothing but Freedom: Emancipation and Its Legacy.* New York, 1983.
———. *Reconstruction: America's Unfinished Revolution, 1863–1877.* New York, 1988.
Garlock, Jonathan, comp. *Guide to the Local Assemblies of the Knights of Labor.* Westport, Conn., 1982.
Gaston, Paul M. *The New South Creed: A Study in Southern Mythmaking.* New York, 1970.
Gerteis, Louis S. *From Contraband to Freedman: Federal Policy toward Southern Blacks.* Westport, Conn., 1973.
Gillette, William. *Retreat from Reconstruction, 1869–1879.* Baton Rouge, 1979.
Going, Allen J. *Bourbon Democracy in Alabama, 1874–1890.* 1951. Reprint, University, Ala., 1992.
Goldfield, David R., *Cotton Fields and Skyscrapers: Southern City and Region.* Baton Rouge and London, 1982.
Goldman, Robert M. *"A Free Ballot and a Fair Count": The Department of Justice and the Enforcement of Voting Rights in the South.* 1990. Reprint, New York, 2001.
Gould, Elizabeth Barrett. *From Fort to Port: An Architectural History of Mobile, Alabama, 1711–1918.* Tuscaloosa and London, 1988.
Hamilton, Peter J. *Mobile of the Five Flags.* Mobile, 1913.
Hahn, Steven. *The Roots of Southern Populism: Yeoman Farmers and the Transformation of the Georgia Upcountry, 1850–1890.* Oxford, 1983.
Hearn, Chester G. *Mobile Bay and the Mobile Campaign: The Last Great Battles of the Civil War.* Jefferson, N.C., and London, 1993.
Higginbotham, Jay. *Mobile, City by the Bay.* Mobile, 1968.
Hildebrand, Reginald F. *The Times Were Strange and Stirring: Methodist Preachers and the Crisis of Emancipation.* Durham, 1995.
Hirshson, Stanley P. *Farewell to the Bloody Shirt: Northern Republicans and the Southern Negro.* Chicago, 1961.
Holt, Thomas C. *Black over White: Negro Political Leadership in South Carolina during Reconstruction.* Urbana, 1977.
Hoogenboom, Ari. *Rutherford B. Hayes: Warrior and President.* Lawrence, 1995.
Horsman, Reginald. *Josiah Nott of Mobile: Southerner, Physician, and Racial Theorist.* Baton Rouge, 1987.
Hunter, Tera. *To 'Joy My Freedom: Southern Black Women's Lives and Labors after the Civil War.* Cambridge, Mass., 1997.
Kolchin, Peter. *First Freedom: The Responses of Alabama's Blacks to Emancipation and Reconstruction.* Westport, Conn., 1971.
Kousser, J. Morgan, and James M. McPherson, eds. *Region, Race, and Reconstruction: Essays in Honor of C. Vann Woodward.* New York, 1981.

Litwack, Leon F. *Been in the Storm So Long: The Aftermath of Slavery.* New York, 1979.
McFeely, William S. *Yankee Stepfather: General O. O. Howard and the Freedmen.* New York, 1968.
McLauren, Melton. *The Knights of Labor in the South.* Westport, Conn., 1982.
McMillan, Malcolm C. *The Disintegration of a Confederate State: Three Governors and Alabama's Wartime Home Front, 1861–1865.* Macon, 1986.
McWilliams, Tennant S. *Hannis Taylor: The New Southerner as American.* University, Ala., 1978.
Mills, Gary B. *The Forgotten People: Cane River's Creoles of Color.* Baton Rouge and London, 1977.
O'Brien, Sean Michael. *Mobile, 1865: Last Stand of the Confederacy.* Westport, Conn., 2001.
Osthaus, Carl R. *Freedmen, Philanthropy, and Fraud: A History of the Freedmen's Savings Bank.* Urbana, 1976.
———. *Partisans of the Southern Press: Editorial Spokesmen of the Nineteenth Century.* Lexington, Ky., 1994.
Owen, Thomas McAdory. *History of Alabama and Dictionary of Alabama Biography.* 4 vols. Chicago, 1921.
Painter, Nell Irvin. *Exodusters: Black Migration to Kansas after Reconstruction.* New York, 1976.
Perman, Michael. *Reunion without Compromise: The South and Reconstruction, 1865–1868.* Cambridge, 1973.
———. *The Road to Redemption: Southern Politics, 1869–1879.* Chapel Hill, 1984.
Powell, Lawrence N. *New Masters: Northern Planters during the Civil War and Reconstruction.* New Haven, 1980.
Rabinowitz, Howard N. *Race Relations in the Urban South, 1865–1890.* New York, 1978.
———. ed. *Southern Black Leaders of the Reconstruction Era.* Urbana, 1982.
Rachleff, Peter J. *Black Labor in the South: Richmond, Virginia, 1865–1890.* Philadelphia, 1984.
Rogers, William Warren, and Robert David Ward. *August Reckoning: Jack Turner and Racism in Post–Civil War Alabama.* Baton Rouge, 1973.
Rousey, Dennis C. *Policing the Southern City: New Orleans, 1805–1889.* Baton Rouge and London, 1996.
Russell, James Michael. *Atlanta, 1847–1890: City Building in the Old South and the New.* Baton Rouge, 1988.
Saunders, Robert, Jr. *John Archibald Campbell, Southern Moderate, 1811–1889.* Tuscaloosa and London, 1997.
Sefton, James E. *The United States Army and Reconstruction, 1865–1877.* Baton Rouge, 1967.

Summers, Mark W. *The Era of Good Stealings.* New York, 1993.
———. *The Press Gang: Newspapers and Politics, 1865–1878.* Chapel Hill and London, 1994.
———. *Railroads, Reconstruction, and the Gospel of Prosperity: Aid under the Radical Republicans, 1865–1877.* Princeton, 1984.
———. *Rum, Romanism, and Rebellion: The Making of a President, 1884.* Chapel Hill and London, 2000.
Thomason, Michael V. R., ed. *Mobile, the New History of Alabama's First City.* Tuscaloosa, 2001.
Thornton, J. Mills, III. *Politics and Power in a Slave Society: Alabama, 1800–1860.* Baton Rouge, 1978.
Trudeau, Noah Andre. *Like Men of War: Black Troops in the Civil War.* Boston and New York, 1998.
Walker, Clarence E. *A Rock in a Weary Land: The African Methodist Episcopal Church during the Civil War and Reconstruction.* Baton Rouge, 1982.
Wang, Xi. *The Trials of Democracy: Black Suffrage and the Northern Republicans, 1860–1910.* Athens, Ga., 1997.
Webb, Samuel L. *Two Party Politics in the One-Party South: Alabama's Hill Country, 1874–1920.* Tuscaloosa, 1997.
Wiener, Jonathan M. *Social Origins of the New South: Alabama, 1860–1885.* Baton Rouge, 1978.
Wiggins, Sarah Woolfolk. *The Scalawag in Alabama Politics, 1865–1881.* University, Ala., 1977.
Willis, John C. *Forgotten Time: The Yazoo-Mississippi Delta after the Civil War.* Charlottesville and London, 2000.
Woodman, Harold D. *King Cotton and His Retainers: Financing and Marketing the Cotton Crop of the South, 1800–1925.* Lexington, Ky., 1968.
Woodward, C. Vann. *Origins of the New South, 1877–1913.* Baton Rouge, 1951.
———. *The Strange Career of Jim Crow.* 3d rev. ed. New York, 1974.
Wrenn, Lynette Boney. *Crisis and Commission Government in Memphis: Elite Rule in a Gilded Age City.* Knoxville, 1998.

Articles

Altschuler, Glenn C., and Stuart M. Blumin. "Limits of Political Engagement in Antebellum America: A New Look at the Golden Age of Participatory Democracy." *Journal of American History* 84 (December 1997): 855–85.
Amos, Harriet E. "From Old to New South Trade in Mobile, 1850–1900." *Gulf South Historical Review* 5 (spring 1990): 114–27.
———. "Trials of a Unionist: Gustavus Horton, Military Mayor of Mobile during Reconstruction." *Gulf South Historical Review* 4 (fall 1989): 134–51.

Bailey, Mrs. Hugh C. "Mobile's Tragedy: The Great Magazine Explosion of 1865." *Alabama Review* 21 (January 1968): 40–52.

Brent, Joseph E. "No Compromise: The End of Presidential Reconstruction in Mobile, Alabama, January–May 1867." *Gulf South Historical Review* 7 (fall 1991): 18–37.

Ellis, Mary Louise. "Improbable Visitor: Oscar Wilde in Alabama, 1882." *Alabama Review* 39 (October 1986): 243–60.

Feldman, Glenn. "Lynching in Alabama, 1889–1921." *Alabama Review* 48 (April 1995): 114–41.

Fitzgerald, Michael W. "Another Kind of Glory: Black Participation and Its Consequences in the Campaign for Confederate Mobile," *Alabama Review* 54 (October 2001): 243–73.

———. "Emancipation and Military Pacification: The Freedmen's Bureau and Social Control in Alabama." In *The Freedmen's Bureau and Reconstruction: Reconsiderations,* edited by Paul A. Cimbala and Randall Miller. New York, 1999.

———. "From Unionists to Scalawags: Elite Dissent in Civil War Mobile." *Alabama Review* 55 (April 2002): 106–21.

———. "Radical Republicans and the White Yeomanry during Alabama Reconstruction, 1865–1868." *Journal of Southern History* 54 (November 1988): 565–96.

———. "Railroad Subsidies and Black Aspirations: The Politics of Economic Development in Reconstruction Mobile, 1865–1879." *Civil War History* 39 (September 1993): 240–56.

———. "Republican Factionalism and Black Empowerment: The Spencer-Warner Controversy and Alabama Reconstruction, 1868–1880." *Journal of Southern History* 64 (August 1998): 473–94.

———. "Wager Swayne, the Freedmen's Bureau, and the Politics of Reconstruction in Alabama." *Alabama Review* 48 (July 1995): 188–218.

Folmar, John Kent. "Reaction to Reconstruction: John Forsyth and the *Mobile Advertiser and Register,* 1865–1867." *Alabama Historical Quarterly* 37 (winter 1975): 245–64.

Griffin, Richard W. "Cotton Frauds and Confiscations in Alabama, 1863–1866." *Alabama Review* 7 (October 1954): 265–76.

Hardin, Stephanie. "Climate of Fear: Violence, Intimidation, and Media Manipulation in Reconstruction Mobile, 1865–1876." *Gulf South Historical Review* 2 (fall 1986): 39–52.

Hinson, Billy G. "The Beginning of Military Reconstruction in Mobile, Alabama, May–November 1867." *Gulf South Historical Review* 9 (fall 1993): 65–83.

Johnson, Kenneth R. "The Peabody Fund: Its Role and Influence in Alabama." *Alabama Review* 27 (April 1974): 101–26.

Kyriakoudes, Louis M. "The Rise of Merchants and Market Towns in Reconstruction-era Alabama." *Alabama Review* 49 (April 1996): 83–107.

Lash, Jeffrey N. "A Yankee in Gray: Danville Leadbetter and the Defense of Mobile Bay, 1861–1863." *Civil War History* 37 (September 1991): 197–218.

McCrary, Peyton. "History in the Courts: The Significance of *The City of Mobile v. Bolden*." In *Minority Vote Dilution,* edited by Chandler Davidson. Washington, D.C., 1984.

Meier, August, and Elliot Rudwick. "The Boycott Movement against Jim Crow Streetcars in the South, 1900–1906." *Journal of American History* 55 (March 1969): 756–75.

Mills, Gary B. "Miscegenation and the Free Negro in Antebellum 'Anglo' Alabama: A Reexamination of Southern Race Relations." *Journal of American History* 68 (June 1981): 16–34.

Mobley, Joe A. "The Siege of Mobile, August 1864–April 1865." *Alabama Historical Quarterly* 38 (winter 1976): 250–70.

Morgan, David T. "Philip Phillips and Internal Improvements in Mid-Nineteenth Century Alabama." *Alabama Review* 34 (April 1981): 83–93.

Partin, Robert. "Dr. Jerome Cochran, Yellow Fever Fighter." *Alabama Review* 13 (January 1960): 21–39.

Robinson, Armstead. "Beyond the Realm of Social Consensus: New Meanings of Reconstruction for American History." *Journal of American History* 68 (September 1981): 276–97.

———. "'Plans that Comed from God': Institution Building and the Emergence of Black Leadership in Reconstruction Memphis." In *Toward a New South? Studies in Post–Civil War Southern Communities,* edited by Orville V. Burton and Robert C. McMath. Westport, Conn., 1982.

Rogers, William Warren, Jr. "'The Past Is Gone': Ulysses S. Grant Visits Mobile." *Gulf South Historical Review* 5 (fall 1989): 7–20.

Sizemore, Margaret Davidson. "Frederick G. Bromberg of Mobile: An Illustrious Character, 1837–1928." *Alabama Review* 29 (April 1976): 104–22.

Spencer, C. A. "Black Benevolent Societies and the Development of Black Insurance Companies in 19th Century Alabama." *Phylon* 46 (fall 1985): 251–61.

Thompson, Alan Smith. "Southern Rights and Nativism as Issues in Mobile Politics, 1850–1861." *Alabama Review* 35 (April 1982): 127–41.

Weisenfeld, Judith. "'Who Is Sufficient for These Things?': Sara G. Stanley and the American Missionary Association, 1864–1868." *Church History* 60 (December 1991): 493–507.

Wiggins, Sarah Woolfolk. "The 'Pig Iron' Kelley Riot, May 14, 1867." *Alabama Historical Quarterly* 30 (spring 1968): 51–64.

———. "Press Reaction in Alabama to the Attempted Assassination of Judge Richard Busteed." *Alabama Review* 21 (July 1968): 211–8.

Unpublished Works

Alsobrook, David Ernest. "Alabama's Port City: Mobile during the Progressive Era." Ph.D. diss., Auburn University, 1983.

Barucki, Wesley Brian. "Yankees in King Cotton's Court: Northerners in Antebellum and Wartime Alabama." Ph.D. diss., University of Alabama, 2001.

Berkstresser, Alma Esther. "Mobile, Alabama, in the 1880s." Master's thesis, University of Alabama, 1951.

Bhurtel, Shyam Krishna. "Alfred Eliab Buck: Carpetbagger in Alabama and Georgia." Ph.D. Diss., Auburn University 1981.

Burnett, Lonnie Alexander. "The Pen Makes a Good Sword: John Forsyth and the *Mobile Register*." Ph.D. diss., University of Southern Mississippi, 2000.

Calametti, John A., Jr. "The Catholic Church in Mobile during Reconstruction, 1865–1877." Master's thesis, University of South Alabama, 1993.

Cantrell, Kimberly Bass. "A Voice for the Freedmen: The *Mobile Nationalist*, 1865–1869." Master's thesis, Auburn University, 1989.

Davis, Barbara Joan. "A Comparative Analysis of the Economic Structure of Mobile County, Alabama, before and after the Civil War, 1860 and 1870." Master's thesis, University of Alabama, 1963.

Ewert, George H. "Old Times Will Come Again: The Municipal Market System of Mobile, Alabama, 1888–1901." Master's thesis, University of South Alabama, 1993.

Gould, Lois Virginia Mecham. "'In Full Enjoyment of Their Liberty': The Free Women of Color of the Gulf Ports of New Orleans, Mobile, and Pensacola, 1769–1860." Ph.D. diss., Emory University, 1991.

Isbell, Frances Annette. "A Social and Economic History of Mobile, 1865–1875." Master's thesis, University of Alabama, 1951.

Jones, Allen Woodrow. "A History of the Direct Primary in Alabama, 1840–1903." Ph.D. diss., University of Alabama, 1964.

Mannhard, Marilyn. "The Free People of Color in Antebellum Mobile County, Alabama." Master's thesis, University of South Alabama, 1982.

Mobley, Joe A. "Flush Times, War, and Reconstruction in a Southern Town: Mobile 1850–1867." Master's thesis, North Carolina State University at Raleigh, 1976.

Nordmann, Christopher Andrew. "Free Negroes in Mobile County, Alabama." Ph.D. diss., University of Alabama, 1990.

Spiers, Jennifer Kaye. "Educating Blacks in Reconstruction Alabama: John Silsby, the American Association, and the Freedmen's Bureau." Ph.D. diss., Auburn University, 1991.

Thompson, Alan Smith. "Mobile, Alabama, 1850–1861: Economic, Political, Physical, and Population Characteristics." Ph.D. diss., University of Alabama, 1979.

Index

African Americans: class divisions within, 3–4, 6, 9–10, 22, 75–6, 86, 101, 101*n*48, 103, 131, 168; and Mobile politics generally, 5–7, 266–7; rural-urban migration of, 5, 21–5, 35–6, 68, 71–2, 117–8, 217–8; population of, in Mobile, 10, 11*n*4, 18, 21, 24, 36, 218, 218*n*69; as Civil War soldiers and veterans, 13, 16–7, 18, 25–6, 30–2, 34, 42, 53, 59, 60, 74, 75, 87; freedpeople's relationship with Creoles, 13, 14, 15, 17; freedpeople's relationship with non-Creole free people of color, 15–6; and Emancipation Proclamation, 20; under Union occupation of Mobile, 27–34, 44–5, 49–50; curfew for, 30, 45; white allies of, 36–51, 55–7, 60–1, 84–5, 93, 99, 100, 117, 124, 130–1, 145–6, 173; and Unionists in Mobile, 37–41, 90; and northerners in Mobile, 42–3, 55–7; court testimony by, 45; and July Fourth disturbances, 45, 53–5; and self-determination rhetoric, 51, 81; community organizations of, 52–3; homelessness of, 68–9; diseases of, 69; housing for, 70; and crime, 74–5, 96–8, 106, 108, 118, 218; police brutality against, 74, 88, 106, 142; concern of, for social order, 75–6; self-defense for, 78; direct action by, 86–98, 108, 117, 121, 122–4, 264–5; and Union League, 87, 90–5, 98, 130–1; and labor organizing, 88–9, 207, 241; as police, 89, 100–6, 123, 124, 125, 151–2, 152*n*76, 204, 219, 230, 263; poor relief and food relief for, 90, 106, 118, 126; as jurors, 112, 203, 226, 250–1; and economic-development proposals, 139–41; and Spencer-Warner feud, 176–92; and National Guard, 188–91, 193; militia of and martial drilling by, 204, 207, 211, 212*n*49; lynching of, 246, 248, 251–2, 252*n*22, 265; and New South, 246–67; and Citizens ticket, 254–5. *See also* Churches; Civil rights; Creoles; Education; Elections; Employment; Free people of color; Freedmen's Bureau; Integration; Segregation and discrimination; Slaves; Suffrage for African Americans; and specific African Americans

Afro-Creoles. *See* Creoles

Alabama: state constitutional convention for, 109–10, 112–3, 136; constitution of, 112–3, 115, 116, 117; readmission of, to

Union, 117, 176; economic development for, 119. *See also* Mobile, Ala.; and other Alabama cities
Alabama and Chattanooga Railroad, 161, 169
Alabama legislature: African Americans in, 12, 17n28; 1868 election for, 114; and Mobile legislation, 119, 122, 125, 145–7, 149n71, 153; Harrington as Speaker of the House, 120, 148; and streetcars, 123, 124; and railroads, 135, 151; and Mobile city budget, 253, 257
Alcohol, 12, 19, 63, 259
Alexander, Allen: as slave, 19; on Horton administration, 99; and municipal employment for blacks, 102; jobs of, 103, 105, 129, 208, 234, 235, 237–8, 247; and streetcar desegregation, 107, 123, 208; and emigration to Liberia, 115, 122; and Myers, 120, 121–2; economic status of, 122; physical appearance of, 122; political career and style of, 122, 192, 210, 225, 233–8, 242, 258–9, 266–7; and black-labor convention, 126–7; criticism of Berry by, 126–7; on Republican party membership of blacks, 139; on education, 145; and *Mobile Nationalist*, 147; and Nicholson Pavement proposal, 156; and Miller, 175; as Spencer supporter, 183, 183n44; arrests and police record of, 189, 213, 234, 237, 237n155, 238; and civil rights legislation, 208, 209, 234; and Moulton, 208; and steamboat segregation, 208; as candidate in 1874 election, 210–1, 213; and 1874 riot, 213, 234; and 1876 election, 221, 222–3; and 1877 election, 225; death of, 238; gambling by, 238; and 1880 presidential election, 243; and 1884 election, 258–9, 261
Alexander, Charlotte, 208
AMA. *See* American Missionary Association (AMA)
American Colonization Society, 115
American Missionary Association (AMA), 42–3, 47, 63, 127, 217

Ammunition explosion, 22, 30, 66, *167*
Anderson, Jacob, 16, 83, 84, 120, 130
Andrews, C. C., 43, 45
Antidiscrimination. *See* Civil rights; Integration and antidiscrimination
Arson, 52, 61, 72–3, 83, 110, 217
Arthur, Chester A., 195, 242
"At large" voting procedures, 215n59, 233
Austin, Henry, 120
Avendorph, Louis, 182n43, 190
Avery, Moses B., 50, 50n3, 56

Banks. *See* Freedmen's Bank
Banks, Nathaniel, 28, 50
Bates, W. B. F., 121–2, 156, 174–5, 183, 183n44, 186, 192, 195, 255
Bay St. Louis, 140n39
Baymen's Association, 69
Berry, Lawrence S.: as slave, 20, 79, 79n95; and *Mobile Nationalist*, 62, 79–82, 84, 130, 139, 153, 169; and Jewett's Sawmill strike, 88; and integrated Republican meetings, 92; and streetcar desegregation, 94, 107; on Horton administration, 99; and municipal employment for blacks, 102; and soup kitchens, 106; criticism of Turner by, 109; as delegate to 1868 state convention, 121; on black-labor convention, 126–7; on colorblind equality, 126–7; finances and jobs of, 128, 145, 153, 168–9; and federal patronage post for Harrington, 130; and economic development and railroads, 140, 141, 159; and chain gang, 142, 153; and education, 153; and health care for the poor, 153; and Nicholson Pavement proposal, 155, 156; death of, 169
Bidgood, T. S., 74
Birmingham, Ala., 136, 250
"Black nationalism," 51
Black Republican, 50
Blacks. *See* African Americans
Blair, Francis, 126
Board of Trade. *See* Mobile Board of Trade

INDEX 289

Boyd, Alexander, 171
Boyd, W. J., 182*n*43
Boyd, Wilborne, 152*n*76
Bragg, James, 41, 58, 121, 124, 129, 143, 145–7, 150, 177, 181–2, 182*n*43, 195, 209
Branch, E. C., 47, 48, 52, 56, 59, 62
Brazil, Walter, 182, 196
Bribery, 129, 130, 155, 156–8, 162, 169, 192, 229, 235
Bromberg, Francis, 39, 110, 119
Bromberg, Frederick G.: as ally of African Americans, 39–41, 110–2, 124–6; in Civil War, 39; and Union League, 90–2, 95, 131; as school board member, 107, 114, 127, 144–5; and Dog River rape case, 108; financial reversals of, 110–1; and 1868 election, 113–4; as city treasurer, 114, 150; as state legislator, 114, 119, 145–6; and Coale as mayor, 119; and economic-development proposals, 138, 139, 145, 151; and race riot in August 1869, p. 143; and Mobile reorganization bill, 145–6; as postmaster, 172, 175, 179, 238; denunciation of Putnam by, 178; and Warner, 180, 188; as congressional candidate and congressman, 188, 190, 191, 214, 220–3, 223*n*95, 228; and Grant, 188; as Liberal Republican, 188, 190, 191, 220; on lynching, 252
Brown, John M., 40–1
Brown, Wiley, 41
Brown, Wylie, 88
Bryant, Carrie, 262, 262*n*56
Bryant, Wiley, 246
Buck, A. E., 142, 151
Bureau of Free Labor, 27–8, 49–50
Burke, Joseph W., 237, 247, 248, 249–50
Burke, Peter, 224, 235
Business community: and cotton trade, 10, 12, 12*n*7, 24, 36, 65–7, 134; and Unionists, 37–40; and *Mobile Nationalist,* 58, 62, 93; employment of African Americans by, 69–71, 257–8; and economic development and railroads, 76–7, 134–9, 147–9, 151, 159–62; Bromberg's financial reverses, 110–1; and Horton administration, 135; and Harrington administration, 148–9; and federal bureaucrats, 173; and Taylor proposal, 232; homes of, in 1880s, 256–7; and Citizens ticket, 258. *See also* specific businessmen
Busteed, Richard, 34, 95, 99–100, 107, 111
Butler, Richard, 61*n*34

Canby, E. R. S., 26–7, 49
Canty, Columbus, 183*n*44
Carpetbaggers: and factionalism in Republican party, 1, 2–3; in Mobile generally, 5; Governor Smith's denunciation of, 119; Myers as, 120; and Harrington, 132–3, 158. *See also* Republican party
Carraway, John: and Civil War, 16–7; as free man, 16; political career of, 16, 17*n*28, 114, 121; as state legislator, 16, 17*n*28, 153, 154–5, 169; patriotic song written by, 17, 17*n*27; and *Mobile Nationalist,* 58, 80, 81, 84, 108, 130, 139, 153; and street confrontations by blacks, 92, 108; and Turner, 92, 108, 109; and Busteed, 100; on civil rights, 108; and Horton administration, 108, 117; and streetcar desegregation, 108, 113, 122–3, 152, 153; and state constitutional convention, 109, 112–3, 169; on white candidates in 1868 election, 113; and presidential election of 1868, p. 124; as city officeholder, 128, 138–9, 150, 169; and Price administration, 128–9; and Griffin, 129–30; and federal patronage post for Harrington, 130; and economic development, 138–9, 154–5, 159; and Mobile Board of Trade, 147; and Nicholson Pavement proposal, 155; bribery charges against, 169; death of, 169; finances of, 169; and Miller, 175
Catholic church. *See* Churches
Cavanah, H. V., 259
Chain gang, 24, 29, 61, 72, 75–6, 78, 89, 94, 106, 142, 153

Chase, Salmon P., 35, 43, 176
Churches: Catholic church, 11, 12, 16, 17, 69, 145, 178; Baptist church, 16, 42, 75; black churches, 16, 42, 50–3, 56, 59–61, 61*n*34, 72–3, 75, 78–80, 89, 108, 230, 264; Methodist church, 16, 42, 50–1, 59, 78; for non-Creole free people of color, 16, 42; for slaves, 16, 20; Congregational church, 57; and *Mobile Nationalist*, 59; white trustees of black churches, 59, 60; arson against, 61, 72–3; Horton's resignation as Presbyterian elder, 111; title to black church property, 113
Citizens Democratic ticket, 201–2, 254–5, 258–61
Civil rights: and Radical Republicans generally, 2, 3; Johnson's conflict with Congress over, 64, 82; Carraway on, 108; in Alabama constitution, 113; and Harrington, 126; antidiscrimination in railroads, 141; and federal employment, 176, 184, 194–5; legislation on, 208–10, 216, 252. *See also* Integration and antidiscrimination; Suffrage for African Americans
Civil Rights Act, 208–10, 216, 252
Civil War: black soldiers in, 13, 16–7, 18, 25–6, 30–2, 34, 42, 53, 59, 60; Creoles during, 13–4; espionage during, 13, 41; Mobile's defenses during, 14, 18, 20–1; non-Creole free people of color in, 14, 17–8; siege of Mobile during, 14, 21, 25–6; slaves during, 20–1, 27; Union occupation of Mobile, 25–36, 44–5, 49–50; white women during, 34–5; Unionists during, 37–41; and Mobile's economy, 65–6; Spencer in, 176. *See also* Ex-Confederates
Clarke County, 20
Class: divisions among African Americans, 3–4, 6, 9–10, 22, 75–6, 86, 101, 101*n*48, 103, 131, 168; Silsby on, 91; and People's Democratic party, 227–8; and Democratic party loyalty, 254; and livestock debate, 255–6; homes for wealthy, 256–7; and public services, 256–8

Cleveland, Ulysses, 260
Coale, R. W., 119–22, 127
Cochran, Jerome, 220, 228
Collector of the port. *See* Customhouse
Colorblind equality, 80–1, 84, 110, 126–7, 130, 182
Colored Orphan Asylum, 83
Committee of Public Safety, 144
Community organizations, 52–3
Confederacy. *See* Civil War; Ex-Confederates
Congress: conflict between Johnson and, 64, 82; and rejection of southern representatives in 1865, pp. 64, 82; and black suffrage, 82; Busteed on, 100; and defeat of Alabama constitution, 115, 116; and readmission of Alabama to Union, 117; and Warner-Spencer feud, 176–92; and civil rights legislation, 208–10. *See also* Congressional Reconstruction; Elections
Congressional Reconstruction, 48, 83, 86–98, 100, 198, 266
Conway, Thomas, 27–8, 44, 49–51, 55, 90, 91, 91*n*13
Cottin, George, 244
Cotton trade, 10, 12, 12*n*7, 24, 36, 65–7, 69, 134, 184
Courts: black testimony in, 45; Freedmen's Courts, 72; and jury duty, 112, 203, 226, 248, 250–1
Crampton, O. L., 258, 259, 261, 264
Creole Fire Company, 12, 13, 73–4, 78, *164*
Creole Social Club, 12, 13, 93
Creoles: characteristics and ethnic heritage of, 10–1, 10*n*3; statistics on, 10, 11*n*4; Catholicism of, 11, 12, 16, 17; legal status of, 11–2; in Louisiana, 11*n*5, 13, 50, 51; and slaves, 11, 13, 14; social position and social life of, 11–3, 73–4, 78, 262–3; education of, 12; during Civil War, 13–4, 50; freedpeople's relationship with, 13, 14, 15, 17; and African emigration, 16; and segregation, 17*n*28; and Union occupation of Mobile, 50, 51–2; and *Mobile Nationalist*, 58–9; employ-

ment of, 70, 184; and Withers, 74–5; political involvement of generally, 93, 96, 115; as police, 103; as city officeholders, 128, 150; and Warner, 182; and Knights of Labor, 241. *See also* specific Creoles
Crime, 74–5, 118, 154, 218. *See also* Police
Cruzan, W. E., 190
Cumming, Kate, 26, 29, 34
Cummings, L. W., 263–5
Curfew for African Americans, 30, 45
Customhouse, 170–88, 192–6, 201, 208, 234, 237, 238, 240, 242, 247

Danner, A. C., 241, 257
Davis, Durham, 146, 182*n*43, 185
Davis, Joshua, 55, 56, 99, 120–2, 183*n*44
Davis, S. S., 230
Democratic party: and black leaders in Mobile, 5, 196, 235–6; interracial rally in 1867 by, 95–6; and police partiality toward blacks, 106; and 1867 election, 109; and Gibbs, 110; boycott of 1868 election by, 113, 115, 119; black membership of, 124; and 1868 presidential election, 124, 126; and city officeholders, 128–9, 148, 159; and Radical faction in Mobile, 129, 131; and economic development and railroads, 141, 160, 162, 199–200; and Committee of Public Safety, 144; and education, 145; and Harrington administration, 148; and bribery, 157, 162; in 1870 elections, 158, 178; customhouse jobs for Democrats, 173, 174; and Joseph, 190; and Wickersham, 195; and Redemption, 198–215; and Mobile economic problems, 199–200; in 1872 election, 200–2; Citizens Democratic ticket, 201–2, 254–5, 258–61; and Withers, 201; in 1873 city elections, 205–6; in 1874 election, 210–5; and black militia companies, 211; "White Line" campaign of, 211; in 1876 elections, 220–3, 228; in 1877 election, 223–30; People's Democratic party, 224–31, 224*n*97, 233, 235,
236, 239; Straightout Democrats, 224–5, 228, 235–6, 254, 258, 259, 263; in 1878 elections, 230–1; in 1879 election, 233; and 1880 presidential election, 245; in 1884 election, 258–61. *See also* Elections; Ex-Confederates
Depression of 1873, pp. 204, 218, 219
Desegregation. *See* Integration and antidiscrimination
Dick, Washington, 61*n*34
Digg, Samuel, 183*n*44
Dillard, A. W., 194
Dimon, C. A. R., 101–5, 107, 108, 118
Discrimination. *See* Segregation and discrimination
Dockworkers, 70, 88, 118, *163*
Dog River case, 96, 108
Domestics, 18–9, 33–4, 40, 207
Douglas, Steven A., 37
Doyle, Don H., 4*n*11, 7*n*13
Draymen, 52, 63, 70, 152, 241
Du Bois, W. E. B., 6
Duffee, George G., 224, 225, 227–33, 236, 239, 263
Duskin, Geo. M., 194

Eastburn, J. R., 156–7
Economic development, 76–7, 134–41, 147, 148–51, 154–62, 176. *See also* Railroads
Economy of Mobile, 10, 24, 36, 65–70, 117–8, 125, 132–5, 145, 154, 159–60, 199–200, 202–4, 206–7, 219–20, 227, 231–2, 253–5, 257, 265, 267
Education: of Creoles, 12; and free people of color, 14; segregation of schools, 17*n*28, 107; founding of Mobile public school system, 39; and Horton, 39, 107; of African Americans, 42–3, 46–8, 52, 72, 107, 108, 127, 145, 217, 251, 259, 263–5; and Mobile Medical College, 46–8, 52, 61, 72, 127; and Emerson Institute, 47, 127, 129, 144, 147, 189, 217; and black teachers, 48, 48*n*95, 78, 251, 259, 263–5; arson against black schools, 52, 217; and

black churches, 52; and *Mobile Nationalist,* 63; support for/opposition to free public education, 113, 127, 145, 153, 178; rival school boards in Mobile, 127, 144–5, 178; and Catholic schools, 178; in Mobile County, 259; boycott of schools, 264–5

Elections: for state constitutional convention (1867), 109–10, 112; Democratic boycott of 1868 election, 113, 115, 119; 1868 elections, 113–5, 119, 124, 126; harassment of Republican voters in 1868 election, 115; presidential elections, 124, 126, 221, 236, 242–5; 1869 election, 142; 1870 election, 147, 158, 177–8; fraud in, 156, 205, 210n39, 249–50, 258; 1871 election, 185; 1872 election, 200–2; and Citizens ticket, 201–2, 258–61; 1873 election, 204–6; and violence, 205, 206, 210, 211–4, 225, 260; 1874 election, 210–5; 1876 election, 220–3, 223n95, 228; 1877 election, 223–30, 235; and U.S. marshals, 224, 248; 1878 election, 230–1; 1879 election, 233; 1880 election, 236, 242–5, 249–50; 1884 election, 258–62; 1885 election, 263

Elliot, John, 125

Emancipation of slaves, 20, 27–8, 33–4, 90. *See also* Slaves

Emerson Institute, 47, 127, 129, 144, 147, 189, 217

Employment: of African Americans, 27–9, 44, 68, 69–72, 118, 141, 151–2, 218–9, 218n73, 255, 257; of domestics, 33–4, 40, 207; discrimination against draymen, 63; and wages, 68, 69–70, 88, 89, 118, 140, 140n39, 152, 153, 207, 257; of white workers, 69–70; of Creoles, 70; city and county offices for African Americans, 99, 125, 128–30, 132–3, 139–41, 150, 159, 185, 196; patronage for African Americans, 100–3, 126, 168–97, 226–7, 229, 233, 239–40, 247–8, 266; of police, 100–6, 151–2; of street workers, 100, 257–8; Horton's city jobs program, 107; and railroads, 140, 140n39, 141; racial politics of federal employment, 168–97, 240, 247–8, 265; at customhouse, 170–6, 192–6, 240, 247

Enfranchisement. *See* Suffrage for African Americans

Espionage, 13, 41

Europe, Henry J., 183, 183n44, 221–2, 229, 247, 249

Europe, James Reece, 183

Europe, Robert, 208

Eutaw rioters, 189

Evans, Augusta, 33, 34, 133

Ex-Confederates, 37, 39, 113, 117, 125, 149, 176, 177. *See also* Civil War

Explosion of munitions warehouse, 22, 30, 66, *168*

Fears, George, 120, 182n43

Federal employment. *See* Employment

Fernandez, Charles, 145–6

Fernandez, Joseph, 113–4

Fifteenth Amendment, 152

Fifth Ward, 22, 23, 205, 223n95

Firemen, 12, 13, 60, 73–4, 162, *164,* 219–20, 254

First Ward, 22, 23, 245, 254–5

Foner, Eric, 1, 6

Food relief, 90, 106, 117–8, 126

Food sales, 106–7

Forsyth, Charles, 135

Forsyth, John: as mayor, 45, 68, 71; as newspaper editor, 45, 67–8, 72, 135, 162, 200, 202; and economic development, 67–8, 68n57, 135, 138; on Freedmen's Courts, 72; and Democratic rally in 1867, p. 95; on black police, 105; on race riot in August 1869, pp. 143–4; on Harrington administration, 149–50; on Nicholson Pavement proposal, 155; on 1873 city election, 205, 206; death of, 251

Fort Blakely, 25, 27, 42

Fort Pillow, 25

Fourteenth Amendment, 82
Fourth of July disturbances, 45, 53–5, 189
Fourth Ward, 22, 23, 213
Free people of color (non-Creoles), 10–2, 11n4, 14–8, 15n21, 42. *See also* African Americans; Creoles
Freedmen's Bank, 40, 52, 87, 222
Freedmen's Bureau: predecessor of, 28; white allies of freedmen in, 37, 43–6, 55, 91; and jobs for blacks, 44, 63; and vagrancy policies, 44, 72; arrest of agents of, 45; and Mobile Medical College, 46–8, 72; and community organizations, 52; and *Mobile Nationalist,* 56–7, 62, 63, 64; and Withers, 72; Johnson's veto of extension of, 82; and direct action, 90–1; and rape case, 96; and Horton administration, 106; and soup kitchens, 106, 118; and emigration to Liberia, 115; on Miller, 171. *See also* Swayne, Wager T.
Freedmen's Courts, 72
Freedpeople. *See* African Americans

Gaillard, Sam, 61
Gallatin, Albert, 183n44
Garfield, James A., 195n82, 242
Garrison, William Lloyd, 43
Gibbs, James B., 101, 109–10, 110n75, 115
Gillette, James J., 112, 118, 157, 236, 243
Goldfield, David R., 7n13
Gomez, Joseph, 70, 182n43, 190
Goodloe, Calvin, 195
Grant, Ulysses S.: election and inauguration of, in 1868–1869, pp. 120, 128, 135, 171; reelection of, 169, 180–1, 187, 188, 189, 191, 192; and Collector Miller, 172, 176, 179; Warner's influence with, 177; and Warner nomination for collector of the port, 179, 184, 187; and Liberal Republicans, 187–8; and black patronage, 194; and 1880 presidential election, 236, 243, 244, 249n8, 251
Greeley, Horace, 188, 190, 209, 244, 245
Greenback party, 239, 240

Gregory, Ovid: in Creole Social Club, 12, 93; political career of, 12, 17n28, 93, 95, 114, 121; social profile of, 12–3; on segregation of schools, 17n28; on Horton administration, 99; and Busteed, 100; as assistant police chief, 103; and state constitutional convention, 109, 112–3; and presidential election of 1868, pp. 120, 124; and streetcar desegregation, 123; and federal patronage post for Harrington, 130; death of, 144
Griffin, Albert A.: as printer of *Mobile Nationalist,* 62; as editor of *Mobile Nationalist,* 64, 77–85, 87, 90, 95, 128, 129; on African Americans, 70, 84, 93, 95, 129, 173; and Harrington, 92, 130; and Union League, 92, 131; on streetcar segregation, 94, 122–3; and rape case, 96; and Horton administration, 99; and Busteed, 100; patronage posts for, 100, 130; and state constitutional convention, 109–10, 113, 136; and disfranchisement of ex-Rebels, 113; and 1868 election, 114; on defeat of Alabama constitution, 116; and delegates for 1868 state convention, 121; and Governor Smith, 125; and McKinstry, 128, 129, 130; and removal of Mayor Price, 128; salary of, 128, 129; Carraway's criticisms of, 129–30; temporary expulsion of, from *Mobile Nationalist,* 130, 139–40; on economic development, 137; and race riot in August 1869, pp. 143–4; flight from Mobile by, 144, 146–7; photograph of, 165; on federal jobs, 173, 175

Hahn, Steven, 255
Hamilton, "Crab Alf," 238
Hampton, Wade, 228
Haralson, Jeremiah, 169, 210, 214
Harbor improvement and wharves, 136, 138–9, 151, 157–8, 160, 199
Harmount, George, 30, 44–6, 54, 56
Harrington, George F.: as lawyer for freedpeople generally, 42, 222; and Smith case,

60; and USCI veterans, 75; and Union League, 87, 91–2; and Jewett's Sawmill strike, 88, 89; *Mobile Nationalist*'s criticism of, 95; and Horton, 102–3, 124; political career of, 109, 114, 120, 122, 129, 148, 158; and black migrants from rural areas, 118–9; and Grant, 120; in state legislature, 120, 148; and civil rights issues generally, 126; federal patronage post for, 130; as mayor, 132–2, 148–58, 149*n*71, 159, 161, 172, 175, 201, 203, 207; and Bromberg, 145; and railroads, 148, 151; and economic development, 150–1; and police, 151–2, 152*n*76; and streetcar desegregation, 152; on carpetbaggers, 158; finances of, 158–9; death of, 159

Hayes, Rutherford B., 195, 221, 223*n*95, 228, 233, 235, 241–3, 246

Health care, 153, 206, 220

Hildebrand, Reginald F., 51

Holt, Thomas, 4

Hopewell, Eli, 182*n*43

Horst, Martin, 136, 158, 159–60

Horton, Eliza, 111

Horton, Gustavus: and state constitutional convention, 13, 109; as Unionist, 38–9, 40, 98, 111; and education, 39, 107; as moderate Republican generally, 41, 93, 126, 221; racial views of, 41; and Union League, 90–2, 98, 131; as mayor, 98–117, 135; and Busteed, 100; and police force, 100–6, 124, 151; as school board member, 107, 127, 144–5; African American support for, 108–10, 112, 117, 131; and Dog River rape case, 108; as county probate judge, 114, 117, 151; in 1868 election, 114; death threats against, 116–7; and Governor Smith, 119, 125; successor for, 119–22; and delegates for 1868 state convention, 121; and Price administration, 126; social ostracism of, 133; and railroads, 138; resignation of, from city government, 150; and economic development, 151; prewar employer of, 171; and Grant, 188; and Warner, 188; and 1874 election, 214

Horton, Gustavus, Jr., 143

Hospital, 106, 202

Housing, 70, 256–7

Houston, George S., 214

Howard, O. O., 47, 48, 62

Hurtel, John, 214, 218–9, 223

Hurter, William, 40, 119–20

Immigrants, 13, 39–40, 69, 100, 257, 258

Integration and antidiscrimination: in Republican meetings, 92; in police force, 100–5, 151; in streetcars, 121–4, 147, 152–3, 153*n*80, 208–10, 216, 217*n*65; in railroads, 141; legislation on, 208–10; in public facilities, 216; Rabinowitz on, 217*n*65. *See also* Civil rights

Internal Revenue Office, 172, 179, 195, 221, 242, 243

James, Frank, 60*n*28

Jewett's Sawmill, 88

Johnson, Andrew: Reconstruction plan of, 32, 37, 39, 43, 45–6, 47, 49, 62, 64; conflict between Congress and, 64, 82; veto by, on extension of Freedmen's Bureau, 82; removal of Pope and Swayne by, 115; failed impeachment of, 116; Myers as supporter of, 120; and federal employment of blacks, 171; scandals under, 196. *See also* Presidential Reconstruction

Johnson, Archie, 111

Jones, James T., 220, 223*n*95

Joseph, Philip: espionage charges against, 13; and slavery, 13; political career and style of, 93, 124, 177, 185, 190, 192, 204, 210–1, 233–4, 238–42, 243; and Mobile reorganization bill, 145; and *Mobile Nationalist*, 146, 147; and Nicholson Pavement proposal, 156; federal employment of, 172, 181, 182, 192–3, 195, 238, 242, 247; and Collector Miller, 175; as Warner supporter, 181, 182, 182*n*43, 184; and

INDEX   295

Ku Klux Klan, 184; as congressional candidate, 190–1, 191*n*73, 193; and black patronage, 194; as newspaper editor, 194, 209, 238, 238*n*158, 239; arrests and imprisonment of, 209, 242; and civil rights legislation, 209, 210; and People's Democrats, 239; death of, 242; drug addiction by, 242
July Fourth disturbances, 45, 53–5, 189
Jury duty, 112, 203, 226, 248, 250–1

Kansas, 77, 250
Keffer, John, 91
Kelley, William D., 96–7
Kellogg, F. W., 114, 128, 129, 171
Ketchum, G. A., 125, 155
Ketchum, William, 134
Kinney, Thomas, 30
Kinney, William, 213
Knights of Labor, 241, 241*n*173
Ku Klux Klan, 1, 78, 116–7, 171, 184, 189, 252

Labor movement, 69, 88–93, 152, 207, 224, 224*n*97, 239–41, 241*n*173
Lankford, Major W.: during Civil War, 18, 18*n*30; direct action by, 18; barbershop of, 102, 122; as police officer, 105; and Myers, 120–2; and streetcar desegregation, 123; and race riot in August 1869, p. 143; and *Mobile Nationalist*, 147; and Harrington administration, 149*n*71; and Nicholson Pavement proposal, 156; and Collector Miller, 175; as Warner supporter, 182*n*43
Law enforcement. *See* Police
Leavens, Reverend Charles, 56, 121
Lee, Robert E., 75
Legislature. *See* Alabama legislature
LeVert, Octavia, 35
Lewis, David P., 191
Liberal Republicans, 187–8, 190, 193
Liberator, 43
Liberia, emigration to, 16, 115–6

Lincoln, Abraham, 17, 37, 38, 50, 79
Lindsey, J. T. M., 252–3
Lindsey, Robert B., 158, 161
Livestock debate, 255–6
Lomery, James, 203–5, 208
Lord, E. P., 217
Louisiana, 11*n*5, 13, 27, 28, 44, 50, 51, 238–9
Louisiana Purchase, 11
Loyal League. *See* Union (Loyal) League
Loyal Newspaper Society, 57–8, 81, 84. *See also Mobile Nationalist*
Lynching, 206, 246, 248, 251–2, 252*n*22, 265

Macon, Ga., 77
Magill, Samuel, 103–4
Mahone, William, 216*n*61
Mann, William D'Alton, 135–8, 141–3, 149, 151, 155, 157, 161–2
Maury, Dabney H., 14
Mayer, Charles, 224*n*98, 248
Mayer, Louis H., 160, 195*n*82, 201, 221, 224*n*98, 228–9, 239, 243, 248, 249, 249*n*8
McCloudis, Isadore, 183*n*44, 186
McGregor, Gregor, 224*n*97
McKinstry, Alexander, 128, 129, 130
McWilliams, Joe, 259
Medical care. *See* Health care
Medical College, 46–8, 52, 53, 55, 61, 72
Memphis, Tenn., 78, 97, 155, 155*n*86, 231
Merchants. *See* Business community
Military Reconstruction, 17*n*28, 86, 171
Militia: black militia, 204, 211, 212*n*49; white militia, 212–4
Miller, William, 156, 171–4, 177–80, 183, 185–90, 192–3, 196
Mills, Gary B., 11*n*5
Missionaries, 16, 42–3, 46–8, 50, 51, 56, 78
Mobile, Ala.: factionalism in general, 4–10, 25; economy and financial condition of, 10, 24, 36, 65–70, 117–8, 125, 132–5, 145, 154, 159–60, 199–200, 202–4,

206–7, 219–20, 227, 231–2, 253–5, 257, 265, 267; population statistics of, 10, 11n4, 21, 24, 24n41, 36, 218, 218n69; during Civil War, 13–4, 18, 20–1, 25–36, 65–6; postwar social developments in, 21–5; maps of, *22, 23;* Union occupation of, 25–36, 44–5, 49–50; economic development for, 76–7, 134–41, 147, 148–51, 154–62; charters of, 89, 265; public services in, 154, 206–7, 219–20, 227, 253–4, 256–8; photographs of, *following p. 162;* and charter repeal, 231–2; Port of Mobile, 232, 233, 253, 254; reestablishment of, in 1887, p. 265. *See also* African Americans; Elections; and specific mayors

Mobile Advertiser and Register, 36, 45, 67–9, 72, 73, 88, 89, 96, 97, 101, 102, 103, 135. *See also Mobile Register*

Mobile and Alabama Grand Trunk Railroad, 67, 136–8, 140, 141, 154–5, 161–2

Mobile and Northwestern Railroad, 161–2

Mobile and Ohio Railroad, 65

Mobile Bay, 136, 220

Mobile Board of Trade, 133, 135–7, 144, 147, 148, 151, 158, 160, 199, 200, 218, 240, 257

Mobile College, 111

Mobile County, 1n4, 10, 90, 252, 259

Mobile Daily Register. See Mobile Register

Mobile Gazette, 239

Mobile Herald, 183, 184, 185, 187, 188, 189

Mobile Item, 258, 259, 263

Mobile Medical College, 46–8, 52, 53, 55, 61, 72, 127

Mobile Nationalist: beginning of, 55–7, 62; Silsby as editor of, 56–8, 62–4, 77–8, 81; directors/trustees and stockholders of, 57–9, 61n34, 83–4, 129, 130, 146–7; finances and fundraising for, 57–8, 63–4, 79, 81, 83, 109, 114, 128, 129; and Carraway, 58, 80, 81, 84, 108; and black interests, 61–2, 78, 84–5, 87; Berry as agent for, 62, 79–82; publication schedule of, 62; staff of, 62; subscribers of, 62–3, 79; accomplishments of, 63; and moral uplift, 63, 77–8, 81; Griffin as editor of, 64, 77–85, 87, 90, 95, 109, 128, 129; arson attempt against, 83; and Congressional Reconstruction, 83; restructuring of governance of, 83–4; and Union League, 87, 91; temporary closure of, after Kelley riot, 97; and Horton administration, 99; and state constitutional convention, 109–10; as daily, 129; temporary expulsion of Griffin as editor of, 130, 139–40; and Griffin's flight from Mobile, 144, 146–7; end of publication of, 147; physical confrontation at, 147; Woodward as editor of, 147

—articles: on Withers, 75; on strikers, 90, 93; on Democratic rally in 1867, p. 95; on direct action by African Americans, 95; on rape case, 96, 108; on Kelley riot, 97; on skin color of blacks, 101n48; on public markets, 106; on Harrington and Turner, 109; on Myers, 121–2; on rally supporting Grant and Myers, 121; on black-labor convention, 126; on black city officeholders, 129; on economic development, 137, 139–40; on race riot in August 1869, p. 142; on federal employment, 171–4

Mobile News, 42, 59, 60–1

Mobile Register: on Creoles, 115, 205; on African Americans, 118, 159, 172, 192, 193, 196, 204, 205, 208, 209, 218n73, 223, 250, 251; on poverty, 118, 218; on segregation, 123, 253; on violence and threats of violence, 123, 143–4, 184, 189, 216, 225, 260; and Harrington, 132–3, 148–50, 149n71; Forsyth as editor of, 135, 251; Mann's purchase of, 135; on economic development and railroads, 136–8, 140, 141, 155, 161–2; on elections, 156, 202, 214, 220, 229–30, 235, 251, 258–61; on Horst administration, 159; on economic problems of Mobile, 160, 206–7, 232, 253, 255; Mann's sale of, 161; on Berry's suicide, 169; on federal employment, 172, 173, 175, 192, 196, 208; on Collector Miller, 175; on Warner-Spencer feud, 184, 185, 189; criticism of, 200; on Moulton administration, 203, 204; on lynching, 206, 252, 252n22; on labor organizing, 207, 240–1; on Republican conventions, 210, 210n39; on Emerson Institute, 217; on whites-only city employment, 218–9; on education, 251, 264; on independent Democrats, 254. *See also Mobile Advertiser and Register*

Mobile Republican, 147, 171, 178, 183, 188
Mobile Times, 36, 61, 67, 69, 73, 96, 98, 101, 105, 109, 111, 135
Mobile Tribune, 35, 96, 200, 209, 212, 213, 216, 218n71, 221
Mobile Watchman, 194, 209, 210
Montgomery, Ala., 26, 66, 81, 94, 120
Montgomery Alabama State Journal, 172
Moore, R. M., 244–5
Moore, Willis, 182n43
Moral/racial uplift, 63, 77–8, 81, 87
Morrow, Thomas J., 252–3
Moulton, Cleveland F., 71, 124, 157, 201–8, 201n7, 211–5, 224n98, 234
Moulton, J. J., 193, 194, 196, 224n98
Mulattoes, 15, 15n21, 151, 152n76, 182, 191, 191n73. *See also* Creoles
Munitions warehouse explosion, 22, 30, 66, 167
Murphy, Peter, 245
Myers, H. Ray, 120–4, 145, 176, 190

National Guard, 188–91, 193
Nationalist. See Mobile Nationalist
Native Guard, 14
Nepotism, 224n98
New Orleans, 75–6, 88, 97, 262
New Orleans, Mobile, and Chattanooga Railroad, 137, 138, 140, 141, 151
New Orleans Tribune, 50, 50n3, 51, 53, 54–6, 58
New South, 7, 246–67
New York Herald, 26

New York Times, 43, 134, 192, 237
New York Tribune, 244
New York World, 54
Newspapers. *See* specific newspapers, such as *Mobile Nationalist*
Nicholas, C. D., 182, 182n43, 185, 247
Nicholson Pavement proposal, 155–6
Non-Creoles. *See* Free people of color (non-Creoles)
Nordmann, Christopher, 11n4
North Carolina, 7, 216n61, 267
Nott, Josiah, 46–8, 61, 133

O'Connell, John, 103
Oliver, Kate, 33
Opera House, 262–3
Overall, G. Y., 125
Owen, Recorder B., 257, 264

Parker, Gideon M., 99, 106, 125, 133, 135, 136, 155, 173, 200, 202
Patronage, 2, 4, 40, 99, 100–3, 111, 126, 168–97, 202–4, 226–7, 229, 233, 239–40, 243, 247–8, 266. *See also* Employment
Patton, Robert M., 64–5
Paving of street, 155–6
Pearson, Timothy, 179, 186
People's Democratic party, 224–31, 224n97, 233, 235, 236, 239
Perez, Constantine, 74, 145–6, 150, 182, 182n43, 185, 194, 196, 205, 247
Perman, Michael, 2, 3
Pillans, Harry, Jr., 257
Pillans, Laura, 34
Pillans, P. J., 152
Poillon, W. A., 46
Police: during Union occupation of Mobile, 31, 35, 36, 46; and July Fourth disturbances, 54; black demands on, 55; disturbance between black soldiers and, 59, 60; arrests of whites versus blacks by, 74–5, 104–5, 106, 118, 204; brutality of, against blacks, 74, 88, 106, 142; and strikes, 88, 93; African American police,

89, 100–6, 123, 124, 125, 151–2, 152n76, 204, 219, 230, 263; and Kelley riot, 97, 98; mayor's control over, 98, 100; under Horton administration, 100–6, 124, 151; and citizen's patrols, 101; dismissal of, 104, 105, 125, 141–2; and streetcar segregation, 107, 123; and elections, 115, 225, 260; under Price administration, 123, 125, 141–3, 146; and race riot in August 1869, pp. 142–3; under Harrington administration, 151–2, 152n76; Turner as police chief, 151, 156; wages of, 153, 227; under Moulton administration, 203–4, 205; militia company of black police, 204; under Hurtel administration, 220; in 1880s, 253–4, 256
Pontiac, C. C., 233, 243
Pope, John, 91, 94, 98–9, 101, 103, 107, 112, 115
Populists, 7, 216n61, 267
Port of Mobile, 232, 233, 253, 254
Post office, 172, 175, 179, 193, 194–6, 234–5, 237–8, 247
Poverty, 68–9, 90, 106–7, 117–8, 126, 140, 140n39, 153, 218
Presidential Reconstruction, 32, 37, 39, 40, 43, 45–6, 47, 49, 62, 64
Price, Caleb: as county commissioner, 114, 151; as president of Board of Aldermen, 114; as mayor, 122, 123, 125–6, 128–30, 135, 136, 139, 141–2, 144, 146; and police, 123, 125, 141–3, 146; and streetcar desegregation, 123; reelection of, as mayor, 128–30, 141; and economic development, 135–6, 139, 151; recommendation for reappointment of, as mayor, 148; arrest of, 149, 149n71
Prisoners, 203. See also Chain gang
Protestant churches. See Churches
Public markets, 106–7
Public services, 154, 206–7, 219–20, 227, 253–4, 256–8
Putnam, George L., 124, 127, 144–5, 153, 178, 179, 193

Quigley, Ann, 33

Rabinowitz, Howard N., 7, 7n14, 217n65
Race riots, 65, 75–6, 97–8, 142–4, 212–4
Racial uplift. See Moral/racial uplift
Racism. See Segregation and discrimination
Radical Reconstruction. See Congressional Reconstruction
Radical Republicans: blacks as, 2; carpetbaggers as leaders of, 2; civil rights advocacy by, 2, 3; in urban areas generally, 4; in Mobile generally, 5; "black nationalists" contrasted with, 51; interracial formulations of, 51, 53; and colorblind Republicanism, 80–1, 84, 110; and rape case, 96–7; and mayoral appointment in 1868, pp. 120–2; and Harrington, 132–3, 150. See also Republican party
Railroads, 65, 66, 67, 76, 119, 133, 135–8, 140, 140n39, 141, 148–9, 151, 154–5, 160–2, 169, 199–200, 204, 224, 241, 252–3
Rape and sexual molestation, 96–8, 108, 206
Ravesies, Paul, 228–30
Ray, Harrison, 183n44
Readjusters, 7, 216n61, 242, 267
Reconstruction: factionalism during generally, 1–10, 25, 49–50, 86; overview of scholarship on, 1–8; reasons for collapse of, 1–5; scalawags vs. carpetbaggers during, 1, 2–3; Military Reconstruction, 17n28, 86, 171; Presidential Reconstruction, 32, 37, 39, 40, 43, 45–6, 47, 49, 62, 64; Unionists as officeholders during, 40, 128; Congressional Reconstruction, 48, 83, 86–98, 100, 198, 266; Radical Reconstruction, 48; Lincoln's plan for, 50; contempt for, by white conservatives, 133–4. See also African Americans; Congressional Reconstruction; Mobile, Ala.
Redemption, 3, 6–7, 194, 196, 198–215
Reed, David, 142
Reid, John, 136, 205–6
Religion. See Churches
Republican party: factionalism within, 1–10, 25, 121–2, 177–8, 183–4, 192, 204–5,

INDEX   299

208, 258–9; Unionists in, 40, 128; and colorblind equality, 80–1, 84, 110, 126–7, 130, 182; in 1866 elections, 82–3; black resolution on integrated meetings of, 92; and Creoles, 93; Busteed excluded from 1867 state convention of, 99–100; social and financial persecution of Republicans, 110–2, 116–7, 133, 174; and 1868 election, 113–5; and mayoral appointment in 1868, pp.119–22; delegates to 1868 convention of, 121; and city officeholders, 128, 133–4; and 1869 election, 142; and race riot in August 1869, p. 144; and Warner-Spencer feud, 176–92, 201, 204; in 1870 election, 177–8; Liberal Republicans, 187–8, 190, 193; in 1872 election, 200–2; and 1873 city elections, 204–6; and civil rights legislation, 208–10; in 1874 election, 210–5; and local elections after 1874, pp. 215, 224, 249, 254; in 1876 elections, 220–3, 228; and 1877 election, 224–6, 228–30; in 1878 elections, 230–1; and 1880 presidential election, 236, 242–5; in 1884 election, 258–9. *See also* Radical Republicans

Reynolds, William C., 70–2
Riots. *See* Race riots; Violence
Roberts, Cyrus, 213
Royal, Abe, 183*n*44, 184, 186, 196
Runaway slaves, 20, 20*n*34, 21, 21*n*37. *See also* Slaves
Rural-urban migration, 5, 21–5, 35–6, 68, 71–2, 117–8, 217–8

Sailors, 14
St. Paul, Henry, 59, 69, 73, 96, 109, 133, 220, 231
Sawmill and sawyers, 88
Scalawags: and factionalism in Republican party, 1, 2–3; blacks' relationship with, 3, 188; in Mobile generally, 4–5, 91; and Unionists, 40; in 1867 election for state constitutional convention, 110. *See also* Republican party

Schools. *See* Education
Schroeder, Martha, 33
Schurz, Carl, 43
Segregation and discrimination: and Creoles, 17*n*28; of schools, 17*n*28, 107; residential segregation in Mobile, 21; in employment, 63; and wages, 68, 69–70, 88, 89; of streetcars, 78, 93–4, 104, 107, 108, 113, 122–4, 147, 152–3, 153*n*80, 208, 209–10, 217*n*65; of Union League councils, 91, 92; racism of conservative whites, 133–4; by Price as judicial officer, 146; racist newspaper illustration, *166;* black patronage and racism, 194; legislation outlawing, 208–10, 216; of steamboats, 208; de facto segregation after Civil Rights Act, 216–7; in early twentieth century, 246; on railroads, 252–3
Selma, Ala., 26, 57, 66
Selma Messenger, 88
Semmes, O. J., 250–1
Semmes, Raphael, 133, 250
Seventh Ward, 21, *22, 23,* 70, 142, 144, 154, 156, 190, 210, 213, 214, 235, 249, 261, 264
Sexual molestation. *See* Rape and sexual molestation
Sharecropping, 66–7
Shaw, James, 62, 77, 78, 84, 114, 125
Shaw, Robert Gould, 16
Shelton, James A., 224, 226, 229, 230, 235, 239
Sherman, John, 243–4, 244*n*192, 249*n*8
Silsby, John, 56–8, 62–4, 77, 78, 81, 91
Sixth Ward, *22, 23,* 178, 223*n*95, 225
Slaves, 11, 13–21, 20*n*34, 21*n*37, 27–8, 33–4, 41, 64, 90, 109
Slough, R. H., 34, 36, 43, 45, 60
Smith, Rev. Ferdinand, 59–61, 72–3
Smith, William Hugh, 117, 119, 120, 122, 125, 147–50, 149*n*71, 177, 178, 189
Social class. *See* Class
Soup kitchens, 106, 118, 126
South Carolina, 4, 7, 228

Southern Loyalist Convention, 82
Southworth, J. P., 189
Spencer, George E., 176–80, 183–93, 183*n*44, 195, 196, 201, 204, 221, 228, 236, 238, 239, 243, 249*n*8
Squires, W. I., 129, 154, 155, 217
Starke, Frank, 40–1
State legislature. *See* Alabama legislature
Steamboats, 208
Stewart, F. A., 263–5
Stewart, John, 109, 110*n*75, 115
Straightout Democrats, 224–5, 228, 235–6, 254, 258, 259, 263
Streetcars, 78, 93–4, 104, 107, 108, 113, 122–4, 147, 152–3, 153*n*80, 208–10, 216, 217*n*65
Strikes, 88–93, 152, 224, 241. *See also* Labor movement
Strong, Wilbur, 141, 172, 182*n*43
Suffrage for African Americans, 7, 24–5, 43, 62, 84, 86, 87, 95–6, 100, 109–10, 124, 214, 215. *See also* Elections
Summerville, James A., 59, 181
Sumner, Charles, 55–6, 244
Supreme Court, U.S., 136, 215*n*59, 252
Swayne, Wager T.: and Freedmen's Bureau, 45–8, 91, 115; and Slough, 45; and Mobile Medical College, 47–8; on community spirit of freedpeople, 52; and *Mobile Nationalist*, 56, 63; and employment discrimination, 63; and Silsby, 64; and Freedmen's Courts, 72; and Union League, 91, 95; and streetcar segregation, 94; and Dog River rape case, 96, 108; and Horton administration, 98–9; and Kelley riot, 98; and Busteed, 100; and black police, 102, 103. *See also* Freedmen's Bureau

Taxes and taxation, 145, 154, 160, 202, 219, 227
Taylor, E. D., 61*n*34, 121, 128, 226
Taylor, Hannis, 231–2
Tenure of Office Act, 243

Terrell, Spencer, 183, 183*n*44, 192, 194, 196, 208, 221, 229, 243, 244
Third Ward, 22, 23, 223*n*95
Thomas, James, 61*n*34, 83
Thomas, Roderick B., 94, 104
Thompson, Holland, 81
Thompson, Robert, 31
Threatt, Frank, 236, 243
Tilden, Samuel, 221
Towle, Amos, 40, 111
Tracy, George, 89, 90, 92, 94, 97
Treasury Department, U.S., 170, 185, 193, 234
Treasury Department, U.S, *See also* Customhouse
Trenier, John, Jr., 74
Truyer, John, 182*n*43, 205
Tunstall, York, 211
Turner, Benjamin S., 179, 185, 188, 190, 191, 191*n*73
Turner, George, 224, 224*n*98
Turner, Jack, 248, 252
Turner, Moses, 248
Turner, W. W. D.: as lawyer for freedpeople, 42, 116; and Union League, 87, 91; and Jewett's Sawmill strike, 88, 89; criticisms of, 92, 95, 108, 109; and streetcar segregation, 94; and Horton, 102–3, 111; political career of, 109, 120, 122, 222–3, 228; and employment outside of Mobile, 116; as police chief, 151, 156; and Collector Miller, 175; on Ku Klux Klan, 189; marriage of, 222

Union (Loyal) League, 55, 87, 90–5, 91*n*13, 98, 102, 104, 110, 111, 130–1
Union occupation. *See* Civil War
Unionists, 37–41, 90, 95, 98, 110, 112, 122, 128
Unions. *See* Labor movement
U.S. Colored Infantry (USCI), 25–6, 30–2, 34, 42, 53, 60, 74, 75, 87
Universal suffrage. *See* Suffrage for African Americans
USCI. *See* U.S. Colored Infantry (USCI)

INDEX 301

Vagrancy policies, 36, 44, 71–2, 75, 106, 203
Veatch, James C., 32
Vigilantes, 144
Vincent, Henry, 182*n*43
Violence: during Union occupation, 29; July Fourth disturbances, 45, 53–5, 189; arson, 52, 61, 72–3, 83; against Rev. Smith, 60; against Sam Gaillard, 61; race riots, 65, 75–6, 97–8, 142–4, 212–4; at festivities of Creole Fire Company, 73–4, 78; police brutality, 74, 88, 106, 142; at black church meeting, 75; and streetcar disturbances, 94, 123; rape case, 96–8, 108; at *Mobile Nationalist,* 130, 147; and Spencer-Warner feud, 184–5; Eutaw rioters, 189; and National Guard, 189, 190–1; election violence, 205, 206, 210, 211–4, 225, 260; lynching, 206, 246, 248, 251–2, 252*n*22, 265; and Civil Rights Act, 210, 216; and segregation of railroads, 253. *See also* Ku Klux Klan
Virginia, 7, 216*n*61, 242, 267
Voting rights. *See* Elections; Suffrage for African Americans
Voting Rights Act, 215*n*59

Wages. *See* Employment
Waring, Moses, 136, 138, 148–9, 151, 157, 201*n*7
Warner, Charles Dudley, 262–3
Warner, Willard, 172, 176–92, 182*n*43, 194, 201, 204, 238, 243–5
Water supply and water drainage, 219, 256–8
Wharves. *See* Harbor improvement and wharves
White League, 2
"White Line" campaign, 211
Whites: nonslaveholding whites in antebellum period, 19, 20; and emancipation of slaves, 20, 33–4; population of, in Mobile, 24, 24*n*41, 36; and Union occupation of Mobile, 32–6; as refugees in Mobile during Union occupation, 35; as allies of African Americans, 36–51, 55–7, 60–1, 84–5, 93, 99, 100, 117, 124, 130–1, 145–6, 173; Unionists in Mobile, 37–41, 90, 95, 128; northerners in Mobile, 42–3, 55–7; and *Mobile Nationalist,* 55–9; jobs for, 69–70; and labor movement, 69, 88, 224, 224*n*97, 240–1; and festivities of Creole Fire Company, 73–4; arrests of, 74, 104–5; militant whites and blacks' direct action, 86–98; and Union League, 91–5, 131; and Democratic rally in 1867, pp. 95–6; as city officeholders, 99, 125, 128; harassment of white Republican voters in 1868 election, 115; flight from Mobile by, 117; contempt for Reconstruction by, 133–4; and race riot in August 1869, pp. 142–4; customhouse employment of, 193–4; patronage for, 193–4, 202–3; lynching of, 206; militia of, 212–4; as vagrants, 218; as independent Democrats in 1880s, 254. *See also* Business community; Democratic party; Elections; Republican party; Segregation; and specific whites
Wickersham, Morris D., 123, 158, 158*n*92, 194–5, 195*n*82, 210, 234–7, 243, 247, 248
Williams, Price, Jr., 196, 222, 264
Williams, Price, Sr., 144, 148, 200
Wilson, Samuel, 152*n*76
Winney, Frank, 260
Withers, J. M.: as mayor, 71–7, 94, 97, 98, 106, 134; and Harrington, 148; and financial conditions of Mobile, 200, 203, 206; and mayoral nomination in 1872, pp. 200–1; as City Treasurer, 203, 206; in 1874 mayoral election, 214, 215
Woodward, C. A., 87, 147
Woodward, C. Vann, 265
Woodward, Sara Stanley, 147

Yarrington, G., 42
"York," 92

www.ingramcontent.com/pod-product-compliance
Lightning Source LLC
Chambersburg PA
CBHW070300240426
43661CB00057B/2605